# Practical Ethics
# in Public Administration
## Third Edition

# Practical Ethics
# in Public Administration
## Third Edition

Dean Geuras
Charles Garofalo

**MANAGEMENT**CONCEPTS

**ƒƒƒ**
**MANAGEMENT**CONCEPTS
8230 Leesburg Pike, Suite 800
Vienna, Virginia 22182
Phone: (703) 790-9595
Fax: (703) 790-1371
Web: www.managementconcepts.com

Printed in the United States of America

Library of Congress Cataloging-in-Publication Data

Geuras, Dean
   Practical ethics in public administration/Dean Geuras,
   Charles Garofalo.—3rd ed.
      p. cm.
   ISBN 978-1-56726-295-7
      1. Public administration—Moral and ethical aspects.
      I. Garofalo, Charles.   II. Title.

JF1525.E8G47 2010
172'.2—dc22

                                                              2010030622

# About the Authors

**Dean Geuras** is Professor of Philosophy at Texas State University in San Marcos, Texas. In addition to articles in philosophy, Dr. Geuras has authored interdisciplinary publications relating philosophy to other fields, including theology, counseling, and, in collaboration with Dr. Charles Garofalo, ethics in public administration. Together, in addition to *Practical Ethics in Public Administration*, they have published *Ethics in the Public Service: The Moral Mind at Work* and *Common Ground, Common Future: Moral Agency in Public Administration, Professions, and Citizenship*.

**Charles Garofalo**, Professor of Political Science at Texas State University, teaches graduate and undergraduate courses in public administration, public policy, administrative ethics, and business-government relations. He has co-authored, with Dean Geuras, *Ethics in the Public Service: The Moral Mind at Work* and *Common Ground, Common Future: Moral Agency in Public Administration, Professions, and Citizenship*. His work has also appeared in *The American Review of Public Administration, Administrative Theory & Praxis*, the *Journal of Management History*, the *Innovation Journal*, *Global Virtue Ethics Review*, the *International Journal of Public Sector Management*, and *Public Integrity*. His career includes both governmental and university administration.

# Table of Contents

# Preface

We assume that you, the reader, want to be ethical. This book is not intended to preach to you or to assume that we, the authors, are in a morally superior state encouraging you to join us in being better people than you are. As human beings, most of us are trying to be the best people that we can be. Unfortunately, however, acting ethically and intending to be ethical are not always the same.

Surely you have found yourself in difficult personal situations in which you want to do the right thing but are unsure of what action would be the right one. For example, you may have been uncertain of which charity you should give money to, how much to give, or whether, in the interests of your family, you should contribute anything; you may wonder whether you should tell a friend of the untrue gossip that others have reported about her; or you may debate within yourself about how much time to spend at home with your family while there are other obligations vying for your attention.

Sometimes ethically problematic cases occur at the office. Ethical questions may occur concerning whether an employee ought to be fired, how departmental funds ought to be allocated, or how to rate an employee on a yearly evaluation. In all ethical cases, whether personal or professional, your intent may be to take the best course of action, but you may not know what the best course of action is.

We would like to find a magic formula that would solve all our ethical problems, but no magic formula exists. We must think through ethical problems with the best information, understanding, and skill that we have. The purpose of this book is to help improve those capabilities so that you will be better prepared for the ethical issues that arise in the course of your work, decide them with greater self-assurance, perform your duties in a more ethically justifiable manner, and be able to explain your actions more reasonably.

## IS PROFESSIONAL ETHICS DIFFERENT FROM PERSONAL ETHICS?

Ethics exists apart from one's profession, but no profession exists apart from ethics. There may appear to be a vast difference between the personal ethical matters of whether to speed on the highway or to buy speed from a drug pusher and the budgetary and personnel matters that confront one at work. Nevertheless, there are universal values and principles that govern ethics in all areas. These values and principles include respect for other people, human equality, honesty, and fairness. Some people may "check their consciences in at the door" when they go to work, but such people do not provide evidence that ethics varies from one environment to another. They demonstrate only that they are not fully ethical. The work context may be different from the home context, but the governing notions are the same. This book will focus on those universals.

## IS ETHICS IN THE PUBLIC SECTOR DIFFERENT FROM ETHICS IN THE PRIVATE SECTOR?

Just as the context in which ethical principles apply varies between the personal and the professional environment, the context also varies, at least to some extent, between the public sector and the private sector. As we indicate in Chapter 2, different factors exist in each environment to alter both the details of the decision-making process and, at least on occasion, the decisions themselves. For example, a private company may recognize a moral responsibility to donate some of its profits to charity, but a public agency may be ethically prohibited from such largesse with public funds. A public agency may be ethically bound by the will of the general public to hire employees at union wage scales, but a small private company with very little capital may be unable to afford such salaries without firing people or risking bankruptcy. In this book, our concern is with ethics in the public sector.

Within the public sector, there are innumerable agencies with different tasks, reporting lines, levels of responsibility, and ethical cultures. Thorough discussion of each agency is beyond the scope of this book. However, the understanding of ethics in general and in its application to public service as a whole can be applied to the conditions of specific agencies.

## TIPS AND CAUTIONS

When discussions of ethics arise, people often have reactions that seem appropriate to the subject matter but hinder investigation rather than enlighten it. We mention a few of those reactions here.

**Don't get uptight:** The purpose of our discussing ethics is to help you and not to judge you. Try to keep an objective distance from the subject matter.

**Don't be an ethical faultfinder:** When people study a new subject matter, they often apply it to anything and everything they encounter. If you visit with a first-year psychology student, he or she will interpret all of your actions as signs of mental disorders. Someone who is new to the study of logical fallacies will "find" them in practically every sentence that you utter. There is also a tendency among people deeply engaged in the study of ethics to find an ethical aspect, most often an ethically questionable one, in everything that everyone does—or does not do. It is not the purpose of this book to make you a moral judge of other people's behavior; its purpose is to help you decide what you should do.

**Don't take it personally:** The tendency to be overly judgmental is often self-reflexive. We do not propose to make you neurotic in your self-criticism of your motives or behavior. We hope that you will learn something from this book that you can apply to your future professional and, possibly, personal behavior, but there is little value in ethical self-deprecation.

**Remember that no one is perfect:** Perfection is an ideal but it is not a reasonable goal. No baseball player can hit a home run in every at-bat; no attorney can win every case; and no one can perform the perfect action every time, even if he or she has every intention of doing so. We all, however, can improve and help others improve. The importance of an ideal is not so much that it serves as a state to be attained, but that it is something to work toward as a means of improvement.

**Sometimes there will be no clear solution to an ethical problem:** Aristotle said that one cannot expect too much precision from the study of ethics. It is not an exact science. The greatest minds in history have disagreed on how to solve ethical dilemmas, so we cannot expect a clear, logical, and unambiguous answer to every ethical question. We can, however, learn to examine an ethical issue in a manner that is most likely to provide the best result.

## THE GENERAL STRUCTURE OF THE BOOK

In Chapter 1, we examine the problem of encouraging public administrators to take ethical concerns seriously in the work environment by introducing serious ethical concerns into the consciousness of the public administrator. At one level, there appears to be great concern for ethics in the public service. According to the survey results, a great majority of managers believe that ethical concerns can be empowering in organizations, and few believe that a concern for ethics is either meaningless or harmful. Nevertheless, getting people to confront ethical issues seriously is a major challenge in the "real world" of the public administrator, who has deadlines to meet, budgets to justify, and a clientele to serve. As Chapter 1 notes, "In such a setting, raising ethical questions can be unsettling, if not risky. If we stick to such issues as financial disclosure, bidding and procurement, and conflict of interest, we are on safe ground. If we shift to questions of judgment and justification, of principles and integrity, then we travel into alien territory."

The problem cannot be resolved unless public administrators realize that ethics is at least as much a part of their profession as any other facet, including budgeting, personnel evaluation, and promptness in meeting deadlines. Moreover, as we will argue in the later chapters of the book, ethics enters into all facets of the public administrator's job. Managers realize the importance of ethics when they answer survey questions, but they do not always apply their concern for ethics on the job.

In Chapter 2, we examine the special importance of ethics in public administration, as opposed to private business. No one is exempt from ethics, and we do not mean to imply that private organizations are either unethical or unconcerned with ethics. Nevertheless, ethics plays a different role in the public sector than in the private sector. The aim of the private corporation is, in general, to make a profit. In a free-market system, the result of people seeking their own best interest, under reasonable laws and regulation, should—at least in theory—produce a fruitful and materially abundant society. Still, the immediate aim of the private firm is profit for itself.

The work of the public agency, however, expresses more directly the values of the society as a whole. Public agencies are created and funded to perform a function that the society as a whole, through its political system, deems important enough to merit governmental attention. The public agency is therefore responsible to the society as a whole, rather than to a special clientele. Even when the agency, such as a department of mental health, serves only a small number of people, the work of the agency is conducted at the behest of the society as a whole. The public agency is the steward of public money and not of private interest. While the private firm operates to make a profit, profit is essentially irrelevant to most public agencies.

The different roles of ethics in the private and public sectors are evident in several organizational ethics statements cited throughout Chapter 2. Private ethics statements often suggest that ethical behavior has good public relations as at least one of its aims; statements of agencies in the public sector treat ethics more as an end in itself.

The chapter concludes with the suggestion that, because ethics is so central to public service, it is an ethical calling as well as a profession. It is therefore not surprising that well-researched evidence, cited in the chapter, suggests that public service generally attracts professionals who are more interested in the betterment of society than are those who enter the private sector.

The first two chapters suggest a paradox. While both chapters emphasize the importance of ethics to public administration, Chapter 1 notes the reluctance of public agents to focus sufficiently on ethics. Among the more evident reasons for placing ethics "on the back burner" are both the anxiety that one experiences in discussing matters pertaining to one's character and the complicated, sometimes vague, notions that enter into ethical analysis.

Chapter 3 attempts to address those issues by familiarizing the reader with the historically important ethical theories and drawing from them a method of addressing ethical problems. The chapter summarizes five general ethical theories: relativism, teleology, deontology, virtue theory, and intuitionism. The first, relativism, may seem attractively "nonjudgmental," but we argue that relativism is unacceptable to most people when they realize that its full impact is to deny the truth of any moral judgments, including the belief that murder is wrong and, ironically, that it is wrong to pass judgment on other people. We further argue that the four others—teleology, deontology, virtue theory, and intuitionism—are not really as distinct as they have generally been thought to be. They can be unified into one ethical system.

The unity of the four provides the basis for the application of ethical theory to practice. Each theory suggests different questions for the ethical thinker to consider in reaching an ethical conclusion. We combine all four sets of questions into a list to be applied to any ethical issue that one might encounter. Consideration of the questions on the list does not offer a formulaic solution to all ethical problems, but it does provide a framework in which to make informed and well-reasoned decisions in which one can have confidence.

Chapter 4 applies that framework to actual cases in which professionals in the public service have made ethical decisions. The cases include the Tuskegee syphilis study, the "Saturday Night Massacre" that took place during the Watergate affair, and a more obscure issue concerning a possible invasion of privacy involving an employee of a public library. While the chapter provides the reasoning behind the decisions that were made, it invites the reader to come to his or her own conclusions based upon the framework that emerged from Chapter 3.

That framework is also the foundation of the ideas discussed in Chapter 5, which returns to the "real world" of the public administrator. After reviewing the literature on the ethical organizational culture in public administration, the chapter attempts to move public administration from a state of minimal concern for ethics to a state of ethical maturity. That maturity requires advancing beyond the prescribed rules of ethics codes to the fundamental ethical reasoning behind ethics in general, as expressed in the unified ethic. That reasoning, in order to function effectively, must be developed throughout entire agencies in their organizational cultures.

Chapter 6 develops the theme of an ethical integration more fully, applying the notion to the individual, the organization, and the society as a whole. Robert Wuthnow (1996) argues that the American Dream is concerned with ends in themselves as well as with material success. Ethical values are ends in themselves and are therefore inseparable from the rest of one's concerns. When those ethical values are challenged in the workplace, one experiences moral stress—the discomfort we feel when we know things are not right, when we try to rationalize our way out of a morally distressing situation. Moral stress disrupts not only the individual, but also the organization and the society that it serves.

While the total elimination of moral stress is impossible, we argue that it could be alleviated if ethics were an integral part of organizations. We argue that moral stress in public administration largely originates in the absence of clear constitutional legitimacy for the behavior of the organization, its neglect of ethical complexities, and the occurrence of daily ethical quandaries. In organizations that are ethically integrated, both within themselves and with the society of which they are a part, moral stress can be kept to a minimum. In such organizations, the individual can attain a state of personal equilibrium that enables him or her to provide a satisfactory answer to the questions asked in the title of the chapter: Who am I? Who do I want to be? What do I want?

Chapter 7 attempts to bridge the previous chapters and the subsequent chapters by providing a more comprehensive decision-making framework for moral choices. We refer to that framework as the enhanced unified ethic, which supplements the unified ethic with behavioral and organizational perspectives. The enhanced unified ethic offers at least six advantages to public administrators: (1) a functional philosophical, behavioral, and organizational framework for ethical decision making; (2) a broader and deeper understanding of the ethical dimensions and implications of decisions; (3) a reduction of moral stress; (4) insight into moral dilemmas, which oppose two apparently correct moral values; (5) a basis for reasoning and justification concerning moral dilemmas, rooted in prudent compromise, cooperation, and consistency; and (6) a redefinition of ethics from the alien to the familiar, comforting, and productive.

Chapters 8 and 9 consider hypothetical cases that might arise and ask the reader to resolve them, using the enhanced unified ethic as the framework. The cases involve common ethical dilemmas that one might face in the course of one's work as a public agent.

In Chapter 8, the importance of character in ethical decision making emerges. In examining the ethically problematic hypothetical cases, one notes that, for the sake of an organization, the character traits of the administrator are at least as important as the decisions that he or she reaches. Sometimes, an issue is so complex or ambiguous that the decision maker cannot provide definitive reasons for an ethical conclusion, but if he or she exhibits moral virtue in making a choice, the organization is well served. Sometimes a decision is made on feelings or intuitions, but if they are those of a decision maker of good character, both the individual and the organization can have confidence in them.

As Chapter 8 comes to a close, the reader is drawn yet further from a formulaic basis of moral decision making to a greater reliance on well-informed and well-developed judgment. Since each person has different ways of arriving at such judgments, we introduce the notion of an ethical style, which is the individual's own approach to making ethical choices.

Chapter 9 develops the notion of an ethical style more fully. We introduce Robert Solomon's (1999) definition of an ethical style as the individual mix of virtues and vices that makes up each one of us and defines the perspective through which we plan and judge our actions and those of others. We tentatively develop it further to include one's values, but finally conclude that when one's ethical style is fully developed, it constitutes his or her entire personality. Thus, the unified ethic ultimately leads us to a deeper understanding of ourselves.

In Chapter 9, we also provide exercises to help the individual determine his or her own ethical style. We conclude that, while theoretically the best ethical style would be the embodiment of the entire unified ethic in one person, in practice, there is no single best ethical style. The individual should work within his or her own ethical style to reach his or her potential as an ethical person.

In Chapter 10, we turn our attention to two different aspects of ethical conflict. The first part of the chapter discusses the conflict between public and private morality, which some philosophers, such as Bernard Williams, claim reflects distinct and often contradictory moral systems. We, on the contrary, argue that conflicts between the two allegedly different systems are actually disagreements within the context of one overarching moral system, which we have identified as the unified ethic.

The second part of Chapter 10 concerns conflicts between conscientiously held ethical perspectives within public organizations. The unified ethic cannot put an end to such conflicts but can ameliorate them with the assistance of the Ethics Impact Statement, as discussed by Carol Lewis, and the Ethical Conscience Statement, which we introduce as a means for an individual to express his or her morally based reasons for ethical disagreement with organizational policy.

In Chapter 11, we explore leadership development and moral agency in contemporary governance, including the need to develop and sustain the next generation of ethical public service leaders. Through a comparative approach, we consider leadership development in several member countries of the Organization for Economic Cooperation and Development, with special emphasis on the United States. We also propose the unified ethic as a framework for leadership development in general and the development of ethical leadership in particular. In this context, we offer a two-stage ethics training initiative focused on values clarification and justification of policies, programs, and practices in light of those values. Finally, we conclude this chapter by suggesting that leadership development should become an integral part of capacity-building in governance, and that public servants are moral actors whose decisions inevitably require the exercise of responsible judgment and discretion.

Chapter 12 examines attempts to reform government to make it more efficient and businesslike. An examination of the results of such efforts suggests, however, that the zeal for reform has little supporting evidence. For example, the chapter shows that careful studies reveal that the attempt to "reinvent government" produced few, if any, verifiable results.

More troubling than the lack of empirical support for such innovations, however, is the largely uncritical acceptance of the notion that government agencies should be run in the manner of private businesses. As we note in earlier chapters, there are essential differences between public and private agencies. It would be no more reasonable to run government agencies as businesses than it would be to run private businesses as public agencies. Although efficiency is a value in public agencies, it conflicts—more than in private companies—with other values, such as fairness and compassion.

*Managerialism, neomanagerialism, and entrepreneurialism,* three terms that denote efforts to move public agencies toward a more private model, emphasize the efficacy of notions such as self-interest and competition. Although those notions may function well in the private sector, they do not translate well into the more altruistic, socially concerned, and cooperative environment of public service.

The fundamental problem with such attempts to reform the public sector so that it resembles the private sector is the failure to realize the essentially ethical nature of public service, as discussed in Chapter 2. The same clash of "ethical cultures" also emerges in attempts to "privatize" public agencies by allowing them to be contracted to private firms.

In Chapter 13, we examine efforts to tie ethics to quality and performance. Although there are some hopeful studies by scholars such as Frances Burke, Amy Black, Willa Bruce, and Donald Menzel that point to such a link, the empirical evidence concerning ethics is hard to stipulate.

We conclude Chapter 13 with the suggestion that if ethics is to result in verifiable productivity benefits, they must emerge from a triad, that is, a model for clarifying and connecting ethical principles, for joining those principles to the fundamental purpose of public management—the creation of public value—and for drawing on well-established, reasonably successful methods to make that union real. That triad, like ethical theories in general, would apply differently in different organizational contexts.

Chapter 14, new in this third edition, considers the ethical implications of hybrid organizations, which today encompass various types of public-private partnerships and arrangements, including contracting out or outsourcing of many governmental functions. The chapter begins by examining hybrid organizations in general and then focuses on privatization and its effect on decision making and public values such as accountability, transparency, and freedom of information. The issues in privatization are exemplified via analysis of two major governmental functions: prisons and national security. We conclude that moral agency and moral competence are critical to effective and responsible management of outsourcing and the preservation of public values.

In Chapter 15, also new in this edition, we consider several features of moral agency as a key facet of good governance and professionalism, including the links between public service motivation and moral competence and the unified ethic and moral competence, as well as education and training issues associated with moral development. We explore the context of moral competence, which comprises the competing values inherent in ethical dilemmas; the motivation, skill, and resources required to resolve them; and the disincentives in public organizations to shift from compliance-based to integrity-based ethics programs.

Chapter 15 ends with three conclusions that are predicated on a level of moral competence and conviction that requires (1) reframing administrative ethics and (2) recognizing that reform has been driven not only by economic or rational forces but also by demands for democratization and empowerment of public service.

## GENERAL COMMENT

It would be wonderful to find undeniable proof of the efficacy of ethics in producing better public organizations, but we recognize that ethics is not merely a tool for productivity. On the contrary, ethics is a good in itself. Even if proof existed—and we doubt that any could ever exist—that ethical organizations are no more productive than unethical ones, the quest for ethics in the public service would still be of paramount importance. Even if an ethical organization does not perform better, an ethical organization, by definition, is better. While attempts to relate ethics to productivity are welcome, fixation on productive aspects might detract from the inherent value of ethics itself.

As the book progresses from beginning to end, the scope of ethics is revealed as increasingly broad and comprehensive. We hope that the reader will, after reading this book, no longer think of ethics as a judgmental, punitive threat, but as the defining factor in the good life and in the unity of the individual, the organization, and the society. That unity is especially evident in the public service, which combines all three facets.

We hope that this book will challenge you to discover your own ethical values and your own ethical style. We firmly believe that such a discovery will benefit you, your agency, and your community, none of which can be separated fully from the others. We also hope that you will complete the book for us. As you develop your understanding of ethics, you can add chapters that apply to your own personal, professional, and social situations. We also hope that you can add entire sequels that will develop the ideas in this book beyond the level at which we leave them.

*Dean Geuras*
*Charles Garofalo*
September 2010

# CHAPTER 1

# The Real World

Different people at different levels of different public organizations define their work environments in different ways. If you are at or near the top of a health or human services agency, you tend to see things in one way. If you are in the middle of a public works hierarchy, then you probably see things somewhat differently. If you are just starting your career in an environmental bureaucracy, you probably see things in a still different way. But public managers, veterans and novices alike, live in what is often called "the real world"—a world of agendas, budgets, and meetings, a world of strategies, internal and interagency political games and power plays, a world of turf battles and empire building. It is a world of relationships with private contractors, interest groups, citizens' organizations, and the media. It is what academics might call an instrumental world, characterized by goal-setting, priorities, and deadlines. It is a world in which you may sometimes need to sit with your back to the wall in order to survive. It is a world of climbers, jungle fighters, and even statesmen and women. It can be exciting, tedious, fulfilling, monotonous, inspiring, or dull, depending on the day, the people around you, the mood you are in, the conversation you just had with your boss, or any number of other things. It is, in other words, the world of work in American public service.

But what makes this world real? Or to put it another way, real compared to what? Is the reality of this world based on the fact that there are consequences that go with decisions and actions, consequences that affect people's lives or agencies' futures? Is it based as well on the explicit and implicit power relationships that tend to govern behavior? Does it also include the focus on getting the job done?

If these are at least a few of the relevant considerations in determining what makes the administrative world real, then we must note that these characteristics can be found in other worlds as well. For example, despite its image as a protected and placid environment of navel gazers, even the academic world is replete with the very attributes associated with so-called more practical settings. On university campuses, the issues of accountability and responsibility are real and enduring in the lives of students and academic staff, and we must not forget that, despite its ivory tower image, the academic world continues to hold the keys to the kingdom, namely, the credentials that many, including public managers, seek to advance their careers. The point here is twofold: first, to locate public administration in the larger landscape of work, and second, to explore the real world of contemporary American public administrators.

## CHALLENGES OF PUBLIC ADMINISTRATION

Because many practitioners and scholars have described American public administration, taking at least a brief look at some of their contributions is required for situating it within the spectrum of organizations and activities in the early twenty-first century United States. This brief look should help us understand better both the immediate environment and the larger world of public service.

For example, in a primer for public managers entitled *How to Manage in the Public Sector,* Gordon Chase and Elizabeth Reveal (1983) depict the reality of public administration and provide practical advice to managers at all levels of government. Chase, who died in 1980, and whose work was completed by Reveal in 1982, began his career as a foreign service officer. He then served in the White House in national security affairs, moved to the Equal Employment Opportunity Commission, and then served as New York City's health services administrator. In addition to his government service, Chase taught at the Kennedy School of Government as well as Brandeis University.

In six short chapters, Chase and Reveal characterize the relationships between public managers and their bosses, other managers, legislators, communities, interest groups, and the media. After noting that government, which is ultimately about implementation, or turning policy into practice, consists of an extraordinary cast of characters, Chase and Reveal maintain that "what makes public management so hard" and so interesting "is that all these players act simultaneously, with few clear lines of authority, constantly changing public mandates, and frequent turnover of people" (15). Thus, to be effective, a public manager must master this world, and not become befuddled by the politics or disconcerted by the mixed signals, or unsure of one's agenda and purpose. This environment is political and complex, and in order for managers to deliver or produce, they must turn this environment to their advantage. They must be able to anticipate conflict, promote their agenda, and earn the respect of both friends and adversaries. The only alternative is failure.

The public organization, however, is not distinctive, let alone unique, because of its hierarchical challenges, personnel problems, or daily demands and pressures. Private organizations experience similar vagaries and vicissitudes. What is notable about public organizations, of course, is their special responsibilities to citizens, elected officials, and political appointees and the different levels of scrutiny, oversight, and accountability expected of them. In this context, the question of managerial effectiveness is a constant. It is an indelible element in the study and practice of public administration, although the meaning of effectiveness and its connection to other variables remain perplexing issues. For example, there seems to be no consensus on a definition of effectiveness, nor is it clear at what level in the organization effectiveness is to be measured. Nonetheless, there is agreement that managerial effectiveness is somehow linked to the attainment of specific results or outcomes. Furthermore, a public manager's effectiveness is believed to be associated with several variables such as skills, education, personality, management style, and, not surprisingly, experience, although the degree to which each of these variables is related to effectiveness is still unclear. In any event, effectiveness, however defined, is a matter of continuing concern in the real world of public managers.

Such concern is reflected, for example, in the Government Performance and Results Act of 1993. This initiative, as well as similar ones at the state and local levels, requires public agencies to conduct strategic planning, to identify performance outcomes, and to measure these outcomes through performance reviews. Agencies need specific performance indicators, in order to assess their activities and make better decisions. Planning, benchmarking, and evaluation are among the essential tools of public managers in this national emphasis on increasing governmental productivity, performance, and accountability. They are part of the high-pressure world of contemporary public service, in which intergovernmental and public-private relations, technological complexity and change, and cultural diversity are important ingredients in the daily diet of the public manager.

Many observers describe the world of the public manager as varied, fragmented, and hurried. In this environment, public managers play many roles, such as leader, negotiator, and conciliator. They function in the midst of competing claims about the distribution of resources, interpretations of legislative intent, policy, and process, and conflicting views of the management of personnel, information, and budgets. Public managers, therefore, need a wide range of attributes, attitudes, and skills to survive and to succeed.

Gordon Chase (1984) identified five particular skills and characteristics that public managers should have: (1) negotiation and persuasion skills, (2) a thick skin, (3) an ability to learn and move quickly, (4) leadership skills, and (5) a willingness to live with uncertainty. Whether you are a public manager at the national, state, or local level, you are undoubtedly involved in all of these activities in one way or another. Furthermore, you are well aware that the higher you are in the hierarchy, the more important these skills and characteristics tend to be, especially in the face of increasing ambiguity. As the old saying goes, "The political winds blow hardest at the top."

## ETHICS IN PUBLIC ADMINISTRATION

Clearly, public managers have their hands full. Their environment is complex and complicated, involving multiple constituencies, responsibilities, and challenges. Their skill, competence, and commitment are tested daily as they try to respond to those constituencies, fulfill their responsibilities, and meet the challenges they face. Nonetheless, there is another set of challenges and another set of skills that are equally implicated in effective public management: the ethical dilemmas that all public managers confront and the skills they need to resolve them in an effective manner.

Ethics in American public service is by no means a new topic; it extends back to the founding of the Republic, through reforms of the late nineteenth and early twentieth centuries, and finally to the explosion of the study and practice of ethics in recent years. Public administration practitioners and scholars, individually and collectively, have turned their professional spotlights on the exercise of ethical public administration, including the challenges of discretion, choices, and accountability, partly in response to what Carol Lewis (1991) calls "catastrophic irrationalities such as two world wars, genocide, and atom bombs" that "taught us the power of organization." She argues that "bureaucratic atrocities, misguided efficiencies, errors, and blind spots begged for explanation" (8). Other observers trace the current interest in governmental ethics to Watergate and the other "gates" that followed, which, in turn, led to such developments as the creation of the Independent Counsel, the Ethics in Government Act, the Office of Government Ethics, designated agency ethics officials (DAEOs), ethics commissions on the state and local levels, and ethics advisors—indeed, a veritable ethics establishment (Morgan and Reynolds 1997), including a cottage industry of administrative ethics specialists on university campuses and in consulting firms.

For some, ethics is, ironically, big business. Regardless of the sources, motivations, and incentives behind the recent surge of interest and initiatives concerning ethics, the words of James Madison in *Federalist Paper No. 51* (1787–1788) still have a contemporary resonance:

> If men were angels, no government would be necessary. If angels were to govern men neither external controls on government would be necessary. In framing a government which is to be administered by men over men, the greatest difficulty lies in this: you must first enable the government to control the governed; and in the next place to oblige it to control itself. A dependence on the people is, no doubt, the primary control on the government; but experience has taught mankind the necessity of auxiliary precautions.

It is clear, his omission of women notwithstanding, that Madison's ideas ring true today. The presence of values in administrative choices, the importance of administrative decisions, and the impact of public policies on citizens are undeniable. The question for public managers and agencies, however, is how to respond to "the old philosophical proposition that, ideally, government is ethics institutionalized for pursuing the public good" (Lewis 1991, 7). With this proposition as a backdrop, as well as the specific events that have led to the current resurgence of ethics in the public sector, what can be said about government's response to both citizens' expectations of moral behavior by government officials and internal institutional pressures for reform?

Ethics is one of the proverbial motherhood-and-apple-pie issues. Who can be against it? In policy terms, it is analogous to protecting the environment or providing equal opportunity. But as public managers know, it is one thing to favor environmental protection or equal opportunity; it is quite another to deal with the particulars of either. For example, although most Americans support the general goals of environmental protection and equal opportunity, there are deep divisions among them concerning the specific ways to achieve them. When framed in "either-or" terms as in jobs or the spotted owl and affirmative action or reverse discrimination, we tend to find that, indeed, the devil is in the details. Ethics is similar. Even though we are all for it, on some level, actually doing it—especially at work—is another matter.

But therein lies the rub. What does "doing ethics" mean, especially at work? How is ethics understood and interpreted in the real world of public administration? These are tough questions, partly because the answers vary, depending on the particular agency involved, and partly because they imply multiple approaches and perspectives. Nonetheless, despite the variety of responses, public administration tilts toward the legalistic, or compliance, mode. John Rohr (1989) calls it the "low road" or "adherence to formal rules" (60). "Ethical behavior is reduced to staying out of trouble," which results in "meticulous attention to trivial questions" (63). In Lewis' words, the compliance mode is "largely proscriptive, coercive, punitive, and even threatening. . .designed to spur obedience to *minimum* standards and legal prohibitions" (9). What this means for public managers, not surprisingly, is oversight, controls, and sanctions. For, after all, this is familiar terrain. Compliance is embedded in government operations; it is fundamental to how public organizations function; and public managers are expected to be accountable.

Since, at this point, our focus is on understanding and interpreting ethics in the real world of public administration, we will not now explore alternative perspectives. Those will come later. For now, let us examine in more detail the nature of the compliance mode and the ways in which it is reflected in the thinking, deciding, and doing of real public administrators. This should give us a benchmark for understanding ethics and quality and the connection between them in the American public service.

In considering the compliance mode in public sector ethics, we first must acknowledge its value. Again, to cite Lewis, "compliance is fundamental to the way the public business is conducted. As guardians of political relationships and political goals, *controls are accountability implemented*" (10). Such controls, for example, can be found in the traditional managerial functions of budgeting and personnel. Indeed, American government has emphasized accountability since its inception. Therefore, the importance of accountability is unquestionable. The essential issue, however, concerns the nature and scope of accountability, whether it translates into simple compliance or obedience to statutes or regulations, as though they are clear in and of themselves, or whether public administrators should be expected to demonstrate independence of mind by exercising judgment and discretion in meeting their obligations as public servants.

Clearly, as the alternatives are framed, the latter is preferable to those of us who see ourselves as mature, responsible, experienced managers. But life in the bureaucracy is seldom that simple. The choices confronting the public manager usually call for both compliance and judgment, thus requiring the manager to attempt a balance between the two. It is not an either-or matter. Yet, in the real world of public administration, it is often difficult to exercise independence of mind if such independence is not part of the institutional culture. Independence is permissible only if it is exercised within the accepted organizational and policy framework—the constellation of norms, assumptions, and technical requirements associated with a given agency's official mandate and particular culture. It is, in other words, hard to think outside the box.

Ethics, in this sense, may appear paradoxical: It buttresses traditional notions of accountability but also encourages independent thought and judgment in the context of objective moral standards. This is a tall order for anyone, particularly public managers whose professional preoccupation is with difficult and demanding choices. It is easy to understand, therefore, why the moral dimensions of public issues tend to receive short shrift in administrative circles. But the apparent paradox is misleading.

Consider, for example, the case of the U.S. Postal Service's money-order operation (Starling 1998). The question, as presented by the agency, was how to make money orders more profitable. How would you, as a member of the task force responsible for addressing this question, have replied? In all likelihood, you would have recommended changes in marketing strategies such as a new publicity campaign to increase use of money orders, or might you simply have recommended raising the price of money orders? Or, as Starling suggests, might you have raised a different question, namely, *should* money orders be made more profitable, in recognition of the fact "that money orders are used primarily by lower-income Americans who do not have checking accounts" (190).

As this case suggests, public managers are continually confronted with both value-laden choices and the question of whether and how those values should be made explicit. On the other hand, it is easier to ignore the values underlying the choices before us if they are either not perceived at all or perceived as beyond our bailiwick as public managers. Later in this book, we will explore the implications for public managers of confronting the panoply of values underlying both organizational and policy choices. For now, let us simply acknowledge that values are ever-present and that the compliance mode addresses only some of them.

Consideration of ethics in the public sector must include organizations themselves, especially what scholars refer to as organizational cultures and structures. An organization's culture is widely acknowledged as a powerful influence, perhaps even a determinant, of public managers' beliefs and behaviors. On both the formal and informal level, it encompasses the norms, assumptions, rituals, and other aspects of an organization's life that contribute to the creation of the organization's climate and set the tone for particular attitudes and actions. Organizational structure refers to the hierarchy, the specialization of tasks, the distribution of authority and power, and the other commonly recognized characteristics of the modern bureaucracy. Organizational structure, too, particularly with respect to a manager's level and position in the hierarchy, exerts a powerful, even determinative, influence on attitudes and actions. Taken together, organizational culture and structure are vital elements in the thinking, doing, deciding, and ethical perspective of public managers.

Given the importance of organizational culture and structure in the public service, we might ask how public organizations have tended to respond to the emphasis on ethics in recent years. For example, let us examine the results of a 1996 survey of members of the American Society for Public Administration (ASPA), to help in developing our understanding of their perceptions of ethics in society and government, integrity in public agencies, and ASPA's code of ethics (Bowman and Williams 1997). A questionnaire, with a copy of the ASPA code of ethics, was mailed to a random sample of 750 administrators who belong to ASPA. Fifty-nine percent, or about 450 responses, were usable.

The results of the survey indicate, first, that these public managers believe that contemporary interest in ethics is not just a passing fad, that "incidents of outright criminality in government distract attention from more subtle, genuine ethical dilemmas," and that private enterprise is not a standard for conducting the public's business. At the same time, nearly all of the respondents agreed that public managers encounter ethical dilemmas at work. Ethical issues go with the territory in public agencies. (518)

According to the survey results, 76 percent of these public managers believed that ethical concern can be empowering in organizations; 60 percent disagreed with the statement that "expressions of ethical concern. . .evoke cynicism, self-righteousness, paranoia, and/or laughter"; and 60 percent disagreed with the statement that ethics is "meaningless because organizational cultures encourage a Machiavellian philosophy of power, survival, and expediency." On the other hand, nearly 50 percent of the respondents claimed that "supervisors are under pressure to compromise personal standards" and that the "source of this stress appears to be the top levels of the organization." In the same vein, almost 90 percent disagreed with the notion that the ethical standards of senior management were higher than their own. "To summarize, these practitioners encounter dilemmas, believe that ethics can be empowering in organizational cultures, are able to surmount social taboos about discussing ethics, and perceive tension between top officials and careerists." (518-519)

The participants in this survey were asked to characterize organizational approaches to ethics. Nearly a fourth said that institutions have a reactive, primitive, low road approach that focuses on wrongdoing and staying out of trouble. Only about 10 percent suggested that organizations have a high road, or affirmative, strategy that encourages ethical behavior and deters, rather than detects, ethical problems, and almost 60 percent indicated that most organizations have no consistent approach to ethics. This lack of consistency, furthermore, relates directly to the fact that employees are often left to flounder when confronted with ethical challenges. As Bowman and Williams state, "many offices either ignore, shift responsibility, or simply have no strategy whatsoever for dealing with ethics. An incoherent, frequently passive, and/or reactive philosophy is not likely to support, nurture, or benefit those seeking to carefully resolve ethical dilemmas" (519). Finally, in this regard, when asked what works best in fostering ethics and deterring ethical lapses in their own organizations, the majority of respondents noted the importance of management by example.

Turning to codes of ethics, more than 90 percent of the respondents endorsed them. According to Bowman and Williams, one possible reason for this high level of support is that both business and government executives see codes of ethics "as an important indicator of professionalism." With regard to the code of ethics of the American Society for Public Administration in particular, again, more than 90 percent of the respondents affirmed that the "code provides an appropriate set of standards," but about two-thirds suggested that for the ASPA code to be effective, it "must be supplemented by an agency-specific code." Furthermore, more than 90 percent agreed that top management must take the code seriously for it to be given weight. (521)

In discussing codes of ethics, Bowman and Williams distinguish between codes of ethics and codes of conduct, a distinction that will be important for us later. They argue that rule-based codes of conduct are often found in statutes or executive orders. They are directive and top down, "typically imposed on (and often resented by) employees with no advice for effective implementation, training and development, or recognition of the importance of leadership modeling." Bowman and Williams describe codes of conduct as a "coercive, quick-fix strategy" that "reduces ethics to legalism by focusing on both the lowest common denominator and penalties for deviations." This strategy, in their view, "does little to promote a philosophy of excellence or to engender a sense of personal responsibility," and it does not work. "In contrast, codes of ethics demand more than simple compliance; they mandate the exercise of judgment and acceptance of responsibility for decisions rendered—the real work of ethics." What codes of ethics do, according to Bowman and Williams, is acknowledge the ambiguities and complexities of public service, and "offer interpretative frameworks to clarify decision-making dilemmas." (522)

It seems reasonable to conclude that these survey results reflect the attitudes and experiences of American public administrators as a whole with regard to ethics in the public service. Everyone, as noted earlier, supports ethical government. The nettlesome questions, however, concern the definition and scope of ethics as applied to administrative challenges, the expectations of citizens, elected officials, and public managers themselves regarding the meaning of ethical thinking, doing, and deciding in the public service, and the resolution of ethical dilemmas consistent with those expectations. As the survey data indicate, we are far from a consensus on the answers to these questions, although the general tendency among public organizations has been to respond to expectations concerning ethics in legalistic, compliance-oriented terms.

For example, one of the standard responses of public organizations to the demand for attention to ethics has been ethics training. Indeed, ethics training has become the conventional method for promoting ethical climates and behaviors in public organizations. It is required by many states and municipalities as well as the federal government. As Carol Lewis (1991) observes in regard to ethics training, however, typically, it "exclusively targets compliance with minimum statutory or administrative standards written into codes of conduct." It fails to acknowledge that public managers already use discretion and judgment every day and, thus, fails to provide them any guidance or advice on this crucial aspect of their responsibilities. (18)

In their daily activities, public managers routinely distinguish among rules, law, and actual behavior. Adaptation, innovation, and leadership require such distinctions. Selective enforcement, or bending, and sometimes even breaking, the rules to get the job done, is commonplace. Confronting complexity, ambiguity, competing values, a disconnect between going by the book and achieving goals—none of this is surprising or unusual in the public sector.

Thus, the intellectual agility, the mental prowess, and the organizational skills needed to exercise ethical analysis and judgment are already in place. The missing ingredients are (1) the recognition that compliance alone is, at least, inappropriate and, certainly, counterproductive for public managers, and (2) the institutional recognition that ethical judgment and sophistication are essential for effective public service.

Job descriptions generally do not include moral creativity, innovation, or judgment. Problem-solving ability is often limited to technical or professional problems that, although perplexing, remain within the familiar boundaries of conventional public administration. The agency expects the new employee to be morally compliant and to raise no questions about the inevitable ethical complexities inherent in the policy and organizational decisions that will arise on a daily basis. To the extent that ethics is acknowledged, it is usually perceived not as a serious matter to be attended to in a serious manner but, rather, as an added burden on an already overloaded agency. Ethics means developing or, more frequently, contracting with a consultant to conduct a legalistic training program. On the organizational level, it is another square to fill.

In such a setting, raising ethical questions can be unsettling, if not risky. If we stick to such issues as financial disclosure, bidding and procurement, and conflict of interest, we are on safe ground. If we shift to questions of judgment and justification, of principles and integrity, then we travel into alien territory. We change the viewpoint and the vocabulary, and we change the set of expectations. We go from ethical compliance to ethical consciousness, discernment, and choice. In an important sense, we move from our heads to our hearts.

In the remainder of this book, we argue that it is crucial for public managers to strive to lift the moral fog that envelops most of us, and to live in moral consciousness and choice, alert to the ethical implications and meaning of our decisions and actions, prepared to exercise moral judgment and leadership. In the following chapters, we sketch the characteristics and qualities of ethical public managers, who are clear about and close to their values and commitments. We confront the anxiety that living in moral consciousness can provoke, and we explore with you issues of decision making, problem solving and resolving, character, and excellence. In the process, we hope that principled reasoning and judgment will become somewhat like learning how to operate a computer or a new software program: At first, it is unfamiliar and, perhaps, unnerving, but ultimately you become more comfortable with it, and as your confidence increases, so does your willingness to perform in public. And, after all, the public interest and the public trust deserve no less.

# CHAPTER 2

# Why Is Ethics in the Public Sector Different from Ethics in the Private Sector?

This book is, as the title states, about ethics in public administration. But one might question the need for ethics specifically for those in the public sector because ethics, it would seem, applies to everyone, regardless of whether one is employed in public, private, or charitable organizations—or not employed at all. Ethics is pervasive. Why restrict the discussion to public organizations?

Unquestionably, everyone should be concerned with ethics, and ethics is not an entirely different subject depending upon one's employment status. However, several factors influence the differing ways that ethics applies under various conditions. A doctor, an attorney, a university professor, and a priest may all share the same ethical beliefs but under different professional assumptions. Each is ethically required to keep the confidence of those under their care or ministry, but in each case, the type of information to be kept confidential, the limits of the confidentiality, and the reasons for it are different.

Within public administration, there are many specific professions with their special ethical environments. The environments may vary even among those in the same profession, depending upon factors such as a job's specific duties, the culture of the organization, and the significant conditions that pertain at a specific time. Nevertheless, factors are at work in public administration in general that are different from those in the private sector or in charitable organizations. In this chapter, we will examine those factors and discuss their ethical import.

## WHO OWNS THE SHOP?

A private company is owned by one person or a small number of people, and they run their business as they see fit within the law for their own private interest. A corporation is run by a relatively large number of shareholders, who, like the private company owners, are legally permitted to govern the organization in their collective interest. A public organization cannot be said to have an owner, at least in the traditional sense of "owner." We may use the cliché "owned by the people," but the phrase is largely devoid of meaning because if everyone owns something, no one owns it. We can say, however, that public organizations are responsible to the general public in a manner roughly similar to that in which a company is ultimately responsible to its ownership. The company or corporation does what its owners tell it to do, but the public organization must answer to a public charge specified by people speaking for the entire society.

The private company or corporation must make a profit; the public agency must serve the public. The owners of the private company or corporation seek to benefit financially from their venture. If a private corporation loses money consistently, it eventually closes down unless subsidized, at which point it ceases to be an independent entity. Public agencies are very different in this regard. The public agency is generally not required to make money but only to respond to a public charge that the public is willing to fund. The public agency is successful when it uses money productively rather than when it makes money.

While one might say that the public as a whole owns the public agency and the few owners or stockholders own the company, the difference in ownership bespeaks a major distinction. For the owners of the company, its productivity is a means to financial benefit. But for the "owners" of a public agency, the productivity of the organization is a final end rather than a means to an end. The public wants the agency to do a job that the public deems worthy and is willing to pay for. The owners of the corporation pay dollars in order to make more dollars.

The difference in the nature of the ownership has deep ethical implications. The public agency is created to serve values that the public considers worthy. In funding groups such as those that oversee the environment, assist the impoverished, or provide care for the aged, the public is asserting a moral value in saying that these social benefits are worth the sacrifice of public funds. Although there might be some self-interest that motivates people to fund such activities (such as the self-interest of cancer patients in the advancement of cancer research), most people support the activities of government to help the society as a whole rather than just themselves. A society must be moved by values above mere profit to charge a public agency with tasks and provide funds for those tasks.

While it might be said that a society's values are ultimately evident in the products that it buys, those values are more directly expressed in the agencies that it deliberately creates. Societies permit private companies and corporations to exist, but societies mandate the work of their public agencies. A society can allow an industry, such as the tobacco industry, to exist without approving of its products or encouraging people to buy them. But when the society creates and funds public agencies, it expresses a value that the society in general considers worthy.

The society's values are implicit not only in the public organizations that it creates, but also in the manners in which it requires those organizations to function. The people may choose to demand more ethical treatment of employees, respect for the environment, or financial disclosure from public agencies than from private firms. The governmental limitations on private organizations, even when they are imposed, express the society's ideas of how an organization is permitted to do its business, but the mandated structure of public agencies, in that they are created, maintained, and ultimately run by the society, expresses how they should conduct business.

In commenting upon the difference between public and private organizations, we do not mean to imply that private organizations are inherently unethical or amoral. The owners and stockholders of a private organization may, and often do, make ethical choices. Moreover, a private organization might even be founded upon ethical values. A private firm must, however, make a profit in order to stay in business. The public organization, by contrast, need not make a profit but must further the society's values as expressed in the organization's mission. Furthermore, even when the private organization chooses to advance ethical values, they are those that the owners, stockholders, and organization as a whole consider worthy. The public agency must advance the values that the public considers worthy.

## WHO'S RUNNING THE SHOP?

The employee implicitly acknowledges the values of the society in choosing to work in a public organization. He or she may not personally accept all of those values but must assume them as the foundation of his or her professional environment. That assumption is especially important in the case of the public administrator, who must make professional decisions on behalf of the society and its values.

Public administrators have often been characterized as public stewards, or people who manage the property and finances of the society on its behalf. As such, the public administrator must act as if he or she represented the public as a whole. But the role of public steward extends beyond just protecting property and paying bills. The steward must make evaluative decisions for the public at large.

The ethical commitment of the public agent is most critical in the stewardship capacity. The public administrator must consider more than the "bottom line." While efficiency and frugality are values that societies largely accept, they value other things as well. In making budgetary decisions, the public administrator must consider not only the cost, but also the importance of the activity under consideration. For example, the building of a shelter for the homeless may not be a cost-effective project. It could never "pay for itself," it requires expensive maintenance, and, because of a limited capacity, it serves relatively few people. A for-profit corporation would be extremely unlikely to enter the "business" of homeless shelters unless the government were paying for the project. The public administrator must make decisions relative to the building, repair, and maintenance of such projects with a view not only to saving public funds but also to what the public is willing to pay for.

The public administrator is also often forced into an ethical decision when the public interest conflicts with that of his agency. It may be in competition with other agencies for public funding. As committed as the administrator may be to the goals of his or her own division, the first consideration of the public steward is attainment of the society's values. The ideal public administrator would sacrifice his or her own interests for those of the public. While the ideal public administrator, like the ideal human being, may not exist, the acknowledgment of ideals has a magnetic appeal.

We do not imply that the manager of a private firm is not also a steward. However, the public administrator and the administrator in the private firm differ significantly in that the first is a steward of the public and the second is a steward of private interest.

In general, the private organization exists to make a profit, and the public organization exists to promote values that the public as a whole deems worthy. The public administrator expresses those values in stewardship. The difference can lead to different mind-sets among private and public administrators. The private administrator can rationalize his or her own pursuit of professional self-interest, even to the point of inhibiting or opposing the interest of the organization by an act of "twisted consistency." The private employee can argue that the firm is "in it for the money" and that he or she is therefore justified in operating on the same motive. The twisted consistency of the private employee becomes a virtuous consistency for the public employee, for whom the rationale would be transformed into: "The organization exists to serve the public, and therefore, so must I."

Research has provided evidence that public employees differ in significant ways from private employees. Two well known studies, one of graduate students preparing for positions in the public service (Rawls, Ulrich, and Nelson 1975) and the other of public employees (Rainey 1983), indicate that people who choose to work in public administration usually value money less and social improvement more than do private employees. If the results of those studies are accurate, public service attracts people who come into the profession already strongly influenced by ethical values. Such people would be well matched for a profession with significant ethical demands.

## WHAT DOES THE SHOP SELL?

Private businesses provide goods and services that the public chooses to purchase. Those goods and services include chewing gum, massage therapy, radar detectors, tattoos, and anything else that can turn a profit. Unless a question arises concerning whether a product is harmful, there is usually no need for the private firm to justify the existence of its product. One does not have to show that licorice, nose rings, or whitewall tires benefit the public at large for an entrepreneur to sell them. While private businesses often provide products that benefit the general population, such as housing and means of transportation, a private business need not demonstrate that it can provide such benefits to establish its legality or legitimacy.

In contrast, public agencies generally exist only because they provide a service that the public at large considers worthy. Defense, education, and programs for the disadvantaged may be questioned by some citizens, but most people would recognize the importance of those universally recognized governmental functions as self-evident. But if the government were to go into the cocoa business, one would ask, for a good reason, why. Governmental involvement in such an enterprise would need justification. In some cases, such a justification could exist; if a nation were highly dependent upon cocoa for its economic survival, the government might be entrusted with producing it. However, unlike private firms, government must justify its activities as being in the public interest. The services that public agencies provide are therefore usually socially very important. The importance of providing those services imposes a moral burden on the providers.

There are exceptions to nearly all generalizations, and we must mention some here. In some cases, public agencies may provide goods and services that are seen as inessential. If a business that employs many people is in jeopardy of failing, the government may step in to keep the organization alive. In such a case, the product may not be important to the society in general, but the existence of the business itself may be. Also, government may be entrusted with the sale of potentially harmful products in order to control them. In the UK, for example, the government provides drugs to addicts. The state of New Hampshire controls the sale of alcoholic beverages by means of a government monopoly. But the apparent exceptions prove the rule. For government to justify participation in such businesses, it must cite a significant public benefit.

In heavily socialized countries, government may provide most or all goods and services. But the existence of such societies does not refute the claim that governmental involvement must be justified as being in the public interest. Socialized societies are founded upon a system based on the assumption that governmental control of the means of production is important for the progress of the society as a whole. A private firm in a free-market society does not, as a rule, have to justify its existence by citing any such progress.

Succinctly stated: If government does something, it must be important. That importance imposes a special ethical demand upon public organizations and their employees. Moreover, that importance may be a major factor in attracting people with a strong social commitment to public service.

We do not mean to imply here that business does not do things that the society considers important. Business provides the wealth of goods and services in a free-market economy and thus benefits society immeasurably. However, it is not a prerequisite of business that it supply products that the society in general considers valuable. Business can supply food and clothing, which is of generally accepted social value, but business can also supply nose rings, which appeal to only a few and may even be disdained by most of the society. The sale of such items by a private business may be considered fully legitimate, but few people would consider them suitable matters for public agencies.

Private business benefits society by the products that it offers, the jobs that it supplies, and the vitality of the economy that it promotes. In theory, what is good for business is, on the whole—though not necessarily in every instance—generally good for a society. But even the strongest supporters of capitalism and the free market recognize that the intent of a private business is to make profits for itself. The net effect of a complex of businesses pursuing their private interest is, if all goes well, a more productive society. Nevertheless, the foremost concern of the private business is its own success. If the society is properly structured, the best interests of the whole will result, but the whole is a remote concern for the private organization. Individually, private organizations need not justify their existence by demonstrating a direct benefit to the society, but the public agency must justify its existence by showing that it has a general public charge.

Nor do we intend to suggest that private businesses ought not be ethical. On the contrary, everyone should be ethical. We argue, however, that there is an important difference between the nature of the ethical commitment of the two types of organizations. The private organization should obey ethical principles in the course of its activities, but the fundamental basis of the public organization is the ethical commitment to a value that the society deems important. Private business should operate within ethical restraint, but public organizations are ethical in their very being.

## SOCIAL VALUES ARE ESSENTIAL TO PUBLIC ADMINISTRATION

Barry Bozeman (1987) has argued that the distinction between the public and the private organization is somewhat blurry. He points out, for example, that private organizations are often under public regulation and political pressure. He prefers to speak of degrees of "publicness" and argues convincingly that virtually all private firms are public—that it, possess publicness—to some degree. If so, employees of private organizations are not exempt from some of the ethical pressures that apply to government agencies. Nevertheless, even if the difference is one of degree, government agencies have a much higher degree of publicness than most private sector companies.

Public agencies express public values, and managers of public organizations are responsible to those values. While private concerns may be influenced by those values and may show respect for them, public values are intrinsic to the public agency. Social values are not merely the context in which the public agency operates; they form its essence. It is therefore not surprising that those attracted to careers in public service are generally more committed than their counterparts in the private sector to social concerns. Their own personal fulfillment, that of the organization, and that of the society at large are in a harmonious unity.

Public service must rely heavily upon that unity to function properly. In a competitive environment like that under which some, though not all, private firms operate, the competition encourages quality performance. Public agencies must rely on two kinds of pressures for excellence, one external and the other internal. The external is the political pressure, often inspired by public dissatisfaction or at least skepticism. That pressure is often difficult to marshal against entrenched public agencies. But perhaps more importantly, that pressure is usually negative, in the form of threat. The internal pressure is that applied by public administrators to themselves in the quest for excellence. This pressure is positive because it is inspired by the desire to perform one's job well. This positive pressure comes from one's ethical values, and public administration depends upon them heavily.

## ETHICS STATEMENTS IN PRIVATE AND PUBLIC AGENCIES

Public administration is not one profession but innumerable professions combined to work for the public interest. Each has its own specific functions, problems, social benefits—and ethical issues. But since these professions are all included within public agencies, one would expect them to share some common ethical features that are different from those in private organizations. An examination of the ethics statements of public and private organizations confirms that such differences exist.

## Medical Ethics Statements As Models

One of the earliest, if not the earliest, ethics statements on record is the Hippocratic oath (see Exhibit 2.1).

---

**Exhibit 2.1** Hippocratic Oath

### Hippocratic Oath

I SWEAR by Apollo the physician, and Aesculapius, and Health, and All-heal, and all the gods and goddesses, that, according to my ability and judgment, I will keep this Oath and this stipulation—to reckon him who taught me this Art equally dear to me as my parents, to share my substance with him, and relieve his necessities if required; to look upon his offspring in the same footing as my own brothers, and to teach them this art, if they shall wish to learn it, without fee or stipulation; and that by precept, lecture, and every other mode of instruction, I will impart a knowledge of the Art to my own sons, and those of my teachers, and to disciples bound by a stipulation and oath according to the law of medicine, but to none others. I will follow that system of regimen which, according to my ability and judgment, I consider for the benefit of my patients, and abstain from whatever is deleterious and mischievous. I will give no deadly medicine to any one if asked, nor suggest any such counsel; and in like manner I will not give to a woman a pessary to produce abortion. With purity and with holiness I will pass my life and practice my Art. I will not cut persons laboring under the stone, but will leave this to be done by men who are practitioners of this work. Into whatever houses I enter, I will go into them for the benefit of the sick, and will abstain from every voluntary act of mischief and corruption; and, further from the seduction of females or males, of freemen and slaves. Whatever, in connection with my professional practice or not, in connection with it, I see or hear, in the life of men, which ought not to be spoken of abroad, I will not divulge, as reckoning that all such should be kept secret. While I continue to keep this Oath unviolated, may it be granted to me to enjoy life and the practice of the art, respected by all men, in all times! But should I trespass and violate this Oath, may the reverse be my lot!

*Source: Center for Study of Ethics in the Profession, Illinois Institute of Technology, http://csep.iit.edu/codes/coe/oath.html. Accessed July 17, 2001.*

---

There are several noteworthy factors in the oath. For example, there are no specified punishments, at least from earthly sources. While there is an invocation of possible divine punishment, there is little evidence to suggest that the oath-takers, including Hippocrates, feared such powers. While one might complain that such an oath has no "teeth" in it, the absence of any penalty identifies the oath as ethical rather than a legal or quasi-legal requirement. If the oath were enforced by punishment, those who adhere to it would do so out of self-interest rather than ethics.

In addition, we recognize that today many people would reject some of the specific prohibitions, such as that against abortion. However, taken as a whole and understood within the context of Hippocrates' time, the oath encourages the doctor to be altruistic and principled in his or her behavior. The general tone of respect for the life and health of patients and for the responsibilities of medical practice are more important than any of the more detailed statements. The intent, or "spirit," is more important than the letter.

A modern statement of medical ethics focuses more on the spirit than on the details (see Exhibit 2.2).

---

**Exhibit 2.2** International Code of Ethics

**The World Medical Association, Inc.**
**INTERNATIONAL CODE of MEDICAL ETHICS**

Adopted by the 3rd General Assembly of the World Medical Association, London, England, October 1949, and amended by the 22nd World Medical Assembly Sydney, Australia, August 1968, and the 35th World Medical Assembly Venice, Italy, October 1983.

DUTIES OF PHYSICIANS IN GENERAL

A PHYSICIAN SHALL always maintain the highest standards of professional conduct.

A PHYSICIAN SHALL not permit motives of profit to influence the free and independent exercise of professional judgment on behalf of patients.

A PHYSICIAN SHALL, in all types of medical practice, be dedicated to providing competent medical service in full technical and moral independence, with compassion and respect for human dignity.

A PHYSICIAN SHALL deal honestly with patients and colleagues, and strive to expose those physicians deficient in character or competence, or who engage in fraud or deception.

The following practices are deemed to be unethical conduct:

a) Self advertising by physicians, unless permitted by the laws of the country and the Code of Ethics of the National Medical Association.

b) Paying or receiving any fee or any other consideration solely to procure the referral of a patient or for prescribing or referring a patient to any source.

A PHYSICIAN SHALL respect the rights of patients, of colleagues, and of other health professionals and shall safeguard patient confidences.

A PHYSICIAN SHALL act only in the patient's interest when providing medical care which might have the effect of weakening the physical and mental condition of the patient.

A PHYSICIAN SHALL use great caution in divulging discoveries or new techniques or treatment through non-professional channels.

A PHYSICIAN SHALL certify only that which he has personally verified.

DUTIES OF PHYSICIANS TO THE SICK

A PHYSICIAN SHALL always bear in mind the obligation of preserving human life.

A PHYSICIAN SHALL owe his patients complete loyalty and all the resources of his science. Whenever an examination or treatment is beyond the physician's capacity he should summon another physician who has the necessary ability.

A PHYSICIAN SHALL preserve absolute confidentiality on all he knows about his patient even after the patient has died.

A PHYSICIAN SHALL give emergency care as a humanitarian duty unless he is assured that others are willing and able to give such care.

DUTIES OF PHYSICIANS TO EACH OTHER

A PHYSICIAN SHALL behave towards his colleagues as he would have them behave towards him.

A PHYSICIAN SHALL NOT entice patients from his colleagues.

A PHYSICIAN SHALL observe the principles of the "Declaration of Geneva" approved by the World Medical Association.

*Source: Center for Study of Ethics in the Profession, Illinois Institute of Technology, http://csep.iit.edu/codes/coe/World_Medical_Association_International_ Code_of_Medical_Ethics_October_1994.html). Accessed July 17, 2001.*

The World Medical Association's (WMA's) statement may appear more vague than the Hippocratic oath, but its generality is its strength. The WMA provides the principles for medical professionals to follow while leaving the judgment concerning how they are to be applied in specific cases to the professional. The WMA statement therefore includes more "spirit" than "letter" and is not as closely tied to a particular society or culture. The Hippocratic oath used specifics to express general ideals, while the WMA statement articulates the ideals themselves.

That difference notwithstanding, there are significant similarities between the two statements. Like the Hippocratic oath, the WMA statement specifies no penalties and is therefore ethical rather than legalistic. Moreover, neither contains any statement suggesting that the medical practitioner follow ethical principles to promote more business from the general public. The statements are intended not to improve public relations but to express concern for the public welfare and reverence for the ideals upon which the profession is founded—which themselves promote the public welfare. The statements promote ethics for the sake of the people served rather than for medical salesmanship.

The statements are also similar in the important respect to which the philosopher J. L. Austin (1975) refers as the "performative" aspect. Austin observed that many linguistic utterances, including those that have the grammatical form of descriptive statements, are not as important for what they say as for the linguistic act that the speaker performs in speaking them. For example, when someone says, "I do" in the course of a wedding service, one is not merely describing one's state of mind at the time but, more importantly, committing to a marriage. When a Muslim says, "God is Great," he or she is not only describing God or offering an opinion about him, but also expressing a commitment to the Islamic faith. And when someone on a beach yells, "I'm drowning!" he or she is not merely providing information for the curious, but calling for help.

Despite their differences at the literal level, the Hippocratic oath and the WMA statement are essentially the same at the performative level. Both strongly express the commitment that medical practitioners should have to the welfare of the patient rather than to themselves. As we examine ethics statements in other professions, both in the public and private sectors, we will note their important performative implications.

One might wonder why a medical statement should be considered a model for public administration. Doctors are not public administrators, but the profession has significant connections with public service. While doctors in the United States are largely privately employed, they often work in public hospitals. Furthermore, in countries that have national health care systems and that are included within the scope of the WMA, medical professionals are public agents. The Hippocratic oath and the WMA statement can apply in both a public and a private context and therefore provide models for both public and private professions.

In summary, we have identified three characteristics that are desirable in an ethics statement: (1) absence of specified penalties; (2) expression of general principles; and (3) commitment to the interests of those that the profession serves rather than to the interests of the professionals.

### Ethics Statements in the Private Sector

Ethics statements in the private sector generally express broadly recognized ethical ideals and are therefore similar to the Hippocratic oath and the WMA statement at the performative level. For example, the following is an excerpt from an ethical statement of the American Association of Advertising Agencies (AAAA):

> We hold that, to discharge this responsibility, advertising agencies must recognize an obligation, not only to their clients, but also to the public, the media they employ, and to each other. As a business, the advertising agency must operate within the framework of competition. It is recognized

that keen and vigorous competition, honestly conducted, is necessary to the growth and the health of American business.

*Source: Center for Study of Ethics in the Profession, Illinois Institute of Technology, http://csep.iit.edu/codes/ coe/aaa-b.htm. Accessed July 17, 2001.*

The excerpt expresses admirable sentiments: concern for clients; concern for the public at large; concern for the health of the national economy. However, the very next sentence of the statement suggests that, in addition to honoring those concerns, the statement performs a very different linguistic act:

However, unethical competitive practices in the advertising agency business lead to financial waste, dilution of service, diversion of manpower, loss of prestige, and tend to weaken public confidence both in advertisements and in the institution of advertising.

In this portion of the statement, we find an allusion to the financial interests of advertisers, who would be injured by negative publicity if advertisers were to engage in wanton unethical behavior. That allusion is made more explicit later in the statement.

These Standards of Practice of the American Association of Advertising Agencies come from the belief that sound and ethical practice is good business. Confidence and respect are indispensable to success in a business embracing the many intangibles of agency service and involving relationships so dependent upon good faith.

Here, the implication is unmistakable: Be ethical and business will be better for all of us.

Let us not be cynical, however. In the entire statement, much concern is expressed for ethics in general and for the public interest, as well as for the interest of clients. The statement is not merely a recommendation of business policy but, in large measure, an admirable expression of ethical concern. But while it is not only an appeal to self-interest, it is at least in part such an appeal.

But even in the matter of self-interest, we should not be too critical of AAAA. Its mission includes advancing the interests of advertisers, and in performing that mission, AAAA is doing exactly what it is expected to do. One might even argue that it has an ethical responsibility to the welfare of its members. We do not criticize AAAA's statement. On the contrary, we recognize that its combining of ethics with professional interest is perfectly legitimate for a private advertising business. The mere concern for ethics as included in the statement is admirable.

But advertising is not medicine. We do not observe such an appeal to business interest in either the Hippocratic oath or the WMA statement. We might have been dismayed if we had found such a statement, as for example "These standards of practice of medical profession come from the belief that sound and ethical practice in saving lives is good business."

The AAAA is not alone among private organizations in combining business with ethics. The Building Owners and Manager's Institute, which offers educational programs for people who own or manage buildings, provides a strong ethics statement but also includes the following:

> This code of professional ethics and conduct is designed to foster trust and mutual respect among those working in the industry, as well as the public at large. It is not intended to discourage fair and healthy competition within the industry, but to increase the esteem of the designations and the individuals who have earned them. We consider industry relationships critical to the industry's success.
>
> Source: Building Owners and Managers Association, http://www .bomi-edu.org/ethics.html. Accessed July 17, 2001.

The last sentence especially suggests that ethics is a means to a profitable end. By contrast, the American Association of Cost Engineers provides a detailed ethics code that makes no statement to the effect that ethics is good business. The inclusion of such a statement in one ethics code and not the other may reflect the nature of the professions. While the welfare of the public depends upon good ownership and management of buildings, the construction of buildings and other edifices is a more important matter.

The American Society of Appraisers is another association of private businesses with an ethics statement that makes no obvious mention of ethics for self-interest. (See: Center for Study of Ethics in the Profession, Illinois Institute of Technology, http:// csep.iit.edu/codes/coe/asa-a.htm.) However, the profession of appraising has close ties to public agencies, as any building owner is reminded when the property tax arises. It is possible that appraising is influenced as much by the public sector as by the private.

The concern for ethics as a matter of good business policy is evident also in the statements of specific firms. Here are some examples.

## Cummins Engine Company:

The Code of Business Conduct is an important foundation for Customer Led Quality. Our pursuit of Customer Led Quality will lead to Cummins being the best there is in products, customer support and business operations, and, as a result, growing our profitability to the benefit of all of our stakeholders.

Our success in realizing Customer Led Quality depends in large part on the trust that our stakeholders—customers, employees, suppliers, shareholders and the countries and communities in which we live and work—have in Cummins.

*Source: Center for Study of Ethics in the Profession, Illinois Institute of Technology, http://csep.iit.edu/codes/coe/Cummins.code_of_buss_conduct .html. Accessed July 17, 2001.*

## Caterpillar Tractors:

The company's most valuable asset is a reputation for integrity. If that becomes tarnished, customers, investors, suppliers, employees, and those who sell our products and services will seek affiliation with other, more attractive companies. We intend to hold to a single high standard of integrity everywhere. We will keep our word. We won't promise more than we can reasonably expect to deliver; nor will we make commitments we don't intend to keep.

*Source: Center for Study of Ethics in the Profession, Illinois Institute of Technology, http://csep.iit.edu/codes/coe/Caterpillar_Buss_Code_Old.html. Accessed July 17, 2001.*

## Pittsburgh Plate Glass Company:

Supply personnel must exercise sound business judgment and maintain a high ethical and moral standards in their business and personal conduct. Therefore, supply personnel must avoid any conflict of interest or other behavior that might mar PPG's reputation for integrity.

By observing absolute honesty in all transactions and correspondence, respecting supplier companies' confidences, and avoiding compromising obligations to supplier companies or representatives. Supply personnel can advance PPG's good name.

*Source: Center for Study of Ethics in the Profession, Illinois Institute of Technology, http://csep.iit.edu/codes/coe%5CPittsburgh_Plate_ Glass_Company.html. Accessed July 17, 2001.*

The references to profitability in the Cummins statement and to competitive advantage in the Caterpillar statement clearly indicate that promotion of business interests is one of the purposes of ethical behavior. The Pittsburgh Plate Glass Company statement is not so obviously commercial in its intent, but the two references to improving the company's reputation suggest a concern for more than merely ethics for its own sake.

One must keep some points in mind when examining these ethics statements by private companies. First, self-interest is not the only reason that private businesses, including those that we have noted, offer for ethical behavior. The inclusion of self-interest statements does not nullify the other aspects of the statements that may be purely ethical. Furthermore, since private companies are generally in business to make a profit, they are not to be condemned for advertising their ethical behavior to impress their clientele, so long as they also recognize that ethics is good in itself.

There is a notable difference between reasonable self-interest and selfishness or egotism. We expect private firms to pursue self-interest within an ethical framework and with respect for the public. A firm becomes unethical when it pursues self-interest without regard for ethics or the public interest.

What is most important in these statements is not their inclusion of self-interest as a motive for ethical behavior but that there is nothing especially surprising or shocking about such inclusions. One expects that private firms will behave in a manner that increases their competitive status. But as we noted earlier, we would be disappointed to find such inclusions in medical ethics statements. One would also assume that statements in public administration would make little reference to ethics as a means of financial success. A random selection of ethics statements from professions closely associated with public service supports that assumption.

## Ethics Statements in the Public Sector

The centrality of social values to public service is evident in the nature of the ethics statements of public agencies. Like the statements of private agencies, those of public agencies usually evoke general ethical ideals in the context of the work that the agency does. And also like private sector statements, those of the public sector usually preserve the purely ethical aspect by specifying no punishments or rewards. But unlike many private sector statements, public sector statements generally do not refer to material benefits that might accrue to the organization in return for ethical behavior. We would do well to begin with the broadest such organization in the United States, the American Society for Public Administration. It provides the following statement, quoted in full in Exhibit 2.3.

---

**Exhibit 2.3** American Society for Public Administration Code of Ethics

### American Society for Public Administration

*Code of Ethics*

*The American Society for Public Administration (ASPA) exists to advance the science, processes and art of public administration. The Society affirms its responsibility to develop the spirit of professionalism within its membership and to increase public awareness of ethical principles in public service by its example. To this end, we the members of the Society, commit ourselves to the following principles:*

### I. Serve the Public Interest
Serve the public, beyond serving oneself. ASPA members are committed to:
1. Exercise discretionary authority to promote the public interest.
2. Oppose all forms of discrimination and harassment, and promote affirmative action.
3. Recognize and support the public's right to know the public's business.
4. Involve citizens in policy decision-making.
5. Exercise compassion, benevolence, fairness, and optimism.
6. Respond to the public in ways that are complete, clear, and easy to understand.
7. Assist citizens in their dealings with government.
8. Be prepared to make decisions that may not be popular.

### II. Respect the Constitution and the Law
Respect, support, and study government constitutions and laws that define responsibilities of public agencies, employees, and all citizens.
ASPA members are committed to:
1. Understand and apply legislation and regulations relevant to their professional role.
2. Work to improve and change laws and policies that are counter-productive or obsolete.
3. Eliminate unlawful discrimination.
4. Prevent all forms of mismanagement of public funds by establishing and maintaining strong fiscal and management controls, and by supporting audits and investigative activities.
5. Respect and protect privileged information.
6. Encourage and facilitate legitimate dissent activities in government and protect the whistle-blowing rights of public employees.

7. Promote constitutional principles of equality, fairness, representativeness, responsiveness, and due process in protecting citizens' rights.

### III. Demonstrate Personal Integrity

Demonstrate the highest standards in all activities to inspire public confidence and trust in public service.

ASPA members are committed to:

1. Maintain truthfulness and honesty and not to compromise them for advancement, honor or personal gain.
2. Ensure that others receive credit for their work and contributions.
3. Zealously guard against conflict of interest or its appearance: e.g., nepotism, improper outside employment, misuse of public resources or the acceptance of gifts.
4. Respect superiors, subordinates, colleagues, and the public.
5. Take responsibility for their own errors.
6. Conduct official acts without partisanship.

### IV. Promote Ethical Organizations

Strengthen organizational capabilities to apply ethics, efficiency, and effectiveness in serving the public.

ASPA members are committed to:

1. Enhance organizational capacity for open communication, creativity, and dedication.
2. Subordinate institutional loyalties to the public good.
3. Establish procedures that promote ethical behavior and hold individuals and organizations accountable for their conduct.
4. Provide organization members with an administrative means for dissent, assurance of due process, and safeguards against reprisal.
5. Promote merit principles that protect against arbitrary and capricious actions.
6. Promote organizational accountability through appropriate controls and procedures.
7. Encourage organizations to adopt, distribute, and periodically review a code of ethics as a living document.

### V. Strive for Professional Excellence

Strengthen individual capabilities and encourage the professional development of others.

ASPA members are committed to:

1. Provide support and encouragement to upgrade competence.
2. Accept as a personal duty the responsibility to keep up to date on emerging issues and potential problems.
3. Encourage others, throughout their careers, to participate in professional activities and associations.
4. Allocate time to meet with students and provide a bridge between classroom studies and the realities of public service.

*Source: Center for Study of Ethics in the Profession, Illinois Institute of Technology, http://csep.iit.edu/codes/coe/aspa-c.htm. Accessed July 17, 2001.*

The ASPA statement strongly supports ethics for its own sake. Particularly noteworthy are the entries, "Service to the public is beyond service to oneself," and, "[s]ubordinate institutional loyalties to the public good." The statement, in its overall performative aspect, suggests a profound respect for the public, which deserves the highest ethical treatment.

One of the entries could be interpreted as self-interested. Section III speaks of inspiring public confidence and trust, so one might infer that the purpose of such safeguarding is to promote the interests of public administration as a profession. However, the entry does not indicate that to be the purpose. In the context of the whole statement, a more reasonable interpretation is that the entry is merely stating that the public trust is essential to the social order, and, for that reason, ethical principles must be observed.

The legal profession has close connections to public service. Although police officers are not administrators, they are public agents, and their ethics statements are composed by law enforcement administration. The ethics statement of the Michigan Police Department, shown in Exhibit 2.4, is typical of departments throughout the United States.

---

**Exhibit 2.4** Michigan Police Department Ethics Statement

AS A LAW ENFORCEMENT OFFICER, my fundamental duty is to serve the community; to safeguard lives and property; to protect the innocent against deception, the weak against oppression or intimidation and the peaceful against violence, or disorder; and to respect the constitutional rights of all to liberty, equality, and justice.

I will keep my private life unsullied as an example to all and will behave in a manner that does not bring discredit to me or my agency. I will maintain courageous calm in the face of danger, scorn, or ridicule; develop self-restraint; and be constantly mindful of the welfare of others. Honest in thought and deed in both my personal and official life, I will be exemplary in obeying the law and the regulations of my department. Whatever I see or hear of a confidential nature or that is confided to me in my official capacity will be kept ever secret unless revelation is necessary in the performance of my duty.

I will never act officiously or permit personal feelings, prejudices, political beliefs, aspirations, animosities, or friendships to influence my decisions. With no compromise for crime and with relentless prosecution of criminals, I will enforce the law courteously and appropriately without fear or favor, malice, or ill will, never employing unnecessary force or violence and never accepting gratuities.

I recognize the badge of my office as a symbol of public faith, and I accept it as a public trust to be held so long as I am true to the ethics of police service. I will never engage in acts of corruption or bribery, nor will I condone such acts by other police officers. I will cooperate with all legally authorized agencies and their representatives in the pursuit of justice.

I know that I alone am responsible for my own standard of professional performance and will take every reasonable opportunity to enhance and improve my level of knowledge and competence.

I will constantly strive to achieve these objectives and ideals, dedicating myself before God to my chosen profession—law enforcement.

*Source: Michigan State Police Post #38 Lapeer, http://www.msp.state.mi.us/lapeer/ ethics.html. Accessed July 12, 2001.*

---

Nothing in the police statement suggests any motive other than devotion to duty.

Attorneys represent another portion of the legal profession. They are, to some extent, similar to doctors in their relation to public administration in that both attorneys and doctors are generally in private practice in the United States, but, because of the importance of their work, they are public agents in many other countries. However, attorneys may be more influenced by the public mind-set because attorneys often become members of the judiciary or public prosecutors.

Ethics statements in the legal profession are longer and more detailed than police department statements, as one might expect from legal scholars, but their performative aspect is similar. By specifying minimal numbers of hours to be spent in providing free legal services to the needy and requiring attorneys to lower their fees for those who cannot pay, the profession makes evident its recognition that the attorney is to serve the public before himself or herself. Also, in enjoining attorneys to refrain from frivolous proceedings in behalf of clients, the statements imply that the legal system is more important than the attorney's private interest or those of his or her client. (*http://www2.law.cornell.edu/ cgi-bin/foliocgi.exe/modelrules/query=[group+rules!3A]+free+legal+ service/doc/{t251}?* Accessed July 12, 2001.)

While higher education is not necessarily a part of public administration, a very large portion of institutions of higher learning are public, and an even larger portion of students in the United States attend public colleges and universities. Their ethics statements reflect the commitment, more evident in public statements than in private industry statements, to social mission over personal or institutional interest. The excerpt shown in Exhibit 2.5 is from a statement by the American Association of University Professors.

---

**Exhibit 2.5** American Association of University
Professors Ethics Statement

I. Professors, guided by a deep conviction of the worth and dignity of the advancement of knowledge, recognize the special responsibilities placed upon them. Their primary responsibility to their subject is to seek and to state the truth as they see it. To this end professors devote their energies to developing and improving their scholarly competence. They accept the obligation to exercise critical self-discipline and judgment in using, extending, and transmitting knowledge. They practice intellectual honesty. Although professors may follow subsidiary interests, these interests must never seriously hamper or compromise their freedom of inquiry.

II. As teachers, professors encourage the free pursuit of learning in their students. They hold before them the best scholarly and ethical standards of their discipline. Professors demonstrate respect for students as individuals and adhere to their proper roles as intellectual guides and counselors. Professors make every reasonable effort to foster honest academic conduct and to ensure that their evaluations of students reflect each student's true merit. They respect the confidential nature of the relationship between professor and student. They avoid any exploitation, harassment, or discriminatory treatment of students. They acknowledge significant academic or scholarly assistance from them. They protect their academic freedom.

III. As colleagues, professors have obligations that derive from common membership in the community of scholars. Professors do not discriminate against or harass colleagues. They respect and defend the free inquiry of associates. In the exchange of criticism and ideas professors show due respect for the opinions of others. Professors acknowledge academic debt and strive to be objective in their professional judgment of colleagues. Professors accept their share of faculty responsibilities for the governance of their institution.

IV. As members of an academic institution, professors seek above all to be effective teachers and scholars. Although professors observe the stated regulations of the institution, provided the regulations do not contravene academic freedom, they maintain their right to criticize and seek revision. Professors give due regard to their paramount responsibilities within their institution in determining the amount and character of work done outside it. When considering the interruption or termination of their service, professors recognize the effect of their decision upon the program of the institution and give due notice of their intentions.

V. As members of their community, professors have the rights and obligations of other citizens. Professors measure the urgency of these obligations in the light of their responsibilities to their subject, to their students, to their profession, and to their institution. When they speak or act as private persons they avoid creating the impression of speaking or acting for their college or university. As citizens engaged in a profession that depends upon freedom for its health and integrity, professors have a particular obligation to promote conditions of free inquiry and to further public understanding of academic freedom.

*Source: Center for Study of Ethics in the Profession, Illinois Institute of Technology, http://csep.iit.edu/Codes/coe/aaup-g.htm. Accessed July 17, 2001.*

---

The samples that we have considered suffice to demonstrate a difference in tone between the public and private sectors, as expressed in ethics statements. In the philosophical language of Austin (1975), they perform both the act of asserting the importance of ethics in itself and also the act of recommending ethics to make business more profitable. Public sector statements also assert ethics for its own sake, but not for profit. Instead, public sector statements imply that ethics is central to the public service of which each public agency is a part. But it is not merely important that public sector statements contain little reference to the use of ethics as an instrument for personal or organizational advancement, but that any such statements would appear unseemly, as they would in the Hippocratic oath or in the WMA declaration. The context of private business is much more welcoming to the notion that ethics is a means to a material end.

## THE NEED FOR ETHICAL JUDGMENT

In emphasizing the public good rather than personal reward or negative consequences, public sector ethical statements treat the public employee as a moral individual who is capable of making the choice to do that which is right, regardless of self-interest. The statement tells the public agent what is right and leaves the responsibility for choosing it up to the individual.

In addition, the statements most often express general principles, values, and concerns rather than designating specific actions. The principles must be interpreted and practiced with good judgment in individual cases. The public agent cannot be a mere rule follower, but must look to the intent of the rule in order to properly understand and apply it. An example illustrates the result of following rules too rigidly.

The United States National Park Service requires permits for demonstrations at national monuments. Any group of twenty-six or more people who attract an audience constitutes a demonstration. Both the requirement and the definition of a demonstration appear to be reasonable, but even the most reasonable rules often must be applied with good judgment.

A group of high school students, numbering more than the specified twenty-six, were gathered at the Jefferson Memorial in Washington, D. C. They were winners in a nationwide essay contest conducted by the Veterans of Foreign Wars. Overcome by patriotic pride, the students spontaneously began singing the United States National Anthem and, in doing so, attracted a crowd. A park ranger, applying the Park Service regulations literally, silenced the students' unlawful demonstration just as they were singing the last stanza. Ironically, the topic of their essay contest was "What price freedom."

The National Park service reprimanded the ranger, who was described as a new employee.

One can sympathize with the ranger, who knew the rule and followed it. What the ranger lacked—probably because of inexperience, was the judgment needed to apply a rule properly. There is a well known fallacy called "Misuse of a General Principle," which, as the name implies, is the application of a principle to cases in which it does not apply. Using a principle properly, determining how and when it applies, and understanding the intent of a principle require judgment. The public sector ethics statements that we have examined, as well as some of the private sector statements, presuppose good judgment. The ethical public administrator must understand the nature of ethical values in order to exercise such judgment, rather than blindly following regulations. But developing and refining ethical understanding is a difficult, lifelong process.

In this chapter we have noted significant differences between ethics in the private sector and ethics in the public sector. Early in the chapter, we noted that the Hippocratic oath and the ethics statement of the World Medical Association express a commitment to ethics in itself because the medical profession is ethical to its very core. We noted, by contrast, that many private organizations, while acknowledging the importance of ethics, often treat it as a means to better business. The general environment of the public agency, as evidenced in its ethics statements, is closer to that of the medical profession than to that of most private firms. Public agencies' statements reflect more unqualified concern for ethical values in themselves.

The greater concern for ethics among public agencies is a natural concomitant of the nature of public service. The public agency is ethically bound to the society, which expresses its most important values by entrusting them to the public service. The public agent must embody those values, and they must motivate him or her in a more positive and noble way than the profit motive and competition drive private enterprise. People in private business are ethical because they are human beings, all of whom have the responsibility to be good, but in the public service, ethics is not only in the nature of the human animal, but also in the nature of the profession. Ethics should influence, limit, and, at least to some degree, inspire private enterprise, but ethics is at the heart of public administration. The following chapters will develop the concept of the essentially ethical nature of the public agency.

Our paradigm examples of good ethical statements are from the medical profession, which is, in some countries such as the United States, largely in private hands. Other private professions, such as the law, also place a strong emphasis on ethics. One might argue that the concern for ethics as an essential aspect of a profession exists within the private as well as the public sector.

We reply by agreeing that private professions may also partake in the same ethical commitment as public service. The public sector has no monopoly on professions in which ethics is essential. But in professions such as those mentioned, the ethical commitment follows from the specific nature of the profession itself and not from its status as a private business. Medicine is essentially ethical because it is medicine and not because it is a business. Like the priesthood or the ministry, medicine may be considered a calling more than a mere means of employment. Public service may likewise be considered a calling.

# CHAPTER 3

# What Is Ethics, Anyway?

Discussions of ethics often evoke more emotion than reason. Typically, when the subject is introduced to an audience of professionals, they display what we call "ethics aversion syndrome," which we will designate as EAS. They clench their fists, look askance, and remain silent for a moment until one of them makes a comment such as, "Let's get back to the real world"—as if ethics were not part of their world. In this chapter, we examine the reasons for EAS and why people seem so uncomfortable discussing ethics. We will also scan the history of the study of ethics to make it more familiar and less mysterious.

## WHY DOES ETHICS MAKE ME NERVOUS?

Among the first reasons for EAS is the recognition that it is impossible to behave in a fully ethical manner in an ethically flawed organization. Wouldn't it create a hellish mess to be really honest and fair on personnel evaluations by calling an average worker average, a good worker good, and a bad worker bad! Can you imagine how ludicrous it would be to return voluntarily a surplus in your departmental budget? And isn't it absurd to expect public money to be treated as if it came from the public? Purification of government organizations is as likely as purification of the nation's entire food and water supply.

But despite obvious and unavoidable ethical flaws in organizations, they must have some ethical basis if they are to function effectively. If personnel evaluations were written so that no one could infer anything from them, good performances would be no more acknowledged than poor ones. The reward system would be rendered useless, and the organization would suffer. It suffers also when budgets are padded by individual departments so that funds are not allocated in the most productive manner and responsible fiscal planning is reduced to a set of turf battles. And if public funds are treated in a totally cavalier manner, the public will eventually reduce or eliminate them. Ethics, even in imperfect form, is already a part of the organization, and, like any aspect of the organization, can be improved by the efforts of committed individuals. We advocate neither ethical metamorphosis nor ethical perfection, but ethical improvement.

A second cause of EAS is the sense that ethics would add an unnecessary complication to one's job. The burden of even incremental ethical improvement would add to an already complex occupation. To labor over the ethical aspects of matters such as evaluation, funding, and maximization of service to the public might be seen as introducing a new layer of professional concern. But, far from introducing a new factor, concern for ethics is already a part of one's professional responsibilities. Ethical issues are present, at least potentially, whenever one person makes decisions that affect others. Although there are laws, regulations, and written policies that govern such decisions, no formalized rules can possibly cover all cases. Ethics is already part of the job. To simplify a job by ignoring its ethical aspects is unprofessional.

Furthermore, ignoring ethical aspects may ultimately complicate a job. Ethical principles do not exist merely to restrict and complicate one's behavior. Ethics is the culmination of human experience regarding important issues. As evidenced by the Watergate affair, application of that experience is more likely to simplify the effects of one's actions in the long term. If ethical people had prevented the Watergate burglary, the country and the Nixon administration would have avoided enormous problems. The ensuing coverup, which ethical action also would have prevented, caused even more difficulty for the nation and the government. The public official who ignores ethics is almost certain to create or contribute to problems. He or she may no longer be with the organization when they occur, but they will occur.

A third source of EAS is the complaint that "I know my job, and I don't need so-called ethics experts telling me what to do." But the point of this book is to help you to make your own ethical decisions without the need for reputed experts or anyone else. We hope to help you in learning *how* to think about ethics rather than *what* to think.

This leads us to another source of EAS: "I am an ethical person; the notion that I need to learn to be ethical is a personal insult." Indeed, most people are well-meaning and generally intend to be ethical. But some issues, especially unforeseen ones, can be very confusing and complicated from an ethical perspective. For example, when sudden layoffs are required, even when all efforts to avoid them have been explored, should the younger, less experienced but lower-salaried workers be fired, or should the older, more experienced and more expensive workers, who will have greater difficulty finding new positions, be removed? To what extent should race, ethnicity, or gender be considered in a worker's favor? Should a person's status as needing only a few months to qualify for significant retirement benefits be considered?

People with the highest ethical intents have vastly different opinions on ethical issues such as these. To have ethical intent is not enough; one must be prepared to think through the difficult cases.

But thoughts of difficult cases give rise to another fear that contributes to EAS: What can one do if, after analyzing the difficult case, one comes to a conclusion unwelcome to colleagues and supervisors? Like the prophet in his own land, the ethical public administrator can become a pariah. He or she could discover ethically questionable activity of individuals in the organization or even entrenched in the organizational culture. It is difficult and professionally risky to tell others in the workplace that they have been unethical. But if they persist in their unethical ways, the ethical thinker might, in extreme cases, be tempted to blow a whistle.

If our recommendations are followed, the whistle will not need blowing—at least not as often. Our aim is to make the organization more ethical, so that even when the occasional and inevitable ethical violation occurs, the organization will respond appropriately. But if it does not, we can only respond with the unfortunate but obvious: Sometimes one ought to blow a whistle.

Finally, there is the prospect that perhaps causes the deepest EAS-related anxiety: Perhaps one might discover one's own unethical behavior. This prospect is especially threatening to those of us who have hitherto regarded ourselves as perfect. The discovery of one's own ethical flaws is like one's first dental cavity, one's first gray hair, or the first realization that there really are some people in this world who do not care to date you. The antidote for this form of anxiety is a modicum of realistic modesty. No one is perfect. If one expects the organization to accept one's criticism, he or she ought to be willing to accept it also.

Unquestionably, ethics is very complicated at many levels. But all professionals have complicated tasks, and for the public administrator, ethical decisions are a necessary part of the job. Unfortunately, that part has been relatively neglected. Therefore, a brief scan of what history's great thinkers said on the subject of ethics would be useful.

## THE GREAT HISTORICAL TRADITIONS

Nearly all ethical theories can be divided into several categories. Any such division, such as the political divisions of liberal, conservative, and moderate, may oversimplify, but may also make the subject matter easier to understand. For the moment, we are not concerned with subtleties, but with general structures, so we will examine the general categories and leave the minutiae to the scholars.

### Relativism

The first class of theories, ethical relativism, is often publicly espoused by people who really do not believe it. We are not accusing these people of dishonesty. They truly think that they are ethical relativists, but they do not realize that they are not what they consider themselves to be. This peculiar state of affairs and the reasons for it will become clearer when we examine ethical relativism.

Ethical relativism is the belief that there is no single ethical standard that applies to all people at all times. The ethical relativist believes that different societies have different standards and that there is no one universal standard that applies to all. On the surface, ethical relativism is very appealing. It would seem very unfair and chauvinistic, for example, for Americans to apply their standards of morality to everyone else. It would even be unfair for one person to impose his or her standards on others in his or her own society. Suppose, for example, that James considers polygamy to be morally wrong. Should he therefore condemn Muslims and Mormons, who believe in polygamy?

There are innumerable ethical issues, such as capital punishment, abortion, and gay rights, that divide people in our society today. Wouldn't we all be happier if everyone were free to believe according to his or her own conscience? The ethical relativist seems to say that everyone should apply and be judged by his or her own standards, and therefore the ethical relativist seems to be open-minded, nonjudgmental, virtuous, and correct.

But the issue is not so simple. The ethical relativist, in stating that there is no single ethical standard that applies to all people, also removes the possibility of any universally valid reasons for the choice of an ethical standard. For example, let us imagine an ethical relativist listening to a discussion among three people on capital punishment.

Alex claims to believe in capital punishment because, in his opinion, justice requires that a person suffer the same injuries that he or she imposes on others. Therefore Alex believes in capital punishment for murder. The ethical relativist, considering Alex's position, concludes that capital punishment is right for Alex, though not necessarily right for anyone else. Bertha thinks differently from Alex. She thinks that capital punishment is wrong because human life is sacred and should never be taken for any reason. As in the case of Alex, the ethical relativist concludes that capital punishment is wrong for Bertha but not necessarily wrong for anyone else. Cletis then offers his opinion. Cletis judges all moral issues by throwing dice. If the dice roll an even number, he is for capital punishment, but if the number is odd, he is against capital punishment. The dice comes up even, so he is for capital punishment, at least until he throws the dice again. He used this procedure when he was on a jury that sentenced the defendant to death. The ethical relativist must say the same thing about Cletis that he said about Alex and Bertha: Cletis's coin flip is just as valid as Alex's reliance on retributive justice and Bertha's belief in the sanctity of human life. The coin flip is right for Cletis, though not necessarily right for anyone else.

But, one might protest that there is nothing morally relevant about a coin flip. At least Alex and Bertha base their conclusions on morally relevant factors. However, the relativist will ignore the protest because it applies an allegedly universal ethical standard. The protester argues that it is universally true that a coin flip is an inadequate reason for an ethical decision, but the relativist allows no universal standards.

Darla now enters the conversation with her own unusual ethical approach. She points out that many people base their ethical decisions on role models, such as Muhammad, Buddha, or Jesus. Functioning as her own role model, she chooses her own behavior as her standard. She stipulates that whatever she does is right because her own behavior constitutes her standard. Consequently, she proudly proclaims her own perfection. The ethical relativist duly congratulates her because he recognizes her own moral opinion as the only standard that can apply to her.

It would be difficult to imagine a society built on relativism. One person would pay taxes as a moral duty; another would be equally morally justified in refusing to pay taxes because he considers them optional. A third considers it her moral duty not to pay taxes at all. Two people conspire to murder a third, but the two murderers are not equally responsible. One is morally reprehensible because he considers murder to be morally wrong, but the other is blameless because she sees nothing wrong with murder. The society might be seen to agree on only one statement: No one should impose his or her moral beliefs on others.

But if the society is truly relativistic, its members could not agree even to that statement because of the occurrence of the word "should." The statement, "No one should impose his or her moral beliefs on others," is itself an absolute moral statement. To be consistent in one's relativism, one would refuse to apply any moral terms or moral concepts, including admonitions against imposing moral judgments.

One can now see why we claimed that many people who claim to be ethical relativists really are not. Although many people will superficially maintain that there is no single true ethical standard, few people, if any, refuse to make any moral judgments. If such people exist, they would deny that mother Teresa was better or worse than Adolf Hitler, that the Red Cross was better or worse than the Soviet KGB, or that a society of equally free citizens was better or worse than a slave state. As easy as it is to proclaim ethical relativism, it is much more difficult to be a relativist. Most people who claim to be relativists are unaware of the problem.

But those who reject relativism in favor of the belief in a universal ethical standard also have a problem. They must answer the questions "What is the correct standard?" and "How do we know that it is correct?" Those are the most difficult questions for ethical absolutists, who, unlike the ethical relativists, believe that there is a universal ethical standard. Ethical absolutism can be divided into four subgroups: teleological theories; deontological theories; intuitionist theories; and virtue theories. We now will examine the differences and similarities among those subgroups.

## Teleology

We all want to be happy. We also want those whom we love to be happy. We would want everyone to be happy if it were possible for them all to be so. Such desires for happiness for ourselves and others are the bases for utilitarianism, the theory that happiness is the good and that we ought to do whatever is necessary to promote the greatest happiness. Utilitarianism is the predominant teleological ethical theory, which is the group of ethical theories that justify the morality of an action on the basis of its consequences. Teleological theories let "the end justify the means," and utilitarianism is teleological because it considers happiness to be the end that always ought to be produced. (Mill 1979)

The centrality of happiness as a value is clearly evident in the professional life of the public administrator. The aim of public organizations such as those concerned with health, education, safety, and poverty is to make the lives of people happier. The notion of happiness as justification for public action is included in the statement in the Declaration of Independence, in which the pursuit of happiness is described as an "inalienable right." George Frederickson (1997) has strong evidence for his claim that public administration, at the level of service providers, is relentlessly teleological.

Nor should we overlook the importance of the happiness of the public administrator. The profession would not be attractive to capable, productive people if they could not find happiness in it. That happiness would come from remuneration, good working conditions, and, perhaps most importantly, the satisfaction of providing happiness for others. In the ideal condition, the work of the public administrator would unite his or her own happiness with that of the people that the organization is intended to serve.

Utilitarian philosophers such as Jeremy Bentham (1970) and Mill (1979) would envision an ideal world in which the happiness of all people is unified so completely that the activities that make any individual happy would also promote the happiness of all. However, the world is not ideal, and there are many conflicts. A corporation's management, its labor force, its customers, and its investors all have different interests that may converge but will often conflict. So also will the interests of the managers of a public organization, its service providers, those to whom it provides services, its funding sources, and individual members of the organization. How can one find a balance among all of these conflicting considerations?

The utilitarian can only give a broad answer to the question: When the happiness of all members of a group cannot be fully provided, promote the greatest total happiness. Although that suggestion may seem satisfactory, it provides only a general approach but no clear method of assessing happiness to determine what constitutes the greatest happiness.

Suppose, for example, that within one society, the happiness of poor people depends upon social programs, the happiness of many of the more numerous wealthy and middle class people would be increased if taxes are lowered, but the happiness of other wealthy and middle class people who work for government agencies would be improved with higher social spending and thus greater taxation. But even this three-way conflict is greatly oversimplified. In any existing society, the conflicts would be greater and more complex. For example, there may be some altruistic people among the middle class or wealthy who would be made happier if the poverty of others were removed. There may be also some among the needy who would rather not make use of social programs. It is easy enough to claim that conflicts should be resolved by promoting the greatest total happiness, but it is often virtually impossible to determine what constitutes that happiness.

The problem is exacerbated by the vagueness in the notion of happiness. Mill (1979) found it necessary to introduce the concept of quality in happiness because he recognized that more happiness is not necessarily better happiness. The life of a carefree "satisfied fool" may be more enjoyable and less painful than that of a "dissatisfied Socrates," whose wisdom produces enormous burdens and pains, including the commitment to principles that leads him to condemnation and execution. To avoid concluding that the life of a satisfied fool is better than the life of the dissatisfied Socrates, Mill argues that the lesser quantity of the happiness of the dissatisfied Socrates is outweighed by its greater quality.

But Mill provides neither any clear definition of happiness nor any means of measuring the quality of one happiness against the quality or quantity of another. How, then, are we to measure the quality of the happiness of the altruistic people who wish to remove poverty, against the quantity of happiness of those who wish to keep their money to finance material possessions and promote their financial security?

The number and nature of seemingly irresolvable conflicts is overwhelming. They occur on matters concerning public support of, among other matters, the environment, education, the arts, and social security. Utilitarianism provides little wisdom by recommending solutions that may be theoretically sound but practically useless.

But even the theoretical soundness of utilitarianism has been questioned. Some theorists, such as Immanuel Kant (1959), have argued that there are cases in which happiness should be sacrificed for higher values. For example, let us suppose that there is legislation before Congress that would promote the greatest happiness—however happiness may be measured—at the expense of the poorest members of the society. The legislation would lower the taxes of all citizens who pay taxes but will remove a subsidy on housing for those who cannot afford it. Is the happiness of the whole more important than providing a minimal existence for the poor? Do individuals not have rights that should be honored even at a cost to society in general?

Other cases are equally troublesome. Administrators of public agencies may be tempted to misrepresent facts to secure increased funding. Those administrators may privately defend their actions by pointing out, perhaps accurately, that those who make funding decisions are not knowledgeable enough to properly understand the actual facts, so they must be presented with misleading information, for the ultimate public good. Should the good end justify such questionable means?

Similar cases are very familiar to those who work in public agencies. Managers often discover departmental "needs" at the end of a funding cycle to justify spending surplus funds and, thus, to avoid cutbacks in the next cycle. In evaluation of personnel, terms such as "excellent" and "superior" are often used with little concern for their conventional meanings. The benefits of attendance at distant conferences, however worthy, are often exaggerated to ensure that the uninformed funding sources will not err on the side of frugality. Are such distortions ethical? Most people would at least question them, but for the utilitarian, there is no question: Promoting the greatest happiness is more important than any other principles.

## Deontology

In contrast to the utilitarian, teleological position, we often find ourselves saying, "It's the principle of the thing." There is something in us that says that we should not only produce the right results, but we must do things in a principled way. That is the position of the deontological theorist. A deontological ethical theory is one which maintains that the ethics of an action does not depend upon the consequences, but upon an important feature of the act itself. For most deontological theories, that feature is the obedience of an action to a principle. Kant is the most notable deontological influence on contemporary ethics and perhaps the most important deontologist in all of human history. His stature is so significant that his theory is designated by his own name, "Kantianism."

According to Kant (1959), the most important aspect of any principle, whether in mathematics, physics, or any other field, including ethics, is consistency. Human beings are naturally rational, and they reject contradictions. Human beings therefore cannot believe in square circles, immovable objects that meet irresistible forces, and applying rules to others that you refuse to apply to yourself. To Kant, the golden rule, "Do unto others as you would have them do unto you," is a common sense expression of this concept of consistency.

While favoring the intent of the golden rule, Kant realized that its wording could be abused. For example, if I am a vegetarian,

I might do unto others as I would have them do unto me by favoring a law that would prohibit the sale and consumption of meat. On the other hand, a cattle rancher may favor a law that prohibits the sale of all meat other than beef. In both of those cases, people apply the golden rule for selfish purposes. The intent of the golden rule is not egocentric, but its wording allows selfish manipulation.

Kant claims that we all recognize that we must be consistent, but there is no foolproof way of formulating consistency in a way that infallibly describes moral action. His first formulation of his "categorical imperative," which means "absolute moral command," was "I should never act in such a way that I could not also will that my maxim should become a universal law" (18). For example, one could not will lying to be a universal law without contradiction. If we all acted according to the rule "You must always lie," a conflict would result. In many cases, we could lie successfully, even if everyone expected us to do so because they anticipated that we would be following this rule.

If someone asked where we live, we could give false information that would impart nothing. If someone asked our age, we could again lie successfully. But if someone asked a question, such as "Do you have a living parent?" for which there are only two alternatives, no lie would be possible. A lie is a false statement that, unlike a statement in a drama or a joke, is intended to deceive. To make a false statement in this case would not be a lie because everyone, anticipating that a falsehood is forthcoming, would infer the truth. On the other hand, a true statement intended to deceive would not be a lie because such a statement would not be false.

Kant's objection to lying is different from that of the utilitarian, whose primary concern is promoting happiness. For Kant, lying is not bad merely because it usually—though not always—fails to support happiness. Kant rejects lying because of the logical contradiction in making a rule that one must lie all the time. That contradiction is evident in the statement, "This statement is a lie." If the statement is true, it is also false; if it is false, it is also true.

One could not make a consistent universal law of "Stealing is morally acceptable" either. If stealing is acceptable, property rights would no longer exist, so there would no longer be any stealing. The rule would thus defeat itself. Similarly, the rule, "It is acceptable to make a false promise," would contradict itself. A promise is, by definition, an obligation, but a false promise, which does not obligate, would not be a promise to begin with.

To be consistent requires not only that one obey consistent laws but also that one apply laws consistently. A rule such as "Everyone except me should be considerate" would offend not only our sense of common courtesy but also our sense of logic. One would ask, "If everyone else should be considerate, why, logically, should you not also?" Therefore Kant says that one should not only obey a universal law, but also follow a law that one could *will* to be universal. One could not will a rule to be universal if one were to make an exception for himself.

But despite Kant's attempt to improve on the golden rule, his first formulation of the categorical imperative has similar problems. One could still will an egocentric law, such as the cattleman's "Everyone should eat at least one pound of beef a day" to be universal. Kant realizes that problem, so he offers a second way of formulating the notion of consistency. To understand this second formulation, we must begin by acknowledging the slight that we all feel when we realize that we have been manipulated. We take offense when we discover that someone, be it a telemarketer, a teacher, or a parent, has used us. As human beings, we resent being treated as inanimate objects or material commodities. Such treatment denies our humanity. But if we consider such abuse to be an unacceptable degradation, consistency requires that we avoid treating others in an equally manipulative manner.

Kant therefore states his second formulation of the categorical imperative as, "Act so that you treat humanity [i.e., rational beings], whether in your own person or that of another, as an end and never as a means only" (47). The value of a rational human being is intrinsic, so human beings should not be used as if they were instruments for some ulterior purpose.

There are two especially noteworthy points concerning the second formulation. First, it presents a point of contact between Kant and the utilitarian concern for happiness. To treat someone as an end in himself or herself entails taking that person's happiness fully into consideration, as a utilitarian would. Secondly, to treat people as ends in themselves rather than as instruments of another person's will requires that one treat people as free, responsible agents. If I were to treat someone merely as a means to my own ends, I would be depriving that person of the freedom to pursue his or her own ends.

Kant's second formulation has much appeal. No one likes to be used. We all recognize that the birth and death of a human being is of a different order from the creation or destruction of an automobile, a building, or an insurance company. People are important because they are people. Administrators in public service realize that the people they serve are not means to the administrator's employment, but people who are to be served because of their own inherent value.

Nevertheless, Kant's second formulation is not without problems. It is not always clear when we are treating people as a means, and, sometimes, treating one person as an end in himself or herself may require treating another as a means. For example, taxing one group of people for the welfare of others appears to be a case of using the first group as a means. Would Kantianism therefore prohibit all taxation that helps one group at the expense of another? One might reply that such taxation is needed to treat the beneficiary as an end, yet the person who bears the burden of taxation is still a means.

Kant realized that there were deficiencies in his second formulation, as in his first. He therefore attempted to formulate a third statement to cover problematic cases, though it, too, like all human creations, is imperfect. The third formulation is not as clearly stated as the first two but it attempts to capture the notion of a society entirely consistent within itself. The third formulation may best be stated as, "Consider all of your acts as if they were laws in a realm of ends," with a "realm of ends" understood as a society in which all ends unite into a coherent whole. The notion of the realm of ends captures the idea of consistency because it is a society in which all people's ends are consistent with all others. The realm also captures the notion of people as ends in themselves because, since the aim of such a realm is to render each person's ends consistent with all others, each person's ends, and therefore each person, are treated as inherently valuable. The general thrust of the third formulation is to suggest that we all attempt to produce and perpetuate an ideal society.

The third formulation seems to overcome the aforementioned problem concerning taxation. If one is attempting to create a realm of ends, taxing one group in a manner that is not overly oppressive to provide others with the basics of life may be in order. Indeed, if the people who bear the burden of taxation think of themselves as acting in a realm of ends, they would probably willingly contribute.

Nevertheless, even the third formulation has its weaknesses. It provides us with the image of an ideal to guide our actions, but ideals are notoriously ambiguous when applied to practical cases. The image of an ideal provides little guidance concerning moral problems such as capital punishment, abortion, or war. In the ideal world, such things would not exist, but they do exist in our world. The image of an ideal tells us where we want to go but it does not tell us how to get there.

Rather than look to Kant's categorical imperative or any of its formulations as a formulaic solution to all ethical problems, it is perhaps best to consider his idea of rational consistency as a theoretical foundation for ethics and to consider his formulations as guidelines to assist in our moral thinking. Both the general notion of consistency and the formulations must be interpreted when applied to specific cases. There will be many cases of ambiguous interpretation, but they do not suggest that we abandon the general Kantian concepts. The Constitution of the United States admits of great ambiguity of interpretation, but its flexibility may be understood as a strength rather than a weakness. Perhaps it is best that we ask Kant or any other ethical theorist to provide us not with a formula, but with a general understanding—to tell us how to think about ethics rather than what to think.

## Intuitionism

In examining the theories of utiltiarianism and Kantianism, we relied heavily on our basic, gut-level moral feelings. If a theory coincides with those feelings, we tend to agree with it, and if a theory offends our moral sensitivities, we tend to reject it. We may even consider those feelings to be more important than logic. If a theory seemed perfectly logical but concluded that Hitler's behavior was better than Mother Teresa's, we would reject the theory and perhaps even logic itself. But if we use a moral sensitivity to evaluate ethical theories, why not consult it as the ultimate source of moral evaluation? Such is the thinking of the intuitionist.

Intuitionism is the belief that human beings have a moral sense that recognizes the moral character of an act. G. E. Moore (1976), the best-known modern intuitionist, compares the moral sense to color perception. We know that an object is yellow when we see it. We do not reach the conclusion that the banana on the grocery table is yellow by means of abstract argumentation or reasoning; we merely see that it is yellow. Similarly, our moral sense, and not some esoteric theory, tells us that helping people is better than torturing them in concentration camps.

The intuitionist appears to be on firm ground in claiming that moral judgments depend upon feeling more than upon theories and arguments. If theories and arguments were the source of ethics, then the best theorists and arguers among us would be the most moral. The opposite is just as likely true.

Yet intuitionism is problematic. The intuitionist tells us, on the basis of a moral sense, that some actions are ethical and some are not. However, there are controversial ethical issues on which people's moral senses differ. One would hope that a moral theory would help in these difficult cases, but the intuitionist provides no way to decide among the different intuitions. Furthermore, the intuitionist would not allow rational argument to decide among intuitions; if rational argument decided among conflicting intuitions, then reason, rather than intuition, would be the ultimate source of ethics. The intuitionist appears to be correct in asserting an important role for the moral sense in ethics, but the intuitionist appears to be mistaken in claiming that the moral sense is the only or the ultimate ethical source.

## Virtue Theory

The fourth major group of ethical beliefs, strongly associated with the ancient philosopher Aristotle (1980) and the modern philosopher Alasdair MacIntyre (1981), is called virtue theory. As the name suggests, virtue theory considers an act to be good on the basis of the character trait or virtue that the act evidences. For example, saving a child from a burning building is a good act because it evidences courage, giving money to the poor evidences generosity, and returning an overpayment from a bank teller evidences honesty. Unethical actions, such as cheating on income taxes or always letting someone else pick up the restaurant tab, evidence poor character traits.

Virtue theory emphasizes the importance of the whole person in ethical evaluation rather than the details of action. But, like the other theories, virtue theory has questionable aspects. One may ask the virtue theorist why certain traits, such as honesty and generosity, are good while other traits, such as cowardice and selfishness, are bad. At first, such questions may seem easy to answer, but the answers may suggest an incompleteness in virtue theory. For example, it may seem obvious that honesty is good because it is important for maintaining a cohesive, trusting civil society. But that answer would suggest that the ultimate reason that a virtue is good is really a teleological one. Honesty is not just good in itself, but it is good because of its promotion of a happy society. The virtues that the virtue theorist extols are not good for arbitrary reasons. But to answer the question "Why are these virtues good?" leads beyond virtue theory itself to some other foundation.

## COMBINING THE GREAT HISTORICAL TRADITIONS INTO A UNIFIED PROCESS

Consideration of these theories can be confusing. They all differ, but they all seem strong in some respects while wanting in others. Deciding among them may be great fun for academicians, but we have the more pressing task of discovering among the theories something that can help us in making ethical decisions. Perhaps rather than choose among them, we should acknowledge that each has valuable insights that we can use.

We may compare the differing ethical theorists to the proverbial group of blind people each trying, from a different standpoint, to discover the nature of an elephant. Each sees a different part, but the whole might be better understood if all the parts were combined into an overall description. Even then, the understanding of the whole may be incomplete but would, nevertheless, be much better than that of one standpoint, e.g., teleology or deontology, or no standpoint at all, e.g., relativism.

In combining the different ethical standpoints, we may compile the questions that each theory would ask. In preparing for such a compilation, a brief comparison of the theories on the basis of their main points, as represented in the list below, may be helpful.

- **Teleology:** Act in order to produce the greatest happiness as a consequence.

- **Deontology:** Act according to the proper principle, and be consistent in applying it.

- **Intuitionism:** Act according to your inner sense of what is right or wrong.

- **Virtue theory:** Act as a person of good character, and set a good moral example for others to follow.

This list enables us to construct another that compares the questions that each theory, as we have previously discussed it, would have us ask.

### Teleology:

- What are the consequences of my action?

- What are the long-term effects of my action?

- Does my action promote the greatest happiness?

### Deontology:

- What principle applies in this case?

- Can this principle be applied consistently in this case and in all similar cases?

- Can this principle be considered as a possible universal principle of behavior?

- Which course of action best exemplifies the ideal of treating all people as ends in themselves?

- Which course of action best exemplifies and most fully promotes the ideal of a society of free, responsible people whose ends promote each other rather than conflict with each other?

### Intuitionism:

- What does my conscience tell me about this action?

- Do I feel good about this action?

**Virtue theory:**

- What character traits does this action express?

- What effect will this action have on my character?

- What effect will this action have on the character of other people?

- Is this the action of a person whose character I would admire?

The list of questions is not intended to be complete but forms a strong foundation for moral decision making. Additional factors may include one's ethnic, cultural, and religious values, and the ethical codes of one's profession.

Moral decision making would be easy if the answers to all of the questions led, in all instances, to the same conclusion. For example, let us consider the question, "Should I lie on my income tax return to save myself thousands of dollars?" Although the lie may make me happy in the short run, the tax system is devised to promote the greatest social happiness. To cheat would therefore, in all likelihood, produce negative answers to the teleological questions "What are the consequences of my action?" What are its long-term effects? Does my action promote the greatest happiness?

The deontological questions would also refute cheating on the tax form. When one asks, "What principle applies in this case?" the answers may include, "One should be honest," "The society must collect taxes in order to exist," and "All must pay their fair share." The policy "I lie in order to place my interests above the general public" is not a moral principle. With respect to the second and third questions, "Can this principle be applied consistently in this case and in all similar cases?" and "Can this principle be considered a possible universal principle of behavior?" the tax cheater's policy would fail on both counts. If everyone were permitted to cheat on taxes, there would be no tax system on which to cheat. The cheater would also fail the test of "Which course of action best exemplifies the ideal of treating all people as ends in themselves?" because the cheater is using the honest taxpayers to pay his or her share. And it is obvious that cheating is not the course of action that "best exemplifies and most fully promotes the ideal of a society of free, responsible people whose ends promote each other rather than conflict with each other." The cheater is setting up his own financial interest in contrast to the interests of the other members of the society.

Answers to the intuitionist's and virtue theorist's questions align with those of the teleologist and deontologist. Only in perverse cases would someone feel good about lying on income taxes or suggest that such behavior exemplifies good character.

It would be unrealistic to suppose that all cases would be so simple. There are many instances in which the answers to all of the above questions will not, at least initially, imply the same course of action. There is no foolproof formula for deciding such cases, but there is a general process to apply to them. The first aspect of that process is to determine if the apparent conflict can be reconciled. In many cases, reconciliation is possible when the questions are examined in depth. Let us suppose, for example, that, in attempting to garner public support for a project, a public agency is tempted to overstate its benefits and understate its likely costs. The rationale for this deception includes the familiar refrains: It is a good project whose benefits the public cannot understand; when the project succeeds, everyone will forget our initial assessment; every agency is deceptive, so we must be deceptive in order to compete.

The deception, however, appears to present a conflict among the ethical factors in our list of questions. The teleological considerations appear to favor the deception on the basis of its consequences, but the deontological considerations seem to favor a more honest approach on the basis of the principle that one always ought to tell the truth.

In this case, reconciliation of teleology and deontology is possible. The teleological considerations, which seem to favor the deception, might oppose it when the consequences are examined more closely. Even if the deception is temporarily successful, it is likely to be discovered eventually, and, as happy as the society may be with the results, it will tend to distrust the agency's word in the future. When considered together with the common deception of other agencies, the society will find ample evidence to distrust government in general, and the consequences of that distrust are certain to be harmful. Yet even if the deception is never discovered, the consequences may be negative. The need to perpetuate the deception throughout the agency is likely to cause its members stress and distrust. Furthermore, a successful deception, like a successful day at the race track, is likely to encourage future similar activities with less fortunate results. For the teleologist, honesty is still, in the long run, the best policy.

The possibility of a unification of the ethical standpoints may lie in human nature itself. The considerations of the teleologist, deontologist, intuitionist, and virtue theorist are all natural to human beings. As the teleologist suggests, they value happiness in themselves and in others. But they are also rational beings with a respect for rules, as the deontologist asserts. People, furthermore, have a moral sense evident not only in their seemingly intuitive ethical judgments, but also in conscience and feelings of guilt. People also admire human virtues and disrespect vices, as the virtue theorist argues. As the authors have maintained in another work, it is unlikely that those aspects of a human being would exist in conflicting, disunified form (Garofalo and Geuras 1999):

> Humanity could not have evolved so successfully over thousands of years if all of those aspects were independent. The physical parts of a human being have evolved to work together in mutual dependence. Human beings would be strange evolution-defying natural enigmas if their inherent mental functions were naturally in conflict rather than in unity. Human reasoning, love of happiness, benevolence, respect for moral character, and intuitive reactions are almost certainly parts of a unified, evolved human nature. If so, deontology,

teleology, character theory, and intuitionism must be in a unified harmony. (125)

Nevertheless, there may still be cases in which the different aspects of ethics may seem in inescapable conflict. Pontius Pilate was faced with a choice between justly freeing an innocent person and preventing a revolt. Whether one agrees with his action or not, one must sympathize with his dilemma. In a less dramatic but more common case, a manager may be faced with the option of firing, for the sake of productivity, older, loyal employees, who are more expensive, in order to hire younger, cheaper ones. The manager must choose between treating people as a means or sacrificing the best interests of the organization and those whom it serves.

Conflicts can occur not only between ethical standpoints but also within them. The deontologist may be faced with a conflict between principles. Public administrators as well as private citizens in Nazi Germany were often forced to choose between the principle that one ought always to tell the truth and the principle that innocent people should not be murdered, even if one must lie to protect them from a beastly government. The more civilized world of the contemporary United States is not immune to conflicts of principle, though they may be less dramatic. In hiring, one must often balance the conflicting principles of equality with the principle that historically abused or deprived groups should be favored over slightly better qualified, advantaged groups.

We will consider such cases of conflict more fully in later chapters, but, for now, it is sufficient to recognize that they exist. Unfortunately, there is no formula to resolve them. One must consider the issues implicit in our list of ethical questions and reach some reasonable balance among them. Since Kant's ideal realm of ends does not currently exist, it is impossible to always find a clear solution to every moral dilemma. One must use judgment. Justices on the United States Supreme Court must use their best judgment in applying the ideals of the Constitution when those ideals are in apparent conflict. Similarly, the moral actor must use judgment to best interpret and apply varied moral ideals.

The judgment need not be made in isolation. Ethical issues involve an entire organization, and should be discussed among colleagues. The advantages of such discussions are obvious: They provide the benefit of the opinions of others; they emphasize the importance of group participation in decision making; and they increase awareness of ethical concerns. Organizations may attempt to formalize the process of ethical discussion in numerous ways. An ethics committee may be appointed. The entire organization or divisions within it may convene periodically to discuss ethical issues. An ethics officer may be available for consultation. In addition to such formal structures, discussions with trusted colleagues are invaluable. Dialogue on ethics must be part of the entire culture of an organization.

But even after an ethical matter has been fully discussed, its ambiguity may still remain. The decision maker must take all opinions into account, but must reach his or her own judgment. Those who bear the responsibility for the judgment may often disagree with the majority of their colleagues, no matter how enlightened they may be. Likewise, members of a group who disagree with the final decision must acknowledge that, while their opinions must be taken into consideration, they must accept contrary but seriously considered conclusions, even on matters as vital as ethics. In keeping with the Kantian notion of people as ends in themselves, one must accord the ultimate decision maker with the right to make his or her own judgments, so long as they are reached in an honest, well-intended manner.

The absence of any formulaic solution to moral dilemmas does not preclude the attainment of reasonable solutions. If one answers all of the questions on the ethics list, conscientiously attempts to reconcile them, and uses one's best judgment when they cannot be reconciled, one still has no absolute guarantee that he or she will find the most ethical solution. But even if one does not reach the ideal ethical conclusion, one would have reached it in the best possible way. If a mistake is made, it will be the result not of one's ethical intent or diligence, but of the difficulty of the issue at hand.

The aim of ethical decision making is not the impossible goal of always performing the finest action but of always deciding in the most ethical manner. If decision makers use the process that we have outlined, their ethics cannot be faulted even if their decisions ultimately prove wrong. One of the stated aims of this chapter was to combat EAS (ethics aversion syndrome). We cannot do so by promising that all ethical decisions will be carefree or easy. However, a major step toward overcoming EAS is taken when one realizes that, no matter how intractable an ethical problem may be, it can be managed properly, even if not perfectly.

## TAKING YOUR ETHICAL TEMPERATURE

Before proceeding, it would be advisable to examine where you are ethically within your profession. We now ask you to consider the questions below for your own analysis. They are for your benefit, and there are no prescribed right or wrong answers. The questions are intended only to stimulate thought.

1. How many of the ethical questions on our list do your regularly ask in your professional activities?

2. Do you have occasion to ask them?

3. Do you favor teleology, deontology, intuitionism, or virtue theory? Do you use them in combination with each other?

4. Do you think about ethics more often outside of work than at work? If so, why?

5. Does your organization have a formal structure for discussing ethical issues?

6. Does the organizational culture at your workplace encourage consideration of the ethical aspect of issues?

7. If the answers to questions 5 or 6 were negative, is there anything that you can do to increase concern for ethics in your division or department?

8. Does ethics in your workplace consist primarily of legalistic compliance with ethics codes?

9. What are the most important professional ethical issues that arise in your work environment?

10. Do you believe that ethics has greater significance in the public service than in private industry?

As a thought exercise, let us consider the following case in which a manager must make an ethical decision. As with the above questions, there is no prescribed correct or incorrect analysis; the case is offered only for your consideration.[1]

Ansel, a retired resident in an apartment building, has not been receiving social security checks because, according to the records of the Social Security Administration, he is dead. He has tried repeatedly to inform the social security office that he is still alive, but because of miscommunication, paperwork errors, and delays, he has been unsuccessful. Fortunately, he has a neighbor, Frieda, who works in the social security office. Ansel asks Frieda to intervene for him, and she does so willingly. As a result of Frieda's efforts, the Social Security Administration learns that Ansel is alive, pays him all that he is due, and begins sending the monthly checks. All is now well for Ansel.

But all is not well for Frieda. To her astonishment, her supervisor informs her that she is to be suspended while a committee considers possible punishment. She has broken administrative rules intended to prevent influence peddling. The rules state clearly that no employee should assist any private citizen who attempts to communicate with the Social Security Administration. Her assistance to Ansel was such assistance, so she may be disciplined or even fired for an ethics violation.

---

[1]This example was suggested by Stuart Gillman at the 1995 Symposium on Ethics and Values in the Public Administration Academy, Tampa, Florida.

Consider the following questions:

- Did Frieda do anything unethical?

- Is there good reason to punish her?

- If you were a member of the disciplinary committee, what response would you consider to be appropriate in this case?

This chapter demonstrates that ethical thinking is not easy. It forces us to examine concepts that have challenged history's greatest intellects. In thinking ethically, we may complicate our jobs by introducing concepts that hitherto we have ignored. The ethical professional may ask questions that irritate coworkers and supervisors. Worse yet, those questions may have no clear answers. We may wish to avoid ethical matters because they present such difficulty. But to avoid them would be like solving a technical problem by taking a coffee break to help one forget the issue. The problems exist, and one must respond to them.

The most honest remedy for ethics aversion syndrome is not the coffee break or the wishful belief that ethics is easy, but the recognition that ethics is difficult. When one recognizes that a task is impossibly challenging, one realizes that success is measured by the quality of one's efforts rather than the discovery of an ultimate solution. In this chapter, we have discussed the general form that those efforts should take. In succeeding chapters, we will explore them in more detail.

## CHAPTER 4

# Raising the Right Questions: Ethical Approaches to Five Important Cases

In this chapter, we will examine five ethical decisions made by public administrators on difficult issues. We will present the essential details concerning the decisions and the reasoning behind them. You will then be invited to reach your own conclusion on the case on the basis of your answers to the ethical questions introduced in Chapter 3.

The cases were chosen because they are interesting, and some are well-known. Because many of the people involved in these cases are high-ranking officials, it may at first appear that their decisions have little relevance to the issues that public administrators at lower levels face. But the level of the administrator's authority is not as significant as the principles that are relevant to his or her decision. Those principles apply at all levels. For example, in signing the Emancipation Proclamation, Abraham Lincoln made a momentous decision based upon the equality of all human beings. The affirmative action officer in a public agency is in a much less dramatic situation than Lincoln, but the concept of equality is an essential ingredient in the job, as well as for those within the organization whom he or she advises. In one of the cases we discuss, Robert Bork must choose between firing the special prosecutor in the Watergate affair and disobeying the president of the United States. Few public administrators receive their orders from presidents of the United States, but many may be asked to choose between following their own consciences and the orders of a supervisor.

Furthermore, even if one never reaches the lofty administrative levels of a surgeon general or chief health officer, one still might serve on the staff of such an official. Staff members often participate in decision making and are often invited to express their opinions. While higher rank in an organization entails greater power and professional prestige, official rank does not determine moral authority. That is determined by the power of one's moral convictions and one's ability to argue convincingly for them. As you examine the cases, you might consider how you would have advised the official who made the decision.

In examining the cases, it is important to understand fully the deciding administrators' reasoning. They had the responsibility to make the decision, and they had to make the decision in a timely manner. The cases are not intended as opportunities to second-guess people but to learn from the moral problems that they encountered.

It is also important to bear in mind that the cases are to be considered from an ethical point of view rather than from a legal point of view or from the standpoint of someone primarily concerned with following organizational policy. Ethical decisions are not always dictated by law and policy. For example, neither law nor policy may dictate exactly how a manager allocates money under his or her authority, but some uses may be ethically better than others. Furthermore, sometimes policy and even law are unethical, as the history of the Nazi party demonstrates.

## THE TUSKEGEE SYPHILIS STUDY

In 1928, the United States Public Health Service (PHS), together with the private Rosenwald Fund, attempted, with public support, to identify and treat African Americans who had syphilis (Jones 1981). Subjects in the study voluntarily submitted to tests to determine whether they had the disease and were given free general medical examinations and other health benefits. The subjects who had contracted the disease expected to receive treatment for it.

The study also provided benefits to Tuskegee Institute, a traditionally African American institute of higher education, which assisted in the project. Tuskegee was given needed money, training for interns, and jobs for nurses.

In the 1930s the Rosenwald Fund withdrew its support, so the program was in jeopardy. Most importantly, the treatment phase had not been implemented. Without support from Rosenwald, the original study could not continue. But Dr. Taliaferro Clark, one of the doctors heading the study, found a way to continue funding from the PHS and to find additional support from Macon County, Alabama, by conducting a new, more limited study. Without informing the African American subjects, the study, whose original intent was to cure the disease, was converted into a study of the effect of untreated syphilis on African American men.

Although Tuskegee Institute eventually withdrew its support for the study, the reasons why the new study appealed to any of the agencies supporting it are unclear. The African American subjects who had tested positive in the original study were included in the new one but were not told that they had the disease. The PHS used extraordinary measures to prevent the subjects from discovering that they were sick, including the exemption of otherwise required syphilis examinations by the United States Army. Furthermore, the PHS worked with local health officials to ensure that the subjects were denied treatment for the disease.

Burial costs were included among the benefits for subjects.

Public and congressional pressure ended the study in 1972. In attempting to justify the program, one of the PHS administrators involved in the study maintained that the subjects were not patients but subjects and were "clinical material, not sick people," and their status did not warrant ethical debate. (Jones 1981, 179)

This case brings up a number of ethical issues and involves several ethical decisions. These decisions are "ethical" in that they were concerned with ethical matters, but they were obviously not all ethical in the sense in which "ethical" suggests "ethically correct." On the contrary, some of the decisions were monstrously unethical. Nevertheless, we will consider the ethical arguments that might be given in their favor, even if the arguments are extremely weak.

The argument for the original study was humanitarian. It was intended to identify people with syphilis and cure them. But when funds became scarce, the study was converted into something quite different because of the fear that the study would have to be abandoned for lack of funds. As a result, the medical research would be halted, the benefits to Tuskegee Institute would cease, and the scholars conducting the study would be removed from their positions.

Under the new plan, the subjects of the study would continue to receive medical examinations and treatment, but with the exception of treatment for syphilis. It could be argued that they also benefited from the newly altered study. Although they were not cured of their syphilis, it could be argued that the study did not really deprive them of any medical treatment that they would have received if the study had not been conducted. If there had been no study to begin with, they would not have known that they had the disease, anyway.

There is at least one possible factual error in the above argument. If the subjects had not been using the study as a medical clinic for other ailments, they might have sought treatment from other medical sources. The subjects thus would have discovered that they had the disease. Furthermore, rather than merely providing medical treatment and thus dissuading use of other medical sources, the study actively prevented other health agencies from diagnosing and treating the subjects.

But what would we say of the argument even if we ignore that possible factual error? Let us consider the questions on our ethical questions list, composed in Chapter 3 and adapted to this case.

## Teleology:

*What are the consequences of continuing the study in its new form?*

What are the long-term effects for both the subjects of the study and for those who benefit from the new information concerning the effects of untreated syphilis on African Americans?

*Who could benefit from such a study?*

Does the newly reformed study promote the greatest happiness, when all factors, including the benefits to those conducting the study, are considered?

## Deontology:

*What principle applies in this case?*

Consider the following possibilities: Nothing should be done to prevent the search for scientific knowledge; subjects of scientific studies are not patients and should not be treated as such; benefits to research teams should be considered more important than consideration of subjects; researchers should not lie to subjects; a prior agreement should not be altered without informed consent of all parties; human life should not be sacrificed. Are there other principles that you would include? Would a combination of principles be considered most appropriate in this case? If so, what are they?

*Can the principle that you chose be applied consistently in this case and in all similar cases?*

Once you have answered the previous question, try to imagine other cases to see if your answer would also apply to them. If not, why not?

*Can this principle be considered a possible universal principle of behavior?*

Would there be any logical contradiction in making the principle or complex of principles a universal rule?

*Which course of action best exemplifies the ideal of treating all people as ends in themselves?*

Were the subjects treated as ends in themselves? (Consider, for example, the statement from the administrator suggesting that the subjects were not patients but merely subjects and "clinical material, not sick people.") Might the researchers have used race as an excuse to regard the subjects as something less than ends in themselves? Were the researchers and medical personnel considered ends in themselves?

*Which course of action best exemplifies and most fully promotes the ideal of a society of free, responsible people whose ends promote each other rather than conflict with each other?*

Were the subjects treated as members of such a society? But was their mistreatment justified by the project of building such a society? Did this project, even to the extent that it succeeded, help build such a society?

## Intuitionism:

*What does my conscience tell me about this?*

If you had been a researcher in this study, would your conscience have bothered you? Some of the researchers and organizers of the study apparently were not bothered by their consciences. Does their lack of a conscience on the matter offend me?

*Do I feel good about this action?*

## Virtue theory:

*What character traits does this action express?*

Were the researchers noble seekers of scientific knowledge? Did they display callous disregard for the welfare of others? Were they so concerned about their own self-interest that ethical considerations did not matter to them?

*What effect will this action have on my character?*

If you had been one of the researchers, would the project have made you a better person?

*What effect will this action have on the character of other people?*

Is this the action of a person whose character I would admire?

It is not enough merely to acknowledge that the research project was monstrous and despicable. One must examine the full reasons why the study was so morally corrupt to be sure that those reasons are not overlooked in other, perhaps less blatant, cases. You might ask, for example, if there have been, in your professional experience, projects whose original worthy intent was replaced by another, less worthy, aim merely to keep the project going. Perhaps, in your experience, the benefits to the people conducting a project were considered more important than the publicly justified intent of the project. Perhaps you have encountered cases in which people, either within an organization or outside of the organization, have been treated as means rather than as ends. Do you recognize any of the ethical problems in the study in any professional experience, including the projects and activities in which you are currently involved?

While one might dismiss this case as a matter of the systematic prejudice of another age, one must recognize that every age, including the present, has its questionable but insufficiently questioned assumptions. But perhaps more importantly, the case does not merely express the biases of a particular era. Nor does it express abuse by an impersonal entity called "a study," "medical research," or even merely "government." The case expresses bias and abuse rendered by flesh-and-blood people working as public administrators.

## ARE LEAKY CONDOMS BETTER THAN NONE?

When Dr. Joycelyn Elders was Director of the Arkansas Department of Public Health, she strongly supported the distribution of condoms to high school students as a means of preventing venereal diseases and unwanted pregnancies (U.S. Congress 1993). The distribution plan appeared to be working well until December 1990, when an Arkansas high school clinic informed Dr. Elders that the condoms were breaking at an alarming rate. Although a small failure rate among condoms was considered acceptable and inevitable, the rate appeared to be higher than expected. Further evidence accumulated for the next year and a half. By June 1992, several additional complaints surfaced, including a report of three HIV-infected people who claimed that their condoms had failed repeatedly.

Throughout that period, Dr. Elders neither recalled any condoms nor issued any public warnings. She believed so strongly in the distribution program that she was very reluctant to do anything that would undermine confidence in either the program itself or condoms in general. Later, in explaining her inaction, she maintained that it was better that a very few young people use defective condoms than that all young people lose their trust in condoms and, perhaps, choose not to use them at all.

In June 1992, Dr. Elders sent a sample of the condoms in the distribution plan to the U.S. Food and Drug Administration (FDA) to test the validity of the complaints. After conducting tests, the FDA concluded that the failure rate was ten times above its limit, and that all condoms made by the manufacturer should be seized. Approximately one month later, the manufacturer voluntarily recalled the condoms.

Several ethical questions arise from this case. First, one might consider the matter of whether condoms should have been distributed at all, even if the failure rate had been within FDA limits. In defense of the program, one might argue that the net effect of the distribution was positive because, in the end, more good than harm would result. While some unwanted pregnancies would result and some venereal diseases, including AIDS, might be transmitted, more pregnancies and infections would occur without the distribution. We refer to this argument as the "net benefit argument."

The use of the net benefit argument introduces another moral issue. While the argument is ethically plausible, reasonable people in the state of Arkansas might not find it convincing. Some might argue that it would be wrong for the state to supply condoms unless there were no chance of failure because the use of a defective condom might encourage a student to feel secure in having sex, which the student might otherwise not have had, to his or her peril. Even if Dr. Elders considered the net benefit argument to be ethically convincing, one might still ask whether the state has the moral authority to impose its own ethical thinking on the society or on the particular student.

The most notable ethical issue is Dr. Elders' response to the discovery that there were unexpected condom failures. She withheld the information because she believed that it would discourage people from using condoms, and use of possibly defective condoms would have better consequences than unprotected sex. She, in effect, made a decision for both the population in general and for the individual condom user.

Several ethical issues emerge from her decision. One such issue is that of paternalism. Dr. Elders considered her decision to be in the best interests of the people of Arkansas, but she deprived them of the information necessary to make their own informed decisions. She decided for them. She may have been correct in her assumption that her decision was better than theirs would have been, but one must still consider whether she had the moral authority to take the decision out of their hands.

Secondly, in making her decision, she endangered individuals who, if properly informed, might have chosen to purchase condoms from a different manufacturer or abstain from risky behavior entirely. She may have been correct in her belief that few people would have made such choices, but those who would have may have been severely damaged by a choice that she, in effect, made for them.

A third issue is that of secrecy. Even if she were correct in her supposition that the people of Arkansas benefited from her decision, its effectiveness depended upon secrecy. As an officer of the government, she had a responsibility to carry out her duties honestly and openly. But honesty and openness in making this decision would have defeated the decision itself. Deception was an essential part of it.

We may now return to our list of moral questions to examine how they would apply in this case. This time, we will not consider all of the questions but will concentrate upon those most relevant to Dr. Elder's decision.

## Teleology:

*What are the consequences of my action?*

*What are the long-term effects of my action?*

*Does my action promote the greatest happiness?*

These three questions may be taken as a group. In answering them, you should consider several factors, among others that you yourself may notice: Would the withholding of the information reduce venereal disease and unwanted pregnancy as effectively as Dr. Elders believed? Even if it did, would the deception set an unfortunate precedent that encourages secrecy in other policies as well? Would the society lose faith in the honesty of government if the deception was discovered? Would

there be unfortunate consequences of a systematic attempt to conceal the deception?

## Deontology:

*What principle applies in this case?*

Among the principles to be considered are the following: Should government make secret decisions that do
not involve national security? Should government deprive citizens of information necessary to make intelligent decisions? Should government make decisions
on behalf of the less wise members of the society at the
expense of those who would make wise decisions with
the proper information? Do the interests of the whole
override the interests of the individual members of a
society?

*Which course of action best exemplifies the ideal of treating
all people as ends in themselves?*

Did Dr. Elders' decision to save people from their own,
possibly bad, judgments treat people as ends in themselves? As rational beings? As complete human beings?
Would providing people with the information to make
their own decisions have better expressed the notion
of people as ends in themselves? Would sacrificing the
welfare of those individuals who would make proper
informed decisions for the sake of the welfare of the
majority violate the notion that people are valuable in
themselves?

*Which course of action best exemplifies and most fully pro-
motes the ideal of a society of free, responsible people whose
ends promote each other rather than conflict with each other?*

Does Dr. Elders' decision conform to the notion of such
a society by emphasizing the welfare of the society as a

whole over the interests of the individuals who would make the best-informed choices? Does the decision conflict with the notion of a society of free, responsible people?

## Intuitionism:

*What does my conscience tell me about this?*

*Do I feel good about this action?*

These two questions may be taken together: If you had made Dr. Elders' decision, would you feel good about it?

## Virtue theory:

*What character traits does this action express?*

Does the action express benevolence because of Dr. Elders' concern for the welfare of the people of Arkansas? Does it express a lack of honesty? A lack of trust? A lack of trustworthiness?

*What effect will this action have on my character?*

If Dr. Elders' policy succeeded, would it tend to make her a less honest person? Would it strengthen a possible disrespect for the judgment of common people?

*What effect will this action have on the character of other people?*

Would such actions, if routinely taken by government, tend to make people more dependent upon government experts and less self-reliant?

*Is this the action of a person whose character I would admire?*

The case of Dr. Elders is especially important for public administrators to consider because the proper function of government is at the root of the issue. One's reaction to her decision expresses one's beliefs regarding the point at which legitimate actions by government become unwarranted paternalism.

## MASSACRE OR BE MASSACRED

In 1974, President Richard Nixon resigned to avoid almost certain impeachment and conviction in the Watergate scandal (Moore and Sparrow 1990). Although he was never conclusively connected to the break-in itself, his own tape recordings proved that he participated in a massive coverup. Nixon might have been able to retain his office if the proof from the tapes had not been exposed. He might have saved his presidency if he could have kept the content of the tapes secret, even after their existence had been revealed.

The legality of Nixon's argument in favor of keeping the tapes secret is unclear. He might or might not have had a good legal case for withholding them. However, our concern is not with the legal issue or even with the ethics of Nixon's own actions; our concern is with the ethical decision of Robert Bork, the solicitor general who fired Special Prosecutor Archibald Cox at Nixon's request in his effort to hide the content of the tapes.

Cox insisted upon reviewing the tapes to determine if any illegality had occurred. Nixon refused to supply them on the basis of presidential confidentiality. Since Cox had been appointed by Attorney General Elliot Richardson, who himself had been appointed by the president, Nixon instructed Richardson to fire Cox. Richardson refused to comply and resigned as attorney general. The deputy attorney general, William Ruckelshaus, assumed the duties of the attorney general but also refused to fire Cox. Bork, the next in line, complied with the request to fire Cox.

Bork considered his position different from those of Richardson and Ruckelshaus in two ways that, in his opinion, morally exempted him from any moral imperative that they may have been under. First, Richardson and Ruckelshaus had promised the Senate not to fire Cox except under extraordinary circumstances, which did not hold in this case. Bork had made no such promise. Secondly, Bork did not consider his office of solicitor general to have the same moral responsibilities as that of attorney general. He considered the office of solicitor general to be more beholden to the president than to the general public, although he considered the reverse to be true of the attorney general. He therefore reasoned that it was constitutionally imperative that someone carry out the president's orders, and that he, as solicitor general, was the agent of the president required to implement the order. Even if he resigned, he argued, someone would have to fire Cox, or the president would be denied his powers under the United States Constitution. To deny those powers would fail not only the president, but also the American people, because the Constitution is designed on their behalf.

Bork evidently applied a different concept of public service to his official position from those of Richardson and Ruckelshaus. They were under the executive branch, but since they made promises to Congress, they also were in part under the authority—moral if not legal—of the legislative branch. Their ultimate allegiance was, technically, to the executive, but their de facto lines of moral and professional responsibility were unclear. Furthermore, the high level of the office that they occupied may be seen to imply responsibility directly to the people. Bork evidently understood his position to be more that of a bureaucrat, and, as such, an agent of the will of his ultimate superior, the president of the United States. He appears to have considered Richardson and Ruckelshaus, on the basis of the ambiguity of their ultimate allegiances and the high level of their authority, to be more justified in asserting their own moral judgment than he was; he considered himself a presidential agent without moral autonomy.

We have simplified the case by omitting other factors that undoubtedly influenced the entire Watergate affair. Those factors include, among others, political beliefs, career concerns, and personal loyalties. Nevertheless, let us suppose that the facts are as Bork apparently understood them, and apply our list of moral questions to his decision.

## Teleology:

*What are the consequences of my action?*

*What are the long-term effects of my action?*

*Does my action promote the greatest happiness?*

These questions are very difficult to answer, because the long-term effects of the possible courses of action open to Bork are unclear. Honoring the power of the presidency, as Bork did, might, in the long-term history of the country, cause more good than harm by allowing future presidents to act for more positive purposes. On the other hand, disobedience to Nixon might have ultimately produced more beneficial consequences. A decision to disobey might have resulted in a more expeditious and less painful end to the Watergate affair without setting any negative precedent that would deny future presidents the legitimate power of their office. One could speculate on the ultimate results, but it is doubtful that any definitive answers will emerge.

## Deontology:

*What principle applies in this case?*

Is the foremost principle, as Bork seemed to assume, "A public administrator must obey the lines of authority"? Would another principle be more germane, such as "A public administrator should act morally on behalf of the public"?

*Can the principle that you chose be applied consistently in this case and in all similar cases?*

*Can the principle be considered a possible universal principle of behavior?*

Bork may be understood to have considered these two questions. He apparently reasoned that if all public officials in his position were to refuse the president's request, the president could not function with the full authority assigned to him by the Constitution. Do you agree with that reasoning?

*Which course of action best exemplifies the ideal of treating all people as ends in themselves?*

This question has special importance not only to this case, but to one's concept of the function of the public administrator. In regarding himself, a public administrator, as a full agent of the will of the president and as acting without independent, autonomous moral authority, does Bork suggest that the public administrator is a mere means, and not a morally responsible individual who could be regarded as an end in himself? The answer to this question has profound implications for the profession of public administration.

*Which course of action best exemplifies and most fully promotes the ideal of a society of free, responsible people whose ends promote each other rather than conflict with each other?*

The case is one of conflict to begin with. The president, the congress, the special prosecutor, the attorney general, the deputy attorney general, and the solicitor general are all in conflict. Which course of action would set a precedent that would best avoid such conflicts in the future? If, for example, the president came to naturally expect that public administrators answered to a moral authority rather than only to presidential authority, would the president be less likely to give morally questionable orders?

## Intuitionism:

*What does my conscience tell me about this?*

*Do I feel good about this action?*

If you were in Bork's position, where would your intuitions guide you?

## Virtue theory:

*What character traits does this action express?*

*What effect will this action have on my character?*

*What effect will this action have on the character of other people?*

Does Bork's notion that, as a public administrator, he has no moral authority to disobey the president in this case have the effect of weakening the moral character of the public administrator? Is it important that a public administrator exercise moral character in his or her profession?

*Is this the action of a person whose character I would admire?*

Is Bork's refusal to impose his own moral values on the society by disobeying the president an admirably disciplined act? On the other hand, is it an avoidance of moral responsibility?

The most fundamental question arising for the public administrator from this case is that of his or her moral authority. Does the public administrator have the authority to apply his or her moral judgment, or must the public administrator remain morally neutral? If the public administrator can exercise moral authority, what are its limits? Can that moral authority interfere with constitutional powers granted to an elected official?

## OPTIMISTIC PROJECTION OR OPPORTUNISTIC DECEPTION?

New York City had a serious heroin addiction problem when Gordon Chase was appointed head of the city's Health Services

Administration in 1969 (Moore and Sparrow 1990). According to some estimates, 200,000 New Yorkers were addicted, and the city recognized a responsibility—not only to the addicts themselves, but also to victims of heroin-related crime—to reduce this number. Both the city and private agencies provided assistance. Chase believed that the best hope lay in a project intended to wean addicts off heroin by means of methadone treatment. The treatment was controversial at the time, as it still is, because its effectiveness had not been proven. Furthermore, there was a legitimate concern that the treatment would only convert heroin addicts into methadone addicts. Nevertheless, Chase firmly believed in the program and sought to implement it. But he needed support from taxpayers, the political establishment, private hospitals, and private donors.

Chase proposed to have 15,600 addicts treated under the program within one year. He considered the figure to be "on the optimistic side" and perhaps "downright unrealistic" (42-43). His reason for publicizing the figure was not a fatuous hope that it might be accurate, but a careful political strategy. He feared that a more realistic, but smaller, figure would garner less support. If the original projections contained only a few addicts, the public would infer that the project was experimental and would have little confidence in its likely success. Furthermore, he believed that the large optimistic figure would encourage the bureaucratic structure to take the project more seriously and behave in a less obstructionist manner.

Chase's strategy appears to have worked as planned. The 15,600 figure proved unattainable, but it fulfilled its intended purposes. The program was instituted in 1970, and by 1971, 2,000 addicts were being treated. The figure grew to 11,000 by 1973. Although figures establishing the success of the program are difficult to interpret, they suggest that heroin use and crime related to it declined significantly as a result of the program.

Chase's optimistic projections bring up ethical questions. His intent in publicizing the projections was not to truly inform the public but to manipulate them, albeit for a good—and apparently successful—cause. There are, in addition to the factors that Chase himself mentioned, other considerations that might be introduced on his behalf. First, one might ask whether some manipulation of the public might be acceptable to help them reach the correct conclusion on an issue that they, for lack of expertise, do not understand. Few private citizens knew the issues as well as Chase himself did, and any attempt to enlighten them would be fruitless. Sometimes it may be acceptable to protect people from their own ignorance. For example, many people would be horrified if they knew of the amounts of probably harmless rat hair and evidence of rat feces that are considered acceptable in some consumer products. A little ignorance might be a helpful thing.

Secondly, it might be argued that Chase was not truly deceptive. The public expects inflated figures from its public officials and adjusts its opinions accordingly. Few people believe the dollar amounts projected to build a new stadium or highway; they know that there will be cost overruns and suspect that, even without them, the stated figures are overly optimistic ploys. If accurate figures are presented, the public will assume that they are underinflated, so the inaccurate figures might represent a truer picture. Similarly, the citizens of New York and its political powers would likely assume that Chase's figures were off. If everyone is expecting a deception, it isn't a deception any more.

Although Chase was a high official, public administrators at lower levels are often confronted with similarly "honest deceptions." When making out a projected budget, a manager might overstate his or her department's needs to seek a greater portion of the available funds. If a manager projects a scrupulously accurate budget, his or her department is at a competitive disadvantage with others who play by the real rules rather than idealistic ones. At the end of a fiscal year, a manager is often considered an incompetent boob if he or she cannot rationalize ways to use leftover funds. Similarly, when evaluating personnel, one must be sure to rate average employees as excellent rather than average, because in the accepted language of evaluation, "average" means "a good candidate for dismissal."

With all factors taken into consideration, we may return to our list of ethical questions.

## Teleology:

*What are the consequences of my action?*

*What are the long-term effects of my action?*

*Does my action promote the greatest happiness?*

There were evidently beneficial effects of Chase's actions. The heroin problem was not solved, but statistics appear to support the effectiveness of the program. But did Chase set a dangerous precedent or reinforce a dangerous policy of "justifiable" deception?

## Deontology:

*What principle applies in this case?*

The principle may be one of many: Never deceive the public; minor, strategic deception is acceptable for the public welfare; people are more important than the truth; a lie is not a lie when people expect it.

*Can this principle be applied consistently in this case and in all similar cases?*

In what respect are the cases to which you would apply your principle similar to this one?

*Can this principle be considered as a possible universal principle of behavior?*

Should one always tell the truth to the public, even if they are unable to properly understand it? If one always inflates figures under the assumption that the public expects them to be inflated, will a spiral of greater inflation and expectation result?

*Which course of action best exemplifies the ideal of treating all people as ends in themselves?*

Do Chase's actions treat the citizens as ends in themselves? Did he treat the addicts as ends in themselves?

*Which course of action best exemplifies and most fully promotes the ideal of a society of free, responsible people whose ends promote each other rather than conflict with each other?*

Does the ideal society elevate honesty over treatment of the needy, or the reverse?

## Intuitionism:

*What does my conscience tell me about this?*

*Do I feel good about this action?*

If you were Chase, how would you feel about your actions?

## Virtue theory:

*What character traits does this action express?*

*What effect will this action have on my character?*

*What effect will this action have on the character of other people?*

*Is this the action of a person whose character I would admire?*

Which character trait is more admirable, complete frankness or compassion?

In some ways, Chase may be compared to Elders. They both acted deceptively for the public good. But they differed in some ways also. Elders chose not to warn the public about the condoms, and that decision virtually ensured that some people would suffer unwanted pregnancies or venereal diseases. Chase endangered taxpayer pocketbooks and city budgets more than their bodies. Also, Elders may have been said to hide a complete fact, while Chase may be described as exaggerating. Are there any other differences that you consider relevant?

Chase's actions call our attention to some fine distinctions that public administrators might be forced to make among the following: lying; exaggerating; justifiably deceiving; misleading but not deceiving; and overstating but not deceiving. In an ideal world, such distinctions may not be necessary or even contemplated, but public administrators do not live in an ideal world. Nonetheless, should they behave as if they do?

## THE FBI LOOKS IT UP IN THE LIBRARY

Two agents of the Federal Bureau of Investigation (FBI) were investigating a series of art thefts that, they believed, were committed by amateur art thieves who might have recently acquired some knowledge of art by checking out books from the local public library (Vocino and Tyler 1996). In the process of one of their thefts, they severely beat an elderly woman and left her comatose. The FBI agents went to the library to find the names of people who had recently checked out books on art.

The agents entered the library at the start of a holiday weekend, when the director was on vacation. They asked the reference librarian to provide them information on those who had borrowed art books, but he refused on the basis of the library's policy of keeping such information confidential. He knew that the library director stressed such confidentiality in general, but the director was unable to be contacted for advice in this case. He suggested that the agents wait until the director returned from his vacation, but the agents claimed that they needed the information immediately if there was any chance of finding the criminals. The agents' emphasis on the brutality of the crime and their status as agents of the federal government eventually induced the librarian to provide the information. He later said that, if he had had the time to think about his decision, he would have decided otherwise.

Let us consult our list of ethical questions to determine what the librarian should have done. This time, however, we will supply only the list without hints concerning how the questions may be applied to this case. At this point, your own insights should be better than any hints that we might supply.

## Teleology:

*What are the consequences of my action?*

*What are the long-term effects of my action?*

*Does my action promote the greatest happiness?*

## Deontology:

*What principle applies in this case?*

*Can this principle be applied consistently in this case and in all similar cases?*

*Can this principle be considered as a possible universal principle of behavior?*

*Which course of action best exemplifies the ideal of treating all people as ends in themselves?*

*Which course of action best exemplifies and most fully promotes the ideal of a society of free, responsible people whose ends promote each other rather than conflict with each other?*

## Intuitionism:

*What does my conscience tell me about this?*

*Do I feel good about this action?*

## Virtue theory:

*What character traits does this action express?*

*What effect will this action have on my character?*

*What effect will this action have on the character of other people?*

*Is this the action of a person whose character I would admire?*

Which of these questions do you consider most appropriate to the case? How would you answer them?

In reviewing the cases, we might ask whether any of the people making the decisions would have acted differently if they had used our list of ethical questions in their deliberations. One might suppose that, if they had had no moral scruples whatsoever, they would have ignored the answers to those questions even if they had considered them. But we should not be so quick to dismiss all of them as amoral. Some may have been trying to do their best but lacked a systematic, developed method for making ethical decisions. Such administrators might have benefited from careful consideration of the questions. But even if some of the decision makers were indeed initially amoral, we might still hope that consideration of the questions might have awakened a latent moral sense within them.

A mere strong moral sense or "moral compass" may be enough to direct some decision makers to a good decision. Some people simply seem to know what is right, even without deep thinking. Such people may not need to contemplate the list of moral questions that we have devised. Nevertheless, even those "intuitive" moralists would benefit by examining the questions and providing explicit answers to them.

As good as the actions to which their moral sense inclines them may be, if they are good administrators, they will have to explain the rationale behind their decisions to others who do not accept intuition alone as an answer. Such explanations not only defend the agent from charges of unethical behavior, but also may ethically educate the questioner. Furthermore, in answering the questions, even after the decision has been made, one might learn something important about the inner ethical conceptual structure of one's own mind.

# CHAPTER 5

# The Real World Revisited

We now return to "the real world," the world described in the first chapter—the world of power, priorities, and performance. It is a world of hierarchies, controls, and constraints. It is a world framed by organizational structures and cultures, with formal and informal distributions of authority and patterns of communication. In ethical terms, it is a world of dilemmas, conflicting obligations, competing values, codes of ethics, accountability, and compliance. All things considered, it is a challenging world—with pitfalls and minefields as well as opportunities and rewards.

In Chapter 3, we described the important streams of ethical thought, the ways in which such thought relates to decision making and action, and the integrated ethic, which combines those streams of ethical thought into a unified perspective and approach to ethical public administration. In Chapter 4, we asked you to consider the connections among principles, values, and character in the context of five important cases, and invited you to examine autonomy, responsibility, and accountability. Having described the real world, and having equipped ourselves with some ethical tools, we now approach the real world from a different perspective. We aim to see it through a different lens, to analyze the taken-for-granted environment of public administration, and to raise some new questions about that environment.

## ORGANIZATIONAL STRUCTURE AND ORGANIZATIONAL CULTURE

Let us begin by revisiting the concepts of organizational structure and organizational culture, to determine what they are, their importance, and their connection to administrative ethics.

We focus first on organizational structure, which refers to the design of work, the way in which it is divided into tasks or assignments. A commonplace reflection of organizational structure is the organization chart, which tells us who reports to whom, the chain of command, the span of control. At the same time, we know that organizations do not function only in accordance with their formal design. Organizations, in reality, also have informal structures that influence communication, decision making, and other important features of organizational life. Taken together, both the formal and the informal structures of organizations have a significant impact on individual and group behavior.

Organizational culture includes the values, assumptions, and expectations that influence thinking, deciding, and doing within the organization. As in the case of organizational structure, there is also an informal component of culture that can be equally, if not more, influential than the formal component. As soon as you enter an organization as an employee, the socialization process starts, and you begin to internalize the values of the organization. In both explicit and implicit ways, you learn what is considered acceptable and what is not considered acceptable in the organization. You learn what behavior will likely bring recognition and rewards and what will likely bring criticism or worse. You learn quickly how to survive and, perhaps, even succeed in your new environment.

Our concern here, however, is the relationship between administrative ethics and organizational structure and culture. This relationship is critical to our understanding, since administrative ethics are clearly embedded in the structure and culture of organizations. Without a firm grasp of this relationship, reform efforts will be futile. For example, we need to acknowledge that organizational structures are not neutral or merely technical artifacts. Instead, they reflect and reinforce the overt and covert moral choices and commitments of the organization. They can either protect and promote ethical values or disable them through both intentional and unintentional means. Therefore, it is essential that public administrators understand the crucial nexus linking organizational structure and culture to ethical behavior.

## THE UNIFIED ETHIC

Before delving into the connections among organizational structure, culture, and ethical behavior, it will be useful to review the unified ethic described in Chapter 3. If our ultimate interest lies in reforming or reframing our public organizations, a clear grasp of the unified ethic is vital. Recall that deontology is associated with Kant (1989), who emphasized the rationality of human beings as the basis of ethics. Ethics, according to Kant, involves rules for governing the way rational beings with free will ought to decide the direction of their lives. So deontology stresses principles, rather than consequences or character, as the important things in determining the morality of a decision or an act. The key to the deontological perspective is consistency, which Kant expressed in three formulations of his categorical imperative.

The first formulation, "Act only on that maxim whereby thou canst at the same time will that it should become a universal law" (38), is similar to the Golden Rule, "Do unto others as you would have them do unto you." The second formulation states "So act as to treat humanity, whether in thine own person or in that of any other, in every case as an end withal, and never as a means only" (46), and the third formulation states that a rational being "must always regard himself as giving laws either as a member or as a sovereign in a kingdom of ends" (50). A kingdom of ends is a community in which the ends or goals of all people are combined into a consistent whole.

The second element in the unified ethic, teleology, considers an action good or bad according to its consequences. The aim of moral action is an end or a goal. Therefore, actions that achieve a designated end or goal are good, while others are bad. The popular form of teleology, utilitarianism, is captured in the idea that an action is good if it promotes the greatest good for the greatest number.

The third component of the unified ethic is character theory. The idea here is that the morality of an act is determined by the character traits that it demonstrates. The character of the actor, rather than the act itself, is the object of moral evaluation. Supporters of character theory believe that moral character is inherent in human nature.

The fourth component is intuitionism. As much as one might attempt to explain all decisions rationally, feelings still matter. They must be included in any full account of ethics.

We believe that the unified ethic reflects the unity of human nature. We all respect and require principles that appeal to our rational nature and our need for consistency. So we value deontology. At the same time, our emotional side, especially our desire for happiness, must be acknowledged. So we value teleology. Last, the third aspect of the unified ethic, character, mirrors our instinctive appreciation of excellence. So we value virtue.

Each of these elements is linked to the others and, in our view, can provide the foundation for the moral renewal of our public institutions, which tend to be dominated by "consequentialism," or pressures to get the job done and produce measurable outcomes. We think that the public administrator grounded in the unified ethic is able to raise more probing, subtle, and comprehensive questions than a colleague who is motivated largely by conventional and largely unconscious utilitarianism. The ethically conscious administrator is less likely to accept only technical options or established patterns of authority and more likely to allow the moral dimensions of a problem to emerge.

## ORGANIZATIONAL STRUCTURE, CULTURE, AND ETHICAL BEHAVIOR

Let us return now to the connections among organizational structure, culture, and ethical behavior. Our specific goal here is to consider the unified ethic as an approach to reframing structure and culture and shifting toward explicit ethical behavior. It has been argued that conventionally managed public organizations are characterized by a number of pathologies (Gabris 1991). One of the most important pathologies is the discontinuity between espoused and actual values, which can be found not only in organizations, but in our private lives as well. In any event, as a result of several structural and cultural attributes, such as hierarchy, specialization, tolerance of suboptimal conditions, and defensive routines, public organizations operate according to a kind of Machiavellian ethics, in which administrators are distinguished by deceit, arrogance, and avoidance of accountability and conflict. This panoply of pathologies might raise serious doubts about the possibility of organizational ethics, particularly in the minds of seasoned and scarred administrators.

This line of reasoning continues with the notion that implicit in hierarchy is the assumption that those in higher positions are smarter and more competent than those working below them. Those in higher positions also tend to feel that those below them in the hierarchy tend to be lazy, unmotivated, and uninterested in hard work. Obsequiousness toward superiors and autocratic behavior toward subordinates is the norm. This results in poor interpersonal relations, poor decisions, and a dysfunctional organizational culture, which tends to be tolerated.

Tolerance of suboptimal conditions is driven by the emphasis on personal survival and avoidance of conflict. Under these circumstances, ethics and excellence take a back seat. For example, Gabris (1991) describes a situation in which a city manager finds the police chief to be incompetent and authoritarian. The police chief's inadequacies lead to problems in motivation, stress, and turnover. But the chief is a veteran of the force and is well-connected in the community. So it may be difficult for the city manager to fix the problem. Taking corrective action might well lead to the dismissal of the city manager. "It is easier and safer to ignore the police chief and act as if no problem exists—in other words, tolerate a suboptimal condition knowing it is damaging the administrative infrastructure" (212–213). Such tolerance makes personal survival sense, and such behavior may be rooted in the organizational culture.

The final pathology we address here is defensive routines or "the tendency to ignore problems and act as if they did not exist." Defensive routines are "short-term solutions to organizational threats and pain that are not solutions to the underlying causes of problems." In fact, defensive routines perpetuate problems while avoiding short-term conflict. An example of a defensive routine involves "the constant complainer or negativist who damages the productivity of staff members but for some reason is the apple of the boss's eye. Ordinary employees will often suffer this employee's ineptitude so as to avoid upsetting the boss with seemingly trivial squabbles, even though the individual is a major threat to morale" (Gabris 1991, 213).

As an alternative to conventional management practices and their pathologies, Gabris proposes organization development or OD, which entails such ideas as trust, ownership, and openness. OD, according to Gabris, may provide the basis for rethinking an organization's culture and for building meaningful administrative ethics. Narrow personal interests and concern for survival can be transcended, and organizational excellence can be conceived as achievable. "Organizational reforms will be more than cosmetic, and employees may experience ownership and buy into new ideas" (220).

Whether Gabris' description of the public organization's culture is accepted in every detail, it does outline general organizational behaviors and conditions to which the unified ethic can be applied. Therefore, with the unified ethic in mind, we consider public organizational culture and its potential for ethical behavior as well as Gabris' proposal of organization development as a strategy for organizational change. This consideration also will provide an idea of the distance between actual organizational circumstances and standard reform proposals, and a strategy for reducing that distance.

Ideally, members of an organization whose culture is characterized by a commitment to the unified ethic approach role and value conflicts with clarity, coherence, and consistency. Their ethical framework enables them to clearly identify the nature and sources of such conflicts; to understand the interrelationship of principles, consequences, and character inherent in such conflicts; and to possess sufficient skill and foresight to fashion effective and ethical resolutions of such conflicts. Their choices are both moral and practical; their choices are one and the same. The question, then, is how to move from the organizational culture presented by Gabris toward this ideal.

The transition from a culture of obsequious and autocratic employees and managers, of suboptimal decisions, of avoidance of accountability, of conformity and expedience, of deception and defensiveness, to one of moral courage and conviction, of professional excellence and responsibility, requires both theoretical and practical commitment and action. For example, we believe that administrative ethics should be informed and animated by the unified ethic because the unified ethic is the foundation of moral understanding and development.

Public administrators, without a clear grasp of the practical nature of moral philosophy, will understandably continue to approach the inevitable ethical conflicts they face with the morally superficial and fragmented thinking that characterizes public organizational culture. They will continue to accommodate the conventional realities constructed by dysfunctional and disjointed organizational cultures. For their part, ethics scholars are responsible for transcending the traditional philosophical and moral separation of deontology, teleology, and character, and for formulating fresh approaches to organizational behavior that address moral substance as well as process.

Together, administrators and scholars are responsible for cultivating moral maturity in public organizations and for developing
outlets for public employees to seek safe and grounded moral
advice and guidance. Today, public employees confronted with a
true ethical dilemma involving competing values and conflicting
obligations have no place to go.

Let us return to Gabris' (1991) city manager who is trying to
figure out what to do about an incompetent and authoritarian
police chief and see whether the unified ethic applies. According to Gabris, conventional management practice dictates that,
given the police chief's personal connections in the community,
the city manager turn a blind eye to the problems of motivation,
stress, and turnover caused by the chief's managerial inadequacy
and domineering style. To do otherwise would jeopardize the
city manager's position and, perhaps, even career. Professional
survival requires toleration of this suboptimal condition regardless of its impact on both organizational effectiveness and the
public interest.

Three questions, however, must be asked about this situation. The first concerns whether the city manager can justifiably
overlook the police chief's pernicious effect on the department
and the polity as a whole. Does either professional survival
or careerism qualify as a good reason for neglecting the harm
done by the police chief? A second question concerns the kind of
ethical thinking that underlies the city manager's neglect of the
police chief's disregard of the police department and the city's
welfare. For example, is the city manager focusing entirely on
personal consequences and ignoring relevant ethical principles
and character? Finally, what kind of organizational and community culture endorses the type of thinking and behavior reflected
in the first two questions? What organizational and community
norms license such flagrant violations of even minimal moral
and managerial expectations and practices?

The answer to the first question is clearly no. There is no justification for overlooking the police chief's effect on the department
and the city. The only interests being advanced by such behavior

are the self-serving ones of the city manager, the police chief, and the chief's allies in the community. The larger community, as well as the police department and municipal government, by contrast, are forced to suffer the consequences of such neglect. If, however, a policy were in place according to which this neglect had to be justified to the citizenry as a whole, it seems reasonable to conclude that action would be demanded to rectify what can only be described as an egregious abuse of the public trust. Local citizens, although perhaps unschooled in formal ethical theory, would doubtless recognize the self-serving nature of such consequentialism and reject the moral fragmentation for which the unified ethic can be an effective antidote. They would interpret the city manager's reluctance to confront the police chief's inadequacy and injurious behavior as gross irresponsibility, perhaps even cowardice, rather than a justifiable accommodation to inevitable and unalterable political reality.

With respect to the second question, which concerns the kind of ethical thinking that underlies the city manager's neglect of the police chief's malfeasance, the answer, once again, is the misguided and conventional understanding that separates consequences from principles and character. If, on the other hand, the city manager adopts the unified ethic, then such separation becomes both intellectually and morally bankrupt. Fear, narrow ambition, and perhaps even shame, will be replaced by self-respect, ethical renewal, and a reinvigorated commitment to stewardship of the public interest.

The third and final question concerns the kind of organizational and community culture in which failure by public officials, at least at certain levels, to meet their responsibilities is classified by particular groups as political realism and, therefore, justifiable. As Gabris (1991) observes, it is sensible to tolerate destructive suboptimal conditions, given the nature of the typical public organization's culture. Yet, again, we are confronted with perspectives and practices that, from the standpoint of the unified ethic, are clearly unjustifiable. Furthermore, such perspectives and practices prevail largely because of their limited exposure to the polity. If subjected to the scrutiny of the citizenry as a whole, it is, again, reasonable to conclude that such self-serving behavior would be resoundingly rejected. It would not pass the test of publicity.

Repudiating conventional management practices, as described by Gabris, as well as fragmented ethical thinking in favor of the unified ethic, however, is to address only one side of the coin. We now must ask what might be an effective approach to reframing and reconfiguring public organizational culture and ethical behavior. For example, is Gabris' proposal of organization development as an alternative to conventional management practices and as a method for creating meaningful administrative ethics plausible?

There is widespread agreement on the desirability of trust, openness, and ownership within organizations. At the practical level, however, these qualities tend to be at a premium. They are often difficult to attain because of the constraints and pressures associated with public administration. The perplexing and formidable ethical and policy challenges inherent in administrative practice are not easily resolved and, therefore, the tendency is to remain at the moral surface and permit general ethical misinterpretations and particular individual or group interests to hold sway. Although organization development may have potential for change, we must ask whether it needs to be paralleled or even preceded by an understanding of and a commitment to the unified ethic.

## CODES OF ETHICS AND ETHICS TRAINING

We have shown that the unified ethic recognizes the essential integrity in human nature and that it can help us to raise basic questions about ordinary, but unethical, administrative situations. It is, however, a far cry from the usual approaches to ethics in public organizations. Therefore, we now turn to the two most popular methods used to advance ethics in public organizations—codes of ethics and ethics training—to explore their strengths and weaknesses, both in their own right and in comparison to the unified ethic. In our view, codes of ethics and ethics training, although somewhat useful, tend to remain at an ethically superficial, and therefore limited, level with regard to promoting the development of morally mature and responsible public administrators.

We recall from Chapter 1 that most public organizations have no consistent approach to ethics, and that, as a result, employees are often left to flounder when confronted with ethical challenges. As Bowman and Williams (1997) observe, public organizations are usually characterized by an "incoherent, frequently passive, and/or reactive philosophy" that "is not likely to support, nurture, or benefit those seeking to carefully resolve ethical dilemmas" (519). Therefore, in this morally confused and confusing environment, public agencies as well as professional associations tend to grasp at whatever ethical straws they can find, to be able to create at least a semblance of propriety and professionalism. The fact that their codes of ethics or codes of conduct fail to deal with the need for moral guidance, the development of ethical skill, and the examination of issues is left unaddressed. The important thing is to have a code of ethics on the walls and in the handbooks.

Nevertheless, codes of ethics do have merit, as several observers have noted. Terry Cooper (1998), for example, argues that codes of ethics can project ideals, norms, and obligations. They can be inspirational and aspirational, presenting lofty values and ideals. "Codes can establish an ethical status to which members of a profession may aspire—the moral optimum rather than the moral minimum established by ethics legislation" (151). Codes can also be tailored to agency-specific needs and circumstances and can help socialize employees into a profession.

On the other hand, as Cooper (1998) suggests, codes of ethics have a number of shortcomings. They are often vague, abstract, and lofty and, thus, difficult to apply in specific situations. They fail to connect their general sentiments such as being "honest in thought and deed" to specific behaviors. As Cooper notes in this regard, the "words are noble but subject to widely differing interpretations" (152). Furthermore, codes of ethics often lack teeth. Again, to cite Cooper, codes of ethics "take the form of elegant plaques that are hung on the office walls and thereafter ignored. They may be quoted on ceremonial occasions, but never taken seriously enough to use in assessing the conduct of individual members." Finally, even when enforcement is part of codes of ethics, they may still be meaningless, since most public sector professional associations are not the gatekeepers for their professions. "They do not license practitioners in their fields, so a wayward member's career is not likely to be significantly affected by the actions of a professional association" (153).

Our concern with codes of ethics is not with their purposes or principles. Indeed, we heartily support the sentiments embodied in the codes of ethics found in both public organizations and professional associations. Like ethics itself, they are, as we said earlier, motherhood-and-apple-pie aspirations, with which it is impossible to disagree. On the contrary, our concern lies in the question of what it takes to translate the noble ideas in codes of ethics into concrete skills and behaviors among public employees. This is similar to, but transcends, Cooper's contention that the general language of codes of ethics fails to specify the types of behaviors that are to ensue. We concur with Cooper but believe that deeper examination of this issue is required if public organizations are to move beyond the incoherent, passive, and reactive stance noted by Bowman and Williams (1997).

Recall that Bowman and Williams (1997) maintain that "codes of ethics demand more than simple compliance; they mandate the exercise of judgment and acceptance of responsibility for decisions rendered—the real work of ethics" (522). We agree, but the question is how the exercise of judgment and acceptance of responsibility are to be achieved. Simply urging public employees to exercise judgment and accept responsibility is clearly inadequate. Public employees, like all human beings, need advice and guidance, as well as the opportunity to develop ethical skills and discuss the ethical challenges they face on a daily basis. Without something more than hortatory appeals, little, if any, effective change will occur. To illustrate our position, let us return to the code of ethics of the American Society for Public Administration (ASPA).

As an aspirational document, the ASPA Code of Ethics is exemplary. Its five categories—(1) serve the public interest; (2) respect the Constitution and the law; (3) demonstrate personal integrity; (4) promote ethical organizations; and (5) strive for professional excellence—cover the ethics spectrum, touching on the major areas of concern in public administration. It is, however, when we delve more deeply into the components of each category that we confront difficulties. For example, in the category "serve the public interest," ASPA members are said to be committed to "[e]xercise discretionary authority to promote the public interest" (ASPA Code of Ethics 1994). Presumably, this exhortation means that ASPA members should not be committed to exercising their discretionary authority to promote private interests. So far, so good. But this does not take us very far. How, precisely, or even imprecisely, are public administrators to exercise their discretionary authority in the public interest? The code of ethics cannot help us with this question.

Codes of ethics, of course, are like mission statements: They provide broad direction, not specific details. This is only reasonable, and we do not fault codes of ethics for this characteristic. Our concern rests with the three assumptions that seem to govern attitudes and behavior toward codes of ethics:

1. They provide sufficient or effective direction to enable public administrators to exercise judgment in the public interest.

2. Public administrators already are conversant with effective approaches to the exercise of discretion and other ethical concerns.

3. Organizations, once having developed or displayed a code of ethics, have met their responsibility.

In our view, none of these assumptions is warranted. If, consistent with the ASPA Code of Ethics, public administrators are to exercise their discretion to promote the public interest; to exercise compassion, benevolence, fairness, and optimism; to be prepared to make unpopular decisions; to encourage and facilitate legitimate dissent activities; to guard against conflict of interest; or to subordinate institutional loyalties to the public good, they will require far more support than their agencies now provide. Otherwise, public administrators will continue to be placed in the untenable position of being expected to perform critical tasks without the proper training or tools.

Like codes of ethics, ethics training has become a widespread fixture in public organizations, perceived by many public officials as "a key element to an effective ethics code" (Lewis 1991, 149). Ethics training is required at the federal level, as well as in many states and municipalities. It is "a conventional method for promoting ethical practices," and, as noted in Chapter I, typically "exclusively targets compliance with minimum statutory or administrative standards written into codes of conduct" (18). Discretion, judgment, and independent moral choice are simply not considered.

Codes of ethics and ethics training, together, constitute the official organizational—indeed, governmental—response to expectations of trust, responsibility, and accountability. They are treated as if they are the clear and certain answers to complex, though technical, problems. The ambiguous and perplexing nature of ethical questions is reduced to a legalistic conundrum that can be controlled by legislation and regulations. Conflicting values and competing obligations remain unacknowledged elements in the pantheon of organizational undiscussables. The moral equivalent of Pandora's Box must stay shut.

## ETHICAL ENERGY AND REFORM

Having characterized the real world of administrative ethics as a place of ambiguity and uncertainty, of superficiality and lip service, let us shift our focus from diagnosis to prescription and treatment. As noted earlier, we acknowledge—and even applaud—the familiar goals in public administration of accountability and compliance that are "embedded in rules, guidelines, inspections, reports, and the other impedimenta of ethics enforcement" (Frederickson 1997, 170). Our point is simply that these things do not go nearly far enough if our aim is to create an ethical public service that engenders trust, responsibility, and the public interest. Although such structures and programs, including "whistle-blowing; telephone hot lines for reporting ethics abuses; ethics boards and commissions; ethics education programs for elected, politically appointed, and administrative officials; agency ethics officers; financial or other conflict-of-interest disclosure systems; and professional codes of ethics" (158) are valuable, their utility is limited. They represent moral minimalism, rather than moral maturity and mindfulness. They merely conform to the conventions of the so-called real world.

We can begin the process of moving from moral minimalism toward moral maturity and mindfulness in public administration by considering the question on two levels—individual and organizational—within the framework of the unified ethic described earlier. Both levels, singly and together, are implicated in the ethical shift we are recommending, so both must be taken into account in devising a strategy for constructing and cultivating an ethical public service. If our goal is personal, institutional, and national pride in the quality and excellence of our public service, then we can do no less.

It is often difficult to identify the responsible party in large organizations. Individuals can easily hide behind what Dennis Thompson (1985) calls the "ethic of neutrality" and the "ethic of structure." With the ethic of neutrality, the public administrator is expected to be compliant, even blindly obedient, to the dictates of elected officials and organizational superiors, while the ethic of structure mandates that no single individual may be held responsible for decisions or actions, since it is the organization itself that is responsible. To the extent that the ethic of neutrality and the ethic of structure are operational in public agencies, there is a corresponding absence of individual responsibility.

Ethics, however, is exactly the opposite. As Carol Lewis (1991) observes, it "rests on voluntary moral judgment, with the individual as ethical player." It "means individual responsibility for judgments and choices. Logically, decision making turns on selecting and accepting responsibility. Individual responsibility is not obliterated by collective decision making in organizations and agencies" (63). The so-called many-hands problem does not relieve us from ownership of our own volition.

Lewis also notes that, although the chain of command, with its deference to superior-subordinate relations, characterizes the organizational habitat of public administrators, "neither discipline nor obedience defines the boundaries of subordinates' ethical responsibility." On the contrary, Lewis argues, when confronted with the "I was only following orders" defense, we respond with moral outrage and astonishment. The problem, of course, is to determine appropriate or proportional levels of compliance. This, for example, is the functional challenge of whistle-blowing. But the issue goes beyond whistle-blowing, for "while few indulge themselves in outright evil and fewer still in righteousness, people are evidently influenced by authority, by apathy, by thoughtlessness, and by their environment" (65).

Most of us tend to accept and absorb the spoken and unspoken expectations of our organization, its structure and culture, and generally, those expectations involve compromises, large and small, with the prevailing norms. Often, these compromises are not felt as assaults on our character, but when they are, we may go through the stages associated with grief, including disbelief, anger, and accommodation. We also may, depending on our level of emotional and moral maturity, try to blame our predicament on others, rather than take responsibility for our "wink-and-nod" behavior, our refusal to act. So, as Lewis argues, one principle relating to individual responsibility is that we cannot hide behind our boss or our desk to escape it.

A second principle is that we cannot hide behind our subordinates. As a manager, you are accountable for your subordinates' decisions and actions, regardless of whether you personally were aware of them. Clearly, our assessment of managerial responsibility is affected by proximity, saliency, and gravity, but in the end, as a manager, you are responsible.

This brings us to knowledge and competence. The third principle of individual responsibility is that we cannot hide behind our ignorance. As Lewis contends, "a profession is defined largely by its specialized knowledge, on which its privileges rest. Ignorance here undercuts all members" (68). Furthermore, "specialized knowledge is a source of substantial power in today's information society, and its manipulation increases the handler's exploitative potential" (69). Therefore, as a manager, you must decide and act, in the public interest, on the basis of the most accurate, complete, and up-to-date information available.

Fourth, as managers, we are responsible for what is done as well as how it is done. Our discretion and expertise are critical elements in meeting our responsibilities, whether we are at the top, in the middle, or at the bottom of the organization, whether we are policy analysts, human resources specialists, or so-called street-level bureaucrats such as police officers, teachers, or lifeguards. Our choices count and affect citizens in many different ways. So the responsible use of our discretion and expertise matters.

A fifth idea related to individual responsibility concerns the link between means and ends. The ethical public administrator must pay attention to both, for immoral means to attain moral ends or moral means to preserve immoral ends are unethical. At the same time, we must distinguish between ethical neutrality and policy impartiality. As we said earlier, the ethic of neutrality forecloses the possibility of moral bureaucracies. In Lewis's words, *"ethical neutrality strips the humanity from both the manager and service recipients. Dehumanizing the players serves to deny the ethical element"* (73). Policy impartiality, in contrast, implies unbiased treatment only, not an absence of ethical judgment.

A final concern regarding individual responsibility is incompetence as an abuse of office. In this context, we consider three components of incompetence: (1) perfecting, not perfection; (2) self-victimization; and (3) impossible promises (Lewis 1991, 74–76).

With respect to perfecting, not perfection, we can say that public administrators who operate below their potential are failing to act ethically. Yet, we must also recognize that "the competence standard demands from public managers not perfection but perfecting, that is, an effort to do the best that can be done given the state of the art and within reasonable limits. Expert judgment, after all, is still judgment" (Lewis 1991, 75).

With respect to self-victimization, Lewis maintains that, despite the popularity of bureaucrat-bashing in the United States, "it is unjust and demoralizing for public managers and employees to accept bureaucracy's *inaccurate* street image" (76). The bureaucrat as slouch, bumbler, and bungler, the product of the Peter Principle, by which bureaucrats are promoted to their level of incompetence, the product of Parkinson's Law, by which the incompetent expand work to fill the time available for its completion, and the paradigm of Boren's testimony, in which pondering, delegating, and mumbling are hallmarks, must be addressed by fundamental rejection of such images. Public administrators as objects of satire can do little to improve the public service. Therefore, Lewis suggests that an intolerance of incompetence as business as usual is essential, and she argues that "a manager who swallows employee incompetence to protect the agency in the short run ends up embroiled in cover-up and deception" (76).

The third and final component of incompetence to be considered here—impossible promises—relates to managerial manipulation, exaggeration, and deception, all in service of agency survival. "Padding budgets," as Lewis states, "may be a commonplace practice, but it is deception nonetheless" (76). Public agencies, therefore, must move to a culture of performance and a commitment to competence as an ethical standard—if the idea of advancing the public good carries any weight among serious public administrators.

We now move to the organizational level of moral maturity and responsibility, again drawing on the diagnoses and recommendations of Carol Lewis (1991) and also of Gary Brumback (1991). Lewis offers a number of intervention techniques for integrating ethics into agency operations, including both compliance and integrity training and counseling, briefings for new hires on common ethical problems, attention to value and character in recruitment, and using regular communications channels and meetings to raise ethical concerns. With regard to overall agency operations, Lewis argues that commitment must go beyond talk. Employees follow the flow of resources and will use the budgets allocated to training, incentives, performance, and agency policies "to meter the authenticity of the talk and the priority of public service ethics in the agency." To clarify the significance of this point, she asks, "what do you think is the more meaningful communication, fine words at a staff meeting or disregarded negligence and padded budget estimates?" (180).

One of Lewis' most interesting proposals is the ethics impact statement, or EthIS, modeled on the environmental impact statement. She claims that it provides for a decision-making process that combines analytic methods and tools, and ensures a place for ethical analysis in agency deliberations. Like cost-benefit analysis, cost-effectiveness analysis, or evaluation and statistical analysis, ethical analysis can help public managers in their decision making and sorting through competing values and obligations. Lewis argues that one major difference, perhaps, between ethical analysis and other, more familiar techniques is that "it cannot be farmed out to paid consultants or outside authorities. . . . It is not perfunctory. . . . Ethics responsibilities cannot be delegated, bought, or temporarily rented" (188).

Encompassing seven steps, "the EthIS process begins in planning, when a proposal's initial feasibility is appraised and before a decision is made" (188). Questions such as "Why is this bothering me?" and "Is it my problem?" may lead to the decision that no ethics statement is necessary. We must remember, however, that all significant decisions contain ethical dimensions. The remaining steps involve scoping, i.e., determining the scope of issues to be addressed and the range of actions, alternatives, and impacts to be considered; tiering, or forestalling repetition and checking for consistency; fact-finding; analysis; recommendations; and finally, responsibility, which entails the signing of the ethics statement by the EthIS team members and the agency head. This statement would certify that the ethical dimensions of the policy, regulation, or procedure have been considered. Finally, Lewis suggests that the advantages of the ethics impact statement include helping to set priorities, identifying problems and needed corrections early in the process, and pinpointing unanticipated effects for legislative proposals or executive decisions.

On the other hand, the EthIS process, like the environmental impact statement, can obstruct rather than facilitate decision making and dispute resolution. "As a *disclosure instrument*, it could freeze action by increasing political opposition over newly clarified controversies and stakes" (192). So, as with other methods for analysis and evaluation, the ethics impact statement involves tradeoffs that, in turn, require perspective and judgment on the part of the public administrator.

Before shifting to Brumback's recommendations for institutionalizing ethics in government, let us consider one last aspect of Lewis' discussion of building an ethical agency: five objections to agency action in regard to ethics. These five objections consist of (1) the substitution of ritual for responsibility; (2) ethical behavior as exception, not rule; (3) red tape; (4) behavior modification; and (5) the double-edged threat of vigilante ethics.

According to Lewis, the "first objection views ritualistic compliance as a poor but likely proxy for ethics." In her estimation, this objection is valid but limited. Although it is true that "institutional mechanisms do endanger the broader goal by threatening to substitute formalistic compliance for ethical responsibility" (182), it is not inevitable that they do so. Fundamental principles do not necessarily have to be trivialized when they become part of administrative routines. This is what innovative management means.

The second objection—ethical behavior as exception, not rule—concerns rewarding managers for ethical behavior. Despite the distaste expressed by some managers for linking ethical behavior to professional rewards or financial incentives, Lewis maintains that "this objection undercuts the former by leaving no alternative except routinizing ethics as an ordinary habit in daily operations" (182). She believes that public administration must make a choice.

With respect to the third objection—red tape—Lewis contends that, although regulations and procedures should be instrumental in the attainment of objectives, not valued for their own sake, necessary or desired rules still can be effective. Furthermore, public employees already experience detailed standards and ethics programs with a compliance slant. Nevertheless, to respond to the need of public managers to minimize the administrative burden, Lewis offers three rules of thumb: (1) ethics do's, like ethics don'ts, should be few and simple; (2) ethics programs should be tailored to the circumstances in particular jurisdictions and agencies; and (3) the ethical managers and employees who want to do the right thing are the clients of agency interventions (i.e., the internal players who directly benefit from ethics initiatives).

The fourth objection to ethics action by an agency—behavior modification—"can be raised against all work routines and rules, including laws and standards of conduct" (183). Admittedly, such routines and rules modify behavior because that is what they are for, and some people will spend time trying to circumvent them, either to avoid doing their jobs or precisely to do their jobs.

Finally, the fifth objection—the threat of vigilante ethics—relates to two concerns: productivity and the potential for harassment or coercion. Ethics proposals in this regard are seen as more shackles on the manager as well as more ambiguity and perplexity in the agency. Lewis answers that procedural protections, therefore, are crucial to an agency's ethics program.

According to Brumback (1991), ethics must be both an individual and an organizational responsibility. In his view, unethical behavior stems from an interaction between personal and situational conditions, but ethics is easier said than done because so much of unethical behavior has become ordinary. Consider, for example, the following examples of behaviors commonly found in organizations: scapegoating personal failures, shirking responsibility, acting disingenuously, reneging on promises, dissembling, loafing, and manipulating budgets. As Brumback says, "None of these behaviors is scandalous. But each nonetheless violates a sense of what is the morally correct behavior (e.g., the behaviors of personal responsibility, honesty, fairness, etc.), abets cynicism and distrust, undermines integrity, and can be a stepping stone to egregious behavior" (355).

Brumback (1991) also identifies six conditions that he argues must be targeted if any government ethics program is to be effective: (1) rationalizations; (2) impatient ambition; (3) seductive positions; (4) ignoble expectations; (5) upside-down incentives; and (6) unguarded trust. Regarding rationalizations, Brumback contends that in corrupting situations, such as the ones listed, "people in them may behave unethically and rationalize their behavior as ethical" (355). He refers to this tendency as "mind-over-manner" and suggests that it is a big reason why good people sometimes behave badly. Mind-over-manner, or excuses for wrongdoing, include such statements as "It's not illegal," "You can't legislate morality," "Morality is a personal matter," "It's cutthroat out there," "If I don't do it, someone else will," "We are no worse or better than society at large," and "Ethics is a gray area."

Impatient ambition is an expression of the value placed by society on short-term success. Wanting it now can drive people to cut corners. Seductive positions are those that provide power, discretion, and access to money. These positions test moral character. Ignoble expectations accentuate results and either are silent on the means to achieve them or implicitly or explicitly approve unethical behavior. Upside-down incentives emphasize expectations. "A common example is giving bonuses based on inflated performance ratings. The bonuses further reinforce the dishonesty behind the ratings" (357). Finally, unguarded trust refers to a laissez-faire posture, or taking ethics for granted.

Given these endemic tendencies and behaviors, what can be done to institutionalize ethics in public organizations? A popular prescription in this regard is "Hire the right people." Although it has merit, Brumback (1991) points out that, like ethics itself, appropriate hiring is more easily said than done. The major hurdles include the fact that the polygraph is not a good predictor, and its use is severely restricted; one in every two applicants tends to lie on job applications; and covert questions are unethical.

On the other hand, unguarded trust in the area of hiring seems naive at best, so Brumback suggests several ways out of this Catch-22. First, review background investigation policies and procedures to see if they are ethical, can be improved, and are used for the seductive positions. Second, build the agency's reputation for integrity by attending to moral leadership and ethics training, and by factoring ethics into performance management. Third, do not use surreptitious screening, and explain policies to recruits. Fourth and finally, ask new hires to pledge a commitment to ethics in government in the oath of office.

The important point, in the end, is that the only way to attain desired results consistently is to manage performance, as opposed to aimless performance and crisis management. "Although each public servant must be personally responsible for his or her own behavior on the job," Brumback argues, "given the fragility of the human conscience, government must also be responsible for a workplace that is conducive to ethical behavior" (362). In his judgment, the essential contribution toward achieving this goal is "a comprehensive ethics program that addresses the basic personal and situational causes of unethical behavior" (362–363).

In this chapter, we reexamined the real world and raised some new questions about it. We argued that administrative ethics is embedded in organizational structure and culture, and that structure and culture reflect and reinforce the organization's moral choices and commitments. We also reviewed the unified ethic—the combination of principle, purpose, and character—and contended that public administrators grounded in the unified ethic can go beyond conventional consequentialism and become more adept at moral discernment and decision making. In our judgment, commitment to the unified ethic means moral clarity, conviction, and consistency.

In our application of the unified ethic to the city manager-police chief scenario, we emphasized the importance of asking the right questions and trying to formulate justifiable answers to those questions. We found that some of the commonplace concerns used to justify unethical behavior, such as career-ism, political reality, and fear, do not stand up to scrutiny and disclosure. The net effect of these and other dysfunctional behaviors is to damage both the organization and its members.

We then turned to codes of ethics and ethics training, and argued that, although somewhat useful, they are limited in their ability to create ethical organizations and to cultivate ethi-cal character. We believe that all of us—veterans and novices alike—need help, guidance, and advice in developing our moral capacity. Codes of ethics and ethics training, however, tend to stay at the surface, leaving public administrators with no greater understanding of ethical thinking, deciding, and doing than when they began. Despite the general manage-rial need to appear prepared, tough, and in control, we sug-gest that it is in everyone's short- and long-term interest to acknowledge our natural human need for ethical assistance, just as we do with technical assistance. If you only pretend to be computer-literate, it will be discovered. And so it is with ethical literacy: If you only pretend to understand the ethical complexities inherent in public administration, you will be found out as well. Pretense and self-deception are both un-ethical and ineffective.

Then, after offering an ethical diagnosis of the real world, we turned to the question of how to move from moral minimalism to moral maturity on both the individual and organizational levels. In this connection, the work of Carol Lewis and Gary Brumback provided the context for a number of ideas and recommendations regarding individual and organizational responsibility, as well as responses to possible objections to incorporating ethics into public agencies. Whether it is an eth-ics impact statement, politically induced images of bureaucrats and bureaucracy, seductive positions, or upside-down incentives, the lesson is that ethical public administration is about responsibility, choices, and consequences. It is about taking ownership of one's decisions, actions, and relationships. It is about service in the public interest.

A second lesson, we believe, is that the creation and cultivation of ethical public organizations and ethical public administrators is a diffuse responsibility. Although we readily recognize the role of organizational leadership in helping to meet this responsibility, we maintain that, whether an organization's top management models ethical behavior and supports it with resources, everyone in the organization shares the responsibility for establishing a moral workplace. No one is off the hook. This notion raises a related question: How can ethical thought, decisions, and actions be systematically introduced and sustained in public organizations? Why should we suppose, for example, that organizational leaders, who have succeeded in our current morally anemic system, will be motivated to countenance the creation of an ethical organization, particularly if, as a result, their own perquisites and prerogatives are threatened?

But this question puts a much too narrow construction on public administrators, for the fact remains that public administration, as a profession, is used to dealing with ethics in one form or another. For example, just within the past 20 years or so, we have seen the passage of the Ethics in Government Act of 1978 and the creation of the Office of Government Ethics. In the early 1990s, the Office of Government Ethics issued a set of ethical standards that addressed such subjects as conflict of financial interest, gifts, misuse of office, impartiality, and outside employment.

On the state and local levels, nearly every state has an ethics code that covers similar subjects, including conflict of interest and other prohibited practices. Thirty-six states have ethics commissions, and many local governments have ethics codes and commissions as well. Therefore, ethics is a familiar concern in the American governmental system. The issue, however, is the depth of ethical understanding on which public agencies operate, the degree to which this understanding permeates public agencies, and whether public administrators have an ethical framework to use in meeting their daily obligations. We have suggested that the level of ethical understanding tends to be superficial and legalistic, that a "thou shalt not" approach characterizes formal organizational cultures, and that the promotion of moral maturity, integrity, and democratic values is random at best.

In response to these ethical deficiencies, we have offered the unified ethic as the framework that may provide public administrators a firm foundation for skillful ethical analysis as well as justifiable and defensible decisions. Application of the unified ethic, we believe, can assist the public administrator in developing an identity as a moral agent, a steward of the public interest, a professional citizen. Although the unified ethic does not guarantee ethical behavior, just as ethics codes and ethics training do not, it does offer clarity of ethical thought, which may increase the likelihood of ethical behavior.

In the face of organizational and policy complexity, adoption of the unified ethic as the framework for public administration can also provide criteria for assessing organizational and policy choices, as well as the reasons offered by way of explanation, defense, and justification of those choices. If, for example, we believe that morally mature organizations acknowledge the presence of conflicting values and priorities and provide opportunities to resolve them openly and safely, then we must recognize that, in the context of those conflicts, an explicit ethical basis for judgment and choice is essential. Otherwise, efforts directed toward organizational change will be merely cosmetic and thus ineffective.

Finally, let us turn to the question of whether ethics matters in organizations and whether it makes them more effective. In trying to answer this question, Nicholas Henry (2001) argues that data from both the private and public sectors support affirmative replies. In the private sector, ethics seems to be good business, and in the public sector, we find similar results. For example, in a study of city managers and chief administrative officers in the 544 American cities with populations of 50,000 or more, responsible risk-taking by senior managers "correlated positively with both a high sense of ethics and better managed cities. That is, the responsible risk takers' cities . . . had fewer lawsuits, better bond ratings, and were more likely to implement state-of-the-art productivity improvements than were cities managed by 'at-risk entrepreneurs'" (417). Henry concludes that "ethics . . . is better business and good government" (418). Despite the obvious utilitarianism embodied in Henry's conclusion, we could not agree more.

# CHAPTER 6

# Who Am I?
# Who Do I Want to Be?
# What Do I Want?

Our journey thus far has taken us to the real world of public administration, the major ethical schools of thought, the value of the unified ethical perspective, and the moral aspects and implications of five important cases. Now, in this chapter, before we move to decision making, ethics exercises, and conclusions, we ask you to step back and reflect on the connections among your principles, values, and character. We explore questions concerning our identity as public servants and as citizens, our personal and professional goals, and the place of trust, quality, and excellence in our careers. Our overall intent is to contemplate the meaning and direction of our lives, to try to make sense of our present and our future.

We begin by considering our lives and careers from a broad social perspective, examining the relationship between our work and our integrity in the context of dominant American values. We then move to our organizational lives and the link between organizational and individual needs and requirements. We conclude with a look at the particular environment of public administration and the interplay between that environment and our autonomy, authenticity, and accountability as stewards of the public interest and as moral human beings.

## HOPES AND DREAMS IN MODERN AMERICA

If you are like most Americans, you carry in your mind an image of the American Dream, the good life, as passed on to you by your parents, your peers, the culture. Much of your thinking about the good life may be focused on material growth and well-being: home ownership, followed by a newer and bigger house, the annual vacation, perhaps an SUV, physical and financial security for both you and your children. If you are a woman or a member of a minority group, you may aspire to economic equality, which includes access to the same material success that the dominant culture celebrates. You, like most Americans, tend to think in economic terms when, for example, you discuss work, family, and fulfillment with your colleagues or neighbors. But you, like many Americans, men and women of all races and ethnicities, may also feel that, although your work is meaningful, you still feel pressured, dissatisfied, and uncertain about how it fits with the rest of your life.

Today, people worry about money, but they also worry about being worried. There is a tension between the material side of our lives and the spiritual side. On some level, we often wonder about our spiritual life, our moral nature, and we ask ourselves how we should live, how much we should work, how much money we need, what we are trying to do in our lives.

Robert Wuthnow (1996) argues that the American Dream is a moral framework that encourages people to work hard and to hope for rewards. But he also maintains that it is about more than materialism, a high-paying job, a home in the suburbs, and opportunities for your children. Although the "American Dream promotes the endless pursuit of more prestigious careers and a more comfortable life" (3), it also "supplies understandings about why one should work hard and about the value of money" (4). In Wuthnow's view, the American Dream supplies these understandings "in a way that guards against money and work being taken as ends in themselves" (4). If Wuthnow is right, then, despite the difficulty of integrating moral considerations into economic life, such considerations are implicit in everything we do. Indeed, Wuthnow believes that, this difficulty notwithstanding, "much of the moral strength embedded in the American Dream remains intact" (5). To put this idea into the language of the unified ethic, principles and values are not confined to our personal or professional lives, but relate directly and deeply to our overall purpose, character, and happiness.

Recognizing the inherent unity in our moral nature, however, is clearly not enough. To adapt the moral strength of the American Dream to our economic striving requires us to confront the powerful cultural imperatives that engulf us every day. This is no easy task, for, as Wuthnow observes, "the advice we receive on all sides encourages us to think in economic categories, rather than giving us ways to transcend these categories" (8–9). Nonetheless, given our moral nature, it is possible to move beyond narrow economic assumptions, including careerism, consumerism, and competitiveness, and achieve some equilibrium between our material and spiritual sides.

The attainment of such equilibrium involves asking hard questions. It involves, for example, questioning what we take for granted as natural, unchangeable, somehow ordained. It involves wondering, to use economic terminology, how much our integrity is worth, and whether it is worth sacrificing for the sake of a job or career. It involves pondering the real significance of getting ahead, making it, being number one.

The point is that, although daily compromises and accommodations are necessary, a balance in our lives between the material and the spiritual is equally necessary. There is nothing ethically wrong with ambition, accomplishment, or even acquisition. The issue is whether there are any limits to these things, and whether a high standard of living, technological expansion, and creature comforts constitute the purpose of our lives. If, at the end of our days, all we can point to are our possessions as the sum total of our time on the planet, the answer will be depressingly obvious. The challenge, therefore, lies in trying to align our economic aspirations with our spiritual needs.

We believe that many Americans are willing to try to meet this challenge, but there are, predictably, many differences of opinion as well as great confusion and uncertainty about how to proceed. This is natural and not to be feared. Indeed, it is the essence of freedom, which necessarily entails responsibility exercised through the political process. But, as a first step, particularly given the evidence around us of environmental damage, personal distress, and many other individual and social pathologies, it seems reasonable to insist that moral discourse be taken seriously in whatever venue it may occur.

For example, instead of simplistic pronouncements about the need to bring values back into our classrooms or to introduce values-based management into our organizations, we must acknowledge the need for a firm and explicit moral foundation for our personal as well as policy decisions and actions. As Wuthnow (1996) contends, "The current crisis of values hinges on the simple fact that we have no basis on which to make these choices. Calling for more attention to values is merely to identify the problem. To move positively toward its resolution requires paying closer attention to the way in which choices are actually made" (12). We suggest that the unified ethic—the integration of principle, purpose, and character—provides a practical as well as moral basis for making both the personal and collective choices that we all must make.

## ORGANIZATIONAL LIFE

Let us begin our consideration of organizational life by looking at your typical day. As a manager, what do you do? How do you spend your time? What do you accomplish? The answers to these questions, of course, depend on where you are in your organization. But, according to a number of management studies, despite the differences across levels and positions within an organization, there are some common elements in a manager's typical day. For example, managers are leaders, even of, perhaps, small numbers of people. Managers monitor behavior and information; they plan and allocate resources; and they motivate, direct, and evaluate other individuals in the organization.

One of the things that managers do is spend a great deal of time in meetings. Yet, in spite of the ink that has been spilled on complaining about meetings, they continue to be the major vehicle for brainstorming and decision making. So it may not be meetings as such that frequently evoke grumbling and groaning. Rather, it is the way that meetings are organized and managed. The effective manager has an agenda, knows when and how much to contribute, and concludes the meeting with some concrete next steps. But, then, you are probably already aware of the finer points of meeting organization and management, and our purpose here is not to explore managerial strategies and tactics. Instead, we wish to take a more personal look at your life in your organization.

Take, for example, stress. Is your job filled with stress? Are you in a pressure cooker? Are deadlines met? Is responsibility clear? If your answers to these questions are yes, yes, no, seldom, or sometimes, and it all depends, then it may be time to pause and reflect on the sources of the stress as well as the perplexity and uncertainty that characterize your work setting.

For example, it may be worth spending a moment considering such concepts as role conflict and role ambiguity. Management theorists tell us that role conflict refers to incompatible demands made on a person, and role ambiguity refers to a lack of clarity as to the requirements and responsibilities of one's job. Does any of this sound familiar to you? If so, then you know that either or both of these role problems can be very stressful and can lead to serious emotional and physical damage to the individual and organization alike.

At the same time, we are by no means suggesting that a stress-free work environment is either possible or desirable. The essential point is that, as Hans Selye (1974), the premier stress researcher, has said, stress may be good or bad. It depends on the sources of stress, the circumstances under which it is experienced, and how we manage it. According to Selye, we respond to stress in different ways. What may be stressful for you may not be stressful for someone else, and vice versa. So it is important to be able to recognize what makes you feel stressed or, more accurately, distressed, what the signs of your distress may be, and, most of all, what can be done to reduce your stress levels.

We believe that attention to stressors and awareness of appropriate stress-reduction techniques are part of knowing who you are, who you want to be, and what you want. For example, we are all familiar with Type A and Type B behaviors. We know that the Type A pattern includes intense desire to achieve, competitiveness, involvement in many projects, and high levels of mental and physical activity. Type B, on the other hand, suggests a more relaxed or laid-back style, a more measured approach to personal and professional pressures and responsibilities. Which type are you?

Are you a workaholic? Do you often experience information overload? Are you worried about burnout? Fortunately, whether you tend to Type A or Type B, techniques are available to help you identify your behavioral patterns, to reflect on your personal and professional goals, and to improve the quality of your life.

Whether Type A or B, for example, you can benefit from greater awareness of how you react to different circumstances. You can determine the type of manager you are, as well. If you are concerned with detail, you probably are affected by time pressures and information overload; if you are a big-picture person, your stress tends to originate in role conflict or role ambiguity. The point is that if you know what causes you distress, if you understand your work setting more clearly, then you will be better able to anticipate problems, develop and use your support system, and integrate your work and your life more effectively.

Organizations, like individuals, experience stress or the consequences of stress. Managers recognize that stress among employees can decrease productivity, increase the costs of health insurance, and contribute to excessive absenteeism and turnover. As a result, many organizations, at least larger ones, now offer employee assistance programs that deal with drug, alcohol, and tobacco problems, weight control, exercise, nutrition, and psychological counseling. The benefits from such programs are clear.

To help you consider your own behavior patterns, we conclude this section with the following stress profile that is intended to measure Type A behavior. Answer the ten questions with: A: almost always true; B: often true; C: seldom true; D: almost never true (Girdano and Everly, 1979).

1. I hate to wait in lines.

2. I often find myself racing against the clock to save time.

3. I become upset if I think something is taking too long.

4. When under pressure, I tend to lose my temper.

5. My friends tell me that I tend to get irritated easily.

6. I seldom like to do anything unless I can make it competitive.

7. When something needs to be done, I'm the first to begin, even though the details may still need to be worked out.

8. When I make a mistake, it is usually because I've rushed into something without giving it enough thought and planning.

9. Whenever possible, I will try to do two things at once, like eating while working, or planning while driving or bathing.

10. I find myself feeling guilty when I am not actively working on something.

Scoring: A = 4; B = 3; C = 2; D = 1. If your total score is 26 or more, then you tend toward Type A behavior.

We believe that taking a personal inventory is a key step in developing and maintaining a fulfilling personal and professional life. Insight into your own personality, character, and behavior is essential to understanding what motivates you, excites you, touches you. It helps you to formulate answers to questions concerning the direction and meaning of your life, to identify effective strategies for planning how to integrate your life and your work, and to establish ways to monitor and measure your movement toward your goals.

In our judgment, a fundamental element in our personal inventory is our identity as moral agents and as citizens, for, just as we experience mental or physical stress in our organizations, so do we experience moral stress, the discomfort we feel when we know things are not right, when we try to rationalize our way out of a morally distressing situation. Getting a handle on our moral stress is as vital as ensuring that we get enough exercise, sleep, and proper nutrition.

An essential first step in getting a handle on our moral stress is to have in hand a clear and compelling basis for analyzing and assessing moral challenges, and for deciding and acting in morally legitimate ways. Recall Wuthnow's (1996) argument that the current crisis of values relates to the absence of a basis for making moral choices and that we must focus on the ways in which choices are actually made. So if you wish to live a moral life in both the personal and professional spheres, you need to go beyond the superficial and simplistic and consider the subtleties and nuances of morally grounded thought and action. As we have asserted a number of times, our prescription for treating the present moral anemia is the unified ethic, the holistic view that connects what you believe, what you want, and who you are.

Tom Morris (1997) asks what life would be like if Aristotle ran General Motors. Or, to put it more broadly, how would we fare as individuals who spend much of our time in bureaucratic organizations if certain philosophical verities and moral virtues were clearly and consciously acknowledged? What qualities of life would be emphasized? How would our identity as moral beings be defined?

Morris suggests that there are four dimensions of human experience—intellectual, aesthetic, moral, and spiritual—and four corresponding foundations of human excellence—truth, beauty, goodness, and unity. These are the qualities of our personal and professional lives that must be nurtured if we are to achieve the spiritual health that is at the heart of ethics. These are the keystones of trust and collaboration that are central to moral maturity. If, as Morris maintains, ethics is about spiritually healthy people in socially harmonious relationships, then we ignore the dimensions of human experience and the foundations of human excellence at our peril. We, in effect, turn our souls over to the highest bidder.

None of this denotes, however, that we should neglect our self-interest. Indeed, implicit in even the seemingly selfish question often asked about ethics—"What's in it for me?"—are other questions that ultimately link our self-interest to our identity and spirit. Morris (1997) suggests that when people ask, "What's in it for me?", they mean, "How will it affect my immediate physical safety?" or, "What sort of impact will it have on my foreseeable personal comfort?" or, "What will it do for my long-term financial security?" But the key question, in the end, is, "How will it affect my ultimate personal fulfillment?"

People are understandably interested in how their moral identity ties into other facets of their lives, and, again, we contend that the unified ethic provides the philosophical foundation for answering that question. It suggests that the moral life is inseparable from the rest of what we think, decide, and do. As Morris says, although you may wear one hat at work and another at home, you still wear them on the same head.

## MORAL STRESS IN PUBLIC ADMINISTRATION

We described and critiqued the real world of public administration in Chapters 1 and 5. You recall that, in our view, when it comes to ethics, the real world tends to focus on obedience, or compliance with laws and regulations, and you recall that we contend that such a position fails on several grounds, including its diminution of our identity as rational and autonomous persons able and willing to exercise judgment and responsibility.

As Morris (1997) observes, ethics is not about staying out of trouble or avoiding problems. Instead, it is about creating strength in an individual, a family, a community, and relationships. Indeed, ethics cannot be about rule-following, since there are never enough rules to cover every conceivable situation; ethics-as-rules can encourage an exception or loophole mentality; rules can conflict; and rules need interpretation, which must come from somewhere beyond the rules. Thus, the primacy of the unified ethic.

In this context, we now return to the concept of moral stress in the public administration environment. Our aim is to identify the sources of moral stress, its effects on the individual bureaucrat, possible resolutions of moral stress (including the demarcation of what we call the Type E personality), and the need for collaborative as well as individual moral behavior. In our view, as noted earlier, moral stress is as important as mental and physical stress and, therefore, requires institutional networks and support systems similar to employee assistance programs.

We should not expect members of an organization to live the moral life alone. Since, as citizens and employees, we live in communities, it is essential that the organizations where we spend so much of our time become moral communities, able to nurture and sustain moral public servants who are clear about their convictions and commitments and courageous enough to act on them.

### Sources of Moral Stress

Moral stress, we believe, is endemic in the public service. Even the most narcotized bureaucrat cannot fail to experience moral discomfort on the job. On the most basic level of human reason and responsibility, moral quandaries cannot be denied. At the same time, however, organizational structures and cultures, expectations and reward systems, often tend to ignore or invalidate moral stress, leaving conflicted individuals with a Hobson's choice: silence or whistle-blowing. There is little, if any, acknowledgment of the value of creating moral systems, as well as technical or management systems, that can contribute to the promotion of moral community within the organization. The old admonition that "you must go along to get along" captures the idea here.

How can this distortion of our moral nature be explained, let alone justified? To try to answer this question, let us look at what some scholars have said and check it against our own experience. One argument is that the bureaucracy takes away the individual's capacity to judge right and wrong. Our personality is replaced by our function or our role. The organization becomes our conscience and tells us what is real. We are transformed into morally neutral, and even morally neutered, instruments of the bureaucracy. "Bureaucrats are asked to become people without conscience; judgments as to right and wrong are to be left to the supervisor, the manager, or the organization as a whole. Those who submit become people without heart; not only does their sense of moral judgment atrophy but so do their feelings for others" (Hummel 1994, 112). This parallels the obedience or compliance orientation described earlier.

Dennis Thompson (1985) argues that "the ethic of neutrality" and "the ethic of structure" characterize the bureaucracy. The public administrator is expected to conform to the traditional ideal of serving as an instrument of legislative will, exercising independent judgment on only technical matters. Responsibility is diffuse; accountability is vested in the hierarchy. Dissent desists as soon as an organizational position is adopted. Otherwise, resignation is required.

So we see that Hummel and Thompson attribute much of the bureaucrat's moral passivity to organizational structure and culture. Douglas Morgan and Henry Kass (1993) extend this line of reasoning and argue that public administration has drifted from conventional management ideology to ambiguous administrative practice that includes policy making and ethical perplexity. Committed to maximizing efficiency and effectiveness, public administrators often complain about the impediments that obstruct the achievement of efficient and effective practice, impediments such as the growing volume of regulations, "the emergence of more participative management styles, court-mandated due process requirements, various forms of citizen participation, laborious bidding and procurement procedures, the making of decisions based on what 'the lawyers will say,'" among others (180–181). Morgan and Kass quote an administrator as stating "that it is a matter of 'seeing how much efficiency you can get away with'" (181).

Nonetheless, administrators invoke the management ideology of control and efficient allocation of resources "to help them rationalize a very messy situation in which they must act." Messiness refers to "a situation in which they are expected to act" but "do not know what is wanted or even what the issue is." Compounding this messiness are interest group competition, technological change, and public opinion that "all conspire to make the situation both ambiguous and equivocal."

Thus, traditional management ideology provides a rationale and a set of techniques for acting. As a rationale, it "creates a moral obligation for the administrator 'to make things work.'" As technique, "it allows administrators legitimately to insert themselves (or be inserted by political superiors) into the decision making process in the name of technical rationality." The reality, however, is that once an administrator is in the loop, the commitment to making things work goes well beyond the technical. Making things work "may require mediating conflict, tempering public passions, or modifying ill-conceived or precipitous action." As a result, administrators "find themselves drifting into a management setting with a moral framework that is ill-suited to the task at hand" (Morgan and Kass 181).

To put this situation into our terms, administrators continually confront moral stress. The pressure they are under to make things work is relentless as they cope with pluralism—the array of competing interests that characterize American politics and policy making. They must balance these interests and also facilitate consensus. They must manage process and do a great deal of stroking to ensure fairness and access, both in the present and the future.

Morgan and Kass (1993) contend that this aspect of the public administrator's life is the second stage of their odyssey toward role reversal, by which they mean that public administrators have shifted from being on tap to being on top, from carrying out the dictates of political leaders to developing as well as implementing policy. In the first stage, as we noted, the administrator is committed to the established management values of efficiency and effectiveness. In the second stage, this straightforward commitment "gives way to the realities of uncertainty, ambiguity, and complexity that undergird much of the administrative landscape." Pluralist politics emerges "as a legitimate moral claim that competes on equal grounds with administrative efficiency." Finally, stage three represents a move "toward the language of the public interest to help resolve moral dilemmas that cannot be accommodated successfully by a commitment either to efficient management or to pluralist politics" (179).

The public interest, however, is itself uncertain and ambiguous, and lends itself to multiple interpretations. It may be used to affirm underlying community values or the constitutional values of freedom, equality, and property. It may be used "to recognize collective interests over the partial group interests within the community." An example of such a collective interest might be those who are unrepresented by interest groups. "Finally, the public interest sometimes is used to express an obligation by administrators to future generations." In any event, administrators in the public service environment often "tend to view themselves as the lonely guardians of the larger public interest" (184).

Morgan and Kass (1993) claim that the odyssey of the American administrative experience has left administrators with a crisis of legitimacy. Their original moral obligation to execute the will of the people has been enlarged to embrace and to reject aspects of pluralist politics. They are expected both to engage in interest advocacy and to ameliorate the worst excesses of pluralism.

Somehow, as mediators, they are to protect the public interest and constitutional values. In the end, they are left "with a set of multiple and conflicting moral obligations without any kind of ordering framework" (185) and, in the process, roles have been reversed: appointed public administrators have assumed responsibility for policy, while elected officials frequently play an essentially ceremonial role. But there is no language to justify what administrators are called upon to do on a daily basis. When public administrators do take on ethical obligations outside of conventional management, they may be criticized for usurping the rights of elected officials, again raising the question of what justifies the administrator's role in democratic governance.

Morgan and Kass (1993) conclude that, although efficiency and effectiveness have been seen as in conflict with democratic control, public administrators do not necessarily see things in this way. Making things work encompasses efficiency and effectiveness but also responsiveness, accountability, and equity. Democratic government, therefore, is not a series of tradeoffs but, rather, a constellation of values that must be balanced and accommodated with judgment and responsibility. Efficiency and accountability are both necessary for a community of ordered liberty, and public administrators are the primary agents of this trust. Finally, Morgan and Kass maintain that career administrators need a "moral framework that enables them to answer the question they face on a daily basis: By what right can/should I play such an active role in the activities of democratic governance?" (187). We suggest that this question, as well as the inevitable and daily ethical dilemmas, imply a profound and continuing source of moral stress.

## Reducing Moral Stress

Moral stress, like other forms of stress, is experienced every day by public administrators. Unlike other forms of stress, however, moral stress is seldom acknowledged. It is analogous to the various diseases that are referred to as "silent killers." Yet, like those diseases, it is real and relentless and, left unattended, will ultimately take its toll. At the same time, as we said earlier, a stress-free environment is neither possible nor desirable. Moral stress, like physical or mental stress, is inevitable. The question is how we respond to it and what support is available to us as we try to integrate our moral and professional responsibilities.

We argued that moral stress flows from the crisis of legitimacy in public administration, daily ethical quandaries, and organizational neglect of moral issues. We also asked you to check these ideas against your own experience. For example, do you, as a public administrator, experience anxiety or uncertainty about the absence of constitutional legitimacy for your role in governance? Have you experienced the role reversal that Morgan and Kass describe? Does your organization try to rob you of your conscience? Are you expected to be a moral cripple?

If your answer to these questions is yes, or sometimes yes, then your experience comports with our belief that moral stress is inherent in administrative life. But, more important, if your answer is yes, then the moral stress you have felt also supports our position that, despite possible constitutional and cultural deficiencies related to public administration, administrators, like human beings in general, retain their moral identity. For example, regardless of organizational attempts, conscious or otherwise, to assault or suppress our moral sense, most of us try to protect it, even if only privately or partially, as we cope with the ethical challenges in both our personal and professional lives. We believe that acknowledgment of our ineradicable moral sense is the first step toward reducing and resolving moral stress.

The rest of our strategy for the reduction and resolution of moral stress can be divided into three levels—individual, organizational, and societal—which sometimes overlap. For example, on all three levels, an important ingredient is an awareness of the moral strength and complexity of the American Dream. As we saw earlier, this strength and complexity correspond directly with the unified ethic as well as the relationship between our personal and professional lives and our principles, purposes, and character. Together, this strength and complexity provide, respectively, a social context that shapes our hopes and dreams and a clear and compelling basis for making moral choices.

On the individual level, our aim is to encourage the cultivation of what we call the "Type E personality," the combination of the best of Type A and Type B behaviors anchored to a clear and consistent ethical foundation. As we noted earlier, there is nothing ethically wrong with ambition, accomplishment, or acquisition. The question concerns their scope and substance, along with the extent to which they are grounded in justifiable moral choices. The Type E personality is achievement-oriented, competitive, and intense, as well as relaxed, self-aware, and centered. But, undergirding it all, is a depth of moral maturity that fosters restraint and moderation, the fundamental keys to character. In our estimation, developing and sustaining a Type E personality is the second step in reducing and resolving moral stress.

The third step in dealing with moral stress is taken at the organizational level. Again, just as many organizations have recognized the high costs of physical and emotional stress, they are advised to recognize the costs of moral stress. Indeed, we believe it is plausible to assume that what sometimes is presented as physical or emotional stress may well be moral stress in disguise. Like other forms of stress, moral stress can lead to poor concentration, fatigue, absenteeism, chronic illness, and feelings of burnout that, in turn, contribute to declines in productivity, quality, and stability. The answer to this problem, we believe, has several aspects, some of which we have alluded to in earlier discussions: (1) acknowledgment of the moral dimensions of organizational life; (2) appropriate responses to these dimensions, such as broad-based cultural change, including training grounded in the unified ethic; and (3) inclusion of moral stress among the conditions requiring or deserving the services of an employee assistance program.

The last or societal level for the reduction and resolution of moral stress implies political and organizational change that relates to the place and perception of public administration in

American culture. Bureaucracy, for example, would be seen as an asset rather than a liability, and bureaucrat-bashing would no longer be accepted as a viable electoral tactic. Young people would aspire to public service, for working in government would be an honorable profession, a way to serve the public interest, advance our democracy, and nurture moral discourse and community. Public administrators would be able, finally, to hold their heads high.

Moving toward such political and organizational change involves formidable challenges and, once again, all three levels of our strategy for reducing and resolving moral stress. Central to this change is political and administrative leadership at all levels of government. Elected and appointed officials alike are the key players in altering cultural perceptions of public administration and administrators. They are the ones, for example, able to question seriously simplistic prescriptions for administrative reform such as privatization, reinvention, and new public management. They are the ones in a position to separate fact from fiction and to help citizens understand and evaluate the reality of public policies, programs, and processes. Whether the impetus or incentive is there for such public-spirited initiatives, however, is open to question.

Nevertheless, the magnitude of such change notwithstanding, action can be taken at both the individual and organizational levels to deal with moral stress and, in the process, to enliven and enrich the public service. For example, through the judicious use of their leadership and discretion, public administrators can introduce a new direction and determination toward transforming their organizations, bureaus, divisions, and departments into morally mature and responsible places, where honorable men and women perform honorable work, and where trust and collaboration are nourished and cherished in the true spirit of public service.

Public administrators can, in keeping with the unified ethic, habitually raise questions about the principles at stake in any given decision situation, how those principles relate to their character, and what the long-term implications of their decision might be. If, however, these sentiments seem saccharine or surreal, then we invite you to consider the alternative which, essentially, is the real world that we addressed earlier, and to ask yourself whether you are satisfied and wish to continue living there. If your answer is at least a qualified no, then further reflection on our recommendations may be worth your time.

In this chapter, we tried to identify ways to help you answer the questions of who you are, who you want to be, and what you want. We noted that our dominant national values, embodied in the American Dream, combine material and moral aspirations. We also noted that the continuing challenge that we all face is how to integrate the two, and we suggested that the unified ethic is relevant in this regard. Our principles and values are embedded in our personal and professional pursuits and underlie our sense of purpose, our character, and our happiness. More specifically, the unified ethic is especially relevant in our secular, commercial culture, where consumerism, careerism, and competitiveness are celebrated, and where our spiritual and ethical needs are effectively privatized.

On administrative life, we pointed out that the common practices of meeting, motivating, monitoring, and, measuring, among others, often involve conflicting and ambiguous roles which, in turn, can produce stress. We argued that understanding how you deal with stress and how stress can be reduced is essential to both your emotional and physical health. Along these lines, we recommended that you consider taking a periodic personal inventory as a way to foster a fulfilling personal and professional life, and we suggested that our moral identity as public administrators is a fundamental feature of this inventory. In our judgment, moral stress, like emotional or physical stress, must be acknowledged and attended to if we are to establish and maintain our personal and professional equilibrium.

Our personal and professional equilibrium is also strength-ened when we acknowledge the value of the unified ethic, for it provides a basis for our moral choices and for integration of the dimensions of human experience and foundations of human excellence. Here, you recall, we refer, respectively, to the intellectual, aesthetic, moral, and spiritual dimensions and to the foundations of truth, beauty, goodness, and unity. At the same time, however, we are not trying to nominate anyone for sainthood. Self-interest, for example, is as intrinsic to human nature as other, perhaps nobler, qualities. But it is only one among many qualities, rather than the sum total of our character. The point, in any case, is to try to enlarge, not shrink, our souls and spirits, and to do so, particularly at work, involves dealing with moral stress and moving toward developing a Type E personality.

In trying to understand where public administrators' moral stress comes from, we identified three sources: (1) the lack of legitimacy in our constitutional order; (2) organizational structure and culture; and (3) daily ethical dilemmas. Public administrators are pulled or pushed into policy making, mediation, and negotiation, for example, without official sanction; thus, the role reversal between elected officials and appointed administrators. Bureaucracies tend to neglect the moral gray areas and emphasize legalisms, a practice that provides no opportunity for the development of the skills required to address the daily ethical dilemmas in the adminis-trative environment. Ambiguity and complexity are the order of the day, and even retreat to the public interest as a moral lodestar proves difficult, since it, too, tends to be elusive and even ephemeral. In the end, then, public administrators might find themselves wondering who they are, who they want to be, and what they want.

Nonetheless, despite the unwritten or unspoken pressures to surrender or suppress our moral identity, we somehow manage to retain it. We may often stumble and fall, but deep down, we are moral beings. We are capable of understanding and experiencing our moral nature—the connection between our principles, purposes, and character—and, despite our cynicism and real-world ennui, we desire to carry our moral weight. But to do so, we need a strategy, a conscious plan, for moral engagement. Accordingly, we proposed a three-part approach—individual, organizational, and societal—the goal of which is to reduce and resolve the moral stress that we feel as long as we are alive.

Finally, we return to the idea that our moral lives are lived in community and relationships. We are not moral hermits but moral collaborators. Our identity as moral citizens is clearly and consistently implicated in the moral identity of others, and denial of our moral identity or theirs is ultimately impossible. As members of our communities, we are obligated to nurture our moral capacity, to collaborate, and to trust our fellow travelers, regardless of who we are, what status we enjoy, or where we sit in the conference room.

# CHAPTER 7

# Making Choices

Making choices, moral and otherwise, is inherent in both our personal and professional lives. We choose every day, in matters large and small, so we have a lot of practice in making decisions. The question, however, is whether we know which of our decisions have moral aspects. Many of the decisions we make, of course, are not morally important. When you buy ice cream, for example, it is of no moral significance if you choose vanilla instead of chocolate, and even with larger purchases, such as a car, no moral consequences flow from your choice of green over red. Or in the work setting, as Dennis Wittmer (1994) wonders, does ordering pencils for the office constitute an ethical decision? The point is that, despite our experience in decision making, most of us, for reasons of time or skill, or both, do not evaluate our important choices from a moral point of view. Nor are we clear about why taking the time and developing such skill would be worthwhile.

The ethical dimensions and implications of our choices tend to be obscured by our commitment to the commonly accepted values of efficiency and effectiveness, as though they, themselves, are easily understood and measured. But this does not mean that our choices lack ethical dimensions and implications. On the contrary, we either do not recognize them or, if we do recognize them, we do not know what to do about them—thus, the moral stress discussed in the last chapter.

In Chapter 6, we suggested that moral stress in public administration originates in the absence of constitutional legitimacy, organizational neglect of ethical complexities, and daily ethical quandaries. We also suggested, recalling Wuthnow's (1996) point, that having a basis for our ethical choices is crucial, and we suggested, as well, that the unified ethic provides such a basis for all of us, including public administrators. In this chapter, our intent is to bridge the previous chapters and the subsequent chapters, as we try to supplement the unified ethic with behavioral and organizational perspectives. Our goal is to provide a more comprehensive decision-making framework as well as the opportunity for you, in the next two chapters, to test this framework and enhance your skill in making moral choices.

## ETHICAL DILEMMAS, ETHICAL DECISIONS

Public administrators suffering from moral stress, as well as lacking clarity, skill, and experience in ethical analysis and judgment, cannot be expected to make consciously ethical decisions. Therefore, the first step toward ethical decision making entails the development of some understanding of the nature of an ethical dilemma. As Mary Guy (1991) argues: "Equipping staff with the sensitivity to recognize conflicts and assess them in terms of the values that are involved is the most enduring means for actively promoting ethical decisions and actions" (201). The goal, however, is not to institutionalize a mechanical or checklist approach to ethical analysis and judgment, but to internalize a sense of personal responsibility among organizational members and to increase both individual and organizational accountability.

Rushworth Kidder (1995) frames ethics as obedience to the unenforceable, a definition derived from John Moulton (1924), an early twentieth century English jurist. Ethics is the middle ground between positive law and absolute choice, between regulation and freedom, and on that middle ground, we confront ethical dilemmas, which must be distinguished from moral temptations. According to Kidder (1995), ethical dilemmas consist of conflicts between right and right, while moral temptations consist of conflicts between right and wrong. For example, an ethical dilemma might pit environmental protection against economic growth, both right values. Or it might pit respect for the sovereignty of other nations against the right to intervene in other nations' affairs to protect the vulnerable. Or, finally, it is right to punish careless employees but also right to be compassionate toward them.

On the other hand, moral temptations, or right versus wrong questions, are different from ethical dilemmas. For example, whether it is cheating on your income taxes, lying under oath, inflating your expense account, overstating the damage to your car to your insurance company, distorting employee evaluations, or padding your budget, you do not face a genuine moral challenge.

In contrast to ethical dilemmas, or right versus right choices, moral temptations present us with one right choice and one wrong choice, and as Kidder observes, we are not equally attracted to each. "Faced with the alternatives of arguing it out with your boss or gunning him down in the parking lot, you don't see the latter as an option" (17–18). At the same time, we may be tempted to do wrong, if only momentarily and if we rationalize our way toward that end. But, as Kidder says, "For most people, some sober reflection is all that's required to recognize a wolf-like moral temptation masquerading in the lamb's clothing of a seeming ethical dilemma" (18).

Having distinguished between ethical dilemmas and moral temptations, we now turn to the nature of an ethical decision. Consider, for example, Dennis Wittmer's (1994) suggestion that ethical decisions are made in situations that have ethical dimensions, and that ethical situations necessarily involve decisions or behavior that have a significant impact on oneself and the welfare of others. In Wittmer's view, however, this conception does not sufficiently delimit ethical decision situations from nonethical ones, since "*all* management decisions can be said to affect others and involve choice" (350).

Let us return, for instance, to the pencils example. Even the decision to order pencils for the office will have consequences for others. Some employees, perhaps, might prefer a different brand of pencil. Yet, it would be a stretch to call this an ethical decision situation. Therefore, we need to fine-tune our notion of an ethical decision if it is to be practical and is not to trivialize ethical considerations. In this context, Wittmer observes that ethical situations or decisions are thought to involve significant impact on the welfare of others, but they involve other things as well.

These other things that define an ethical situation "are the particular norms, standards or principles relevant in guiding decisions. Moral standards and principles would include fairness, honesty, justice, human dignity, and integrity, among others. Such values and principles, then, could be seen as constituting the 'ethical' dimensions of situations, and a situation could be thought of as 'ethical' to the extent that these values and principles are *relevant and deserve consideration*." Moreover, although we might claim that these values and principles must always be considered, "in many situations ethical standards are not at issue or in jeopardy of being compromised," so we would not consider such situations as ethical. "Unless a situation more directly and explicitly requires or involves considerations of ethical standards and principles," Wittmer argues, "we would not describe the situation as an 'ethical' one" (351).

Wittmer concludes this discussion by identifying the various elements in understanding ethical decision situations: choice, right and wrong, cooperative social life, significant impact on others, justice, rights, and other particular standards and principles. An ethical situation is one in which ethical dimensions *"are relevant and deserve consideration in making some choice that will have significant impact on others"* (351) and ethical dimensions are those norms and principles that provide the guidelines for determining how conflicts are to be settled and for benefiting people living in groups.

## APPROACHES TO DECISION MAKING

With the structure and substance of ethical dilemmas and ethical decisions in mind, we now turn to the major decision-making perspective in public administration: the rational model. Our belief is that some acquaintance with this perspective, in general, will prove useful for understanding the challenges of ethical decision making, in particular, especially given the centrality of decision making to the administrative function. As a number of practitioners and scholars have observed, public administration is fundamentally about decision making. For example, Robert Denhardt (1999) argues that decision making is the most universal managerial activity because it is involved in all the other functions of management. It is impossible to plan, control, staff, direct, organize, or perform any of the miscellaneous management functions without making decisions. All management involves either explicit or implicit decisions" (366).

From this perspective, the chief characteristic of decision making is rationality. "In its purest form," Denhardt says, "the rational model of decision making suggests the following steps: 1. Find an occasion for decision making ('decide to decide') and then formulate the problem in the best way possible. 2. Develop as many alternative solutions as possible. 3. Choose the alternative that maximizes the possibility that we will attain our goals or standards" (366). Essentially, the rational model prescribes analysis of the problem, generation of alternative solutions, and selection from among the alternatives.

To Denhardt, the most important lesson of the rational decision-making model is "becoming aware that a problem exists and correctly defining the problem" (366). Without such initial awareness, the remainder of the process is moot, and the chances of solving the problem are slim. But awareness alone is not enough. The second part of the lesson is problem definition. If a problem is not defined correctly, the chances of solving it are also slim.

According to Denhardt, defining a situation relates to our perception of reality, our need to make sense of things. But our definition of a situation is also important because it is the basis of our decisions and actions. Denhardt even contends that "all mentally healthy individuals behave in a way consistent with their definitions of situations" (366). If this claim is accurate, then it buttresses our concept of moral stress in public administration, given the frequent conflicting perspectives between individual administrators, their colleagues, and the organization as a whole. In any event, in Denhardt's estimation, correctly defining the problem is half the battle.

You might ask yourself at this point if the rational decision-making model fits with your experience. The chances are that it does not, although pieces of it may apply, perhaps in different configurations. But as a description of how public administrators actually make decisions, the rational model leaves something to be desired. In your daily activities, it is probably fair to say that you arrive at solutions in ways that do not much resemble the steps in the rational model. Why? Because "the basis of the rational problem-solving process is the economic assumption that people attempt to maximize their outcomes when they make choices (i.e., decisions)" (Denhardt 1999, 367). In theory, you identify a goal, evaluate all alternatives in terms of that goal, and then pick the alternative that will produce the results you are after. But it is never so simple. Moreover, we must distinguish this usage of "rational" from the Kantian usage in the unified ethic. They are not the same.

Consider, for example, the work of Herbert Simon, Nobel Prize winner and premier student of decision-making behavior in organizations. Simon (1957) maintains that the "economic man" model does not accurately describe actual problem-solving or decision-making behavior. In practice, maximizing outcomes is seldom possible, largely because of constraints on our ability to deal with information, on our time to make decisions, and on the resources available to us.

"Moreover," Denhardt (1999) notes, "because we care more about some problems than others, our motivation to solve problems varies. We are willing to spend more mental and physical energy on some problems than on others" (367–368). Thus, given all these constraints, "Simon argues that human beings attempt to be rational, but they can be rational only within certain limits or bounds." Choices are evaluated in the context of what Simon calls "bounded rationality," which, in turn, "results in a satisficing criterion for evaluating alternatives, rather than a maximizing one" (368).

The expression "good enough for government work" captures the meaning of a "satisficing" decision. A satisficing decision is good enough; it is not ideal, but it does conform to the constraint-driven reality of public administration. Denhardt describes the process as follows:

> When an individual faces a choice situation in which a decision must be made, rather than attempting to garner all possible information, generate all possible alternatives, and choose the alternative likely to produce the best results, the decision maker decides what level of outcome (in terms of some criterion) will be satisfactory or "good enough." The individual then examines choice alternatives one at a time and selects the first one that equals or exceeds the minimal ("good enough") criterion level. The process stops at this point, and the choice becomes the decision. (368)

Denhardt concludes that the rational decision-making process "tells us what we should do to make better decisions, but it does not give us an accurate picture of how human beings actually make decisions." In his view, the satisficing model is more accurate because it describes how things actually happen. Satisficing, in fact, "may be the only way a manager can deal with the constant stream of problems and choice situations that arise daily" (368).

## PERSPECTIVES ON ETHICAL DECISION MAKING

We now shift our focus from decision making in general, with its constraints and compromises, to ethical decision making in particular, which shares these constraints and compromises, and adds a few of its own. Our main goal is not to prescribe or even recommend ethical decision making, but, rather, to point out its advantages, both individual and organizational, for public administrators and public agencies. You can then decide whether you find our position plausible and whether you are willing to apply at least parts of it to your own work setting.

Consider, for example, the notion of satisficing. You probably were already familiar with satisficing, even though you may not have used the term. You already had experienced the necessity of modifying initial positions on an issue in order to achieve some of your objectives. Negotiation, accommodation, and flexibility are all part of the management and policy environment.

As we noted in Chapter 1, public administrators routinely distinguish between rules, law, and actual behavior in order to get the job done, and they routinely exercise judgment in the enforcement of rules as they navigate the bureaucratic terrain. Therefore, as we also noted, public administrators often possess the intellectual agility, mental prowess, and organizational skills needed to exercise ethical analysis and judgment.

What needs to be recognized is that the typical legalistic or compliance approach to ethical issues in public administration is not only inappropriate, but also counterproductive. What needs to be emphasized is that a truly ethical public service requires discernment, choice, and the ability to satisfice, and that these qualities and skills are the same as those customarily associated with effective management.

A number of authors have addressed ethical decision making on both the individual and organizational levels. Their work includes the principles and values implicated in ethical decisions, as well as the procedures and processes to be followed in making ethical decisions. In our estimation, however, none offers as comprehensive or functional a framework as the unified ethic. Therefore, in order to broaden our understanding of ethical decision making, we first summarize a sample of the literature on ethical decision making in public administration. We then return to the unified ethic, supplementing it with behavioral and organizational perspectives. In our view, the enhanced unified ethic offers the most promising model for integrating integrity, clarity, and consistency into individual decision making and organizational processes alike.

## A Sample of the Literature

Let us look again at the work of Guy (1991), for instance, to understand more directly the connection between established administrative perspectives and practices and explicitly ethical approaches and actions. She suggests that ethical satisficing results when personal or organizational values clash, and that it leads to "a compromise that will permit satisfaction of ethical parameters at a minimally acceptable level" (187). In the end, some values are minimized while others are maximized, and, as Guy notes, "[T]his does not necessarily result in an unethical decision," but rather, "it produces decisions that are only as good as the circumstances permit" (187–188).

We believe that this process is no different from the satisficing that occurs in decision making without explicit reference to ethical principles or values. We also believe that this process supports Kidder's (1995) distinction between moral dilemmas and moral temptations. The real work of administrative ethics is about navigating between right versus right challenges, not resisting the blandishments of the unscrupulous.

Consider Guy's (1991) example of the choice of how to distribute an annual bonus to a work team. She suggests four possible alternatives: (1) distributing to each person an equal share; (2) distributing to each person according to individual effort; (3) distributing to each person according to individual need; (4) distributing to each person according to the usefulness of his or her contribution. According to Guy, if we adopt one rule of distribution, it will result in maximizing different values. The first maximizes accountability, in that it is easy to justify the distribution plan, and assumes parity on the part of everyone in the unit. But it does so at the expense of caring about individual contributions and distinguishing between excellence and mediocrity. The second maximizes caring for each person's intensity of effort and respect for each participant. But it does so at the expense of rewarding excellence, since nonproductive employees may devote hours to a task without making a substantive contribution to it. The third maximizes loyalty to individual employees in an appreciation of their unique circumstances but minimizes fairness to others and pursuit of excellence. It rewards people in proportion to what they need rather than what they contribute to the effort. The fourth maximizes the pursuit of excellence while minimizing respect for everyone's individual skills and abilities.

As Guy observes, "While each of these alternatives is designed to achieve distributive justice, each results in different forms of distribution and sends different messages about what values are most important and which work characteristics are rewarded" (189). This is precisely the type of problem that public administrators face on a daily basis. The difference here is that we are acknowledging the need to incorporate explicitly into our decision-making process the principles and values embedded in each alternative and the need to justify our selection of one alternative over the others.

A significant part of the selection and justification process, according to Guy, is the presence of beacons or decision rules that "help define the problem, steer the debate, and guide the selection of alternatives so that the final choice sends a message consistent with expectations for personal performance, the overall mission, and the objectives for achieving it" (189). Beacons serve as rules of thumb that simplify and streamline the decision-making process while keeping it grounded in important principles and values. They are invoked amid the complex and competing perspectives confronted by public administrators, and they permit what Guy calls "constructive satisficing," which, she argues, yields "results that are only as good as the sensitivities and intentions of those making the decisions" (189–190). Ultimately, "[t]he responsibility for making the 'right' decision rests on individual judgment" (190).

Finally, Guy invites us to adopt "high reliability management," a strategy that gets to the heart of the decision-making reality in public organizations. It "emphasizes strong organizational norms, reliance on individual judgment, and personal accountability for the welfare of the whole" (190). Values are in the consciousness of all employees; "all segments of the agency endorse similar values and adopt similar actions when confronted with similar situations" (195); and individuals are empowered and rewarded for practicing principled reasoning. Last, high reliability management benefits an organization in two ways. "It satisfies employees' desire to have control over decisions that affect their work, while it also increases accountability for both individuals' and the organization's actions" (201).

H. George Frederickson (1997) tends to focus on the nature and pattern of decisions, relying primarily on "the deontological tradition of decisions based on fundamental principles" and the "teleological tradition of decisions based on calculations of their likely consequences or results" (167). Thus, Frederickson approaches ethical decision making with two aspects of the unified ethic in mind. The deontological tradition suggests that certain underlying rules are the basis for judging behavior, while the teleological tradition, or utilitarianism, suggests that decisions are judged by their consequences.

Frederickson maintains that a defining feature of American government is the presence of explicit standards of right and wrong that are reflected in the federal and state constitutions and laws, as well as the charters and laws of cities and counties. This, in addition to countless administrative regulations adopted pursuant to laws and with the force of law themselves, tends to support the oft-cited argument that ours is a nation of laws and not of people. Frederickson contends that we "have an impressive deontological array of constitutions, laws, and regulations that codify our values and define the principles of right and wrong as we see them" (168).

At the same time, Frederickson notes that "public administrators live and work in a world that is unrelentingly teleological, a world in which policy and program results rule" (170). Thus, the public administrator practices "bounded ethics," meaning that administrative activities are defined by "enabling legislation . . . limited budgets," and advocacy, or at least support of agency purposes

(170). "Questioning fundamentally the purposes and practices of the agency on the basis of morality issues is seldom found and rarely encouraged. Whistle-blowing is very risky to the whistle-blower and seldom results in fundamental organizational change." Yet, according to Frederickson, within bounded ethics—"within the limits of organizational purpose and funding"—the public administrator is "almost always honest, virtuous, procedurally fair, and efficient" (170).

Terry Cooper (1998) offers an essentially procedural approach to ethical decision making that consists of several steps reminiscent of the rational decision-making model. The first step is to try to ascertain and describe the facts of a situation, including the key players, their respective viewpoints, the issues, the sequence of events, and the risks involved.

The second step involves defining the ethical issue at hand. In Cooper's view, this is the most difficult step for public administrators, not because they are unable to recognize an ethically problematic situation, but because they have trouble "articulating which values and principles are at stake" (22). For example, he indicates that public administrators tend to define problems as practical dilemmas, such as keeping the boss happy, rather than focusing on the ethical dilemma to be addressed.

The third step in Cooper's model is identifying alternative courses of action. In this process, Cooper suggests that after you have described the situation and defined the ethical issue, "the most difficult requirement is resisting the inclination to view the alternatives in dichotomous terms." He rightly cautions against simplistic, either-or thinking, arguing that it is "the most common trap in the ethical process" because "rarely does an ethical issue have only two or three possible solutions" (23).

The fourth step involves projecting the probable consequences of the range of alternatives. As Cooper observes, projecting consequences of alternatives is already part of our informal decision making, and he recommends that we make this process more formal, more conscious, and more systematic. Moreover, consistent with the limitations of the rational model of decision making, Cooper recognizes that constructing scenarios for each alternative is beyond the time that administrators have, at least for every issue. But it may be worthwhile for particularly complex problems.

Cooper notes also that the consequentialist or teleological emphasis here is not the only factor in arriving at a decision. He refers to the deontological approach as well, suggesting that his model includes both perspectives, "as it is never possible to completely separate them in practice. Duty to respect human dignity is inseparable from the harmful consequences of not doing so" (25). Thus, Cooper, like Frederickson, refers to two aspects of the unified ethic in his decision-making model.

The last segment of Cooper's model involves finding a fit or achieving resolution among the four previous elements. At this stage, Cooper contends that the public administrator considers "the *moral rules* that can be adduced to support each alternative and the projected consequences" (25) and argues that the identification of moral rules "will tend to happen quite naturally in a group setting as individuals are allowed to opt for a particular decision alternative and defend it" (25–26). Why this will happen naturally, however, is not explained.

Cooper then moves to the next consideration, which is a *"rehearsal of defenses,"* in which the administrator asks how a particular option would be defended in front of a broad audience. This is the test of publicity, which is followed by the third consideration—"an attempt to discern the implicit *ethical principle* at stake" (26). According to Cooper, "[t]his occurs when the available moral rules are not sufficiently satisfying to permit resolution" and involves justification of one option over another. The goal in this process is to reach resolution, which consists of "an alternative that, first, provides an acceptable balance of our duty to principle and the likely *consequences,* and, second, satisfies our need to have sound *reasons* for our conduct and our need to *feel* satisfied with the decision" (27).

The fourth and final element in finding a fit is *"anticipatory self-appraisal,"* "the test of how well a course of action fits with our own self-image" (27). Cooper concludes that, although no practicing administrator can be expected to apply this model to every ethical issue, the assumption is that if this model is used with more significant problems, "administrators will cultivate over time something like an intuitive decision-making skill that will serve them well when there is no time for such explicit and formal exercises" (28).

## The Enhanced Unified Ethic

Carol Lewis (1991) recounts the "story about a government employee who complains to the teacher that someone at school is stealing his child's pencils. The father explains that it is the *principle* that bothers him, not the pencils—he gets all the pencils he needs at the office" (106). As Lewis observes, "behavior is not always this transparent, but it does seem easier to pin down, without qualification or queasiness, someone else's responsibility than one's own" (106).

Avoidance of responsibility, hypocrisy, rationalization—these are a few of the major features of moral passivity and immaturity. We all do these things from time to time to make things go more smoothly, to avoid rocking the boat, to be safe—at least temporarily. We may not be proud of ourselves when we act in these ways, but we convince ourselves that it was not our responsibility, that we were only trying to do our job, and even though it may not make things right, our job and our survival must come first. After all, we were not hired to be heroes.

Although moral temporizing of this type may be commonplace, it reflects a mistaken understanding of ethical decision making and action. The responsibilities and requirements of ethical decision making must be reframed if we are to move, personally and professionally, toward a more empowered, productive, and accountable public service. As we suggested earlier and as our sample of the literature on ethical decision making confirms, public administrators already have the arsenal of skills and experiences to engage in ethical decision making. What is needed is the recognition that those skills and experiences apply directly and necessarily to ethical dilemmas and ethical situations.

With such a recognition, public administrators will be able to move toward Guy's (1991) high reliability management, the kind of organizational culture in which performance, excellence, and constructive satisficing are routine. But the transition from morally passive to morally active decision making requires the depth and breadth of ethical understanding provided by the enhanced unified ethic.

The enhanced unified ethic is the application of the unified ethic within an organizational context. In any organization, ethical decision making is inevitably influenced by power relationships, rule structures, stakeholders, customary practices, and all the other factors involved in organizational culture. One cannot fairly assess the actions of an individual decision maker independently of such factors. If an organization and its members are to be ethical, the organization's entire structure must be infused with a perspective that encourages moral action. The enhanced unified ethic, when fully instituted, includes the unified ethic in all facets of the organization and, thus, within the organizational culture.

The unified ethic, itself, as you recall, consists of the three principal positions in moral philosophy—deontology, teleology, and character theory. It combines these positions into an integrated whole and, therefore, provides a practical perspective on the ethical challenges faced by public administrators. For example, typically, these components are considered to be separate and, given what Frederickson (1997) calls the "unrelentingly teleological world" of public administration, "in which policy and program results rule" (170), utilitarianism or concern for consequences comes to dominate decision making in public organizations.

The practitioner, understandably, fails to see the underlying interdependence between principle, purpose, and character. The unified ethic, however, joins the three elements of moral philosophy and enables the practitioner to approach decision making with a broader and more ethically sophisticated understanding of the situation at hand.

The unified ethic reflects the inherent unity of human nature. Principles appeal to our rational nature and need for consistency. So we recognize the value of the deontological perspective. At the same time, we acknowledge our desire for happiness, both for ourselves and for others. So we recognize the value of the teleological perspective. Last, character invokes our respect for excellence. So we recognize the value of the virtue perspective. These three elements, linked together, provide the foundation for moral renewal and reform in the public service.

However, to have full practical meaning, the unified ethic needs to be supplemented by an understanding of behavioral and organizational perspectives. For such perspectives, we return to Wittmer (1994), who reviews several of the most recent models, and who observes that "there is a growing awareness among management scholars of the importance of understanding the process and determinants of ethical behavior and decision making" (352).

One model that we think is particularly pertinent to public administrators is the four-component model of James Rest, as discussed by Wittmer. Rest, a moral psychologist, approaches the complexity of moral behavior with this question: "When a person is behaving morally, what must we suppose has happened psychologically to produce that behavior?" (353) His answer to this question is that we go through four psychological processes to produce ethical behavior:

> (1) ethical interpretation or perception of situations in terms of alternative courses of actions and the effects on the welfare of those involved or affected; (2) ethical judgment or formulation of what would be the morally right course of action (that is, reasoning to some conclusion about the ethically right action); (3) selection or actual choosing of the moral values

and actions; and (4) implementation or executing the moral course of action, which [is] the behavioral follow-through or "doing" of what is determined to be morally right (353-354).

To illustrate these four steps, Wittmer (1994) offers the case of an administrator who is asked to hire the son or daughter of a loyal party member and financial contributor. How would this administrator apply Rest's model? The first stage is interpretation or perception, so the administrator might ask questions concerning who will be affected by the decision, what will be the consequences for others, and whether the situation involves fairness. The second stage involves reasoning to some judgment or formulation of the right course of action. Is the right course of action to hire the party member's child because it might lead to the greatest good for all affected? Or is the right course of action to conclude that someone on the civil service list deserves the job and would be harmed if the party member's child were hired? The third stage involves choice, which is difficult, since values are often in conflict. Finally, there is implementation or execution of the judgment and the choice. "Rest contends that proper functioning in all components is necessary for achieving moral behavior" (Wittmer 1994, 354).

On the organizational level, Wittmer observes that among the factors influencing ethical decision making are the "organizational sanctions, or the rewards and punishments of ethical and unethical behavior and decisions" (358). Citing several studies of decision making, Wittmer notes that "subjects whose ethical behavior was punished or whose unethical behavior was rewarded were more likely to make unethical decisions. Ethical decisions were more likely when unethical behavior was punished." Moreover, other significant factors in decision making were one's peer group, organizational policies and codes, and the commitment of top management. One important finding from the research in this regard was that "only when the existence of a code and top management concern was combined with sanctions (dismissal for unethical conduct) was there a significant effect on ethical decision making" (359).

The enhanced unified ethic offers at least six advantages to public administrators:

1. It provides a functional philosophical, behavioral, and organizational framework for ethical decision making.

2. It both broadens and deepens our understanding of the ethical dimensions and implications of our decisions.

3. It helps to reduce moral stress by offering a clear basis for our ethical choices.

4. It helps us to navigate between right versus right dilemmas and to discern the value conflicts embedded in situations that might otherwise appear to be only technical.

5. It offers not only clarification of value conflicts, but also a basis for reasoning and justification of our choices, rooted in prudent compromise, cooperation, and consistency.

6. It redefines administrative ethics from an alien, threatening, high-anxiety activity to a familiar, comforting, high-performance activity, akin to Guy's (1991) high-reliability management.

As we suggested earlier, principle, purpose, and character are already ingrained in public administration. Therefore, the enhanced unified ethic offers a balanced, practical approach to decision making that accords with the administrative, legal, and political circumstances of bureaucratic life.

Decision making, especially ethical decision making, is the linchpin of public administration, the pivotal administrative function. Public administrators decide daily on matters large and small, and thus affect the lives of others as well as themselves. Therefore, it is critical that public administrators approach this vital activity with maximum possible clarity, coherence, and consistency. It is essential that they fulfill this central obligation with judgment, prudence, and integrity.

In this chapter, we have aimed to provide both a practical framework for responsible decision making and the basis for you to test our claims concerning the enhanced unified ethic. In the next two chapters, you will have the opportunity to review a number of cases, first with our reasoning provided, and second with your own reasoning alone, and to apply the logic of the unified ethic as you think appropriate. Our hope is that this experience will help you strengthen your decision-making skills in general, and your ethical decision-making skills in particular.

# CHAPTER 8

# Problems That Might Arise and How to Analyze Them

In this chapter, we will examine hypothetical cases that involve ethical problems. In each case, we will consider different possible ethical reasoning leading to different solutions based upon the list of ethical questions that we have already devised and used in previous chapters. You will then be asked to consider how you would attempt to resolve the problem. Your resolution need not be identical to any of those that were considered, because you may have a better idea.

Some, if not all, of the cases may have no clear resolution. Ethical ambiguity is a fact of organizational life. Consequently, it is impossible to make an unquestionably correct ethical decision every time. But ethical ambiguity does not excuse people from making difficult ethical decisions thoughtfully. Right, wrong, or uncertain, decisions must be made and must be founded on good reasons. The most that one can ask of a decision maker is to have such reasons. We ask neither more nor less in this chapter.

When one has made a decision on the basis of a strong reasoning process, he or she can have confidence in a job well done. Such confidence cannot remove moral stress completely but can alleviate it significantly. Furthermore, a good reasoning process permits decision makers to explain their decisions to others, not only to protect themselves from criticism, but also to edify the moral thinking of the organization to whom they must answer.

We will discuss the teleological, deontological, virtue-theory, and intuitionist aspects of the cases, but we will examine intuitions least. By their nature as intuitions, they cannot be analyzed rationally. If they could be analyzed in a way that would make sense of them ethically, they would be reduced to some other ethical theory, i.e., the theory by means of which they are analyzed. But we do not mean to imply that intuitions are unimportant because, as we indicated in Chapter 3, they are aspects of the unified ethic. They can be very important, but they are simply the least easily given to rational analysis.

We consider your ethical intuitions so important that we suggest that you consult them twice concerning each of the following cases: once immediately after reading the case and a second time after reading and contemplating the analysis that follows the case. Notice any difference that occurs in your intuitions before and after analysis.

## A QUESTIONABLE HIRE

Felicia has been working for five years as an accountant at the office of the state comptroller and has been assigned to a search committee to hire a new colleague. According to the office regulations, which are approved by the state legislature, all committee meetings are to be kept strictly confidential. No member of the committee is allowed to discuss the proceedings of the committee or the files of the candidates with anyone outside of the committee until the committee has completed its work and sent its ranked list of three approved candidates to the office of the director. Even then, only the committee chair is permitted to discuss the proceedings and can divulge them only to authorized personnel. The penalty for violating this policy could range from censure for unethical behavior to dismissal for invasion of privacy or insubordination. The policy has been followed strictly in all the years in which Felicia has worked for the organization.

An African American candidate named Anne, whose academic record and work experience are outstanding, is Felicia's clear favorite. Anne is one of five chosen to be interviewed, and her performance at the interview confirms Felicia's high opinion of her. She is poised, confident, articulate, and current in her knowledge of the profession.

After all five candidates have been interviewed, Felicia is surprised to discover that in a "test vote," Anne is not among the three finalists. When Felicia asks the other six members of the committee why they did not support Anne, the chair replies that Anne's race is a problem. While there is no reason to believe that the committee members are personally racially biased, they voted against her because the division already has enough African Americans, especially African American women, and needs more Hispanics and Native Americans. With the exception of Felicia, the others unanimously rank the top candidate as Xavier, a Hispanic candidate from East Los Angeles. Their second choice is Sylvia, a Native American who spent the first 14 years of her life on a reservation in Oklahoma. Their third choice is Murphy, who is independently wealthy, grew up in the affluent suburb of Pelham, New York, and technically qualifies as a Native American, but has no personal ethnic or social ties to any Native American community. While all three candidates have good credentials, the committee members agree that none is as impressive as Anne. With the exception of Felicia, they also agree, however, that Anne would be "superfluous."

During the proceedings, it becomes clear to Felicia that the other six committee members have discussed the case among themselves outside of committee meetings, when she was not present. The six commonly socialize after work on Fridays at a local pub, where they discussed the hire. There is no rule prohibiting such meetings, so long as the discussion remains private, and no one outside of the committee is apprised of any of its negotiations. By agreeing unanimously among themselves, they virtually eliminated Felicia's voting power.

After the preliminary vote and the ensuing discussion, the committee takes its final vote. It is 6 to 1 in favor of the slate of Xavier, Sylvia, and Murphy.

Felicia is indignant but does not know what to do. She seeks advice from her parish priest, from whom she demands a promise of confidentiality, her husband Muraldo, and her very close friend Bethea. After consulting with them all, she decides to discuss the matter with her division director, Alma.

After listening to Felicia's complaint, Alma indicates that she will accept the committee's selections. Alma admits that she has been under considerable pressure to hire members of protected groups in proper proportion. Her prior record has been very suspect. In managerial positions in both private business and the public sector, she made more than fifty hires, all of whom were white males. Her supervisors have been watching her very carefully to ensure that she shows no biases.

The job is offered to Xavier, but he refuses it. He has learned that his ethnic background was a factor in his hiring, and he is adamantly opposed, on philosophical grounds, to affirmative action or any other program that suggests preferential treatment for any group. No one knows how Xavier learned that he benefited from such a policy, but Felicia discovers that Xavier is the son of her priest's half sister Gina. The position eventually falls to the third choice, Murphy, because the second choice, Sylvia, finds a better position elsewhere.

## Analysis

The case suggests many ethical questions. Was Anne the victim of unfair hiring practices? Was the policy of confidentiality among the committee members appropriate? Did Felicia violate that policy, and, if she did, was her violation excusable? Was it appropriate for six members of the committee to discuss the hire without Felicia present? Were Alma's motives for accepting the committee's decision ethical? There remains also the question of whether the priest violated confidentiality, but since he is not a public administrator, we will not dwell on his actions.

Nevertheless, the reasons that Xavier gave for refusing the position suggest some important ethical issues. The first is the large question of whether hiring to achieve racial, ethnic, or sexual equity is appropriate. However, that may be too large an issue to discuss here. But there is also the issue of whether a well-intended policy should be used to benefit a person who, while a member of a protected group, has little in common with it or its members. Also, one might ask whether it is ethical to hire someone without informing the person of hiring factors he or she might find morally objectionable.

Before analyzing the ethical nature of the case, let us review the list of questions that we devised in Chapter 3:

## Teleology:

*What are the consequences of my action?*

*What are the long-term effects of my action?*

*Does my action promote the greatest happiness?*

## Deontology:

*What principle applies in this case?*

*Can this principle be applied consistently in this case and in all similar cases?*

*Can this principle be considered as a possible universal principle of behavior?*

*Which course of action best exemplifies the ideal of treating all people as ends in themselves?*

*Which course of action best exemplifies and most fully promotes the ideal of a society of free, responsible people whose ends promote each other rather than conflict with each other?*

## Intuitionism:

*What does my conscience tell me about this?*

*Do I feel good about this action?*

### Virtue theory:

*What character traits does this action express?*

*What effect will this action have on my character?*

*What effect will this action have on the character of other people?*

*Is this the action of a person whose character I would admire?*

While we encourage you to ask all these questions, for the sake of brevity, we will examine the issues more generally on the basis of the approaches of teleology, deontology, intuitionism, and virtue theory.

### Was the Policy of Confidentiality among the Committee Members Appropriate?

Committee members were forbidden from discussing their proceedings among unauthorized people outside of the committee. There are numerous reasons for such a policy. From a teleological perspective, such a policy would encourage committee members to speak more frankly without fear that their words might be conveyed, either accurately or distortedly, to applicants or to people with interest in their success. The policy also protects the interests of applicants who may prefer that their qualifications not be discussed indiscriminately. From a deontological perspective, one might argue that respect for individuals requires that their privacy be honored through a policy of confidentiality. From the standpoint of virtue theory, the policy of confidentiality discourages gossip and encourages respect for people's privacy.

But while there are ample reasons for such a policy, there are also reasons for limiting it. If the committee were to be blatantly racist or otherwise unfair in its deliberations, it should be exposed. One might also question whether the organization has the moral authority to bind someone to secrecy. Surely a legal proceeding, such as a discrimination lawsuit, would be justified in abridging the confidentiality. Therefore, since the confidentiality is not absolute, one might consider abridging it for purely moral rather than legal grounds.

Furthermore, the moral and legal issues may become interwoven. If someone were aware of being a victim of racist hiring practices, he or she could take the complaint to court. But if the racist nature of the procedure were protected by the confidentiality policy, there would be no way of knowing that a lawsuit was in order. In such a case, only a moral decision to defy confidentiality would enable justice to be done.

The case of Anne may not have been so blatant as to justify a breach of confidentiality. Felicia did, however, violate the policy, though in a limited way. To seek advice, she spoke to people who she assumed would not betray her confidentiality. Ironically, she expected them to honor her secrecy in her dishonoring of the committee's secrecy. Nevertheless, she cannot be accused of openly and indiscreetly revealing committee secrets to the general public. She spoke to a member of the clergy, whose right to retain confidentiality is supported by law, to her husband, who is in a special relation to her by virtue of the marital relationship, and a close friend whom she could fully expect to keep the information private. In no case did she reveal the privileged information in a wanton manner, but she did so to seek advice on a problem.

In your opinion, was Felicia justified? Why or why not? Are your reasons based on teleology, deontology, virtue theory, intuition, or a combination?

Another problem with confidentiality involves the candidates themselves. It would seem only fair to inform them of factors that influenced their success or failure. In particular, Xavier objected to any hiring practice that favored him on the basis of ethnicity. If he had not learned in some mysterious way that he had been chosen because of his ethnic background, he would have chosen to accept a position under conditions that he found offensive. Was it fair to him to leave him ignorant concerning an issue of importance to him? Do the needs of the organization outweigh his interest in knowing that ethnicity was a factor?

## Did the Committee Act in Good Faith?

Even if one recognizes the validity of the confidentiality policy, there remains the question of whether it was abused. There are strong moral reasons for having such a policy, but its purpose is not that of protecting committee members from criticism for wrongful acts. Did the committee do anything wrong?

We will proceed under the assumption that the affirmative action policy that the committee used was correct. Nevertheless, one might ask whether a good policy was used in the wrong way. The intent of such a policy is to ensure fairness in hiring. The committee appeared to be more concerned with attaining a desirable mix of minority employees than with treating the applicants fairly.

But reasons can be given in support of the committee's decision. They may argue that, once the rule has been established on ethical grounds, whether they be based upon teleology, deontology, or any other theory, the job of the committee is merely to follow the rule. Judges and juries are charged with properly applying laws rather than adopting the legislative role of evaluating and creating them. Likewise, it may be argued, the committee's role is only to apply the policy rather than to attempt to interpret its moral intent. Furthermore, it may be argued that the intent of the committee members is irrelevant. The policy is intended to produce a fair result, and such a result was attained.

On the other hand, one might argue that the committee's intent was morally significant. Even if the members were "playing by the rules" and were therefore not subject to penalties imposed by the organization, their own moral characters are at issue, as virtue theory would maintain. In simply following the rule, they appear to have attempted to exempt themselves from moral decision making, which they left entirely to the rule makers.

But their attempt may not have been successful, at least from a moral standpoint, because ignoring the intent of a principle can result in its abuse. For example, speed limits are not intended to impede people who are rushing injured friends to a hospital; the right of free speech was not intended to provide people with the opportunity for slander; and the affirmative action policies used by the committee were not intended to help people such as Murphy, who has no serious ties to the ethnic community that he was chosen to represent.

From a deontological perspective, to act as a mere unthinking rule follower is to behave below the level of a human being. The defining feature of a human being is rationality, and the highest human aim is to serve morality. If the members of the committee reduced themselves to automatic rule followers, they negated their most noble human functions. One does not render those functions dormant when one checks into work.

In your opinion, did the committee apply the affirmative action policy properly? If not, how would you have applied the policy? In general, do people in your place of work interpret rules before applying them or apply them without using any discretion?

Did the committee act in bad faith in any other of its actions? For example, was its deliberation without Felicia present appropriate, even if it violated no explicit rules?

## General Consideration of Procedure

While numerous specific issues are involved in this case, some of which we have already discussed, it might be helpful to examine the entire procedure in general to determine how it might have been improved, and perhaps to draw some lessons for one's own organization. As we indicated earlier, we may apply the entire list of questions that we have previously considered—feel free to do so if you prefer—but it would be simpler to consider the list in abbreviated form, applying general questions from each of the four ethical theories from which the list is drawn.

## Teleology:

*Was the procedure in the long-term best interests of the people involved? Of the organization? Of society in general?*

## Deontology:

*Was the procedure conducted under valid, universal principles? Were people used only as means, or were they also considered as ends in themselves?*

## Virtue theory:

*Was the procedure conducive to the development of good character traits among the participants?*

## Intuitionism:

*When you have considered all aspects of the procedure, what feelings do you have concerning it?*

It might be helpful to write a brief summary of your thoughts on the case, together with an examination of its similarities and differences from other cases that you have encountered. The other cases need not be superficially similar and may not even involve hiring or personnel decisions, but they might involve some of the deeper issues and principles at work in this case.

Might this decision have had any effect on the moral character or virtue of those who participated, actively or passively, in it? When all things are considered, what course of action would you "feel" best about (i.e., would accord best with your moral intuitions)?

## TAKING A LEAVE OR TAKING LEAVE?

The following example is adapted, with significant revision, from an article by Maureen Moakley and Kathryn Power (1996).

Milo was a longtime tenured professor of history at a state university. Despite his comfortable professional position, he applied for and received a comparable position at a nearby, more prestigious private institution, which offered him a significantly higher salary. Milo also had an important personal reason for moving. He had been living with Flo, his colleague within the department, for two years. They wished to be married, but the university had a rule prohibiting married couples from both having faculty appointments within the same department. The new job would permit the couple to be married, and since the two universities were near each other, they would not have to move from their current dwelling.

Marguerite, the chair of the department, was also happy about the prospect of Milo's finding another job. She had been bothered by Milo and Flo's living arrangement because it obviously violated the intent of the nepotism rule. She knew that the sole reason that they were not married was their employment status. Furthermore, Marguerite shared the concern of other department members that, in faculty meetings, Milo and Flo always voted the same way on every issue. Marguerite also looked forward to replacing Milo with a younger, more invigorated, and less expensive faculty member.

There was, however, a stumbling block. The institution to which that Milo wished to move had not offered him tenure, which is a virtual guarantee of lifetime employment. He felt certain that he could earn tenure, but the possibility existed that he would not. If he did not earn tenure within three years, he would be terminated. Since he already had tenure at his current institution, the move involved considerable risk.

Milo had a possible escape hatch. His current university allowed faculty members to take unpaid leaves of absence for up to three years. The purpose of the leave policy was to enable faculty members to take time off, either to develop new talents or merely to relax away from the job for a while. The institution could not afford to give paid sabbaticals, and the leave option was a substitute. However, in order to take a leave, Milo would have to sign a statement promising to return to the institution for at least one year after the leave was completed. The purpose of requiring such a promise was to prevent faculty members from doing exactly what Milo intended to do, i.e., to use the leave to advance one's employment possibilities elsewhere.

No one had taken the promise very seriously in the past. It was unenforceable because, if the employee chose not to return after the leave, the university could do nothing in response. The ultimate punishment would be termination, but that was not possible for someone who had already quit. Although no faculty members had ever failed to return after a leave, several administrators had taken full advantage of the opportunity. The previous vice president for academic affairs had been one such administrator.

Milo refused to sign the promissory statement. Despite Marguerite's assurance that the statement was not truly binding, Milo continued to refuse merely because he considered it dishonest to sign the statement when he had every intention of violating it. Marguerite asked Cosmo, the new vice president for academic affairs, if he would allow Milo the opportunity to take the leave without signing the promise, but Cosmo refused. He noted that state law required Milo to sign the document before leave could be granted.

After ruminating over the matter for several days, Milo relented and signed the document although he had every intention of leaving permanently. The document was sent to Cosmo for his signature, but he was reluctant to approve it. His previous conversation with Marguerite left him unsure of Milo's sincerity. Cosmo's most convenient option was to support the leave and thus virtually grant it to Milo. But Cosmo's sense of responsibility demanded that he investigate further. He therefore met with Milo to discuss the matter. Milo stated his intention clearly and honestly: Even after signing the document, he would take the new job if he was granted tenure.

Using his discretion, Cosmo denied the application. Milo was disappointed but accepted the decision. He, himself, had been reluctant to sign the document, so he understood Cosmo's position. Nevertheless, Milo considered the decision somewhat unfair because others—all of them administrators—had been treated more leniently. Sensitive to Milo's concern, Cosmo proposed, at the next meeting of the institution's higher administration, that administrators agree never to take a leave without returning. The proposal died for lack of a second.

## Analysis

Milo's case may seem different from most issues that typically arise in public administration because it takes place within an academic context. Public universities are generally much larger than most public organizations, follow different policies, have a different organizational culture, and often are looser in their interpretation of rules. However, the case has some general aspects that apply more broadly. For example, the issue of leaves of absence has been a matter of concern in many public administration contexts.

But perhaps most significantly, an underlying issue in Milo's case is of almost universal concern in ethical decision making. In ruling against Milo's leave, Cosmo, in following the intent of the state's rules, apparently placed honesty and openness above the happiness of the people most directly involved in the case. In doing so, he apparently favored the deontological commitment to duty over the teleological commitment to happiness.

But as we have seen, appearances can be deceptive. The teleological and deontological aspects of these cases become blurred when long-term consequences are considered. In Cosmo's case, those teleologically significant consequences might ultimately prove best under the policy that he pursued. If leaves were routinely offered to employees who had no intention of returning, uncertainty within the organization concerning the need to hire permanent replacements would result. Perhaps more importantly, the institution might suffer a higher turnover rate among its employees. It might not be as able to rely upon a stable work force, and instability could result.

There are also more abstract consequences that are more difficult to measure but may be of greater importance yet. For example, if employees are encouraged to ignore the rules if they prove inconvenient and cannot be easily enforced, a disrespect for the structure of the entire organization could result. Furthermore, as was evidently already the case among administrators at Cosmo's institution, the use of leaves for the purpose, unintended by the state, of furthering one's own career might promote an attitude among employees of placing their careers above the institution. Such an attitude cannot be helpful to the long-term goals of an organization. Honestly following the moral rules within the context of an organization, while seemingly fundamentally deontological, may also be teleological.

The distinction between the teleological and the deontological becomes even murkier when virtue theory is considered. Cosmo displayed a moral virtue in choosing, on the basis of moral considerations, the more difficult alternative. He could have signed the leave request without bothering to ask Milo about his ultimate intentions; that is, he could have swept the matter under the rug. Cosmo displayed a strength of moral commitment. One might ask whether an organization—and furthermore, an entire society—would not ultimately fare better, teleologically, with people like Cosmo, who are committed to deontological principles.

But the case for Cosmo is not so open and shut. Marguerite also expressed a virtue in her flexibility. Might Cosmo have been too rigid? Which virtue is better in the long run? Does it depend upon the individual case?

The relation of virtue to ultimate consequences is also a matter to be considered regarding the case of Felicia and the questionable hire. With the exception of Felicia, all of the people involved in the hiring process appeared to be most concerned with covering themselves—most notably Alma, the director. One again might ask whether an organization composed of characters such as Alma would best perform its utilitarian, teleological function.

Consider the interrelations of virtue, teleology, and deontology as you privately assess Cosmo's decision and as you reassess the other decisions that we have discussed. We will return to the character issue later.

## PRIVACY VERSUS SAFETY

The following discussion concerns an actual case, though the names are false (Leazes and Campanelli, 1996). After reviewing it, we will consider similar hypothetical cases.

Melina is a crack cocaine user who is attempting to overcome her habit. She attends a publicly funded support group for drug users under the direction of Constance, a professional social worker. During one of the group meetings, Melina experienced a hemorrhage. Although she suffered no permanent damage as a result of the incident, she bled profusely on herself, the meeting room, and the women's bathroom. Several people, including those who cleaned the floor, furniture, and Melina, came into contact with the blood. Although Constance was not present to witness the event, she heard of it from the other members of the group, some of whom assisted in the cleaning process.

Melina is HIV positive. Privacy regulations protect Melina from having to reveal her infection, so none of those involved in the bleeding incident except Melina herself were aware of the danger, however slight, that they may have contracted the AIDS virus.

At some time after the incident, Melina revealed her HIV status to Constance in a casual conversation. Constance did not react casually, however. Concerned about what to do next, Constance called her supervisor, Carla, to inform her of the incident. Constance was surprised to discover that Carla, who had not known about the hemorrhage, had already known of Melina's condition, but, because of the privacy laws, had not revealed it to Constance. Constance was extremely displeased.

Constance met with Mona, the department director, and Marco, the regional manager, to discuss the incident. Mona and Marco agreed that Constance was both legally and ethically correct in protecting Melina's privacy. However, there remained the question of what further action to take. Should the people who came in contact with the blood be informed? If they were told that they had been exposed to HIV-infected blood, they would have been easily able to infer that it had come from Melina, even if she were not explicitly identified. They would not have been legally or professionally bound to secrecy since they were not public employees. Telling them would have been tantamount to telling the entire community. On the other hand, the information was important to them, their sexual partners, and anyone who came into contact with their blood. Those who had touched Melina's blood would have been well-advised to be tested for HIV and, until they receive the desired test results, limit some of their activities.

Discussions with legal and medical personnel produced contradictory advice. The chief legal counsel stated that the law was clear in this case: No breach of Melina's privacy would be allowed under the law. But the agency's HIV expert advised that, from a medical standpoint, those who had contacted Melina's blood should be tested.

## Analysis

What should Mona and Marco do? Let us examine the reasoning behind the options.

There are teleological reasons both for and against disclosure. Those for disclosure include consideration of the possibly infected people and anyone who might come into contact with them. There are several teleological factors against disclosure, however. They include the possible negative effect on Melina, the organization, and its individual members who revealed Melina's condition. All could suffer legal action as well as damage to their reputations. Furthermore, since the chance of infection is very slight, disclosure would not likely result in any benefit to the people in contact with Melina's blood but would, instead, cause them unnecessary worry. Which teleological considerations do you consider most compelling?

Deontological considerations also can be used in defense of both sides. The deontological respect for individuals as ends in themselves supports both Melina's right to privacy and the rights of the vulnerable to be warned of possible avoidable dangers that might befall them or that they might cause for others. There is a deontological responsibility to obey the laws of the state, but there is also a deontological responsibility to disobey the laws of the state on the basis of higher, overpowering moral considerations.

Considerations of character enter into the issue in numerous ways. Depending upon their actions, Mona and Marco could display the traits of obedience to law, benevolence to an individual (i.e., Melina), benevolence to society in general, respect for privacy, openness, honesty, and a range of other moral traits. But Mona and Marco could also display more questionable moral traits such as disrespect for the law, disloyalty, dishonesty, and self-protectiveness. Which virtues and vices do you consider as the best and worst that might emerge in this case?

Having considered the teleological, deontological, and virtue aspects of the case, can you find a way to reconcile your conclusions on all three into one overall decision?

Now let us consider some possible variations on this case. Suppose that Constance, the social worker, had known of Melina's HIV status at the time that she hemorrhaged. Suppose also that Constance had been present when several people were preparing to clean up Melina's blood. What should Constance have done? The same laws apply and the same considerations enter into this hypothetical case as in the previous, actual case. In the hypothetical case, should Constance do as you thought Mona and Marco should have done in the actual case? If not, why are the cases different in relevant ways? Does consideration of the hypothetical case cause you to reconsider your conclusion in the actual case?

Let us consider another variation from the actual case. Suppose now that Melina had a contagious disease that was not protected by law or by any organizational policy. For example, would the case be significantly different, from the moral perspective, if HIV-infected people were not legally protected? Would it be moral to reveal Melina's HIV status if there were no law forbidding one from doing so? Does the moral responsibility to protect one's privacy derive solely from the law?

## THE ILLEGAL STRIKE

Omega is the director of the transit system of a large city with a small tax base. Her staff has done an outstanding job of providing good service with a meager budget, but the corner cutting of the past few years is now creating problems. The light rail cars are in disrepair to the extent that the repair service is more overworked than ever and increasingly more cars are in the shop, waiting to be fixed. The tracks are also needing increasing attention. Without additional funds to overhaul the system and purchase new cars, the system will deteriorate below an acceptable level of service. Omega and her staff have publicized the problem extensively and discussed it fully with the city council, but it is politically impossible to find new money. Moreover, the situation seems to be in an unfortunate spiral: Without the money, the service deteriorates; as service deteriorates, the public uses it less and less; as the public uses it less, they take less interest in funding the system.

The only solution lies in allocating more of the department's own resources to upgrade the system. But that solution entails placing a two-year freeze on both hiring and salary increases. She knows that workers are already underpaid and overworked, but she sees no other option.

The furious transit workers seek help from their union, which votes to strike within one week if Omega does not reverse her decision. Serge, the head of the union, understands Omega's plight but realizes that it would be futile to explain the situation in a way that would satisfy the rank and file. He finds no other option but to support their strike.

State law prohibits strikes by public employees and provides criminal penalties ranging from fines to imprisonment. In addition, the city has a law specifically designed to prevent transit strikes. The city's penalty is immediate dismissal. Transit workers have struck several times in the past, but no legal punishment has been applied. As a nearly automatic part of the bargaining process, all striking workers have been pardoned. Omega, Serge, and the union members hope that the traditional bargaining process will be applied in this case.

But this case is different from the past. The current mayor, Cleon, has never been confronted with a strike before, and he is philosophically opposed to strikes by public employees. During his campaign for mayor, he promised never to permit such strikes. He publicly warns the union that he will fire striking workers and asks the state to impose the legal criminal penalties. While he knows that the state will not comply, he fully intends to fire all strikers. He refuses to budge, even to end a possible prolonged strike.

## Analysis

Both Omega and Cleon have teleological arguments for their positions. Omega argues that it would be impossible to hire qualified replacements for fired strikers. Years would elapse before the system could function properly again. Furthermore, she argues, even if the fear of losing their jobs causes the union members to refrain from striking—an unlikely possibility—their morale will be low, their productivity will consequently suffer, and some of the best employees will seek jobs elsewhere. Moreover, she argues, a strike might not be such a bad thing. It might help the public realize that more money is needed to run the system while paying workers a fair wage.

Cleon also has several teleological arguments. Although he recognizes that the workers would be impossible to replace, he fears that if the transit workers succeed, strikes in other city agencies are inevitable. He and his city administration will be seen as weak, especially after the promises that he has made, and he will invite trouble from all quarters. Furthermore, he does not think that the transit workers would stop after one victory. As soon as the transit workers are discontent again—and they will have good reason to be discontent, given the financial state of the division—they will confidently strike again.

Omega recoils in despair as Cleon compares himself to President Reagan, who ended the air traffic controller's strike permanently. Cleon realizes that finding permanent replacements will be difficult but believes that the time needed to retrain people will pay off in the long run. If need be, he says, he will consider privatizing the entire system by hiring a company without union workers. Finally, he argues, he simply cannot raise wages. To accede to their demands even minimally, he says, is impossible. If the money is not spent to upgrade the system physically, it will soon virtually collapse.

Both also have deontological arguments. Omega argues that it would be unfair to fire workers for striking only for wages that, as Cleon would agree, they truly deserve on the basis of their productivity. But Cleon also has deontological arguments for his position. First, he argues, the law requires that striking transit workers be fired; he is an executor of the law, so he is obligated to fire them. Secondly, he has promised the public that he would not permit strikes, and he considers himself morally bound by that promise.

Both Omega and Cleon may be seen as having personal interest in their own positions. Omega has greater personal contact with the workers and is more likely to sympathize with their situations. She is also more dependent professionally upon their support. Cleon has a political stake in showing a strong hand and in living up to his campaign promises. Nevertheless, let us ignore any private interests that they might have and concentrate on their moral arguments.

Whose arguments do you consider to be the most convincing, when all factors are considered? Are there important factors that neither Omega nor Cleon mentioned? Does the workers' assumption, based upon past policy and "organizational culture," that they will be rehired despite the law have any influence on your thinking? If so, can you characterize the influence as teleological or deontological? Does Cleon's notion of privatizing the system with a company whose workers are not represented by a union introduce ethical problems?

## WHO GOES? WHO STAYS?

We will treat the following case as an extension of the previous case, but with some changes. First, we will ignore any union involvement. Secondly, let us suppose that Cleon eventually accepted Omega's arguments, permitted the workers to return, and allowed them a raise. However, the needed physical repairs and replacements had to be sacrificed. Omega, in turn, promised to do anything necessary to upgrade the system within a three-year period. Eventually, the anticipated crunch occurred. The department decided that it must lay people off to pay for the needed equipment and repair. Omega called a meeting of her assistant directors to discuss the process of terminating employees. (For a thorough analysis of the budget cutting process, see Lerner and Wanat 1993, 85–96.)

Delia, who had served longest as an assistant director, argued for even cuts across all divisions of the department. She had endured several such cutbacks in the past—all before Omega arrived—and all had been "across the board." Typically, the layoffs were based upon time of service, with the most recent hires being fired first. She would accept the last in-first out approach if it was successful in retaining enough personnel while reducing the budget sufficiently. Otherwise, she would apply a more complex system in which the highest paid nonmanagement, nonessential personnel would be fired first, and then, if need be, managers would be fired by a similar procedure. Once applied, her approach would be formulaic. It left little to the judgment of division directors, who would be happy not to be blamed for decisions that they otherwise would have had to make. This, she said, was the easy way out. It avoided professional and ethical judgments.

Her reasoning is apparently teleological. Do you agree with her position? Does it, as she thought, avoid ethical judgments?

Arno, who was next to Delia in longevity, had a different approach. He believed that some divisions, either as a whole or in part, should be sacrificed in order to streamline the system. One such division was dedicated to the physical and psychological wellness of employees. Arno agreed that the division performed a valuable function, but it was not central to the mission of the system. Although he did not wish to eliminate the division concerned with employee retirement and insurance benefits, he believed that severe cuts in that division were possible with a minimal impact upon the system as a whole. He therefore suggested a cost-benefit analysis of all divisions within the system. His highest priority was to preserve the physical quality of the system and the number of drivers. He acknowledged to Delia that his solution would require professional decisions, but he believed that it would avoid ethical ones.

Arno's position was different from Delia's but still teleological in that he was concerned with the ultimate consequences of the layoffs for the system. Does his approach avoid ethical decisions, as he thought?

Marlo disagreed with both. She believed that, in thinking that they had avoided ethical decisions, Delia and Arno were making them tacitly—and bad ones, to boot. She claimed that Delia was treating people as though they were numbers or inanimate objects. Delia's system did not consider the personal conditions of the people involved. According to the first of Delia's options, people would be fired because they were the last hired and not on the basis of merit. According to the second option, long-term, higher salaried workers, most of whom would have difficulty finding new positions because of age, would be sacrificed. Marlo believed that those options, far from avoiding ethical decisions, were, themselves, ethical decisions.

Nor, she said, did the third of Delia's options avoid ethical decision making. According to that option, managers would have a possibly unfair advantage because they would be fired only after nonmanagement workers. She criticized both Delia and Arno for ignoring an ethically very important factor: the merits of the employees. Marlo argued for a merit system according to which division directors would use their judgment to evaluate the performance of their personnel and suggest who most deserved to be retained and who was least worthy to remain with the organization.

Delia and Arno strongly opposed Marlo's proposal. They described it as messy and unsystematic. It left too much to the judgment of the division directors, who certainly would not want to take responsibility for their own personal decisions. Delia and Arno believed that if Marlo's proposal were implemented, the division directors would accuse upper management of shoving the responsibility back to them.

Marlo replied, "Yeah, sure. They accuse us of shoving responsibility back to them. They think that the right thing to do is for them to shove their responsibility as managers back to us. Do they want managerial pay without the responsibility that goes with it? I think that you have misjudged them, or at least some of them. I think that they are professional enough to accept judgment as part of the job. Besides, Omega must make the final decisions, anyway; they should be happy for the opportunity to offer their opinions."

Arno considered Marlo's response to be charmingly naive. But, pressing her for more specifics, he asked that she supply more guidelines for managers. For example, he asked, should managers consider merit on the basis of past performance, prospects for future performance, or some combination of the two in considering whom to retain? Marlo replied that she would want managers to favor merit on past performance because to do so was most just, but that she would also entertain the possibility of considering the likelihood of future meritorious performance. Whether in the past or the future, however, merit was her foremost concern.

Delia feared that Marlo's plan would reduce the entire downsizing process to a despotic exercise in favoritism by the division managers. They would retain their favorite workers and purge the divisions of possibly good employees that had conflicts with the managers.

Marlo recognized the potential problem but had two responses. First, she argued, the managers had been chosen because of their managerial expertise, which presumably included concern not only for professional effectiveness but also for ethics. She maintained that they should be trusted unless evidence against them could be established. Furthermore, if the managers prove untrustworthy in this case, the entire organization should pay more attention to the ethics of individuals before hiring them. Secondly, she argued that if managers were discovered to have fired the wrong people, Omega, as the final authority within the system, should exercise her judgment to overrule the managers.

Marlo could not convince Delia and Arno. The three could not agree on a single plan, but their function was only advisory. They submitted three separate reports to Omega. She was disappointed. She asked them to meet again to find a proposal that they could all accept, even if it was a compromise. But this time, she asked them to consider the matter as if they themselves were in one of the divisions to be included in the downsizing.

Arno immediately withdrew his proposal to eliminate the least important divisions in favor of Delia's proposal, with the provision that the most recently hired be fired first. Delia agreed. Marlo withdrew her proposal in favor of Delia's, with the provision that the longest-standing, most expensive employees be fired first. They then laughed at their little game of self-ridicule and began to address Omega's request seriously. As of this writing, they have not come to a decision.

## Analysis

Review of the deliberations among the three assistants suggests that Delia and Arno took differing teleological positions, while Marlo's was primarily deontological. Delia and Arno wanted to get the job done most efficiently, with the least agony, and with greatest concern for the smooth functioning of the organization. They disagreed concerning the best way to achieve their teleological goals. Marlo was more concerned with the deontological issue of evaluating people according to their merits and giving people, as nearly as possible, what they deserve.

Who do you think gave the best arguments? Are there other arguments that were not mentioned but that you would find compelling? What do you think was Omega's purpose in asking her assistants to apply their proposals to themselves? In making that request, do you think that she betrayed any bias toward one of the points of view over the others?

## KEY EMERGING ISSUES

At this point you may become disturbed. All of these ethical cases are confusing, and, taken together, they pile confusion on top of confusion. Nevertheless, there are some issues that are beginning to emerge, and we will address three in particular: (1) the relation of character to ethical decision making; (2) the development of informed ethical intuitions; and (3) the development of personal ethical styles.

### The Relation of Character to Ethical Decision Making

In the preceding cases we noticed a variety of different people with different characters. In the case of the questionable hire, Felicia seemed concerned with ethical commitments and generally would follow the accepted policies of the organization. But, when those policies conflicted with what she thought was right, she was willing to overlook the rules regarding privacy to help her resolve the conflict. On the other hand, Alma and the remaining members of the hiring committee followed organizational policy without letting any personal moral beliefs interfere. In the case of the professor's leave of absence, Milo attempted to follow both the letter and spirit of the organization's laws but was willing to make an occasional exception for his own benefit. Marguerite was more than willing to get around the law, but, by contrast, Cosmo, the vice president for academic affairs, adhered both to the letter and intent of the law, although he could easily have ignored it despite an expectation within the organization to ignore the particular law in question. In the case of the transit workers' strike, Omega favored the expectations of the organizational culture in opposition to Cosmo, who initially favored the literal understanding of the law.

Finally, in the case of Omega's three advisors, Delia and Arno appear to be ethics avoiders and decision avoiders. Unlike Marlo, who prefers to rely on individual judgment and responsibility, Delia and Arno prefer to apply an impersonal and—as far as they could tell—ethically neutral formulaic policy. The ethical decisions of the persons seemed to express their characters, in which you may detect both virtue and vice.

Some of the characters leaned more toward the deontological and some more toward the teleological; some were merely practical people who were trying to do their jobs with minimal ethical involvement; some were ethically rigid; and some were ethically lax. But we must ask, which character type or types would be most helpful to an organization? While the rigid deontologist might make some decisions that seem to be teleologically harmful in the short rum, we must ask whether, in the long run, an organization made of rigid deontologists might produce the best results for both the organization and the public interests that it serves. On the other hand, a character type that favors teleology might ultimately support deontology; the employee of a welfare agency who is solely concerned with the productivity of the organization may serve the deontological concern for the dignity and intrinsic value of the people for whom the agency exists. Ironically, the deontological character may serve teleology and the teleological character may serve deontology.

While specific ethical issues may evoke different specific ethical responses from individuals with different ethical beliefs, managers must also concern themselves with the character traits of the people that the organization employs. Those character traits may be, as we noted, a factor that unifies both teleology and deontology and, in the end, may be more important to the organization than any specific ethical decision that the employee makes.

## The Development of Informed Ethical Intuitions

You may be disturbed by the ambiguity that remains after you have fully considered the cases. Earlier in this chapter, you were asked to consult your intuitions twice: once upon first reading each case and once after analyzing it. But what good is an analysis if it leaves you as before, having to rely on intuitions? Isn't the analysis supposed to remove the judgment factor?

Unlike mathematics, ethics does not provide formulas to resolve problems. Ethical ambiguity is inevitable; therefore, reliance on one's intuitions is inevitable. Nevertheless, your intuitions after the analysis may have been different from before. In some cases, the analysis may have brought about a change in your opinion of how the case should be resolved. In other cases, the analysis may have uncovered factors that were not immediately evident. Even if your conclusions on a case were the same both before and after analyzing it, the analysis likely provided greater understanding, which can be applied in other cases.

We use aesthetic intuitions when we decide how to dress for dinner at an upscale restaurant. Fashion experts also rely on their aesthetic intuitions, but theirs are much better than those of most of us. Their intuitions are informed and supported by years of training and experience. Even if they choose the same outfit for a particular evening as the nonexpert, the professional has the advantage. The professional can make the decision with greater confidence, will more likely make the best decisions over a long period of time, and will be able to give solid explanations for his or her choices.

Doctors must also "play hunches" occasionally when clinical diagnoses are not definitive. The unschooled patient may also play a hunch, as might his great-aunt Emma. But one would do well to rely on the doctor's intuition, because the doctor's is informed by expertise. One might also consider another opinion, but it would be more reliable if its source was another medically trained professional rather than a nonexpert.

Ethical decisions are generally more important than aesthetic ones and less easily confirmed than medical diagnoses. But like aesthetic and medical judgments, ethical decisions are improved by knowledge, study, and experience. In contemplating cases such as those we have considered and those that you are yet to consider, one's judgments become more enlightened and more reliable. As one looks more deeply into an individual case, one notices principles, values, and sources of conflict that are common to other cases. One also becomes more aware of the subtle factors that are easily overlooked. Examining past cases and hypothetical cases, even if they are never definitively resolved, can provide guidance for real future cases. Every public administrator faces important ethical decisions; one might as well consider a range of them ahead of time.

There is no route to infallible ethical decision making. One is often unsure that his or her decision is correct and, more lamentably, one sometimes decides, too late, that one's decision was incorrect. Uncertainty and regret are inescapable. Nevertheless, one cannot be blamed—indeed, one ought to be credited—even in reaching the wrong conclusion if it is reached in the right way. If you examine a range of theoretical cases and learn to apply the essence of, if not the detailed questions in, our list, you can address ethical issues with the confidence that you are performing at your best. To do less would be to fail ethically at a higher level: One is ethically obligated to prepare as fully as possible to confront ethical decisions. One can only imagine the unfortunate state of an organization whose members fail to recognize that obligation.

## The Development of Personal Ethical Styles

Few people are purely teleologists, deontologists, virtue theorists, or intuitionists. While great thinkers may present pure theories, real-life ethical decisions are usually much cloudier than the theoretician's textbook case. Moreover, as we have argued, the four ethical theories are not as distinct as they may at first appear but, rather, form a unified whole. We therefore would discourage rigid doctrinaire applications of abstract theories to actual cases with the expectation that moral resolutions will emerge as if from a well-programmed computer.

Nevertheless, in examining the above cases, you may have discovered that you tend to approach ethical issues in your own characteristic way. If you write your thoughts on each case and compare yours with those of others, you may find that you all think differently in identifiable ways. We call these individual characteristic ways of approaching ethical problems "ethical styles." We will discuss the concept of the ethical style more fully in the next chapter. For now, it is sufficient to recognize that examination of broad ranges of ethical cases help in the development of an ethical style.

In this chapter we have examined several cases that require serious ethical thought and decision-making. The cases reveal the complexity involved in balancing differing, often conflicting, values in reaching reasonable ethical conclusions. There is no formula for reaching such conclusions; they require informed and well-developed judgment. Contemplation of such cases, both real and hypothetical, is a useful exercise in strengthening one's ethical judgment.

The next chapter will also include hypothetical cases for your consideration, but those cases will not include as much explicitly stated analysis. The tone of the next chapter will therefore be less directive, and it will give you greater opportunity to engage in your own free, thoughtful ethical examination. The conclusions that you reach are not as important as the process that you use in reaching them—and your understanding of that process.

# CHAPTER 9

# Developing an Ethical Style: How Would You Analyze Problems That Might Arise?

The primary purpose of this chapter is to use hypothetical ethical cases to help you discover and develop your personal ethical style. In our examination of hypothetical cases in Chapter 8, we gave arguments for and against positions that one might take concerning ethical issues that arose. In this chapter, we will not include the supporting and disputing arguments but ask you to supply them instead. As you analyze the cases, provide your own arguments, and come to your own conclusions, we ask you to engage in a process of self-discovery. After fully considering each case, review your own reasoning and attempt to discern your ethical style. The questions that we will ask after each case are intended to help you in that attempt.

Members of any public organization must endure significant moral stress. Although it can never be eliminated, one can reduce its incidence and severity by recognizing that one is "up to the task" of ably addressing ethical issues. By discovering and developing your ethical style, you can make ethical decisions in which you can have greater confidence.

As we have noted in earlier chapters, better ethical decision making provides benefits for the individual, the organization, and the general public. The ethical individual maintains his or her own integrity, develops a strong sense of personal fulfillment, and commands a high measure of respect. Organizations also improve as a result of the ethical behavior of their members. Both the efficiency and long-term morale of an ethical organization are higher than those of less ethically inclined organizations. The public is also a clear beneficiary of an ethical organization that fulfills its public purpose responsibly, while serving as an ethical model.

## WHAT IS ETHICAL STYLE?

Robert Solomon (1999) discusses the notion of an ethical style in reference to business ethics. He gives a broad definition of an ethical style as "the individual mix of virtues (and vices) that makes up each one of us and defines the perspective through which we plan and judge our actions and those of others" (116). Solomon's definition seems, in its reference to virtues and vices, to favor virtue theory. In keeping with our notion of a unified ethic, we prefer a description that is neutral with respect to ethical theories, so we revise Solomon's definition somewhat. Our definition replaces "virtues (and vices)" with "attitudes, beliefs, and values"; therefore the definition is restated as "the individual mix of attitudes, beliefs, and values that makes up each one of us and defines the perspective through which we plan and judge our actions and those of others."

The definition is intentionally broad, leaving room for differing interpretations and applications. Ethical styles, themselves, are various and idiosyncratic, so they cannot be defined rigidly. They constitute the general approaches that people take to ethical problems. Ethical styles are similar to the styles of musical composers, novelists, business managers, and baseball pitchers, in that styles leave room for variation within themselves and tend to evolve over time. Styles are not rigid formulas but general ways of doing things, either consciously or unconsciously. Sometimes, people are unaware of their own style until they take the time to examine their own thoughts and actions.

Solomon gives some examples of ethical styles, but, since there may be as many different ethical styles as there are human beings, no list can possibly be complete. His list is a good place to begin, however. Four of his styles are closely related to deontology, teleology, virtue theory, and intuitionism. His "rule bound" style is that of the rigid deontologist, who considers circumstances and exceptions as only secondary issues. The "utilitarian" style is, as the name implies, a strong commitment to teleology. The "virtuous" style is that of the person whose thinking is primarily that of the virtue theorist, and the "intuitive" style is that of the intuitionist. The remaining styles do not fall explicitly within the categories of deontology, teleology, virtue theory, or intuitionism, but can be related to them in various combinations. The "professional" style is characteristic of the person whose primary commitment is to his or her profession, institution, company, and its reputation. The "loyalist" may overlap with the professional, but the loyalist is more committed to the company itself rather than to the profession or to the company as exemplar of the profession. The "empathetic" style is that of a person who follows his or her feelings of sympathy and compassion.

We might also refer to Lawrence Kohlberg's (1981) stages of moral reasoning to hint at other ethical styles. The first two of his stages may be dismissed as not really ethical at all. The first, concern for obedience and punishment, is merely a form of self-interest within a punitive system. The second, concern for cooperation and reciprocity in a single instance, is also essentially egoistic in that its primary motive is the material advantage that one acquires in the bargaining and contracting process. Furthermore, since its focus is on a single instance, this level does not assert principles that can be applied generally.

The third stage, concern for enduring personal relationships, may also be considered egocentric if the concern is merely to use such relationships to enhance one's life. But if the concerns are for the relationships per se, a semblance of altruism begins to emerge. The relationship and the people participating in it would then become important for their own sakes. This stage could become part of an ethical style if, in examining ethical issues, one uses the value of personal relations as a factor in arriving at a moral decision.

Consider, for example, the previously mentioned case of the department chair who wanted to allow a leave of absence under questionable conditions. The chair may decide to support the leave, even if the faculty member taking it promised insincerely to return, because to deny the leave risked damage to personal relations within the department. An impartial evaluator of the case might support the chair's decision for the unselfish reason that relationships defined by mutual concern and benevolence are inherently important. If that evaluator consistently considered support for personal relationships to be an important ethical factor, that concern could be part of the evaluator's ethical style.

Kohlberg's fourth stage, concern for law and duty, is more clearly ethical. At this stage, one recognizes the need for law as a basic element of society and recognizes a duty, shared by all, to follow the law. While the person at this stage may question the moral authority of some specific laws, he or she respects the concept of law in general and follows it out of a sense of moral duty rather than fear of punishment alone. Such a person would implicitly recognize a moral value in society itself. A sense of obligation to society and its laws could therefore be part of an ethical style.

Kohlberg's final stage is principled reasoning, defined as impartial moral judgment using justice and fairness as core values. Principled reasoning is clearly moral and can therefore enter into an ethical style.

While we accept the highest three stages of Kohlberg's list as factors within an ethical style, we do not consider any one of the stages alone to describe most ethical styles. Few people think at only one of the stages, either in contemplating an individual action or in their general approaches to a broad range of cases. Ethical styles are more complex than any single stage. Furthermore, we make no qualitative judgment concerning which stage is "higher" than another. Since these stages are only parts of ethical styles, the characterization of any stage as higher or as lower than any other does not necessarily apply to the more complex ethical styles.

We consider an ethical style to be more complex than either Solomon or Kohlberg suggests. When one thinks about ethical problems, one considers many factors in numerous different sequences and structures. To describe a person's common thinking patterns by means of one word or even a few sentences is an oversimplification, as it would be if one tried to so briefly describe the musical style of Mozart, the artistic style of Raphael, the writing style of Hawthorne, or the running style of Walter Payton. In each case, a characteristic mode of performance is discernible but too complex to describe fully in a short formulation.

Your ethical style may be as unique to you as your speech patterns, your sense of humor, or your taste in food. You may not be able to describe your ethical style precisely, but, as in the case of all such patterns, if you examine yourself as objectively as you can, you will discover a roughly defined set of tendencies, though with several variations and exceptions. We suggest that you describe your style as best you can. As you examine the cases to be considered, try to discover and clarify your own ethical style.

We need not assume that any ethical style is better than any other. The notion of a unified ethic suggests that numerous styles may be equally valuable in leading people to the best conclusions. Often, people with different styles will reach the same conclusions, as there may be different routes to the same mountain peak. Rather than suggest that you examine your ethical style with a view to choosing a better one, we suggest that you develop and refine your own ethical style. Instead of trying to think in an entirely new way, try to do things in your own way, but better. If you adopt a different style from the one that you currently have, the new style will gradually evolve from the old.

It is probably possible to have no ethical style. Someone without an ethical style never uses the same pattern of thinking twice. Someone without an ethical style uses an inconsistent pattern of thinking. Such an eclectic approach may seem admirably open-minded, and it is possible for someone to make excellent ethical decisions with nothing common among them. It is also possible for a musician, artist, or writer to operate differently every time, but most experts do things in a characteristic way that they "perfect" over time.

## DETERMINING YOUR ETHICAL STYLE

In trying to discern your ethical style, ask yourself the following questions:

- When I consider an ethical issue, what factors do I generally think about first?

- When I come to my final conclusion, what factors do I consider most important?

- Do I approach each problem with a preestablished system or methodology?

- Do I initially consider the facts of the case from an ethically neutral perspective and let my conclusion emerge after considering the whole case?

- Do I make tentative ethical decisions about each ethical factor as it appears and correct them as the case becomes more complex?

- Do certain factors tend to "jump out" at me?

- Do my feelings or does my logical analysis have the greater impact on my final conclusion?

- Do I tend to compare the case at hand with others that I have encountered?

- Do I tend to make up analogous cases to illuminate the one in question?

- Do I tend to "identify with" some of the people involved in the case, or do I separate myself from all equally?

How does one evaluate one's ethical style? While there is no hard and fast test, there are ways in which one can discover evidence concerning the effectiveness of one's ethical decisions. One test is the confidence test, which is simply that of asking yourself whether you have confidence in the decision. Another test is that of putting yourself in the positions of those most negatively affected by your decision and asking yourself if you consider the decision fair. But perhaps the best test is that of attempting to explain your position in a manner that others can understand. This test is most informative when you provide your explanation both to people with ethical styles similar to yours and to people who have very different styles.

## A PRIVATIZATION MATTER

The following example is based upon a hypothetical case discussed by C. J. Fox (1989).

Waldo, a newly elected mayor, is working with his also newly elected city council to privatize some city services, as he had promised while running for the office. He was not certain that privatization would work, but he knew that it would be a good campaign issue. His strategy was successful. Although a very small portion of the electorate voted, Waldo's message of fiscal responsibility attracted the majority of voters, who, as a group, knew less about privatization than he did.

The prospect of privatization does not appeal to Poinsettia, the city manager. Although she is secure in her position, many city employees are not, and they fear for their jobs. Even if the employees are not fired, they are concerned about any change in management style, especially one that promises to focus unscrupulously on the bottom line. Furthermore, employee benefits, including insurance and retirement funds, may be in jeopardy. There is also a visceral, perhaps irrational reaction against the specter of privatization among the public employees, much like the visceral, irrational reaction in favor of privatization among the general public. Not only is the resultant morale problem inherently undesirable, but it also is encouraging some of the city's best employees to seek early retirement or alternative employment.

Poinsettia fears that the mayor, city council, and voters may not be as concerned as she is about the working conditions of city employees. If she is to persuade the council to oppose both the mayor and his privatization scheme, she must appeal to civic pride. She realizes that there are many good arguments for privatization, but she also realizes that the arguments against privatization are equally convincing. There is no conclusive evidence that privatization is ultimately of any benefit whatsoever, but there is also no conclusive evidence that it has not generally improved government efficiency. Her own opinion of privatization is generally unfavorable, but she is far from certain, and she cannot prove her case by any empirical data. The arguments, when objectively presented, are so inconclusive that she is certain that the city council will ignore them in favor of the mayor's agenda.

How should Poinsettia react to the prospect of privatization? Should she offer an opinion at all or stay out of the argument? If she says nothing in opposition, she risks further morale problems with the city employees, who will consider her a sellout and lose confidence in her leadership.

What ethical issues do you observe in this case? Which do you consider the most important? If you have an opinion concerning what Poinsettia should do, give the best reasons that you can to support your opinion, and explain why you consider them best. Also, give the best reasons that you can find against your opinion.

Consider the suggestion offered by Fox: Poinsettia is faced with a mayor and city council who are insufficiently informed concerning the very privatization that they are about to impose on the city and its employees. She, however, is far better informed. She could make equally convincing cases for and against privatization, but both her own professional judgment and the interests of her employees incline her to keep public service in public hands.

Fox offers the possibility that, since the case cannot be decided objectively, Poinsettia should not make the case objectively. He suggests that, like an attorney arguing in behalf of a client, she emphasize the possible drawbacks of privatization while deemphasizing its benefits. For example, he suggests that she argue that it might increase costs by introducing a possible new layer of bureaucracy, while ignoring arguments that he considers "equally valid" in favor of the mayor's proposal. He justifies his recommendation by pointing out that the city council, lacking in knowledge on the subject and possibly unduly influenced by a business mentality, may not embody the public interest as well as Poinsettia, a knowledgeable public servant. Furthermore, he argues, even if "some deception has occurred, it has been, after all based on real facts, however arranged on the basis of what the manager firmly believes is inductively derived valid hypotheses" (927).

What do you think of Fox's suggestion? Would you call advocacy, based upon Poinsettia's honest convictions of what is truly best for the city "deception," if presented as an impartial analysis? Does Fox's suggestion for Poinsettia remind you of any of the other cases that we have discussed in this book? For example, is the notion of possible "honest deception" present in both Poinsettia's case and the case of Marguerite, the department chair who was willing to approve a leave of absence despite a deceptive promise by the applicant to return? Were your opinions of Marguerite and Poinsettia—assuming that Poinsettia acted as Fox suggests—consistent with each other?

## THE SKOKIE CASE

The following ethical issue is based upon the well-known case concerning a request from a group of Nazis for a parade permit from the town of Skokie, Illinois. We will not be concerned with the details of the case itself, but with the issues that it causes us to consider. The case appears to pit the notion of free expression, guaranteed by the First Amendment to the United States Constitution, against the concerns of many Skokie residents. Some were survivors of Nazi concentration camps, and their sensitivities would be deeply offended if their own community allowed celebration of the forces that perpetrated the holocaust. Other residents fear violence that the marchers might cause, either by their own actions or by inciting those who oppose them. There is also a concern among residents that their town will be smeared with an anti-Semitic reputation.

Imagine that you are the town manager faced with deciding whether to grant a parade permit. The Nazi group has filed for the permit in a legally appropriate manner, and there is no reason to deny the permit, except for the concerns of the residents. While you share the fear that violence will erupt, you realize that the possibility is remote. The concern of the residents is mainly their revulsion at the beliefs of Nazis.

Specify all of the ethical issues that you recognize in this case. Which did you notice first? Which do you consider the most important? How would you decide the issue? In your decision, which of the following seemed most important to you: the law? the principle of free speech? fairness to the demonstrators? the feelings of the concentration camp survivors? the possibility, however small, of violence? concern for the city's reputation? concern for upholding the responsibilities of your office? concern for your own reputation? Are there other factors that you consider important?

Consider the following solution suggested by Gerald Pops (1994). He suggests that the manager refuse the permit for the following reasons: (1) the town manager wishes to serve the citizens of a community that does not include Nazis; (2) the Nazis can express themselves elsewhere; and (3) he wishes to keep his job, and denying the permit will make him a local hero and make the courts, who will undoubtedly overturn his decision, the villains. But, Pops argues, the manager should not publicly state those as his reasons for the denial. To give his decision legitimacy, Pops maintains, the manager should couch his explanation in language about consequence, principles, or any other notions that give him ethical credibility.

What do you think of Pops' reasoning?

What do you think of the following variation on the third of Pops' reasons: Whatever decision the manager makes will be taken to court. The courts will decide anyway, so it does not matter what decision the manager makes. He may as well make the decision that will be to his own best advantage.

Is this variation an improvement on Pops' original analysis? If so, would you consider the argument sound? Would you act in accordance with the reasoning? If you thought that the reasoning was sound, but you would not act in accordance with it, why not? (For example, did it "sound" right but not "feel" right?)

Now consider one more variation on Pops' analysis. Suppose that the manager, realizing that the courts would ultimately decide anyway, denied the permit so that the city would make a statement against anti-Semitism. In this case, the manager is concerned with the interests of the city rather than his own. Would you favor such reasoning?

There is a broader set of questions implicit in both the case of the Skokie city manager and the previous case of Poinsettia. In both cases, a city manager was under temptation to act in a manner that might be considered deceptive. The broader set of questions, then, includes the following:

- Is it ever justifiable to be deceptive toward a public that is too lacking in knowledge and sophistication to make a good judgment on a full, truthful presentation of the facts?

- Is a deception intended to benefit the very public that is deceived really a deception?

- Is a deception intended to lead the public to a more important truth really a deception?

- Is it possible for an individual charged with making important public policy decisions to be both honest and professionally responsible in the face of a public that lacks a professional's understanding?

The problem of possible conflict between honesty and professional responsibility often occurs between professionals rather than only between professionals and nonprofessionals. We are all familiar, for example, with the budgeting process. Divisions within the same organization are often in competition with each other for limited funds. In order to succeed in such competition, each division must make the strongest possible case for the satisfaction of its own needs. The amount of money that is allocated to a division often affects its morale and productivity. Division heads are therefore greatly motivated to present the strongest possible cases for the highest possible budget. Organizations seldom reward managers for admitting that their budgetary needs are less pressing than those of other divisions and thus sacrificing the opportunity to financially strengthen their own division. When making budget requests, there is a fine line between objectivity and advocacy; there is an equally fine line between presenting the strongest possible case and exaggerating.

The manager therefore has an ethical problem deciding what constitutes honesty. If she states her case objectively, without advocacy or exaggeration, she risks the unfair disadvantage of becoming the lone "honest" manager competing with a group of manipulators. Furthermore, her honesty might be misunderstood for incompetence in fighting for the interests of her division. The pressures on her to "play the game" come not only from her subordinates but also from other managers, who evaluate how skillful a game player she is, and from her superiors, who determine the winners and losers of the game. In such an environment, where game playing is expected, i.e., where "dishonesty" is expected, an objective participant may inadvertently represent her division's case as weaker than it truly is. Worse yet, the manager may be accused of dishonesty in her honesty; her own division members may believe that she has, for some perverse reason, betrayed them by "sending a subtle message," under the guise of honesty, that her departmental needs are less than they really are.

The case of the end-of-the-year budget surplus is an example of the pitfalls of pure honesty. Few divisions voluntarily sacrifice their surplus funds to other divisions that might be in greater need or might have more productive uses for a few extra dollars. To make such a seemingly honest sacrifice would not only have negative material consequences for the current budgetary year, but also might result in funding cutbacks for the next year. The temptation of the manager to "play the game" is overwhelming.

Part of the problem is in the nature of communication. In any communication, the speaker and listener must use the same language. When professionals attempt to communicate perfectly honestly to nonprofessionals or to other professionals who are playing a game, the speaker and the hearer use different languages. Honesty in one language becomes misrepresentation in the other. Nowhere is the problem thornier than in the following case of professional evaluation.

## EVALUATING RICO

Rico is a 20-year employee of a public organization. His job performance has been steady but unspectacular, and he has received few merit raises in his career. He is now being considered for such a raise. The process requires an advisory review by his peers and a recommendation from the director of his division.

Margo, the director, calls a committee meeting to discuss Rico's case. The committee consists of the four peers, who will give their collective advice to Margo, a nonvoting member. The committee members are to evaluate Rico according to a four-level rating system. The top rating is "outstanding," followed by "good," "fair," and "poor."

Clarence, who favors Rico's candidacy for the raise, acknowledges that he is not outstanding but also realizes that a rating of "good," though accurate, will hurt his chances considerably. He therefore votes to give Rico the "outstanding" designation.

Daria accuses Clarence of deception. She likes Rico and hopes that he gets the raise, but believes that it would be dishonest to give him a falsely high rating. She believes that to do so would unfairly hurt the chances of worthier candidates. She also argues that, if divisions regularly rate favored candidates more highly than they deserve, rating inflation will result and the entire rating system will become meaningless.

Clarence does not respond happily to the implication that he is being dishonest. In response, he argues that it is Daria, rather than he, who will mislead the higher levels of the organization. He argues that the inflation that Daria is worried about has already taken place, so a rating of "good" will naturally be interpreted as "fair" and will unjustly damage Rico's candidacy.

Daria concedes that "good" will likely be taken as a lower rating than she intends, but she argues, "Just because everyone else is being dishonest, it doesn't mean that we should be. I must be true to my own principles even if I am consequently misunderstood." Clarence replies that principles must be applied in context, and in the context of traditional rating procedures in the organization, a principle of honesty would require an approving "outstanding" rating rather than a "kiss of death" rating of "good."

Quentin, a third member of the committee, agrees to the "good" rating, but for reasons different from those of Daria. He has rated other candidates of Rico's quality as "outstanding" but does not get along well with Rico. Since the case is so close, Quentin applies the "kiss of death" willingly.

Of all of the members of the committee, Zelda has the lowest opinion of Rico's job performance. If she were to rate him objectively, she would give a "fair" rating. However, she believes that his many years of service entitle him to a significant raise, and she strongly decries a system in which dedicated, though average, workers should consistently be given only cost-of-living increases, which often fail to keep up with inflation. She therefore gives Rico an "outstanding" in the hope that he will receive just remuneration for his average, but consistent and lengthy, service. She also argues that Rico would be discouraged if he were turned down, and she does not want him hurt. Furthermore, she argues, if Rico's morale suffers, his performance may suffer also, to the detriment of the entire organization.

Of the four members of the committee, whose position do you favor, and whose do you find weakest? In answering that question, note the values implicit in your own reasoning. If you consistently display similar concern for those values in other examples, your degree of respect for those values may constitute part of your ethical style.

Give a brief ethical analysis of the reasoning of all four of the committee members. Can you discern characteristics in their reasoning in this case that may also recur in other cases? If so, those characteristics may be parts of the ethical styles of the members. In your analysis, consider the following questions: Was Daria really being honest? Was Clarence truly deceptive? Was Zelda honest or deceptive?

If you were the division manager, what would you include in your written report to those who will make the ultimate decision? How would you represent the deliberations from which the ratings emerged? Would you recommend any organization-wide changes in the procedure? Would you set any new rating guidelines for your own division members concerning future deliberations and rulings?

If you have participated in a similar rating procedure in the past, was your reasoning similar to that of any of the four committee members? Does consideration of Rico's case cause you to rethink your decisions in those cases? How do you think you will decide in similar cases that you might encounter in the future?

## FITNESS AND JOB PERFORMANCE

The line between privacy and public interest is often difficult to draw, as evidenced in the issue of fitness. We begin with a case presented by William Timmins (1990) and develop it in several directions. As you examine the case and its variations, try to decide how you would draw the privacy/public interest line and determine how your attitudes toward the distinction reflect your ethical style.

Marianne, whose job was to check restaurants for compliance with a city's food handling regulations, is asked to enroll in a weight reduction program. She was bothered not only that the city would consider her overweight, but also that her weight appeared to have little relation to her job. She might have understood the city's request if she were a police officer, firefighter, or tree trimmer, but she saw no reason for the city's concern for her weight if all she did was check restaurants for proper food handling.

On the surface, Marianne has a good point. Yet the city may have legitimate concerns, also. Although there is no obvious connection between her weight and her ability to determine whether a restaurant's open food is too close to a wash basin or whether clean towels in the lavatory are in good supply, the city may have an interest in her health. There is statistical evidence that overweight people have more heart problems and die sooner than people of ideal weight. If an employee takes numerous sick days, he or she is not as able to serve the city as well as an equally capable employee who seldom misses a day of work. If employees need expensive medical treatment, the city's cost of insuring them rises. Premature death or early health-related retirement of well-established employees requires the city to replace experienced workers with novices, who must take time to learn their jobs. Responsible public servants must protect the public interest, even at the cost of offending government employees.

In your opinion, does a government agency have the moral authority to demand that an employee lose weight or otherwise improve fitness when there is no directly provable connection between the employee's health and job performance? Is a statistical likelihood of future problems a good enough reason for telling an employee to lose weight or be fired? What, in your opinion, are the significant ethical aspects of Marianne's case? What do you consider to be the most important aspects? If you were Marianne's supervisor, what would you do about her weight problem if she were twenty pounds overweight? Fifty pounds? One hundred pounds?

If you concluded that the city has no right to intrude in people's personal lives in such matters, consider the following different, though related, perspectives. If the employee has an absolute right to determine his or her own fitness conditions, the city would have no right to demand that a police officer or tree trimmer be fit either.

Perhaps, however, one might argue that the employee has no such absolute right, but that the city should impose a fitness requirement only if it can be clearly demonstrated to improve job performance. However, the phrase "clearly demonstrated to improve job performance" could provide the city with the justification for its demand on Marianne, after all. If statistics show that, over a period of years, fit people perform better, then the clear demonstration would be established, and she would find herself doing aerobic dancing after all.

It might seem easier to resolve Marianne's problem if there were a definitive way of establishing whether a specific physical condition has a likely effect on an employee's ability to perform on the job. One might be tempted to conclude that, if such an effect can be established, the city can impose a fitness requirement, but, lacking any negative effect, no requirement is in order. However, the issue is not so simple. Even if a condition under the employee's control can be shown to hurt performance, the question remains concerning whether the rights of the employee, as an individual, should take precedence over any demand by a public agency employing her. Do you see a possible deontological-teleological conflict in such a case, as well as a conflict between private rights and public interest? Are there any other examples in this book, and are there any other examples that you have encountered elsewhere in which the same conflicts arise? Can you discover anything common to your analysis of all of them? If so, that common feature may be included as part of your ethical style.

Now, let us examine Marianne's case from another perspective. Some might argue that the interests of the public always override the interests of the employee, so she should be required to attend the fitness program. But under that interpretation of the relative strengths of the rights of the employee and the public, another problem may arise. Suppose that the city's actuary discovers that the city actually profits by early retirement and death of employees. Early retirement enables the city to replace longtime workers who, as a group, are more expensive than newer ones. After the age of fifty, according to the actuary, productivity of employees tends to drop off while salaries remain high and continue to rise. Early death will cost the city less money on retirement pensions. The actuary therefore suggests that, since the city has no economic interest in encouraging employee fitness, all fitness programs be dropped.

What do you think of the actuary's reasoning, under the assumption that his statistics are correct? You may be disinclined to favor such programs for other reasons, but how do you assess the actuary's thinking, from a moral perspective? His analysis appears consistent with the principle that the interests of the city outweigh the interests of the employee.

You may also have noticed another issue emerging. The city may have good reason for encouraging—though perhaps not forcing—Marianne to join a fitness program. The city may consider itself morally responsible to the employee herself, regardless of any concern for the public good. Do you recall any perspective mentioned in an earlier chapter that would justify such an attitude toward the employee? Do you, once again, notice a possible deontological-teleological issue implicit in this attitude?

The case of Marianne and its variations provides an opportunity to develop one's ideas of the relation between private rights and public responsibility and the moral source of both. In developing and articulating your beliefs on that relationship, reexamine the ethical theories discussed in Chapter 3 to determine which you consider most insightful on the matter. Your understanding of this issue may be important in analyzing your ethical style.

## ISSUES IN PRIVATIZATION

In an earlier case, we touched on the issue of privatization. We now consider the issue of privatization in general and without reference to a specific instance. Your conclusions on the issue itself are important, but, for our purposes, your thoughts on the matter are also significant for another reason. Your thinking process may reveal some of the factors that influence your ethical style. The issue of privatization is a good one for our purposes because it is general enough to reveal several such factors. One of them, for example, may be your attitude on the possible conflict, evident in the case of Marianne, between the public interest and the interests of the public employee.

Many members of the private sector react with immediate and unquestioned approval to the term "privatization." Americans are especially proud of the accomplishments of private industry and assume that "if it works at General Motors, it will work in the State House," or that government agencies should be "run like a business." Such thinking fails to account for the important differences between the manners in which public agencies and private corporations must operate. There are reasons for the location of public libraries, schools, police forces, and oversight agencies within the public sector. If they could have been run as profit-making businesses, they may well have been.

But just as there is a bias of some people in favor of privatization, there is, perhaps as misplaced, a bias among others against privatization. Public employees are often fearful that privatization will take away their jobs, their benefits, or at least their accustomed ways of performing their jobs. They would oppose privatization in any context, regardless of whether it be in a prison system, an electric utility, or a homeless shelter. It is best to set aside one's natural biases in this discussion and focus on the issues. It is reasonable to suppose that privatization will work in some cases but will not work for all public functions.

Suppose that you are an official charged with recommending whether a particular agency ought to be privatized. What moral issues would you consider relevant? We suggest some for your consideration.

Let us suppose that, as the official making the recommendation, you are convinced that the agency will run more efficiently if privatized. Is that the end of the matter? Are there other considerations that are relevant? If you believe that efficiency is the only consideration, on what ethical theory do you base your belief? Some who share that belief would argue that the public agency is responsible only to the public interest and that the interests of the employees are irrelevant. What is your response to that argument?

Those who would argue for efficiency as the sole criterion concerning privatization would probably have a strong teleological aspect in their ethical styles.

Perhaps you consider other factors, however. Now, assume the following circumstance to obtain. You are convinced that privatization would result in a more efficient operation, but you recognize that there is another, potentially important, factor. The private company that will be hired will not be under the same restrictions that apply to public organizations in your state. For example, the company will not be required, as the state is, to pay its employees wages equivalent to those of union workers, to promote diversity in hiring practices, to limit employee working hours, and to provide a full range of employee benefits, including domestic partner health insurance. Would you consider the company's exemptions from these requirements relevant to your decision?

Some may favor privatization not merely despite the exemptions, but because of them. The ethical style of people with such an opinion varies with the reasons for the opposition to the exemptions. People who see only hindrances to efficiency but nothing valuable in the restrictions probably have the same aforementioned teleological aspect in their ethical styles.

Others, however, might object to the restrictions for other reasons. Some might believe that the limitations on working hours prevent the worker from fulfilling his or her own potential and thus inhibit the worker's own self-fulfillment. Such people would have a strong virtue theory element in their ethical styles.

Some people might believe that paying union wages has a tendency to standardize the reward system, giving people the same amount of money rather than giving them what they merit. Such a perspective would likely suggest a strong justice-based, deontological aspect in their ethical styles.

Yet another group might object to some aspects of the employee benefits, such as the domestic partner benefit, on religious grounds and thus display a religious aspect to their ethical styles. It must not be assumed, however, that people with religious ethical styles would necessarily oppose the domestic partner benefit; depending upon the content of one's religious beliefs, he or she may favor that benefit.

For the purpose of exploring the issue further, let us now suppose that one opposes privatization because of the removal of those restrictions. What would such an opposition indicate concerning the individual's ethical style? The indications are many and varied.

One might simply favor all of the restrictions, but each for a different reason. To explain the ethical style of such a person would require an investigation of each possible reason for each restriction, and that would be a lengthy process. However, there might be a general reason for one's opposing the removal of the restrictions, even while disapproving of some or all of them, individually.

One might argue that in enacting the restrictions, the community has exercised its moral judgment concerning how it believes those in its employ should be treated. To allow an employer, albeit a private employer, to treat employees working under the auspices of the community in a manner that the community deems less than fair may be seen as a betrayal of the community's wishes.

The argument displays an irony in the notion that public officials should concern themselves exclusively with the public interest. The public interest is often considered to be the material interest of the public, but it also has moral interests. It may be that the public considers the interests of the public employees to be part of its own interest. Those who offer such an argument against privatization would likely have a strong element of public agency in their ethical styles. By "public agency" we mean the attitude that, as a public official, one functions as an agent of the public will. In this case, that public will would be interpreted as a will with a benevolent moral perspective.

There are still more reasons for the rejection of privatization, despite its assumed efficiency. One might simply object because of a concern for fairness to the employee, even at the expense of the public benefit. This position may be easily confused with the prior position because they both favor the interests of the employee, but they are, nevertheless, different.

In the previously expressed reasoning, the employee's interests are served because they are understood to have been supported by the community. Therefore, in that ethical style, concern for the public will is paramount. In the latter case, the interests of the employee are favored simply because they are inherently important, even if the public does not agree. The ethical style implicit in this reasoning would likely have a strong deontological element with an emphasis on individuals as ends in themselves.

The issue of privatization is a large one, containing innumerable related issues. Different instances of privatization will also introduce particular issues specific to their cases. But because privatization is so multifaceted, analyzing it is a good exercise in learning about one's ethical style.

## SELLING PRIME CUTS

Ethical problems have been discovered at the willed body parts program at a major research university. The person in charge of the donated bodies is alleged to have sold some of their parts to other laboratories.

The following letters are entirely fictional. They have no connection, other than the subject of willed body parts, to any actual case. Dr. Scotos, Dr. Mannheiser, and the unnamed university and laboratories do not exist. The letters are presented here entirely for analysis of their ethical reasoning.

In the following imaginary exchange, Dr. Mort Mannheiser is the administrator and sole researcher for a university's willed body parts program. Dr. Andreas Scotos is the Vice President for Academic Affairs at the institution. Dr. Mannheiser's program is housed under Dr. Scotos' division.

Dear Dr. Scotos,

I am very much disturbed by the accusation that I behaved unethically when I transferred my access of somatic resources to several highly professional laboratories worldwide. I did so in the full knowledge that those laboratories had potential for greater use of those resources than I. As you know, my laboratory is best known for its stellar research on intestines and mucous membranes, so I kept those resources, as well as others which our lab can use to fullest advantage, for myself.

Our laboratory has been receiving body parts from donors for several years. We have a profound responsibility to those donors to ensure that their donations advance medical science in the best possible way. We are agents of the deceased and their families, and, as such, we must provide that their wishes be fulfilled. If another lab can use hearts, livers, knees, or genitalia better than we can, we are morally required to allow that laboratory to perform its services. The way I see it, I was only outsourcing on behalf of the donors.

I have been accused of selling the body parts to those laboratories. I categorically deny the charge. I did not own them, so I could not have sold them. I had access to them, but they were not mine, which, I can assure you, are fully functioning within my own body. I merely transferred my access to the better-equipped laboratories. I charged an access fee because, while the other labs would work on the parts, I would be deprived of their use for my own research. Besides, their willingness to pay an access fee was evidence of their sincerity; they would not pay a fee if they did not intend to use the materials productively. Moreover, the transfer took time that I could have been using for my own work, so it was only fair that I receive just compensation. Furthermore, since the laboratory is funded entirely by private contributions, including monies and raw materials, I did not abuse the taxpayers of this state-supported institution.

Finally, the access fees that I received should be considered just compensation for my efforts at this university. As you, yourself, have admitted, my salary is unduly meager. Because of funding limitations, the institution has been unable pay me commensurate with my contributions, which, as you have stated many times, are invaluable. If I am refused the opportunity to make up for the shortfall, I will be forced to resign, to the detriment of the institution and the world at large.

In addition to the access fees, the institutions to which the resources were transferred all willingly gave donations to our program. The donations are a matter of public record. The university therefore benefited from the mutual good will that grew out of the transactions between the labs and me. The university should credit me for aiding in its fund-raising efforts.

In short, my transfer of access fees has been entirely ethical. I have ensured that the interest of the donors in advancing medical science has been served. I have facilitated the advancement of medical science. I have reduced the university's moral debt to me for my work. In doing so, I have made it possible for me to continue my humanitarian work at the institution. I believe that I merit honor rather than criticism.

At no time did the institution conduct an inventory of somatic resources at my disposal. If the institution had wished me to hoard the items in question for my own use, it surely would have monitored then. Its refraining from doing so demonstrates the institution's tacit approval of my policies and procedures. I had every reason to believe that the institution respected my judgment sufficiently to allow me the opportunity to decide the best interests of the deceased without interference.

Sincerely,

Mort Mannheiser

Dear Dr. Mannheiser:

I understand your consternation over the alleged violations of ethical practices in your lab. The charges are serious.

I agree that you are undercompensated and that you have contributed greatly to the university and to the advancement of medicine. However, your past efforts are not license for unethical behavior.

Your assumption that the university tacitly approved your activities because it did not constantly inspect you and your laboratory is egregiously mistaken. The institution does not have the time or money to constantly monitor every program. In addition, the monitoring of your program would be especially unseemly. Would you have us send someone over to the lab periodically to do an inventory of feet, arms, lungs, torsos, etc.? We trusted you, and you betrayed our trust. Now you have brought negative publicity to the university. The harm that you have done to our institution is ethically reprehensible.

The institution is currently considering appropriate ways to respond to your actions. We have convened a Committee on Academic Integrity which will recommend penalties ranging from official reprimand to dismissal. We are also exploring the possibility of legal action. You will be duly informed of their recommendations and of the university's final action.

Regards,

Andreas Scotos

What is your impression of the ethical reasoning in the two letters?

Dr. Mannheiser's arguments are ridiculously self-serving. Nevertheless, some semblance of a case may be made on his behalf. What do you think of his argument that the world would be better served by his relinquishing the body parts to laboratories that could use them more productively than he could? If those laboratories produce results that greatly improve medical science, would the donors have been served or would they have been betrayed? Even if they had been betrayed, would their betrayal have been justified?

It is understandable that Dr. Scotos finds it unseemly to examine the inventory of body parts accumulated by Dr. Mannheim's laboratory. Nevertheless, the Vice President for Academic Affairs is a public agent responsible for the use of public funds. Even though the laboratory is funded mostly by contributions, the land, physical plant, and administrative structure of the institution are paid for, at least in large part, by taxpayers. The personnel and resources, including telephones, stationery, and computers, used to raise private funds are public property. Thus, there is no hard-and-fast distinction between private and public funds in a public institution. Whatever distinction exists is virtually eliminated during budgeting when funds from both sources are intermingled. Dr. Scotos, as a public agent, is responsible for the oversight of the laboratory. Yet he acknowledges no fault in his failure to provide a method of overseeing the program.

What is your impression of Dr. Scotos' ethical reasoning? From the letter, what seems to be his primary concern? If you were in his position, how might your letter of response read?

What penalties, if any, should the institution impose on Dr. Mannheiser? Should any penalties be imposed for ethical violations that are not illegal? Should any penalties be imposed for unethical behavior that violates no specific university rules but that displays poor moral judgment?

## BUILDING CHARACTER THROUGH ATHLETICS?

The pressures on colleges to recruit top athletes are overwhelming. The careers of athletic department personnel, alumni contributions to the institution, athletic budgets, and national prestige can all be affected by a winning or a losing season. As a result, the temptation is strong to push ethical considerations aside in the effort to attract outstanding athletes to a college program.

In 2001, the University of Colorado at Boulder allegedly attempted to recruit athletes by luring them with sex and alcohol (Anas 2009). Eventually, the university settled with two women who claimed to be victims of assault. The victims claimed that the assaults stemmed from the environment created by the recruitment policies. The accusations and the revelations resulting from investigation of the assaults prompted the university to reform those policies.

Without the emergence of such a highly publicized case, how can a chain of habitual, routine, and widespread unethical practice be broken? What would you have done if you were part of the recruiting program at Boulder before the scandal erupted?

The question can be made more general. We must all ask ourselves if we have witnessed questionable practices in our organizations that have two aspects in common with the alleged recruiting abuses: (1) the practices are accepted because they are customary and habitual; and (2) the practices are useful tools in the competition with other organizations that engage in similarly questionable practices. We have mentioned some such practices, including padding of budgets and inflated employee evaluations.

We might also look to the alleged recruiting abuses to help us consider how to discourage such habitual practices. Change is unlikely to result from the lower level employee who bucks the system. Athletic recruiting will improve only when athletic directors and presidents of competing universities agree to police themselves. Leaders must step up and reform their organizational culture.

But reform may be difficult to achieve in the athletic programs of higher education. Winning teams attract contributions to athletic programs and are often assumed (although without proof) to improve the status of institutions (Bok 2003). With intense pressures to win, the potential for abuse will always remain. As is often the case, the private interest of institutions often conflicts with the social purpose they are intended to serve.

## MAKING THE BIG SWITCH

In June 2004, a former Pentagon official was accused of ethical violations for accepting a position with the Boeing Corporation. The job change suggested a possible conflict of interest, especially when the person in question was suspected of informing Boeing of a competing bid while she was still an employee of the Pentagon.

If she did, indeed, convey private information about a competitive bid, she was clearly in violation of the law. But the issue of changing jobs from the public to the private sector is more complicated. On one hand, it would seem unfair to prohibit a public employee from seeking a better job in the private sector. On the other hand, it would be a betrayal of the public trust to use personal connections, inside information, or special status to, in effect, buy a job in a private company.

Such job changes among lower level employees are, in most cases, innocent enough, but upper level public administrators could prove very useful in positioning private companies for advantages in dealings with government agencies. One would suppose, therefore, that the "revolving door" laws should apply more to upper level administrators than to lower level personnel, but in fact, the reverse appears to be true. According to a report from the Project on Government Oversight (POGO), www.pogo. org, "revolving door laws generally do not apply to the most senior policymakers who ultimately have the most power in shaping programs and policies that benefit contractors."

POGO discovered that the practice of high government officials shifting to the private sector is common. More than two hundred of them went to work for private contractors, and one-third of the former officials were in positions that could influence contracting decisions. Even former members of Congress have found gainful employment in lobbying their former colleagues.

The issue of the revolving door suggests many questions. Why are the prohibitions weaker when applied to higher level administrators than to lower level employees? Is it fair to prohibit public administrators from seeking alternative employment if they break no laws? Is it ethical for any public employee to use her public trust for personal advantage, even if she breaks no laws? What specific elements would you include in a fair and effective revolving door law? Would any such law prevent both government and private business from acquiring the experts they need to provide valuable public services?

It may well be impossible to write a law that satisfies all requirements of fairness while preventing abuse of one's office. While laws can complement and encourage ethical behavior, they cannot replace it. But, as in the example of abusive recruiting, the highest administrative levels must take the lead in reforming the ethical climate. Exempting themselves, at both the legislative and administrative levels, from the rules that they apply to lower level employees is not a good place to start.

## PLAUSIBLE AMBIGUITY

The Abu Ghraib prison scandal in Iraq is notorious enough that we need not linger on its details. Nevertheless, some aspects of the situation deserve our attention. The first is the issue of miscommunication, which some might dismiss as ethically insignificant. The most important issue may be who gave the most authoritative order to threaten and demean the prisoners. That issue aside, communication, in itself, has ethical aspects.

Let us suppose (perhaps falsely) that the entire incident was a result of mistaken communication. Perhaps an order to do whatever can be done to extract information was misunderstood to suggest harsher measures than those intended. The person who gave the order might argue that "whatever can be done" entailed only actions that are within the bounds of civilized ethical standards. Perhaps the order was altered in translation to one subordinate after another, so that the prison guards thought that they were obeying instructions that were never issued. As a result, people were abused and humiliated, but no one was truly to blame—unless miscommunication is a blameworthy offense.

But miscommunication, in some instances, is blameworthy. Any form of negligence is culpable if it should have been avoided. A doctor who scribbles a prescription is blameworthy when the patient suffers an overdose. The doctor cannot merely say, "It was not my fault; I just didn't write as clearly as I thought." Carelessness can be fatal.

Yet there may be more than negligence at issue in the Abu Ghraib case. Some of those in the communication chain, including, perhaps, those who issued the initial orders, may have believed that any form of abuse was justified if it would reveal life-saving information. One might argue that such abuse would be proper if it could prevent another 9/11-like attack. Ambiguous orders may have been considered to be an ideal means of accomplishing a worthy goal while protecting everyone in the chain of command.

It would be inappropriate to conclude, without any more evidence than we currently have, that any of the people involved in the Abu Ghraib affair were intentionally ambiguous. But the issue presents some provocative questions. If you were an advisor to the Secretary of Defense and believed, on strong but uncertain evidence, that torture and humiliation of the prisoners stood a good chance of preventing a mass terrorist attack, would you recommend that he issue an ambiguous order intended to be construed as justifying brutal treatment? If so, would you suggest that he signal his true intent to those who would carry his instructions? Would such an order be ethically wrong? What better alternatives would have been open to him? What would happen to a nation's defense system, including its intelligence operations, if no one ever lied or intentionally misled?

## THE ELEGANT OUTHOUSE

John Stossel (2004) provides another example of ethically questionable behavior that becomes part of routine business in a public organization. A national park in Pennsylvania constructed an outhouse at the expense of $330,000. Although it had no running water, the outhouse had a gabled roof, cobblestone masonry, a porch, and a window. While the gables, masonry, and the porch added to the aesthetics of the sanitary facility, the reason for windows in an outhouse is unclear. The park officials claimed that the cost of the structure was in keeping with local real estate and construction costs, but a nearby 15-room "beautifully restored" home cost about the same as the outhouse did.

Stossel's inquiries did not dissuade the Parks Department. After he publicized the case, the Parks Department proceeded to build, in Montana, an outhouse that could accommodate four users at a time, at a cost of one million dollars.

One can easily imagine how an organization can become so cavalier with public funds. The funds belong to no one in particular, organizations use such funds to finance their activities, and the overseers of the funding process are so entrenched in the customary practice that they notice no ethical breach. People who would never steal a dime for themselves thus become unconscious accomplices in organizational misuse of public money. Many people with impeccable personal integrity would feel guilty, ironically, in questioning the ethical climate of an organization to which they feel great loyalty and to whose goals they are fully committed. It is thus not surprising that the Pennsylvania park officials whom Stossel confronted seemed unembarrassed by the affair.

We can also see, in the case of the elegant outhouses, how an insufficiently considered teleology can become ultimately self-defeating. One can imagine that, at the early stages, park officials probably reasoned that the public would be served by attractive, useful, and environmentally sound facilities. No one could estimate the costs precisely, so it would be better to overstate them than to have to make innumerable requests for additional funding. Moreover, most budgeting in public agencies is on a "use it or lose it" basis, so the organization would be well advised to justify as high a budget as possible. The ends truly seem to justify the means, even if some exaggeration is involved. Most of the reasoning leading to ultimate gross abuse of public funds is well-meaning and reasonable, at least within the climate of public funding.

But while the short-term reasoning is teleological, the long-term consequences can contradict the teleological concern for society's best interests. The specifics of the outhouse case and the recruiting case are different, but the underlying process of ethical erosion is similar. For entire public organizations, the line between the ethical and the unethical is blurred. The organization therefore ceases to serve the people to its fullest capacity.

The problem of blurred ethical lines can become systemic. In most of the cases we have considered, we examined individual ethical decisions. But when there is a general ethical breakdown in the overall culture of public service, broader questions need to be addressed. In your opinion, to what degree is each of the following responsible for the general ethical tenor of the public sector: the public worker; the public administrator; the legislative branch of government; the executive branch; the citizenry? In each case, what, if anything, can the members of those groups do, both collectively and individually, to ensure a responsible public service?

## CRIMINAL NEGLIGENCE?

At what point does institution-wide negligence become a criminal offense? According to a Government Accountability Office report, the Pentagon has committed innumerable major clerical errors in the course of the Iraq war (www.nola .com/news/t-p/frontpage/index.ssf?/base/news-1/109040030 564230.xml). These errors include 1.2 million dollars worth of war material lost, mistaken sale of equipment that could be used to make biological weapons, Internet sale of chemical warfare suits worth $200 each for $3 each, and failure to collect millions of dollars from insurance companies. The Pentagon had to pay outside employees to fix errors that it had committed in the year 2002 alone.

The errors are comical, until one realizes that they are the culmination of many of the problems that we have noted: negligence; miscommunication; lax oversight; insufficient concern for public funds; and habitual abuses that become systemic. Most shockingly, all these abuses occurred in the course of fighting a war. If it is difficult for people to keep their minds on what they are doing in a case of such urgency, one must wonder how lax people are in organizations far removed from matters of life and death.

Is carelessness a concern in your organization? If so, can you think of strategies that administrators might use to combat it?

## CYBERSEX AT THE SECURITIES AND EXCHANGE COMMISSION

In late April 2010, David Kotz, the Inspector General (IG) of the Securities and Exchange Commission (SEC), issued a report on his investigations of senior staffers who spent hours surfing pornographic websites on government computers instead of meeting their responsibilities for policing the nation's financial system. Between 2005 and 2010, the IG conducted 33 investigations of employees and contractors; 31 of those investigations occurred during the period of the national financial crisis. While the number of employees implicated in these investigations was less than one percent of the SEC's total staff, 17 were senior officials, including accountants and attorneys.

Media coverage of Kotz's report tended to focus on the viewing and downloading of pornographic websites. Congressional reactions included the comments of Representative Darrell Issa, the ranking Republican on the House Committee on Oversight and Government Reform, who said it was "disturbing that high-ranking officials within the SEC were spending more time looking at porn than taking action to help stave off the events that put our nation's economy on the brink of collapse." (*Los Angeles Times*, April 23, 2010).

Despite the SEC's claim that the IG's report is old news and that reforms have been instituted within the agency, this case raises a number of significant questions concerning moral agency and moral competence in the public service. Indeed, if the IG's report is old news, these questions are even more salient.

It is unclear whether every SEC employee who searched the web for pornography was investigated, so blanket condemnation of the agency is unwarranted. At the same time, however, we do know that, like other government organizations, the SEC provides on-line computer training, which includes the do's and don'ts of using government computers and the Internet. Considering the agency's surveillance and filtering system, the presence of supervisors and IT staff, and the fact that employees surfing the Internet for pornography is not new in either government or the private sector, we wonder about the breadth of this problem.

Whether SEC employees were viewing pornography, playing games, or checking stock prices, they violated not only agency policies and government-wide ethics rules but also their fiduciary responsibility as public servants. Although viewing pornography may be regarded as more egregious a violation than playing games or checking stock prices, the central question is twofold: (1) How did senior public officials come to occupy a place in which unprofessional, even reckless, behavior superseded their obligations as morally competent agents? and (2) How did the SEC's internal oversight processes either fail to detect or ignore such behavior prior to involvement of the Inspector General?

Pornography sites are notorious for implanting malware or viruses; thus, these SEC employees put at risk the agency's computer network as well as financial and personal information. In short, the agency culture and management allowed a situation in which public resources were stolen and the public interest was debased.

One of the complicating factors in efforts to create and cultivate ethical organizations is that most of us believe that we are already ethical; in the public sector, what more proof does one need than the fact that administrators obey the rules? Yet, in the SEC case, a number of officials did not obey the rules. Senior accountants and attorneys, as well as IT staff, supervisors, and managers, apparently lacked a sense of themselves as public servants and therefore failed in their obligations both as professionals and as morally competent agents. How they rationalized their behavior, how they explained themselves to their families, friends, and colleagues, and how they would explain themselves to citizens might provide important insights into their particular ethical styles.

## LEAKS IN THE SHIP OF STATE

In 1971, the Vietnam War was lingering and the American public was confused and polarized on whether the war should continue. Some objected to the war on moral grounds, while others favored the war as a means of opposing the aggression of Communist states, such as the Soviet Union and China. At that time, a military analyst, Dr. Daniel Ellsberg, was in possession of top secret documents that displayed the administration's lack of confidence that the war could be won (Apple 1996) and questioned the validity of the rationale for the war. Ellsberg leaked the papers, which were subsequently published and almost certainly had some influence on the erosion of public support for the war.

The United States Supreme Court eventually ruled that newspapers could publish the documents (*New York Times* 1971). But Dr. Ellsberg's ethical decision to release them is a separate matter from that of the newspapers' right to publish them thereafter.

Should Dr. Ellsberg have taken upon himself the discretion of determining whether top secret information was to be protected? If he released some information relevant to the war, was he under a moral obligation to reveal all the relevant documents, in their entirety, so that the public would have a complete view of the situation? Could the general public, without relying on the competence of military and international experts, properly evaluate the documents, even in their entirety? In releasing the documents, did Ellsberg act as a moral agent, i.e., someone acting with morality as his or her motive? If so, was Ellsberg on ethically stronger ground than those who kept their word to maintain the confidentiality of the documents? What criteria should be used to determine when someone privy to top secret information is ethically permitted or even obligated to release it?

In 2006, the Iraq war was in progress. With increasing doubt over the question of whether weapons of mass destruction would ever be found, the public was becoming increasingly skeptical and weary. From the standpoint of those committed to the war, it was not a good time for unfavorable information concerning the war effort to appear. But the *New York Times* printed leaked classified information suggesting that the war was fomenting radicalism against the United States (Mazzatti 2006). The leaked material included information that was more negative than anything the government had released.

The Bush administration considered the leak to be unfairly selective, as information in the report that may have been more charitable to the war effort was not included. In response, the

Bush administration declassified much of the report, keeping some of it classified for national security reasons (Associated Press 2006).

Here again we are confronted with a number of ethical issues. Should the *Times* have revealed both the favorable and unfavorable information to the public? Was the Bush administration's response—declassifying information for its own benefit—appropriate?

In 2010, the Obama administration appeared ineffective in preventing Iran from pursuing a nuclear weapons program. At a time when confidence in the administration's ability to handle the problem was weakening, the *New York Times* leaked information suggesting that the administration's own Defense Secretary, Robert Gates, may have been uncomfortable with the situation. According to the *Times* account, the administration had no effective long-range strategy to respond to Iran's possible development into a nuclear threat (Sanger and Shanker 2010). While Gates may have been quoted correctly, his statements expressed an opinion that may not have been shared by all involved in decision making regarding the issue.

Many of the same questions can be asked in this case as in the previous leak cases. Should a member of the administration have leaked the information? Is selective leaking potentially misleading? If there is no negative consequence for leaking information, in what sense can any information be considered confidential? What are the long-term consequences of leaking?

## MUST I REALLY TELL YOU WHY I DID IT?

In 2006, the Bush administration fired several United States attorneys. The attorneys serve at the pleasure of the President, so he was within his rights to fire them. Other presidents had also exercised such discretion. A report later concluded that political considerations played an important role in the firing (Kravitz 2008).

Let us suppose that the firings were legal and that the administration was under no legal requirement to give reasons for them. The ethical questions remain, however. Legal or not, is it ethical to fire attorneys for political reasons? Is an administration morally obligated to be open and therefore to give reasons for such firings, even if the reasons are legally permissible?

On Election Day 2008, some members of the New Black Panthers were accused of voter intimidation. One of them allegedly said, "You are about to be ruled by the black man, cracker!" (Fund 2009) The "black man" to whom the New Black Panther allegedly referred was Barack Obama, who was elected president that evening. The Justice Department filed a civil lawsuit against the New Black Panthers under the 1965 Voting Rights Act. The New Black Panthers were accused of intimidating voters with weapons and racial slurs.

The defendants neither responded to the charges nor appeared in court, so a guilty verdict was virtually certain. However, the Justice Department, under President Obama's Attorney General Eric Holder, failed to prosecute two of the defendants and took relatively light action against the third.

The Justice Department has not explained its failure to prosecute the case fully. Furthermore, Justice has refused to allow its attorneys to appear before the United States Commission on Civil Rights, which is charged with investigating voter intimidation.

Although the cases of the firings of the U.S. attorneys and the refusal to prosecute the New Black Panthers are different in many ways, some similar questions may be asked. Under the assumption that Attorney General Holder is not legally required to prosecute, does he nevertheless have a moral obligation to do so? Is the Justice Department acting unethically if its decision is made on partisan political grounds? Should the Attorney General's office explain its refusal to prosecute?

The cases involving the attorneys general bear some resemblance to the cases of leaking. In both sets of cases, public officials may be caught between openness in the public interest and obedience to an organization. While few public administrators will be faced with such dramatic instances of leaking or of complicity in unwarranted secrecy, the conflict between public interest and organizational interest is a serious concern that manifests itself in a wide range of cases.

Several of the cases that we have considered are political in nature. Developing a strong ethical style requires making decisions on impartial, unbiased grounds. If you found yourself consistently supporting one political party or administration, you might consider whether bias has influenced your ethical style.

## LIVING IN STYLE—ETHICALLY

In this chapter we have been using examples to help you identify your ethical style. Ethical styles are impossible to characterize in a simple formulation because they are as complex and as individual as people themselves. The most that we can do is to arrive at some broad generalizations about ethical styles.

There are two basic aspects of ethical styles: content and process. The content includes one's ethical beliefs, values, and commitments, and the reasoning behind one's ethical conclusions. The process is the sequence of behaviors, thoughts, emotions, and psychological events that occurs when one makes an ethical decision. The process is the more difficult to describe because so much of it occurs at a deep psychological level. Nevertheless, it is possible to make some general, superficial observations concerning the process.

When people consider ethical issues, they may begin in very different ways. Some people, for example, may begin very egocentrically, focusing on the issues that they can relate to their own life and preparing to justify their own past behavior. Others may consider a case and react initially in an emotional manner to injustice, inconsideration, benevolence, or some other feature of the case. Still others may begin in a cool, analytic manner.

But, as in a chess game, the opening move may reveal little about the ultimate result. The person who begins egocentrically may settle into a pattern in which she gradually becomes impartial and insightful; the emotional person may proceed to a stage of justifying his emotions, and finally to a principled analysis; and the person who begins coolly and analytically may become frustrated and frantic midway through the process.

From the standpoint of the strength of the ultimate ethical conclusion, the process of one's ethical style matters little, so long as the content of the ethical style is strong.

What, then, is the ideal content of an ethical style? From our earlier discussion concerning the unified ethic, we can infer two conclusions concerning this question. First, the ideal content of an ethical style would include all of the factors in the unified ethic, including teleology, deontology, virtue theory, and intuitionism. We discussed the ideal ethical style in Chapter 4, when we studied examples and systematically considered them from all perspectives. But try as we might to consider all of those perspectives impartially and rationally, we are all different and cannot help but favor one perspective over another. Consequently, few people, if any, are so systematic, impartial, and patient as to express the ideal content of an ideal ethical style.

The second conclusion that we can derive from the unified ethic is that the content of one's ethical style need not be ideal to reach strong ethical conclusions. The unified ethic suggested that any one or any combination of the four basic theories will lead in the same ultimate direction. Furthermore, the unified ethic would suggest that, since the four are not really independent but interdependent, analysis from one perspective will inevitably lead to analysis from the other perspectives. They complement each other rather than compete.

Our message is therefore that, so long as you develop your ethical style fully, it can be any one of a number of possible styles and be just as good, when taken to its highest level. But before taking it to its highest level, one must discover what one's ethical style is. The cases that we have discussed are intended to help you in that process of discovery, but we will now ask some questions to further that process.

In uncovering your ethical style you might consider the following questions regarding moral issues. Only you can answer them, so, depending upon the answers that you give, you will be able to infer at least some aspects of your ethical style.

1. Do you generally favor obedience to principles over other factors?

2. Regardless of your answer to Question 1, when you do take principles into account, which do you consider most important (e.g., always be fair to people, treat people as equals, always be honest, give as much as you can)?

3. Do you consider people's happiness more important than any other factor?

4. Regardless of your answer to Question 3, when you do take happiness into account, what factors do you consider most important in happiness (e.g., material possessions, physical health, mental health, a good conscience, close relationships, a sense of achievement)?

5. Do you consider the virtues and vices that are expressed in people's actions more important than any other factors?

6. Regardless of your answer to Question 5, when you do take character into account, what factors do you consider most important in character (e.g., honesty, benevolence, courage, perseverance, personal loyalty, professional loyalty, personal warmth)?

7. Do you rely on your intuitive feelings more than any other factor?

8. Regardless of your answer to Question 7, when you do take your intuitive feelings into account, what factors generally influence them most (e.g., sympathy for others, respect for people's good traits, the general personalities of the people involved in the case)?

These questions are based upon the four basic ethical theories that we have discussed. The odd numbered questions refer to your tendency in general to be deontological, teleological, virtue theorist, or intuitive. The even numbered questions examine the importance that you place on the factors from each of those four categories.

After answering the questions as best you can, review your responses to the many cases that we have discussed in this book. Are those responses consistent with the responses that you gave to the above questions? If they are, you can congratulate yourself for knowing yourself quite well. If they are not consistent, then you must ask whether your answers to the above questions indicate what you really believe and feel or only what you think you believe and feel.

Answers to the even numbered questions are very open ended. They ask you to designate all of the factors that you consider important. To answer them completely would probably be an endless task. But suppose that you could answer them completely by stating everything that is important to you. Furthermore, suppose there was a measuring device or method enabling you to indicate the relative importance that you place on each factor. For example, as impossible as it may seem, suppose that one could designate that one factor was, say, 1.34 times as important as another. If you could accurately list all of the things that are important to you, together with their relative importance, you would have a description of all that you value and how much you value it. You would have before you an account of your entire value structure.

That value structure is, for the most part, your personality. By "personality," we do not mean an extroverted or engaging manner, as one might mean in saying that someone has "a lot of personality." Instead, we use the word to mean the collection of traits that constitute a person's individual identity. From your value structure, which determines your personality in the sense that we use the term, one could infer such factors as your professional and personal priorities, the choices that you would make, the people whom you admire, those with whom you are most compatible, and those with whom you would most clash.

If you were to compare your answers to the above eight questions to those of others, you would discover how your personality differed from theirs. Your ethical style is, in effect, your personality brought to bear on ethical issues. We earlier suggested that there is no simple formulation to describe one's ethical style, and now one can see why there is none: Ethical styles are personalities, and there are no simple formulations to describe personalities fully.

As our unified ethic has suggested, there is no reason to believe that any single ethical style is inherently better than any other. Each person can function within his or her ethical style to arrive at sound ethical conclusions because there are numerous routes up the ethical mountain. More important than choosing the "right" or "ideal" ethical style is the refinement and development of one's own ethical style by means of increasing experiences, real or imagined, of an ethical nature and increasingly deeper thinking about those experiences.

Our unified ethic would also suggest that different ethical styles are welcome in an organization. Rather than cause discord, the differing ethical styles—in that they are founded on the same unified ethic—will complement each other.

When there is unanimity or at least consensus among the ethical styles in an organization, a sound ethical position is strongly indicated. When there is disagreement, however, the concept of a unified ethic would call for an attempt to find unity in the diversity. Each person's ethical style would be contrasted with others initially, but rather than remain rigid and uncompromising, as a pure teleologist or a pure deontologist would, the unified ethic would call for a mutual flexibility to find a common meeting point. That flexibility should not be viewed as weakness but as open-mindedness.

There will always be cases in which people ultimately disagree, but the instances of them will be fewer under the acceptance of a unified ethic and of differing ethical styles. And even in those cases in which the minds do not entirely meet, they will likely come closer together.

# CHAPTER 10

# Addressing Public Ethical Conflict by Means of the Unified Ethic

In this chapter, we discuss ethical conflicts of two kinds. First, we discuss the apparent conflict between public and private morality. Some scholars, such as Bernard Williams (1978), argue that public morality and private morality are entirely different moral systems with no common foundation. Such a position would contradict the unified ethic, according to which all ethics forms a single, complex structure. We argue, together with other scholars such as Thomas Nagel (1978), that the alleged conflict between distinct moral systems is, in reality, a conflict between differing values within one moral system. We examine several kinds of apparent conflict between public and private morality and argue that they can be rendered consistent with the unified ethic.

The second part of the chapter addresses another ethical conflict of concern to the public servant and perhaps more relevant to the professional life of the public administrator: the conflict between different conscientiously held ethical perspectives within public organizations. Such ethical conflicts are inevitable and frequently irresolvable. The unified ethic offers no formula to settle them all smoothly and without dissent. The unified ethic can, however, offer a framework that facilitates reasonable responses.

We recommend that public organizations support policy and procedure decisions with written ethical analyses. The analyses would have many of the features of Carol Lewis' (1991) Ethics Impact Statements and would employ the unified ethic. We also suggest that such statements accompany actions taken at higher levels of government, including the legislative and executive branches, although we do not consider those branches as likely to do so as are organizations within public administration.

## CONFLICTS BETWEEN PRIVATE AND PUBLIC MORALITY

The problem of conflict between a public official's private moral commitments and the public interest has troubled scholars since the earliest works of literature. The conflict is noted in the *Iliad*, forms the context of Aeschylus' *Oresteia*, and is the main subject of Sophocles' *Antigone*. In modern political theory, it is often characterized as the problem of "dirty hands" (Sartre, 1948). Examples of the problem of dirty hands include that of the head of state who must lie, despite his private belief in total honest disclosure, to protect highly sensitive information. In another example, a social worker recognizes a personal moral obligation to provide funds to an impoverished family but must deny them to keep the agency's budget in balance.

Such conflicts have often been interpreted as oppositions of two distinct and incompatible moral systems, one public and the other private. Some ethicists regard the opposition as so irreconcilable that the moral characters of the private individual and the public official should be different to conform to the different systems to which each is subject (Williams 1978). Under such an interpretation, the head of state and the social worker must choose between two separate moral structures, one private and one public, with no common foundation.

Such a dichotomy between public and private morality contradicts our concept of the unified ethic, which encompasses different conclusions and different styles but subsumes them under the same moral framework. Our enhanced unified ethic is not a combining of a distinct professional ethic with a private morality but the application of one moral structure within the context of professional obligations, which sometimes may be overridden if the ethic so demands.

We maintain that such cases can best be understood, as Thomas Nagel (1978) suggests, as conflicts of values within one moral system. Under our interpretation, the public official would not be in a conflict between two moral systems, one public and the other private. Echoing Nagel (90), we maintain that a public official is, by virtue of his or her office, burdened with special responsibilities that he or she must include in the same moral system that would have been adopted even without the additional burden. We argue that one morality is applicable in both public and private affairs. The apparent difference is not in moral systems but in the additional factors that a public official must consider by virtue of the responsibilities of public service.

We further argue that the moral values of both the public official and the private individual are unified in that both share the designation of moral citizen. As such, the values of both should be compatible and the moral character of both should be essentially the same.

To examine the ramifications, let us suppose that there are two incompatible systems for public officials and private individuals. Consider, for example, the case of a public official forced to lie to protect secret, critical peace negotiations from exposure. Under the supposition of incompatibility, the official would have no criterion for choosing between a private morality that demands that the truth be told and a public morality that demands that the public interest be served. The two distinct systems would each provide its own justification for action using its own reasoning and assumptions. Since the systems would share no common structure of reasoning and assumptions, the arguments of one would not be compelling for the other.

Unless there were a third system, compatible with both, there would be no means of favoring the conclusions of one over the conclusions of the other. But such a "third system" would not, in fact, be a distinct third system but a single one encompassing the other two, as the unified ethic encompasses seemingly distinct ethical aspects (Nagel 79).

The alleged dichotomy between public and private morality also overlooks the importance of private moral convictions in justifying the legitimacy of governmental action. For example, let us suppose that a society is convinced that its best financial interests would be served by the military takeover of a small, powerless nation. Would the public official then be required by the conditions of his office to follow the public's wishes? If our theory is correct, the answer could be negative.

We maintain that the obligation to act in the public interest derives from a prior, more fundamental moral based in the unified ethic. That ethic, because it is more fundamental, would bind the public official more than would public opinion. If he were to ignore it, he would also undermine the basis of any obligation that he had to the public, since that ultimate moral foundation would provide the justification for all obligations. It would therefore be incoherent for him to claim that his moral obligation to the public necessarily overrode his obligation to the more fundamental obligation, whence his obligation to the public derives.

We do not imply here that the public official must always ignore the will of the public in exercising moral judgment. If government receives its legitimacy by consent of the governed, public officials are morally obligated to take the collective wishes of society into account. The public official may, in some instances, consider her own moral judgment to be more compelling than the will of the people, but in other instances defer to their will.

For example, a legislator who personally opposes abortion may vote in favor of a pro-choice measure that is strongly supported by her constituents. She may consider her obligation to adhere to the wishes of her constituents paramount in this case.

In another case, however, the same legislator may vote against her constituents' will. She may, for example, oppose capital punishment even though her constituents favor it. In this case, she may consider capital punishment so morally abhorrent as to override her obligation to the public will.

In either case, the public official must consult her own moral convictions to determine whether the public's beliefs or her own beliefs on an issue have the stronger moral claim (Nagel, 90). Whatever her decision, it is based upon moral reasoning that attempts to balance different values within one overall moral structure. If there were no such structure, she would have no basis upon which to decide.

The issue of private and public morality is clouded by ambiguity in the notion of the public interest: It may not be, and often is not, the same as the public believes it to be. History contains innumerable cases of societies that willfully take action that they eventually regret. But perhaps more importantly, the notion of the interest of the people may include more than their material welfare or even their moral commitments as they understand them. If the public is morally ignorant or perverse, the public official may decide that he has moral stewardship, and that his moral judgment is better grounded than theirs. He may then conclude that he has the moral responsibility to make moral judgments for a society that has judged poorly.

The issue of the relation of private to public morality also emerges in the judiciary. Suppose, for instance, that a judge privately rejects capital punishment but finds herself having to issue a death sentence in accordance with the law as she best interprets it. While she has discretion, she understands the intent of the law as requiring the death sentence in this case. If she imposes the death sentence, is she acting publicly morally but privately immorally? If she refuses to impose the death sentence, is she acting publicly immorally and privately morally?

There is no need for such dichotomous parsing. Although the case is a difficult one that we will not resolve here, the judge should be best and most simply understood as balancing her legal obligation against her belief in the sanctity of life to reach a morally correct overall decision.

The conflict between private and public morality is not restricted to cases in which a public official imposes or considers imposing private morality on public policy. There are also cases in which the public interest threatens to overrule the private morality of individuals. For example, our case of the overweight assessor of food handling may be interpreted as asserting individual rights against a society that seeks to protect itself from the cost of compensating for someone who has the temerity to die of a heart attack while on the public payroll. The union that seeks better working conditions for public employees may also be seen as favoring the moral rights of individuals to a good living over the interests of the general public.

Power relationships may resolve such issues by an appeal to force rather than an appeal to morality. Those in positions of power may dispute that it was the sole determinant in the moral decision and claim that ethics was the true victor. To that effect, they may argue that, since they believe themselves to be morally correct, there is no conflict between might and right; both, they would assert, are on the same side. However, what is needed in such cases is a higher order ethical analysis.

At one level, one decides what one considers to be morally correct on a particular issue. But at another level, the higher order, one must decide whether to impose his or her moral beliefs upon others. Even when someone is correct at the lower level, he or she may be incorrect at the higher level. The ethical organization must function at both levels and balance them against each other within a comprehensive ethical perspective.

We must also consider cases of civil disobedience. In acting against a duly executed and popularly accepted public policy, an accomplice in the Underground Railroad helps southern slaves escape to Canada. Those who would dichotomize private and public morality may be tempted to argue that the agent is acting morally from a private standpoint and immorally from a public standpoint in opposing the publicly supported law. We argue that the agent is not under two different systems that contradict each other but that he is under one moral system with conflicting moral claims. In this case, however, the conflict between the claims is easy to adjudicate. His actions are morally correct, pure and simple, when all factors are taken into consideration.

The moral values of an organization, rather than only an individual, may also clash with the public interest (as the public understands it). The city of Austin, Texas, hired the administrators of Seton Hospital, a Catholic institution, to run the financially troubled public hospital. A problem arose, however, because Seton, following church doctrine but not the will of the people of Austin, refuses to perform abortions. The doctrine of separation of church and state is ambiguous on this issue. The city may argue that the doctrine prohibits imposition of religious values on the public, but the hospital administration may argue, on equally plausible grounds, that the city would be in violation of the doctrine of separation in compelling a religious organization to violate its principles at the city's demand.

While the conflict is, in one respect, between the public interest and the moral convictions of an organization, individuals ultimately make decisions within the organization. If the city prevails, some individuals would be required to perform acts against their consciences. The city's position represents the public's understanding of its own interest, but the hospital argues that it must be true to its principles even if the public overwhelmingly rejects them.

Once again, the conflict need not be understood as an opposition of two incompatible moral systems: a private, religious system and a public system. If such were the case, the issue could only be decided by an imposition of one perspective on people who do not share it. The hospital administration does not accept abortion as a moral practice; in addition to that judgment, however, the administrators must make another judgment. They must ask, "Given both our perspective on abortion and our obligation to the city, what is the right thing to do?" They may decide against providing abortions, but their reasoning process must take their civic responsibility into account. Likewise, the city must ask "What should we do, given not only our responsibility to the residents of the city but also our consideration for the moral convictions of our partners?"

Both sides must include consideration of the other's position as part of their moral reasoning. If they do, they can reach accommodation if not total agreement.

The Bill of Rights in the United States Constitution acknowledges the possibility of conflict between private individuals or groups and the interests of society. The rights included in those ten amendments are not intended to promote the general welfare but to protect those whose inalienable rights are threatened by the interests of society as a whole. The constitution appears to recognize the rights as founded in deontology rather than teleology.

In a broader sense, the conflict implicit in the Bill of Rights suggests the overall teleology-deontology conflict. For example, Terry Cooper (1998) mentions a case in a new law passed in a large western state permitting people with no hope of recovery to die naturally rather than be kept alive against their wishes. For patients to avail themselves of the option of ending their lives, two physicians had to declare that the patient was terminally ill. However, the policy conflicted with the professional values of physicians, who are trained to keep people alive. According to Cooper, "the new act was attempting to get physicians to do something that was inconsistent with the values and norms that they had internalized through medical training and practice, and which would expose them to malpractice litigation in the courts" (186).

We can assume that at least some of the doctors would have refused on the basis of their own moral conviction, even without the threat of court action. If so, the conflict was between the teleological concern to avoid misery and the deontological prohibition against taking a life.

We are now on familiar ground. As we mentioned in Chapter 3, the distinction between teleology and deontology fades upon close examination. If the alleged distinction between public and private morality reduces to that between teleology and deontology, both distinctions dissolve together. In this case, both the seemingly teleological, public concern to relieve suffering and the deontological, private requirement to protect human life derive from the same source, which has both teleological and deontological aspects. The source is the recognition that people are ends in themselves. The question that must be answered is whether respect for people as ends in themselves requires preserving their lives or ending their misery. The answer, according to our analysis of the unified ethic, depends on one's overall judgment concerning how the teleological, deontological, intuitive, and character-based aspects apply in each individual case. The seemingly opposed values are, again, subsumable under one ethical structure.

## CONSCIENTIOUS MORAL CONFLICT WITHIN ORGANIZATIONS

Having put aside the illusory conflict between private and public morality, we now turn our attention to conflicts that occur within the public sector. These conflicts arise between people who have differing conscientiously held moral opinions on issues that affect policy and procedure. Moral conflicts of this kind can occur in any organization, no matter how professionally it is run. Among those issues today are questions regarding policies on diversity, insensitive language, and the rights of parents deemed unsuitable by social agencies. The unified ethic allows for disagreements on such matters because it provides a means of thinking about ethical issues rather than a formula that ensures universal agreement. While the unified ethic cannot decide such issues definitively, it can provide a framework within which they can be analyzed.

Conscientious, honest moral conflict can occur at several levels in public agencies. For example, it can occur between a member of the organization and a superior. The conflict between Milo, the faculty member who wanted a leave, and the dean who denied it was such a case, though it ended relatively felicitously. Such conflicts also occur when a supervisor and a lower level decision maker differ on allocation of funds, hiring, or long-term planning. Morally, might does not make right, but practically, might usually makes policy. Nevertheless, the ethical organization is not content merely to settle an issue but seeks to resolve it in the best possible manner. In the organization that takes the moral high road, right has substantial might.

A second type of moral conflict arises when different individuals of roughly equal power in an organization hold different ethical perspectives. We considered such conflicts in the cases of the questionable hire, the resolution to the problem of the illegal strike, and the termination decision that developed from the strike case. In these instances, people of equal status disagreed in the process of making a decision with ethical implications. Such cases are often decided by a method that reaches a conclusion but does not necessarily make the moral weight of arguments central to the decision. They include appealing to a committee majority, referring the matter to a higher organizational level, and reaching a compromise that partially satisfies the conflicting parties. A decision is thus made on the basis of an accepted procedure but not necessarily on moral grounds. Such decisions may be facile, popular, and easily implemented but, nevertheless, they are ethically flawed.

A conflict of a broader sort can occur when a member of an organization engages in a moral conflict with the organization as a whole. An interesting case of such a conflict within a private organization occurred between AT&T Broadband and one of its employees (http://washingtontimes.com/national/20040407-124312-3261r.htm). The employee objected on religious grounds to a statement requiring that all members of the organization "recognize, respect, and value" differences, including differences in sexual orientation. He was terminated for refusing to sign the statement. We can assume that the employee was a devoutly religious person with honorably intended convictions, regardless of what we may think of them. We can also assume that AT&T was responding to its own moral commitments.

The judge in the case ruled in favor of the employee. Although the conflict occurred within the context of a private organization, similar conflicts in public organizations are certainly conceivable.

## THE UNIFIED ETHIC IN POLICY DEVELOPMENT AND IN ORGANIZATIONAL ETHICAL LITERATURE

Moral conflict will never be eliminated: People have different views of morality, and they will inevitably clash. Rather than attempt to eliminate such conflicts, we will propose procedures that anticipate them and reduce their disruptiveness. The procedures will not aim simply at achieving moral consensus but at allowing deeply held and morally tenable positions to be presented and treated respectfully. Imposing a moral policy merely on the basis of a consensus is moral tyranny of the majority. Such an approach decides a moral issue on the basis of a non-moral reason: that it is favored by most of the people in a group. Sometimes the consensus is wrong. Sometimes, as in the Confederate States of America or in the segregationist South of the 1950s, the consensus is very wrong.

Moral values inescapably enter into policy decisions in any organization, but especially and most significantly in public organizations. Rather than be buried, the moral aspects of policy should be explicitly justified in an organization that claims to be ethical. In making policy, organizations should routinely include ethical analysis in distinctly identifiable sections of policy statements. Thus, not only the practical and professional but also the moral commitments of an organization will be clear to all, including stakeholders, employees, and the general public.

Ideally, such ethical analysis should be included in the legislative process. If congressional debates and inclusions in the congressional record contained discussions specifically addressing the ethical aspects of legislation, the general public would be made aware of the ethical foundations of legislative actions. Furthermore, a legislative emphasis on ethics sets a tone for the entire nation, including private corporations. While it is difficult to measure the impact of leadership by example, there is little doubt of its influence. Nonetheless, it is unlikely that any legislature, state or federal, would encumber itself with such a requirement. Legislators are better at imposing burdens upon others than upon themselves.

Systematic, explicit inclusion of ethics in decision making may be more feasible within public organizations, where models have already been proposed. Among the most notable is Carol Lewis' Ethics Impact Statement (EthIS) (1991), a seven-step procedure to ensure that the ethical aspects of policy are fully examined and seriously implemented. She lists the following aims of EthIS:

> [I]t procedurally secures a role for ethical analysis in agency deliberations, particularly over policies and regulations. Another application is critiquing potent standard operating procedures in the agency. An individual manager can apply the process informally to working through the wrenching dilemma that seems an inevitable part of public service. The design is deliberately slanted toward process rather than outcome because the objective is to integrate systematically ethical analysis into decision making. The goal is to amplify managers' thinking, not usurp it. (186–187)

The first of the five stages is an examination of the feasibility of an ethical action. The second stage considers the likely scope of the ethical analysis, including considerations of the range of actions to be considered and their likely effects. In the third stage, which Lewis describes as tiering, the ethical values under consideration are included within more general ethical core values in public service and within the logical framework already established by relevant precedent. The tiering stage ensures consistency within the organization's ethical framework. The fourth stage includes investigation that entails fact-finding on relevant matters. In the fifth stage, ethical analysis occurs, and the sixth produces recommendations. In the final stage, participants in the EthIs process take responsibility for their recommendations and the process that led to them.

The fifth stage, that of analysis, is crucial to the decision-making process. Lewis describes this stage as follows:

> The EthIS team selects an ethical analytic framework at this stage. Criteria underlying selection are discussed in Chapter Six. A truly momentous issue or having no team consensus calls for the application of several frameworks or one framework that combines different ethical perspectives . . . . (191)

We find the structure of Lewis' impact statement to be impressive and would favor its implementation. Nevertheless, we believe that the account of the fifth stage needs to be supplemented. She suggests that, if team consensus already exists, there may be no need for applying new frameworks or perhaps even for further analysis. But as we have noted, consensus is not always the best means of reaching an ethical conclusion. Only if consensus is based upon good reasons is it authoritative. Moreover, in the case in which consensus is not reached, Lewis recommends applying several frameworks or one overarching framework that combines different ethical perspectives. We caution that such a procedure is dangerous if some of the perspectives are morally flawed.

We do not object to Lewis' inclusion of consensus as an important part of the decision-making process. Rather, we suggest that she has not included enough because she has omitted the ethical thinking process to which the participants should adhere. We suggest supplementing Lewis' structure by including the method we outlined in Chapter 3: applying the unified ethic to analysis of ethical issues. The questions concerning teleology, deontology, virtue theory, and intuitionism could be used to structure the ethical analysis.

In arriving at ethical conclusions, all ethical sides of issues should be expressed and recorded. While the rationale behind the ultimate decision should be stated, including reasoning in favor of alternative positions would permit the fullness of the ethical debate to become part of the record. Perhaps, as in the United

States Supreme Court, both concurring opinions (which agree with conclusions but employ different reasoning) and dissenting opinions could be presented. Over time, the organization would develop a history of ethical thought that could inform later decisions. Each organization would create its own ethical literature and its own ethical precedent. In the process, the organization would develop an ethical style. In the course of the evolution of these organizational ethical traditions, each public organization could refer to and benefit from the experiences of others.

As the ethical literature of an organization emerges in the written records, some of the elements can be included in mission statements, policy statements, and even job descriptions. The ethical literature, which expresses the ethical thinking of the organization over its history, can function as a means of making ethical reasoning systemic.

The results of the process will extend beyond the improvement of ethical decision making, which would in itself be a worthy consequence. The recorded ethical analyses would inform the public of the organization's ethical foundations and commitments. Among the informed would be members and potential members of the organization, who would understand the ethical reasoning to which they must conform. In a more general sense, the concept of the public organization as a moral enterprise with an ethical tradition would emerge.

While we favor Lewis' model, the unified ethic could also be used in the context of other models. For example, the questions generated by our unified ethic are applicable to Terry Cooper's (1998) decision-making model at several levels: defining the ethical issue; identifying alternative courses of action; projecting the probable consequences; and finding a fit, the point at which the ethical conclusion is drawn. The unified ethic questions would also conform to Gerald Gabris' (1991) concept of organization development.

## THE UNIFIED ETHIC AND MORAL CONFLICTS

Inclusion of the unified ethic in decision making and in organizational ethical literature can proactively avoid many moral
problems. One would suppose that if an explicit written ethical
component had been included in policy decisions, many of the
athletic recruitment problems would have been avoided. It is
doubtful that the humiliation of prisoners in Abu Ghraib would
have been justified under an ethical analysis using the unified
ethic. Nor would the sale of body parts for profit likely have been
approved by a university research center.

In addition to avoiding obvious ethical violations, the development of an ethical literature would also obviate some difficult
moral conflicts. If ethical statements had been prepared in the process of developing the law to which Cooper referred, permitting
doctors to end people's lives, the conflict between the proposed
law and accepted medical ethics would have been noted. In the
case of the conflict between Seton Hospital and the City of Austin,
a developed ethical literature in both organizations would have
revealed the problem prior to any agreement to permit Seton to
administer the public hospital. A solution could have been devised before the conflict arose, or, if no solution could be found,
Seton would not have been offered a contract.

The case of the food handling investigator who was required
to meet a weight limit is more complex, because the policy was
developed after she was already employed. Nevertheless, a more
thorough ethical analysis might have suggested several options.
One option would have been simply to avoid such a requirement.
But if the requirement were imposed, despite objections concerning individual rights, the fairness of applying the policy to current employees as well as to new ones would have been refined.

If the policy and its ethical rationale were made explicit,
new employees would be expected to conform to it. However,
existing employees would have joined the organization under

different assumptions, which, in our scenario, would have been stated in the organization's ethical literature. On the basis of the differing explicit ethical assumptions from those imposed upon new employees, existing employees, including the food handling investigator, would have either been exempt or given substantial accommodation. In any event, there would have been forethought—and an extensive written record—behind the ultimate decision.

As reluctant as they may be to do so, legislative bodies would enhance the ethical tone of their proceedings if a separately recorded ethics dialogue accompanied legislation. Ethical aspects are often included within legislative debates but are not accorded separate status whereby the ethical analyses are singled out for special consideration.

The executive branch at the highest levels may also be well advised to issue an ethics impact statement concerning its actions, including legislative proposals and acts specific to executive offices. The impact statements accompanying legislative proposals could be used to initiate ethics debate in the legislature. Impact statements concerning other acts, such as military interventions, would also seem in need of ethical justification.

For example, if the ethical justification for the Iraq war of 2003 had been made explicit, the debate concerning the reasons for military involvement might not have been so vehement after the war was underway. Moreover, if there had been such a debate, there might not have been a war at all. Although there was ethical debate beforehand, it was not presented in one coherent document but in scattered comments by different voices in different times and contexts.

## ETHICAL STATEMENTS BY INDIVIDUALS WITHIN AN ORGANIZATION

Individuals, as well as organizations, may have good reason to present ethics statements concerning their own beliefs. Such statements could be issued under several different circumstances.

In one case, a member of an organization may anticipate conflicts that he or she wishes to address before they arise. For example, a person working in a state's parks and wildlife service may wish to indicate that she refuses, on moral grounds, to participate in any way in the killing of animals. She would therefore likely not be assigned to an agency that oversees fishing and hunting.

In some cases, an employee or potential employee may offer a statement so incompatible with an organization's ethical assumptions that he would be clearly unsuitable as a member. A potential employee, for example, may present a statement so diametrically opposed to an agency's diversity policies that he would not function well within the organization. Such matters could be resolved before a conflict emerges.

But sometimes the conflict cannot be anticipated, as in the case of the AT&T Broadband employee who refused to sign a diversity statement. In such cases, the employee may issue something akin to the request, common in the United States when a military draft was implemented, for conscientious objector status. We refer to such a statement presented within the context of a public organization as an Ethical Conscience Statement (ECS). The individual would present an ECS providing morally based reasons for a substantial ethical disagreement with organizational policy, particularly insofar as it affects his behavior. An organization may be willing to make allowances for people who dissent for worthy reasons.

In many cases, the organization and the individual may reach a mutually satisfactory resolution in which they "agree to disagree." The organization could, in such cases, exempt the individual on grounds of moral conviction. In other cases, termination may be the only option. Regardless, the proper response would be easier to discern if the ethical aspects of the differing positions were presented explicitly in written documents.

Ethics statements from individuals who are unschooled in ethical theory could descend into incoherent verbosity. Consequently, a structure or schema may be needed to ensure that he or she makes the strongest possible case. Here, again, we suggest the unified ethic base structure.

Ultimately, a person or group within an organization must make a final decision concerning ethical conflicts. It is unrealistic to suppose that all decisions will be flawless and uncontroversial. Nevertheless, the presentation of cases of ethical disagreement in a rational format—and evaluation of them by means of the unified ethic—would unquestionably facilitate a reasonable solution.

Disagreement on ethical issues within a public organization is often unpleasant and difficult, if not impossible to resolve. One may be tempted to dismiss many public sector ethical disagreements as conflicts between personal and public morality, but the dichotomy between the public and the private in morality is false. Ethical disagreement often ends either in autocratic imposition of one perspective or in unresolved disputes that leave an organization with no clear ethical standpoint. The latter possibility may lead to a weakening— inappropriate in public administration—of the organization's commitment in the entire ethical enterprise.

Ethical disagreements have an important place in public organizations, and are essential to keeping ethics in the forefront of their activities and their organizational culture. The implementation of the Ethics Impact Statement and the Ethical Conscience Statement allows for ethical disagreement while elevating, rather than reducing, the ethical climate of the organization. We maintain that incorporating the unified ethic into both is essential to their maximal effectiveness.

# CHAPTER 11

# Leadership Development and Moral Agency in Contemporary Governance

A central challenge in contemporary governance is the quiet crisis in human capital: the need to develop and sustain the next generation of leadership in the public service. Driven by demographic changes, as well as strategic, technological, and performance pressures, public officials in a number of nations are grappling with this challenge in a variety of ways. A key, though neglected, element in this challenge is the cultivation of ethical leadership, especially the exercise of moral reasoning, judgment, and discretion.

In this chapter we (1) introduce the literature on leadership in public administration, including ethical leadership; (2) examine leadership development in Organization for Economic Cooperation and Development (OECD) countries; (3) explore the American experience with leadership and leadership development; and (4) propose the unified ethic as a framework for leadership development in general and the development of ethical leadership in particular.

Leadership development, combined with the unified ethic, can enrich succession planning and management by going beyond the simple replacement of individuals, moving toward the strategic positioning of public organizations for the future, and helping align missions and quality. Such positioning and alignment necessarily involve the clarification of values and principles as well as underlying organizational assumptions. Thus, central to this initiative is an effort to reframe organizational cultures and subcultures, including their respective leadership development and decision-making processes, based on adoption of the unified ethic. In conjunction with systematic leadership development, adoption of the unified ethic can be a key element in the global search by public organizations for capacity-building strategies to resolve the quiet crisis, align missions, principles, and quality, and position themselves to deliver public value in a more effective and ethical manner.

## LEADERSHIP

Leadership is central to governance in all polities. It is an essential part of our collective capacity to develop vision and strategy, to formulate, implement, and evaluate policies, to provide stability and continuity, and to deliver services to citizens. Without public leadership, civil society could not be sustained nor could citizens' preferences and needs be satisfied.

The literature on leadership is replete with theoretical approaches, definitions, and expectations. For example, Peter G. Northouse (2001) says that leadership is treated as a trait, a behavior, the focus of group processes, a power relationship between leaders and followers, and an instrument of goal achievement. He views leadership as a process in which an individual influences a group of other individuals to attain a common objective. Thus, leadership is not a trait or characteristic in the leader, but a transactional event between leaders and followers. Leaders and followers affect one another in an interactive, rather than linear, process.

Leadership also has been described as transformational, not merely transactional (Burns 1978). Transactional leaders, according to this formulation, concentrate on technical issues within the boundaries of the status quo, while transformational leaders try to change the status quo, to engage and empower employees, and to encourage communication and growth. The differences may be more apparent than real, however, since proponents of the transactional approach might well support the essentials of the transformational perspective.

Other major themes in leadership literature include the differences and similarities between leadership and management, as well as the demands on leaders amid the pressures and perplexities associated with globalization, technological innovation, environmental issues, privatization, the new public management, and the overriding requirement to manage culture and change.

Despite, or perhaps because of, its complexities, leadership continues to command the attention of both practitioners and scholars. Analysts such as Joseph Rost (1991), Jay Conger (1992), Edgar Schein (1992), Robert Denhardt (1993), Ronald Heifetz (1994), Larry Terry (1995), Ronald Heifetz and Marty Linsky (2002), and Robert Behn (2003) have approached leadership from a variety of perspectives in an attempt to clarify the language of leadership and to promote a more vibrant and valuable leadership conversation.

Part of the language of contemporary leadership revolves around the claim that the world is experiencing a radical transformation—a paradigm shift—in which such established notions as hierarchy, authority, and accountability are undergoing major changes that, in turn, demand changes in established assumptions, practices, and leadership styles. Today, we even hear and read of the need for spirituality, vision, and values in the workplace, and of such concepts as servant leadership.

In general, we can conclude that leadership is many things besides instrumental goal achievement. It involves wisdom, adaptation, conflict resolution, dialogue, influence (rather than coercion), commitment, and community. In short, it involves the continual struggle to make sense of contemporary confusion in the work setting and elsewhere, to reconfigure personal and professional relationships, and to find meaning and purpose in our daily lives. This, in turn, brings us to ethical leadership.

Like leadership in general, ethical leadership can be considered from many angles. But regardless of which perspective we adopt—personal, professional, or political—we are essentially concerned with the character and conduct of present and prospective leaders. We are interested in the virtues that leaders embody in their decisions and actions, and we are attentive to the effect that leaders have on the lives of their followers. Either explicitly or implicitly, we recognize that leadership bears an ethical burden. As Northouse (2001) argues, "ethics is central to leadership because of the nature of the process of influence, the need to engage followers to accomplish mutual goals, and the impact leaders have on establishing the organization's values" (255).

Leadership and ethics, therefore, are inseparable. It is not possible to consider leadership seriously without taking into account its ethical nature.

Nevertheless, the literature on ethical leadership tends to remain at the hortatory level. Although many scholars and others have emphasized the importance of integrity in public administration, for example, the meaning, consequences, and implications of integrity-based organizational or cultural change are either treated without a specific moral framework or ignored altogether.

Some scholars who have written on ethics and leadership, such as William Hitt (1990), seem to believe that the fundamental issues have been resolved, that the requisite commitments and skills are in place, and that linking leadership with ethics is merely a technical task. But, as Denhardt (1993) maintains, "most public organizations have not undertaken active efforts to promote ethical behavior" (242). Most public organizations, in fact, fail to distinguish between the legal and the ethical and thus tend to approach the entire subject from a rules-based perspective.

What is needed to move the public service from a legalistic to an ethical understanding of leadership is a clear moral framework: a normative foundation designed to enhance the critical faculties of public servants, to provide a basis for values clarification and justification, and to promote moral agency in the public interest. Later in this chapter we will sketch such a framework. For now, suffice it to say that ethical leadership in public administration means the capacity and the courage to make hard choices and to explain and justify those choices to legislators, judges, and above all to citizens.

## LEADERSHIP DEVELOPMENT IN OECD COUNTRIES

According to the OECD (2001), leadership development is an increasingly important issue across member countries. A new type of leadership is required in the face of globalization, decentralization, and intensive use of information technology. Policy coherence, negotiating and managing accountability in the midst of privatization, new public management, and other reforms, as well as growing expectations of transparency, adaptability, and flexibility, demand more systematic and sustained attention to the development of a different kind of leadership. As the classic command and control model of leadership loses credibility, authority is questioned, hierarchies are flattened, and employee commitment rather than compliance becomes a high priority.

Historically, the most important role of public sector leaders was to solve problems in a specific environment. The responsibility of contemporary leaders, however, is to solve the problem of adaptation and to close the gap between the real and the ideal. The OECD (2001) argues that citizens expect leaders to promote institutional adaptations in the public interest and to promote certain fundamental values that are embodied in public spiritedness. Although the nature of these values and this public spiritedness is unspecified, the mere mention of such concerns points in the direction of leadership as a function of integrity, vision, judgment, and courage. Indeed, the OECD (2001) asserts a particularly close connection between public sector leadership and public sector ethics, and among public service ethics, trust, transparency, accountability, and governance.

OECD members exhibit a spectrum of leadership development approaches and patterns. At one end, we find France with a high level of central intervention, exemplified by its Ecole Nationale d'Administration (ENA); Japan and Korea employ similar strategies. At the other end of the spectrum are countries with market-oriented approaches, such as New Zealand, in which senior positions are advertised and, in principle, are open to any qualified candidates. Between these poles are countries with a range of approaches, often including the establishment of senior executive systems such as in the United Kingdom and the United States. In most OECD nations, control of leadership positions is retained at the central government level, but departments and agencies have considerable flexibility in adapting leadership strategies to their particular needs and circumstances.

For more specific comparisons among OECD members, we profile five countries: Australia, Canada, New Zealand, the United Kingdom, and the United States. These profiles briefly describe the leadership development programs in each country, as well as each country's ethics infrastructure. Through the profiles, we aim to provide a snapshot of the situation in each country. We then turn in more detail to the American experience. Finally, we offer a proposal for leadership development and moral agency in the public service in general.

Leadership development, including succession planning and management, aims to build organizational capacity, specifically, an organization's human capital. It identifies, develops, and selects an organization's future leaders through strategic, systematic, and sustained processes, rather than through simple ad hoc replacement procedures. To use a sports metaphor, it aims to enhance an organization's bench strength.

To illustrate, in its investigation of succession planning and management initiatives in Australia, Canada, New Zealand, and the United Kingdom, the United States General Accounting Office (2003) found that, collectively, these countries' initiatives share several practices. First, they receive the support of top leadership, including needed financial and staff resources. Second, succession planning and management initiatives are linked to an agency's strategic planning. Third, talent is identified from multiple organizational levels, either early in careers or with critical skills. Fourth, agencies emphasize developmental assignments besides formal training to strengthen high-potential employees' skills and to broaden their experience. Fifth, specific human capital challenges are addressed, such as diversity, leadership capacity, and retention. Sixth and last, agencies facilitate organizational transformation by identifying and preparing future leaders with the requisite skills and experiences. GAO (2003) observes that, in the United States, many federal agencies have yet to adopt succession planning and management initiatives, although increased attention is being paid to strategic human capital management by Congress, the Office of Management and Budget, and the Office of Personnel Management.

The leadership development challenges across the five countries profiled here are similar, ranging from demographic changes reflected in large numbers of impending retirements over the next few years, to pressing diversity needs, to attrition and retention issues. While the incidence of these pressures varies across the five nations, it varies only in degree, not in kind. In Canada, for example, 80 percent of public sector executives are eligible to retire by 2010. The United States faces a similar loss. The United Kingdom is struggling to diversify its senior ranks with ethnic minorities and women; the United States is engaged in this process as well.

Increasingly (if incrementally) in the United States, current public sector leaders are recognizing the benefits of leadership development and succession planning—specifically, the retention of institutionalized knowledge, expertise, and leadership continuity. Whether it is Canada's Accelerated Executive Development Program, the United Kingdom's Fast Stream Program, New Zealand's senior leadership and management development strategy, the succession planning initiatives of Australia's Family Court, or the incipient initiatives in the United States, we are witnessing a shift in leadership development from a risk management tool for the near term to a strategic planning tool for the long term.

With regard to the development of ethical leadership, OECD countries, including the five members profiled here, have followed different but similar paths: different in the details of emphasis, format, and structure, but similar in the absence of an explicit philosophical foundation for the formulation of moral agency and integrity-based leadership and management. Consider, for example, the ethics infrastructure of each profiled country. According to Canada's Office of Public Service Values and Ethics (2002), an ethics infrastructure includes a statement of values or principles, standards of conduct, tools to promote and raise awareness of values, control of wrongdoing, and management and evaluation of values and ethics programs. The framework evolves as agencies, in their own way, attempt to reinforce "the culture of ethics" and maintain public trust.

Each of the five countries profiled here articulates its public service values, its code of conduct, its means for promoting values among public employees, its accountability mechanisms for controlling wrongdoing, and its management and evaluation methods. None, however, articulates the foundation of its values, nor, perhaps more important, the specific approaches by which the actual challenges of moral reasoning, judgment, decision making, and the exercise of discretion are met—the very areas of public service that are the most contentious and confounding as public servants try to sort through the conflicting and competing priorities and agendas they confront every day.

A sampling of the statements of values and the approaches intended to promote values illustrates the point. The statement of values for the Australian public service, for instance, includes the familiar aspirational assertions found in other values statements. The Australian public service is apolitical, it makes decisions based on merit, and it is accountable, responsive, and fair. It promotes values via training, workshops, and integration of the statement of values in the work contract orientation programs of its agencies, in personnel bulletins, and in other publications, and it claims that it integrates values into the "obligation to justify administrative decisions." How trainees are exposed to methods of justification on both the philosophical and political or practical levels is not explained.

Canada distinguishes among democratic, professional, ethical, and people values. Democratic values include loyalty to ministers, accountability, "support for the government of the day," and respect for the Canadian Constitution, the rule of law, and due process. Professional values include competence, efficiency, creativity, innovation, "speaking truth to power, fidelity to the public trust, neutrality/non-partisanship." Ethical values include honesty, integrity, probity, public trust, the common good, and discretion. People values include respect, tolerance, moderation, courage, decency, and civility. Finally, with regard to the promotion of values, Canada provides training and "awareness sessions" for its public servants, including new employees and executives, and it also requires financial disclosure, declaration of possible conflicts of interest, and recourse against administrative decisions.

Public employees in New Zealand are expected to be professional, honest, and respectful, but there is no mandatory ethics training, which may or may not be problematic, given the paradoxical quality of compulsory ethics training. The United Kingdom espouses "Seven Principles of Public Life": (1) selflessness, meaning that public employees "should act solely in terms of the public interest"; (2) integrity, meaning the avoidance of conflicts of interest; (3) objectivity, meaning that decisions regarding appointments, contracts, or individual rewards should be made on the basis of merit; (4) accountability, meaning that public employees "must submit themselves to whatever scrutiny is appropriate to their office"; (5) openness, meaning that public employees "should give reasons for their decisions and restrict information only when the wider public interest demands"; (6) honesty, meaning that public employees must avoid conflicts between their private interests and public duties; and (7) leadership, meaning that public employees "should promote and support these principles by leadership and example." Public employees in the United Kingdom "receive ethics training on the Civil Service Code and the detailed rules of the relevant department."

In its statement of values, the United States emphasizes similar concerns. Public employees are to promote the public interest, respect public property, avoid conflict of interest, and be professional, impartial, apolitical, and loyal. Among other things, they may not solicit or accept any gift or other item of monetary value; they are to disclose waste, fraud, abuse, and corruption to appropriate authorities; and they are to avoid the appearance of impropriety. Ethics training aims to make employees aware of federal conflict-of-interest laws, the principles of ethical conduct for government employees, and the rules specific to their agency. Each organization in the federal government has at least one employee responsible for ethics.

This profile of the leadership challenges and the ethics infrastructures of Australia, Canada, New Zealand, the United Kingdom, and the United States suggests that leadership and ethics development varies across these polities in degree rather than in kind. Whether driven by demographic pressures such as looming retirements, global, technological, and economic change, or a combination of these factors, leadership and ethics development aims to ensure the creation and cultivation of future leaders equipped with an appreciation of the ethical imperatives of public service. The missing ingredient, however, is an explicit framework for the formulation and inclusion of moral agency in the exercise of reasoning, judgment, decision making, and discretion by public administrators.

The five countries profiled here, like OECD members in general, tend to take a structural, rather than normative, approach to the development of ethical leadership. Codes of ethics, anticorruption measures, legal and regulatory prohibitions on certain practices—all legitimate concerns—constitute the principal portion of these nations' programs and practices. Although these efforts (as well as other structural initiatives) are necessary, they are not sufficient for the development and promotion of ethical leadership, including moral agency, in the public service. But moral agency is critical to leadership, and is inseparable from the public interest.

As Charles Garofalo (2003) argues, moral agency "embodies the common good, signifies obligation and accountability, and symbolizes reason and responsibility" (499). It is practical action, an indelible fiduciary quality, and the capacity to probe the issues in the daily struggles over budgets, agendas, and turf wars.

Moral agency includes justifiable decisions, a strategic grasp of organizational politics, and a shrewd sense of timing. It is at the heart of effective leadership.

## LEADERSHIP DEVELOPMENT IN THE UNITED STATES

Leadership development in the American public sector, particularly at the national level, has received considerable attention from a number of sources. Before describing several key treatments, issues, and recommendations, however, we need to capture the context and constraints within which American governmental institutions function. For example, Larry Terry (1995) argues that although bureaucratic leadership "entails the exercise of power, authority, and strategic discretion in pursuit of the public interest" (2), public bureaucracy in the United States has historically been seen as a threat to democracy. In the minds of many Americans, bureaucratic power is illegitimate, unaccountable, and unresponsive, despite the positive experiences that individual citizens often have with particular public organizations and agencies.

As Robert Behn (2003) suggests, in the perennial push-and-pull between Hamiltonian and Madisonian perspectives on the administrative apparatus of government, fear of the abuse of power continues to outweigh commitment to efficient and effective performance. Thus, as Terry (1995) observes, in view of the constraints imposed on the American administrative state, it is possible to think of bureaucratic leadership as an oxymoron.

It is not helpful, however, to consider bureaucratic leadership in that light, given the complexities of contemporary governance. The American democratic system requires that a certain legitimacy attach to the role of public bureaucracies and career civil servants, including administrative leadership. One of our goals in this chapter is to provide a basis for such legitimacy through the adoption of the unified ethic in conjunction with our vision of public administrators as moral agents. But first we turn to a description of the chief themes in leadership development in American government as identified in accounts from a variety of sources, including the National Academy of Public Administration, the PricewaterhouseCoopers Endowment for the Business of Government, and the United States Government Accountability Office.

There seems to be general agreement that leadership development in the United States government has not been a high priority owing to several major barriers, such as organizational culture, insufficient resources, inadequate rewards for initiative, limited mobility, and lack of role models (NAPA, 1997). Senior officials have tended to avoid or ignore the need to move from random or ad hoc replacement of personnel toward the systematic and sustained efforts required for comprehensive leadership development, including succession planning and management. Ellen Schall (1997) argues, for example, that public sector leaders must surmount four impediments to succession: (1) the leader's reluctance to take up the succession task; (2) the assumption that succession issues are beyond the scope of the leader's work; (3) confusion about how the succession task should be framed (i.e., is it a matter of replacing oneself or strategic positioning?); and (4) lack of information about how to implement a succession planning program, particularly in the midst of a shifting political environment as well as regulatory and political constraints.

Schall's (1997) last point is noted by a number of other observers, such as NAPA (1997), which suggests that there is an anomaly in the public sector not found in the private sector, namely, that "top leaders have relatively short tenure, little organizational history, and sometimes brief management experience" (xix). Indeed, the presence of a large political/policy cadre significantly affects the public sector's capacity to change to a leadership culture. Leadership development requires a long-term investment of time and resources, while political appointees tend to remain in office only a short time and therefore focus on the near-term agenda.

In view of this discontinuity, NAPA (1997) maintains that leadership development, including succession planning, should be viewed as a primary responsibility of the career Senior Executive

Service. Not that political leaders should not be involved, but what may be required is a "lead from the middle" strategy. In any event, five years later, NAPA (2002) repeated the litany of the barriers to succession planning in the Senior Executive Service, as well as the anomaly of leaders with short tenure in office, and again called for the implementation of a government-wide succession planning and leadership development program.

Although leadership development and succession planning have yet to be implemented government-wide, several agencies have been identified as exemplars in this process. For example, in *Organizations Growing Leaders: Best Practices and Principles in the Public Service,* a report for the PricewaterhouseCoopers Endowment for the Business of Government, Ray Blunt (2001) cites the Pension Benefit Guaranty Corporation, the U. S. Coast Guard, the Western Area Power Administration, the Veterans Benefits Administration, and the Social Security Administration as particularly noteworthy in their efforts to resolve the quiet crisis in human capital by mounting systematic and strategic leadership development programs. In Blunt's view, these five organizations have been able to overcome the entrenched cultural assumptions or myths that tend to hobble most governmental departments and agencies, and to take relatively bold steps to initiate organizational responses to the leadership crisis.

Blunt (2001) identifies and then refutes six myths:

1. Leaders are born, not made.

2. If leaders can be grown, they develop needed skills by attending leadership development training courses; the more expensive, the better the result.

3. If leaders can be grown, the best people to accomplish this task are (1) trainers, (2) consultants, (3) the human resources (HR) organization, and (4) all of the above.

4. Leaders are people who have gained expertise and capability in their field. (The corollary is that there is serious career risk in moving to another functional area, to another agency, or to the field from headquarters, and vice versa.)

5. Leadership is a "soft" skill that defies the tougher challenges of a performance management orientation and the measurement of hard results. (The corollary is that leader development is a task for those in the "soft" functions—HR and training—and not worth the time of senior leaders who engage in the "hard" functions like internal and external budget negotiations.)

6. Senior executives are not really the change leaders in their organizations; political appointees are. If future leaders are to be grown, this is an initiative for the political cadre.

Blunt (2001) then dispatches these six myths with the following arguments: With respect to Myth #1—leaders are born, not made—he suggests (based on the research of John Kotter of the Harvard Business School, the Center for Creative Leadership, and others) that research and experience demonstrate the falsity of this myth, that it is no more than "an excuse for doing little or nothing and letting nature take its course" (41). On Myth #2, which concerns leadership development and training, Blunt observes that leaders are grown "by the lessons of challenging and varied experiences, by the relationships they forge with senior leaders, and, most surprisingly, by the hardships of career and life experiences" (41). In Blunt's view, training is "a necessary catalyst but a relatively small part that is not tangibly evident in the outcome" (42).

Myth #3 is similar to Myth #2: Blunt again contends that although trainers, consultants, and HR organizations can be helpful, "It takes leaders to grow other leaders" (42). According to Myth #4, leaders are specialists, staying in one career field, in one organization, and often in one location. Blunt believes otherwise, based on his own work, that breadth of experience, coupled with such qualities as character, integrity, courage, and empathy, is the true basis of leadership. Myth #5—that leadership is "soft" and not important enough for senior leaders—is not borne out by experience in either the private or public sector.

Regarding Myth #6—that political appointees are the change leaders in their organizations—Blunt, like NAPA, acknowledges the complexity of this problem. He notes, for example, that the growth in the number of political appointees and Schedule C political support staff, as well as the use of non-career SES positions to augment political appointments, has had two effects on leadership development. The first is that leadership development falls into the hands of those least able to invest sufficient time and energy in a long-term process. The second is that the kinds of experiences so central to leadership development are often provided primarily to political appointees.

Finally, Blunt suggests that, to overcome this myth, senior career leaders must adopt a perspective similar to that of military officers, "who clearly see themselves as the stewards of the development of the next generation to follow them and take that role very seriously" (43). At present, this perspective is absent among most members of the Senior Executive Service, and would require a major redefinition of political-administrative relations.

Blunt (2001) concludes with recommendations both for individual government organizations and for organizations with government-wide program or policy responsibility. For individual organizations, Blunt offers the following:

1. Base succession and leader development practices on proven principles of growing leaders, including challenging, job-based experiences as part of a development strategy, involvement of future leaders with senior leaders in the organization's strategic agenda, and the use of Executive Core Qualifications as a template for development. Executive Core Qualifications involve leading change, leading people, results-driven, business acumen, and building coalitions.

2. Make a business case for succession and leader development and ground it in a real imperative that will urge action by senior leaders. With respect to the succession imperative, Blunt (2001) notes that the strongest incentive for action in the five leading-edge agencies was "the glaring visibility of the number of senior leaders who would likely depart within the next five years and an understanding of the implications that this held" (13).

3. Organizations and their senior leaders must hold themselves accountable for leadership development, which means that they must be involved from the beginning.

For government-wide action, Blunt (2001) recommends, first, that the President's Management Council provide a clear mandate to career Senior Executives to take the lead in succession planning, and that this initiative be incorporated "into a government-wide business case spearheaded by the President's Management Council" (8). Second, for the Office of Personnel Management, Blunt (2001) recommends that mobility be made a requirement for assumption of future SES leadership responsibility, and that a volunteer cadre of retiring and retired Senior Executives be formed to serve part-time as coaches, teachers, and mentors of the successor generations. These are the key lessons learned from the five exemplary organizations that Blunt identified as leaders in growing leaders.

Finally, GAO has produced a number of reports concerning leadership development, including succession planning and management, both in the United States and in several other nations. To reinforce some of the observations of NAPA (1997, 2002) and Ray Blunt (2001), we note that GAO projected in 2003 that more than half of all members of the Senior Executive Service employed by the government in October 2000 will have left by October 2007 and about 15 percent of the overall federal workforce will retire from 2001 to 2006.

Clearly, the need to build future leadership capacity is urgent and must become a government-wide initiative. We believe that of equal urgency in building leadership capacity is the need to create ethical leaders—moral agents—in the career service and to shift from compliance to integrity as the modus operandi of the public service at all levels and in all locations.

## A PROPOSAL FOR LEADERSHIP DEVELOPMENT AND MORAL AGENCY

Our aim is to propose a model of moral agency in public administration that we can reasonably hope will contribute to the development of the new kind of leadership that the OECD, NAPA, the PricewaterhouseCoopers Endowment for the Business of Government, and GAO claim is needed in the 21st century. The need is for leaders who understand and undertake policy coherence, boundary spanning, negotiation, flexibility, adaptation, and transparency. We need leaders who are effective and efficient as well as ethical, who can operate at various levels simultaneously, and who can hold two or more thoughts in their minds at the same time. We need leaders committed to democratic deliberation, discourse, and decision making if we are to reframe administrative culture and attain more responsible and humane governance. In short, we need moral public servants.

As an important backdrop and complement to our position, before describing our model of moral agency and ethics training, we consider in detail Kenneth Winston's analysis of moral competence in democratic governance. Winston (2003) argues that moral competence is one dimension of the professional skills that make for good governance. It includes a set of individual attributes and dispositions, or latent moral resources, that should be identified in recruiting or cultivated on the job through an appropriate organizational ethos and well-designed structural supports that constitute the moral competence of the institutions themselves. Since what a practitioner should be depends on what the organization expects the practitioner to do, the key question concerns the nature of moral competence for a practitioner of democratic governance.

Democracy, which is a moral order of sorts based on reciprocal commitments between and among citizens, has moral foundations, moral ends, and moral structures. Its foundations include legitimacy, the common good, civic goods, and limits on instrumentalism. With regard to ends, citizens are seen in terms of their well-being and in terms of agency. Well-being refers to how well off they are, that is, whether they enjoy favorable life circumstances, including security and prosperity. Agency refers to respect for citizens' ability to set goals, develop commitments, pursue values, and succeed in realizing them. Winston asserts that "In the context of a democratic polity, valuing agency is at the core of self-government" (172). Citizens recognize the moral space within which they can exercise deliberate choice, typically in conjunction with others.

The central criterion for selecting among policy options is that public policy aims to empower citizens and foster conditions for them to engage in meaningful activities together. Moreover, from agency flows citizen participation in decision making, with every decision viewed along this dimension. In this process, the special task of good practitioners is to reconcile partial and general perspectives. Finally, moral structures refer to our capacity as citizens to engage with others in self-rule, applying various decision mechanisms such as elections, contracts, adjudication, legislation, mediation, and regulation.

With these background conditions for the exercise of moral competence, Winston (2003) turns to the five particular attributes or defining features of the practitioner of democratic governance: (1) fidelity to the public good; (2) duty to civility; (3) respect for citizens as responsible agents; (4) proficiency in social architecture; and (5) prudence. Although these attributes vary among individuals, they are the qualities of officials acting in their official capacities as required by the duties of their office.

Fidelity to the public good focuses on the dual responsibility of officials in democratic polities. Officials achieve office via a process that incurs legitimate obligations to individuals or to limited constituencies. At the same time, they have a duty to enlarge their vision beyond these connections to encompass the public good. Thus, we have the requirement to reconcile partial with general perspectives, as exemplified by members of Congress balancing district or state against national considerations, or top administrators balancing allegiances to an administration's agenda against the statutory mandate of their office. The fundamental issue is how practitioners of democratic governance are to weigh their duties to their electoral, constitutional, and moral constituents.

Duty to civility refers to the need for practitioners to transcend the idiosyncratic or personal and to reach out to what can be shared and agreed to by others. Although personal beliefs or convictions may be the inevitable starting points for discussion, common ground is indispensable for collective endeavors. The conscientious democratic official is one whose grounds of decision are beliefs and principles that citizens generally are committed to—or could become committed to after deliberation and reflection.

Respect for citizens as responsible agents—the core of self-government—shifts our focus from citizens' well-being only to their moral agency in governance. A major issue in this context is the style of governance preferred: directive or facilitative. With directive governance, the role of citizens is to choose among competing elites who define policy alternatives. The measure of political power is citizens' compliance with practitioners' goals. In contrast, democratic self-government is too important to leave to elites, which makes facilitative governance preferable. The practitioner's contribution is critical but the process is interactive, with power residing in the practitioner's ability to facilitate citizens' capacity for self-direction and the exercise of effective agency. In effect, the practitioner acts as a transformative leader who sees citizens as whole persons, values their capacity as moral agents, and strives to reconcile partial and general perspectives.

The fourth attribute of the good practitioner, proficiency in social architecture, encompasses deliberative judgment about ends and means as well as institutional craftsmanship. Winston (2003) contends that institutional design is moral legislation that influences how we live, provides access to some citizens but not others, and facilitates certain problem definitions. Good practitioners must always consider means and ends as well as the implications of moving governance responsibilities, for example, from public institutions to private for-profit and non-profit organizations. They need to reflect on the question of whether the market can be used as a means to pursue the ends of governance without changing the ends of governance, or whether contracting out improves citizen participation, transparency, or responsiveness.

Finally, prudence—the cardinal political virtue—refers to the exercise of practical wisdom in governance. It aims to sustain valued relationships so that ruling requires more than technical expertise. Prudence is the capacity to engage in ethical inquiry, skill in managing competing claims, and the ability to tolerate moral ambiguity. Our commitment to core values is balanced by an appreciation of the recurrent perplexities and tensions inherent in democratic governance.

Winston's (2003) sketch of moral competence in democratic governance complements our model of moral agency and ethics training in terms of both structure and process. Individual and institutional characteristics and capacities, grounded in the moral nature of democracy, for example, reflect Kant's kingdom of ends, the realm in which citizens are legislators in political and social reconciliation. The significance of citizens and citizenship vis-à-vis officials, which also figures prominently in Winston's (2003) analysis, comports as well with our understanding of moral agency and moral action, along with fidelity to the public good, principled decision making, and the exercise of responsible discretion.

In general, the two perspectives coincide. What is missing in Winston's analysis, as well as in leadership development initiatives in general, however, is an explicit moral basis for the democratic practice of governance. We turn now to our model of moral agency and ethics training, including the unified ethic, which supplies such a basis.

Philosophically, the framework of the model of moral agency proposed here is the unified ethic. Functionally, this model derives from the application of enhanced principal-agent theory to public administration. Politically, this model represents a countervailing or at least critical perspective on public choice theory and privatization. Together, the philosophical, functional, and political dimensions of this model of moral agency can provide the 21$^{st}$ century public administrator with the concepts and confidence needed to strive toward consistent embodiment and enactment of the public interest.

The unified ethic, as we have shown, consists of the three principal positions in moral philosophy: deontology, teleology, and virtue. It combines these positions into an integrated whole and provides a practical perspective on the key elements that constitute the ethical challenges faced by public administrators. Consider, for example, the nature of moral agency and the characteristics of the moral agent in public administration. Agency means an awareness of the moral connection between ends and means, supplemented by those personal qualities that we call character.

Public administrators, functioning in instrumental organizations, are simultaneously agents, experts, and stewards. They draw no arbitrary lines between principle, consequence, and character, and they do not seek or claim legitimacy based on expertise or hierarchical position. On the contrary, their view of the public administrator's role in governance is the comprehensive moral point of view embodied in the unified ethic (Garofalo and Geuras 1999).

When approaching a problem or confronting a decision, the public administrator, informed by the unified ethic, might pose a series of questions drawn from deontology, teleology, and virtue theory to construct a coherent method of analysis and decision making. From deontology, the administrator might ask: What principle applies in this case? Can this principle be applied consistently in this case and in all similar cases? Which course of action exemplifies the ideal of treating people as ends in themselves? From teleology, the administrator might ask: What are the short-term and long-term consequences of my action? Does my action promote the greatest happiness? From virtue theory, the administrator might ask: What character traits does this action express? What effect will this action have on my character? Is this the action of a person whose character I would admire?

These questions are suggestive, not exhaustive, but they can lead to increased clarity and coherence in administrative decision making, recognizing that the answers to all the questions will not necessarily lead to the same conclusion or course of action. Rather than provide a formula or blueprint for decision making, ethical analysis provides a morally grounded process that can be applied to specific cases, as well as the potential to reconcile conflicts.

Functionally, principal-agent theory provides an important perspective on the role of the public administrator as a moral agent. Generally, principal-agent theorists focus on the question of how employees or contractors can be induced to serve the interests of their principals, particularly when they know more than their principals or have interests different from their principals.

Applying principal-agent theory to the public sector, however, complicates the question, given the concern with the public interest that ideally characterizes the decisions and actions of public administrators. An additional complication is that principal-agent theory tends to assume only one principal and that the principal's identity is clear. In reality, multiple principals are common in both the private and public sectors, ranging from immediate organizational superiors to boards of directors to shareholders to customers to regulators in the private sector, and immediate organizational superiors to legislators to citizens to the public interest in the public sector.

In each case, the manager is confronted with complex questions of loyalty to those commanding some form of authority and control. Moreover, the traditional formulation of principal-agent theory assumes not only a single principal but also a lucidity and a consistency of goals that have been disputed, if not discredited, in the public sector. The public administrator operates in a political environment with general, even vague, goals that in turn lead to multiple interpretations of the meaning of goals and multiple strategies for their implementation and evaluation.

The plurality of principals in the public sector, with their multiple and often imprecise goals, represents a permanent challenge to the public administrator as a moral agent. Obligated and accountable to hierarchical superiors, elected officials, and citizens, the public administrator-moral agent must mediate among these obligations on a daily basis and manage them in ways that contribute to the attainment of both organizational policy goals and the public interest in an effective, efficient, and ethical manner. The unified ethic can provide the public administrator-moral agent with an essential understanding of the interdependence of principle, consequence, and character that, with experience and perspective, can sustain moral conviction and commitment as well as practical wisdom and action. Moral literacy and moral advocacy become the norm.

On the political level, the challenge to public administration of plural principals, varied and vague goals, and limited resources has been expanded and exacerbated in recent years by the global phenomenon of privatization. Whatever its causes— market theory, a desire to curtail or eliminate unions, a wish to reduce the scope of government—privatization contributes to the complexities of public administration in general and to the perplexities of ethical public administration in particular. Public administration's goals of equity, assurance of quality and cost, stewardship of public resources, accountability, and promotion of democratic ideals are all tested by privatization. Thus, the need for moral agency and moral agents in contemporary governance at all levels and in all regions is urgent, especially if public choice theory, globalization, and their externalities are to be managed and the public interest promoted.

The vehicle for creating moral agency in public administration is a two-stage ethics training initiative framed by the unified ethic and designed, first, to clarify universal values such as honesty, loyalty, and fairness, and second, to justify policies, programs, and practices in the context of those values. Inasmuch as most proposals for ethics training tend to emphasize compliance and process over integrity and substance, and thereby fail to identify the interconnected values and challenges underlying political and administrative activity, the first stage is critical. Both trainers and trainees must be clear about the nature, purpose, and function of the unified ethic and of values as ingredients of public policy and administration. In this process, the training of trainers is crucial.

Equally important is the justification of policies, programs, and practices in light of the universal values identified in stage one. The goal here is to make those values explicit, to determine how those values come into play in the policies, programs, and practices under scrutiny, to understand the purpose and process of justification, and to link these elements in a system of discourse and discovery. Public officials need to understand their own value premises and obligations, the implications and impacts of their decisions, and their place as moral agents in democratic governance. Finally, this two-stage ethics training initiative, like other forms of ethics training, is unlikely to have lasting or significant effects without regular reinforcement and visible commitment from both political and administrative leaders at all levels (Garofalo 2003).

Leadership and leadership development must be reconceptualized as an integral part of capacity-building in governance. Public servants are moral actors whose decisions and discretion require consistent application of moral judgment to both the policy and management arenas, rather than mere obedience to hierarchical directives. In short, we propose a shift from compliance to integrity as the *modus operandi* of the public service—a shift predicated on (1) the inherent moral nature of public administrators as human beings who possess dignity, autonomy, and reason; (2) the changing expectations of the roles, responsibilities, and quality of public sector leadership; and (3) both local and global challenges in building democratic governance.

This recommendation for a shift in administrative behavior does not exclude the need for laws, codes, and sanctions. What it does exclude is sole reliance on such legalisms as surrogates for genuine moral leadership. In this context, we recall Rushworth Kidder's (1995) distinction between an ethical dilemma and a moral temptation. We also recognize that reform under any circumstances can be daunting.

Despite the platitudes about the need for leaders to induce and manage cultural change, current and prospective leaders would do well to heed the admonitions of Heifetz and Linsky (2002), who distinguish between technical and adaptive change and emphasize that any type of change, especially adaptive, is likely to cause anxiety, uncertainty, fear of loss, and even resistance among those affected. Leaders, including practitioners of democratic governance, must possess the skill and sensitivity to anticipate, articulate, and adjudicate these responses in a process of trust, transparency, and transformation.

Instilling ethics in governance can itself be viewed as an adaptive change that is also expected to enable administrators to cope with adaptive challenges in the governance process. It is a disruption of the rules-based status quo and, therefore, a threat to the comfort and convenience of many players. On the other hand, it also can be viewed as a sign of civic health, a refusal to collude in the denial of administrative discretion that characterizes the public service script. In this connection, civic health hinges on this initiative in an important way: Citizens are asked both to acknowledge and to honor the value and complexity of public service and their own contributions to the processes of governance.

The unified ethic provides the comprehensive perspective for morally based leadership development in the public service. As the framework for the establishment of moral agency, it can serve as the context for the two-stage training initiative involving clarification of universal values and justification of administrative decisions and actions in the context of those values. The goal is to embed the moral perspective in the political-administrative culture, to advance democratic deliberation and decision making, and to furnish an important building block in the construction and support of civil society.

Clearly, the unified ethic alone is not enough to invoke a reconfiguration of political and administrative thought and behavior. But without it, the likelihood of developing the leadership required by 21st century governance is slim indeed.

# CHAPTER 12

# Perspectives on Contemporary Reform: Reinventing Government and the New Public Management

In our journey together so far, we have covered a lot of ground. We have visited and revisited the real world of public management. We have explored ethics, ethical decision making, and the special place of ethics in government; we have taken a personal inventory of our principles, attitudes, and goals. At this point, then, we are almost ready to shift our gaze and begin to consider ethics, quality, and performance. But before dealing directly with that topic, it will be useful to examine the current reform initiatives that you and your organization are probably experiencing in one way or another.

In this chapter, we focus on reinventing government and the new public management. Our aim is twofold: (1) to provide an understanding of the origins, purposes, assumptions, and outcomes to date of these two reform efforts, which have become the catechism of governments worldwide; and (2) to provide a context for the next chapter's treatment of ethics, quality, and performance.

In the past decade, "reinventing government" has become part of our international lexicon, or at least the lexicon of those with professional interests in the purposes and processes of government. It would be surprising, in fact, if the reinventing government language has not seeped into your organization, and if you and your colleagues have not been exposed to such ideas as customer service, empowerment, and performance. So, regardless of the criticisms that might be leveled at the reinventing government movement—and there are many—we must acknowledge the impact of this latest reform, along with the new public management, on contemporary thought and practice. Like privatization, reinventing government and the new public management have undeniably stimulated consideration of the fundamental issues of governance that continue to challenge governments across the globe.

## REINVENTING GOVERNMENT

David Osborne and Ted Gaebler, the authors of the bible of the reinventing movement, *Reinventing Government: How the Entrepreneurial Spirit is Transforming the Public Sector, From Schoolhouse to Statehouse, City Hall to the Pentagon* (1992), claim that their essential concern is a new form of governance. They are not interested, they say, in what governments do but in how governments operate because, in their estimation, the "central failure of government today is one of means, not ends" (xxi). A later volume by Osborne and Peter Plastrik, *Banishing Bureaucracy: The Five Strategies for Reinventing Government* (1997), elaborates on this perspective.

Osborne and Gaebler's new form of governance is based on ten principles:

1. Catalytic government, or steering rather than rowing

2. Community-owned government, or empowering communities and citizens by changing expectations

3. Competitive government

4. Mission-driven government

5. Results-oriented government

6. Customer-driven government

7. Enterprising government

8. Anticipatory government

9. Decentralized government

10. Market-oriented government.

They label their model "entrepreneurial government," and describe an entrepreneur in this context as someone who uses resources in new ways to maximize productivity and effectiveness. In their view, government can be organized in one of two ways: it can be either rigid, rule-based, and protective of patronage and corruption, or it can be mission-driven, performance-oriented, and customer-focused.

Clearly, when framed in these either-or terms, the second option is much more appealing, and it was this option that inspired the Clinton administration's National Performance Review (NPR), which was spearheaded by Al Gore. Much of the NPR agenda was taken from *Reinventing Government*, including evaluating the efficiency of every federal agency, identifying and eliminating waste and inefficiency, streamlining the federal personnel system, changing the culture of the federal bureaucracy, and empowering employees. The series of reports published by the National Performance Review captures the spirit of this new form of governance. Examples include *Creating a Government That Works Better and Costs Less* (1994), *Putting Customers First '95* (1995), and *The Best Kept Secret in Government* (1996).

Catalytic government, Osborne and Gaebler's first principle, involves separating policy decisions, or steering (away from service delivery) rather than rowing. To students of public administration, this notion is reminiscent of the hoary politics-administration dichotomy, in which elected officials were to express the will of the people in the form of policy while public administrators were to execute the will of the people in the form of administration. The second principle—community-owned government—is predicated on the assumption that communities understand their problems better than service professionals, and that institutions and professions offer service, while communities offer care.

Competitive government, predictably, involves introducing competition in service delivery, while mission-driven government focuses on outcomes rather than rules because, Osborne and Gaebler suggest, rules stifle innovation. Results-oriented government supports outcomes, whereas bureaucratic governments fund inputs, such as school enrollments, eligible welfare clients, or the number of police officers needed to deter crime.

According to Osborne and Gaebler, bureaucratic government pays little attention to results. It does not ask, for instance, how well students perform, how many welfare clients find and keep stable jobs, or how much the crime rate declines. In fact, Osborne and Gaebler contend, schools, welfare departments, and police departments typically receive more money when they fail because their failure emphasizes the importance of the problems they face and the need for even greater support.

Customer-driven government aims to meet the needs of the customer, not the bureaucracy, and Osborne and Gaebler argue that the best way to achieve this aim is to give customers resources and allow them to decide how to use them. An example of this concept is the school voucher program.

Enterprising government emphasizes earning rather than spending, while anticipatory government focuses on preventing rather than curing problems. Osborne and Gaebler illustrate the need for anticipatory government by pointing to the Environmental Protection Agency, which spends 99 percent of its budget on managing pollution, even though effective pollution prevention technology is available.

Finally, decentralized government tries to move from hierarchy to participation, and market-oriented government tries to effect change through the market, for example, by investing capital, pension funds, and cash balances to encourage such things as minority business or energy conservation loans.

We will return to these principles when we review the major critiques of the reinventing movement as a whole. At this point, however, let us summarize Osborne and Gaebler's perspective on government, as presented in their book.

First, they say that they believe in government and do not see it as a necessary evil. Government is the mechanism for making communal decisions about where to build a highway, what to do about homeless people, what kind of education to provide our children. It is the way we deliver services, including defense, environmental protection, water systems, police protection, and a myriad of others. It is the way we solve collective problems.

Second, Osborne and Gaebler believe that civilized society cannot function effectively without effective government, and that the problem we face today is that large, centralized bureaucracies, with their standardized "one-size-fits-all" services, are inappropriate and ineffective in rapidly changing information societies. Third, they believe that the problem is not government employees, but rather, the system in which they work. Osborne and Gaebler emphasize that they are not bashing bureaucrats— they are bashing bureaucracies.

Fourth, Osborne and Gaebler claim that neither liberalism nor conservatism is relevant to the problems that governments confront today. We will not solve our problems by spending more or spending less, by creating new bureaucracies or by privatizing existing bureaucracies. The solution, instead, lies in making government more effective, in reinventing it. Fifth, and finally, Osborne and Gaebler believe in equal opportunity for all Americans, and the way to increase equality is to increase choice and competition through the use of entrepreneurial government.

The central thesis of *Reinventing Government* is that the kind of governments that developed during the industrial era, with their centralized bureaucracies, their preoccupation with rules and regulations, and their hierarchies, no longer work well. They were effective in their time, but eventually became bloated, wasteful, and resistant to change. Osborne and Gaebler describe hierarchical, centralized bureaucracies as ocean liners in an age of supersonic jets: big, cumbersome, expensive, and extremely difficult to turn around.

The bureaucratic model was developed in different conditions from those we experience today. It was an age of hierarchy, when only those at the top of the pyramid had enough information to make informed decisions. It was a time when most people worked with their hands, not with their minds.

Today, we live in a time of astounding change, a global marketplace, an information-based society, a knowledge economy. According to Osborne and Gaebler, therefore, both public and private bureaucracies that developed during the industrial era increasingly fail because today's world demands flexible and adaptable institutions that squeeze more bang for the buck. It requires institutions that are responsive to their customers, that lead by persuasion and incentives rather than commands, that give employees a sense of meaning and control, that empower citizens rather than simply serve them. Our technologies are breathtaking and complex, but our institutions are sluggish and slow. Therefore, they must be reinvented.

## PROFILE OF REINVENTION RESULTS

Before turning to the major critiques of the reinventing movement, let us look at a snapshot of reinvention results at the federal level, in order to get an idea of some of the things that have actually happened and to have a benchmark for reflecting on the critiques. According to Anne Laurent (1999) of *Government Executive* magazine, "government has gone measurement crazy," largely because of the 1993 Government Performance and Results Act. Therefore, "if it's true that what gets measured gets done, then the Government Performance Project should prod top government officials to do more to improve management in federal agencies."

Laurent says that the Government Performance Project (GPP) is the "first-ever attempt to systematically measure federal management performance with the goal of prompting agencies to manager better" (1). Originating in 1996 with a grant from The Pew Charitable Trusts, the project, through the Alan K. Campbell Public Affairs Institute of Syracuse University's Maxwell School of Citizenship and Public Affairs and *Government Executive* magazine, sought the advice of academic experts and government practitioners to develop working criteria for effective government management. Along with *Governing* magazine, another project partner, the GPP tested the criteria in 1997 through a survey administered to four federal agencies, four state governments, and four local governments. The four federal agencies were the Coast Guard, the Food and Drug Administration, the Defense Logistics Agency, and the Veterans Health Administration.

Following the pilot year, the GPP undertook a review of the operations of 15 federal agencies that have extensive interactions with citizens. In 1998, a 93-question survey was sent to the 15 agencies to collect information on 34 criteria in financial management, capital management, human resources, information technology, and managing for results. In addition to the questionnaires, the project probed manager and employee views of the agencies, reviewed documents, and conducted hundreds of interviews with congressional staffers, the General Accounting Office, the Office of Management and Budget, think tanks, the press, advocacy groups, vendors, unions, academic institutions, and government commissions. Then, after digesting the information from all these sources, the project team assigned grades to each agency in each of the areas covered in the questionnaire.

Here are the major findings, organized into the following six categories:

1. Turf and Stovepipes

2. Conflicting Missions

3. Double-Edged Fees

4. Technology Trumps All

5. Clear Vision

6. Culture Cuts Both Ways.

In the first category, Turf and Stovepipes, the project emphasizes the widely known fact that "managing in government is as different from managing in the private sector as it is similar," noting that "as hard as an agency may try to adopt business tools and techniques, political realities sometimes block the results of improved management" (2). For example, the Veterans Health Administration has restructured itself to serve an aging population of veterans who are increasingly located in the south and west, and whose health problems are more related to poverty than combat. "The agency determined that veterans need clinic-based care and nursing homes, not long inpatient stays in large hospitals, so it reallocated resources. But closing hospitals and replacing them with outpatient clinics displaces workers and removes from communities some of the most venerable symbols of government beneficence. It angers constituents and therefore members of Congress, who have fought VHA's decisions in the press and via the appropriations process" (3).

In a similar vein, "the Internal Revenue Service was soundly spanked on Capitol Hill in late 1997 for its efforts to use performance measures to pump up tax collections. Never mind that the IRS was acting at Congress' behest to close the gap between what taxpayers owe and what is collected and that the measures were in line with the 1993 Government Performance and Results Act" (2-4).

In addition, as the GPP notes, "when lawmakers divide up agencies and their missions like turf, they cause structural hurdles to effective management." (2). The EPA, for example, "is hampered by a rigid stovepipe structure dictated by myriad environmental laws creating separate program offices for air, water, toxic waste and other environmental categories." Although experts "say that the problem would be solved by a single generic law giving the agency administrative flexibility . . . legislators on the more than 40 committees and subcommittees overseeing EPA aren't likely to give up their turf to pass such a law" (5).

The second category, Conflicting Missions, illustrates the fact that politics also leads to conflicts in what agencies are to do. For example, the GPP found that the Customs Service:

> . . . is responsible both for speeding trade and preventing the entry of undesirable goods into the United States. But thoroughly inspecting goods coming into the country takes time and the resulting shipping delays cost importers money. Conversely, moving goods quickly reduces the ability to aggressively inspect them for contraband. Hence, those who favor law enforcement see Customs as inadequately aggressive and those who want faster movement of people and goods view the agency as a bureaucratic impediment. The mission clash dooms Customs to constantly shift resources between conflicting priorities, a recipe for management inefficiency. (3)

The third category is Double-Edged Fees, which refers to the fact that some agencies find that fees come at a cost. In some cases, fees can be a boon to agencies faced with declining appropriations, but in the case of the U.S. Food and Drug Administration (FDA), for example, they are proving to be problematic.

In 1992, the FDA began collecting fees from the pharmaceutical industry, which it regulates. The purpose of the law creating the fees was to foster streamlining and speeding the approval process. The Government Performance and Results Act, however, "would have FDA focus on improved health resulting from FDA-approved drugs." As the Government Performance Project observes, "while the two priorities need not be in conflict, FDA's reliance on the regulated industry for an increasing percentage of basic resources does raise public policy questions" (3).

The fourth category, Technology Trumps All, concerns the continuing challenge faced by federal agencies to surmount their management barriers by expanding their use of information technology; the fifth category, Clear Vision, leads to the conclusion that "a single-minded quarterback with a well-crafted game plan can pull an organization out of a dismal slump."

With respect to technology, the Government Performance Project asserts that "it is nearly axiomatic that agencies cannot make great strides in management or overall performance without first solving their technological problems" (4). But solving these problems can be formidable, especially for technology-dependent agencies with millions of lines of computer code, millions of claims to process every year, and heavy reliance on intergovernmental and contractor relationships for program implementation. With respect to clear vision, the GPP emphasizes the importance of experienced administrators, personal intervention, and accountability as essential elements in the articulation and cultivation of a clear and compelling agency vision.

Regarding the sixth and final category, Culture Cuts Both Ways, the Government Performance Project suggests that "culture change is both a common denominator and chief challenge at many of the GPP agencies" (5). The GPP's findings of considerable cultural variation across agencies, including differences in clarity of mission, regulatory and stakeholder relationships, and overall management complexity, led it to observe that external as well as internal forces play a role in the management effectiveness of any given agency. "Whatever its causes," the GPP concludes, "mismanagement clearly cannot be sustained at a time when budgets are dwindling and public expectations are rising. We hope one of the results of the Government Performance Project is that this truth filters up into the political leadership as well as down into the agency management and employee ranks" (6).

The GPP also notes that of equal importance are the examples of good management that it discovered in the agencies studied. Ultimately, it hopes that blame and finger-pointing are reduced and Americans are helped to differentiate between well-managed and poorly-managed government agencies" (6).

## CRITIQUES OF REINVENTING GOVERNMENT

Many analysts have offered critical perspectives on reinventing government. Before exploring two particular perspectives in some detail, however, we should at least briefly acknowledge the four lessons and the four temptations that have grown out of the long history of major efforts to improve the executive branch (DiIulio, Garvey, and Kettl 1993).

The first lesson is that institutional reform is daunting. Whatever our political persuasion or preferences, we must recognize that solutions to administrative problems do not come easily. Second, "despite the difficulty of the job, progress, albeit gradual, partial, and selective, has been made. Government works better today because of these earlier reform efforts" (7). The third lesson is that a strategy and intellectual support help to ensure the viability of reforms. Performance must be buttressed by a strategic plan, a vision, and direction. Fourth, "long-term follow-through matters" (9).

The four temptations that today's reformers must avoid include, first, the temptation "to confuse disagreement over what government ought to do with how well it does it." Given the differences of opinion, for example, over what constitutes fraud, waste, and abuse, we must guard against the danger "that solutions billed as administrative, managerial, or technical may disguise underlying differences of policy or significant competition among disparate interests" (9).

Second, we must avoid "not only rushing to judgment but rushing into action" as well (9). Clarity of purpose along with effective and patient implementation are more likely to prove fruitful than a "do-it-all now" approach, which fails to match required political resources with the objectives sought.

The third temptation is "to promise that management reforms will produce major savings and reduce the budget deficit" (10). Whether we face a budget deficit or not, DiIulio and his colleagues suggest that savings are more likely to be a by-product of improved performance than a direct outcome.

Fourth, and finally, "it is tempting for study commissions to seek The Answer" (11). Seasoned observers and practitioners, however, are quite aware of the incremental, evolutionary, and experimental nature of management improvement and of the improbability of knowing what will work best under all circumstances.

## The Political Theory of Reinvention

Among the many critiques of reinventing government, one of the most important concerns its implications for democratic governance. According to Linda deLeon and Robert Denhardt (2000), "the most basic premise of the reinvention movement is that the accumulation of the narrowly defined self-interests of many individuals can adequately approximate the public interest" (89).

This premise is consistent with the long-standing tradition in public administration that government should be run like a business, meaning that government agencies should adopt practices that have been used in the private sector, such as total quality management. DeLeon and Denhardt maintain, however, that "the reinvention movement takes this idea one step further, arguing that government should not only adopt the techniques of business administration, but it should also adopt the values of business" (90).

DeLeon and Denhardt begin by examining three aspects of the reinvention movement—the market model, the emphasis on customers, and entrepreneurial management. It is in the context of the market model that deLeon and Denhardt press their claim that, according to the reinvention movement, business values, not merely techniques, are to be adopted by government. Such values include "competition, preference for market mechanisms for social choice, and respect for the entrepreneurial spirit" (90).

In this view, an article of faith is "a belief that the free play of market forces will bring self-interested participants—individuals, social groups, agencies, firms—into an equilibrium that represents, in some way, the maximum achievable social good" (91). The public interest can be attained through individuals' pursuit of their own self-interest.

The second important premise of the reinvention movement is customer-driven government. Government must listen to its customers, should offer its customers choices between competing service providers, and should give customers resources to use in selecting their own service providers. From deLeon and Denhardt's perspective, "these ideas go beyond improving the quality of government service and, in fact, represent a particular viewpoint, one that prefers a government that responds to the short-term self-interests of isolated individuals (customers) rather than one that supports the pursuit of public interests publicly defined through a deliberative process (citizens)" (91).

Moreover, the functions of government "do not represent uniform products or even a 'product line' as one might encounter in business. Rather, the work of government is extremely diverse in the way it originates, in the way it is performed, and in the way it is received." Thus, "the relationship between those in public organizations and their customers is far more complex than the relationship between those behind the hamburger stand and their customers" (91).

But it is the third element of the reinvention movement— entrepreneurial government—that deLeon and Denhardt find particularly indicative of its underlying political theory. Besides resourcefulness, creativity, innovation, and a focus on ends rather than means, the ingredient in the recipe for entrepreneurship that deLeon and Denhardt find especially problematic is the idea of "the individual government agent acting on his or her own self-interest (or that of the agency)" (92).

In deLeon and Denhardt's judgment, "the particular political viewpoint represented here is one that glorifies the innovative potential of the single self-interested individual over the powers of established institutional processes or the slower and more hesitating, but more involving and perhaps democratic, efforts of groups." The fundamental problem with entrepreneurial managers, according to deLeon and Denhardt, is that "they can be innovative and productive, but their single-mindedness, tenacity, and willingness to bend the rules make them very difficult to control. They can become loose cannons" whose actions fly in the face of the "tradition of accountability and responsiveness in democratic public administration" (92).

Finally, deLeon and Denhardt conclude that the "political theory of reinvention, founded on a faith in individual self-interest as the engine that drives social good, in fact acts to deny the ideal of citizenship" (94).

## Reinventing the Proverbs of Government

Daniel Williams (2000) examines what he describes as five inconsistencies in *Reinventing Government* and *Banishing Bureaucracy*, assesses the claim that reinvention constitutes a new paradigm of government, exposes the hazards of reinventing government, and evaluates Osborne and his co-authors' research approach. He concludes "that the reinventing government reform movement is seriously flawed, providing both contradictory advice and advice that is outright harmful" (522).

Beginning with competitive government, Williams notes that reinvention advocates recommend competition between private sector providers, between private and public providers, and within government itself. "Competition allegedly improves government the same way it improves the private sector: by increasing the risk of failure for unsatisfactory work, such as work that is less efficient or effective than that supplied by others." At the same time, however, reinvention advocates object to duplication in government agencies, such as, for example, the more than 90 federal programs administered in 1989 by 20 different agencies for the reduction of infant mortality. In this regard, Williams suggests, reinvention advocates "are squarely in the tradition of government reformers who have tried to reduce 'irrational' duplication of government services throughout the twentieth century" (523).

Thus, reinventors want competition but oppose duplication. Unfortunately, however, reformers are given no useful direction for action. It is not clear whether government units and programs should be allowed to compete with each other, whether they should be rationalized to eliminate the duplication, whether some level of duplication is too much, or what should determine if streamlining or competition is preferable.

With respect to privatization, Williams finds reinventors equally indeterminate. Sometimes, according to Williams, reinventors recommend privatization, and at other times, they recommend its opposite. Although, in general, the public sector should defer to the private sector where private goods are produced, the reinventors also recommend that the public sector pay attention to governmental profit making and investment.

From Willliams' point of view, "this conflict reveals an undisclosed agenda. Government is permitted to act like a private business when it raises revenues without direct taxation. It can intervene in the private market to control development. However, it should not intervene in the market to meet socialist employment or income distribution objectives." As a result, Williams asserts, reformers are left without clear guidance as to when intervention is permitted and when it is not.

Nonetheless, despite the lack of guidance, there is a rationale that Williams calls "the hidden agenda," which "is one of centrist social policy dominated by conservative economic policy. Thus economic intervention to achieve economic objectives— that is, nationalization of businesses to maintain employment and economic distribution—is treated as faulty, but economic intervention to protect the property interests of the relatively affluent—that is, nationalization of a single business to control development—is permitted" (524).

The third thematic inconsistency that Williams treats concerns decentralization, which "is an integral component of entrepreneurial government as it allows the devolution of power from central bureaucrats to local public servants who can develop unique solutions to unique problems." Decentralization, Williams tell us, "consists primarily of abolishing rule-based decision processes and requirements for approval from higher authorities for any significant, and many trivial, decisions" (524).

But the decentralization theme, he also tells us, is incompatible with another reinvention theme: "rationalizing of government decisions." "The effective use of rational decision making techniques relies on the existence of a strong centralized authority structure that can require that these techniques be used, assure that the outcomes of rational analysis lead to decisions, and prevent bureaucrats from subverting rational decisions while implementing policies" (524). In other words, it is difficult to understand how such techniques as strategic planning, long-term budgeting, and performance measurement can be implemented in the absence of central authority.

Next is innovation, which entails empowering employees by showing them that they and their ideas are valued. Yet, on the one hand, the reinvention gurus "recommend that governments accept failure as a sign of innovative thinking," "recommend tolerating failure and even rewarding it," and even "recommend avoiding financial penalties for poor performance because such penalties suppress innovation," while on the other hand, they "recommend that governments should pay only for results and that there should be 'real consequences for failure.'" Employees should be held accountable for producing results, and when short-term results are unsatisfactory, agency heads should be fired. Finally, there should be significant risk of layoff as well as suppression of "resistance" (525).

The final inconsistency concerns empowerment, which is an established expression of human development management theory. But, according to Williams, it is also in conflict with many other reinvention recommendations. As noted, "empowerment conflicts with use of rational decision-making techniques and with recommendations to establish real consequences for failure" (527), but "empowerment also conflicts with uncoupling steering and rowing, which refers to dividing policy-making functions from service delivery functions" (526).

Williams argues that empowerment is hollow if it permits public servants to exercise discretion only over the means of attaining hierarchically defined goals, with little or no voice in determining the goals themselves. Thus, the conflict is that empowerment is either in direct conflict with other reinvention recommendations and therefore is incompatible with them, or it is not really empowerment, but merely discretion over relatively unimportant technical matters.

After dismissing reinvention as a new paradigm shift in the understanding of government or the delivery of government services, owing to the hoary nature of such techniques as performance measurement, privatization, and long-range budgeting, Williams moves to the hazards of reinventing government. He maintains that the real problem with reinvention is not merely that it is inconsistent and inaccurate in its claim to be innovative. The real problem is that it "dispenses advice that is antithetical to effective and democratically controlled government and information that is so misleading as to be deceptive" (527). For example, "while Osborne, Gaebler, and Plastrik recommend community empowerment, this advice should not be confused with support of democratic institutions. Their discussion of actual democratic governance suggests hostility" (529).

In essence, Williams believes that the reinventors aim to circumvent accountability mechanisms, the messiness of interest groups, and the involvement of constituents in policies and programs, all for the sake of achieving contradictory propositions and proposals offered under the guise of "fixing government."

Williams concludes his appraisal by positing that "the reinventing government literature . . . is severely flawed." Its advice is inconsistent, and rather than a paradigm shift in public administration thought, it is nothing more than "a popularization of various ideas about government, many of which have been around for 50 years or more, with a few dating to the last century or earlier." Worse still, this literature offers "a number of harmful ideas, such as the reintroduction of the policy-administration dichotomy, advocacy of excessively small governmental organizations, a general hostility toward democratic control of administrative agencies, a simplistic analysis of the benefits of privatization, and an advocacy of excessive and undemocratic administrative discretion" (532).

Based largely not on research but on anecdotes, the reinventing literature and the movement it has spawned represent a simplistic, harmful, and dangerous antidote to the putative problems plaguing the public service. According to Williams, little is to be gained and much is to be lost by attempting to apply this model of government and governance in the twenty-first century United States.

## NEW PUBLIC MANAGEMENT

Like reinventing government, the new public management is a global reform that can be found in the United States, the United Kingdom, Korea, Australia, Brazil, and several other nations. Although variations in the new public management can be identified worldwide, a common element in all these countries is the use of the market as a model for political and administrative relationships.

As Linda Kaboolian (1998) has said, "While the reform movements vary in depth, scope, and success by country, they are remarkably similar in the goals they pursue and the technologies they utilize. Each movement is driven to maximize productive and allocative efficiencies that are hampered by 'bureau-pathology' that is, public agencies unresponsive to the demands of citizens, led by bureaucrats with the power and incentives to expand their administrative empires and 'policy spaces.'" In addition, "across the reform movements it is possible to observe the use of administrative technologies such as customer service, performance-based contracting, competition, market incentives, and deregulation" (190).

Advocates of the new public management assert that "managers need to be liberated from routines and regulation by the various administrative systems, e.g., procurement and personnel." The Gore report on reinventing government takes this position, describing the federal government in the United States as "filled with good people trapped in bad systems: budget systems, personnel systems, procurement systems, financial management systems, information systems" (National Performance Review 1993, 2). The recommended course of action is deregulation, which entails "relaxing the rules, decentralizing authority, and increasing the discretion of managers" (Kaboolian 1998, 190).

In the next section of this chapter, we examine the new public management and its implications for public managers. We inquire into the meaning of the market orientation of these latest reforms, with particular reference to their effect on the role of public managers in the delivery of policies and programs. We also pay special attention to the entrepreneurial model of public management that the new public management encourages, and we consider the implications of the new public management for democratic governance. We conclude with a review of the relationship between the new public management and public ethics.

## New Public Management, Entrepreneurship, and Ethics

The material in this section samples the burgeoning literature on the new public management, drawing specifically from a 1998 symposium on leadership, democracy, and the new public management (*Public Administration Review*, May/June 1998), the work of Linda deLeon (1996) on ethics and entrepreneurship, and the work of H. George Frederickson (1999) on public ethics and the new managerialism. Our goal is to provide a reasonably coherent view of the major streams running through new public management thought and practice, with primary emphasis on American governance. We begin with Larry Terry's (1998) symposium contribution on administrative leadership, neomanagerialism, and the public management movement.

Terry opens his essay with a brief review of various public management approaches, focusing especially on liberation and market-driven management which, he contends, are guided by neomanagerialism. Then, from the perspective of democratic accountability and its dominant assumptions, he critiques the view of administrative leadership that he claims is fostered by neomanagerialism. He closes his essay with an exploration of the implications of neomanagerialism for the study and practice of public administration.

According to Terry, liberation management and market-driven management are popular because they are associated with the so-called global revolution in public management. He notes that liberation management is akin to reinventing concepts, stating:

> [L]iberation management is guided by the idea that public managers are highly skilled and committed individuals who already know how to manage. Consequently, the supposedly poor performance of public bureaucracies is not the result of managerial incompetence or malfeasance. Rather, it is the result of a "bad system," which is overburdened by a plethora of cumbersome and unnecessary rules, regulations, and other constraints. Succinctly stated, liberation management assumes that public managers are "good people trapped in bad systems" (195).

Thus, improving the performance of public bureaucracies demands that managers be liberated from the pervasive red tape.

Market-driven management is influenced, first, by the idea of competition, which is considered to be a viable strategy for public sector performance enhancement because it lowers costs and increases efficiency. The assumption is that "public managers will increase their performance levels if exposed to market forces" (195). The second influence is the notion of the generic character of private-sector management, which takes for granted the superiority of private-sector practices and technologies. Advocates of market-driven management then conclude that management is management and that differences between public and private management are illusory.

Turning briefly to neomanagerialism, Terry notes that the concept draws on public choice theory, which assumes that human beings are rational economic actors driven by competitive self-interest; it also draws on agency theory, which, consistent with this narrow view of human behavior, assumes that the rational economic actor—in this case, the public manager—is inclined to shirk, to be opportunistic, to act with guile, and to maximize his or her self-interest. Terry suggests that "the negative moral evaluation of human behavior deeply ingrained in these theories sends a strong message: Public managers require extensive policing for they cannot and should not be trusted" (196).

Terry then moves to a discussion of neomanagerialism, entrepreneurialism, and democratic governance, noting that "advocates of both liberation and market-driven management hold the entrepreneurial model in high esteem." In their view, entrepreneurial managers cut red tape, empower employees, respond to customers, and transform their organizations into mission-driven, results-oriented enterprises. But Terry warns us of the dangers of public entrepreneurship. For example, he points to the critics who "charge that the public entrepreneur's anti-traditionalist orientation and obsession with self-promotion, rule-breaking, power politics, risk-taking, and radical change conflicts with democratic theory." Public managers are public servants whose acts must be legitimated by the consent of the governed, the Constitution, and laws, not by personal values.

On the other hand, although conceding that accountability may be problematic when dealing with bureaucratic entrepreneurs, defenders of public entrepreneurship argue that it does not threaten democracy if it is "civic-regarding." In Terry's judgment, however, "the public entrepreneur's penchant for rule-breaking and manipulating public authority for private gain has been, and continues to be, a threat to democratic governance. The danger is intensified by the emergence of public entrepreneurs of the neo-managerialist persuasion" (197). The qualities of such managers—the risk-taking and rule-breaking, for example—erode the public interest even further and exacerbate the lack of trust and anxiety that many citizens already feel about government.

In contrast to Terry, Robert Behn (1998), in the same symposium, argues that "Leadership is not just a right of public managers. It is an obligation" (209). It is necessary for several reasons, including the fact that elected chief executives can lead only a few agencies, the fact that the legislative branch provides agencies vague and conflicting missions as well as limited resources, the fact that special interests can capture an agency and use it for their own purposes, the fact that the citizenry often lacks the knowledge and information to meet its responsibilities, and, finally, the fact that the judicial branch often focuses on narrow issues of process rather than broader public purposes.

Behn believes that, given the imperfections of the three branches of government, public managers can contribute to our constitutional system "by compensating for some of the failures of the legislature, the judiciary, and their elected chief executive. By leading, public managers can help to improve American governance" (209).

Behn says that the type of leadership that he advocates is between the "heroic conception of leadership," the reckless, charismatic, antitraditional, and innovative leader, and Terry's model of "conservator" leadership, which preserves the integrity of the agency. In Behn's view, between these two types of leaders are various possibilities and interpretations of responsibility.

For example, how should public managers interpret their responsibility to preserve an agency's integrity? According to

Behn, they could focus on following the rules scrupulously to avoid any taint of ineptitude, profligacy, or corruptibility; they could ensure that agency resources and authority are used for legitimate purposes; and they could defend their agency against attacks. But, to Behn, none of these steps would be enough (220).

To truly preserve the agency's integrity, managers must do more than react defensively; they must exercise initiative. "Responsible public managers not only preserve their agency's institutional integrity. They also use it. They deploy it to accomplish their agency's mission. And, in the process, they add to it." As Behn says, "Values and principles lose all meaning unless they are frequently applied to help resolve real problems" (220).

Behn also asks, "Why would we assume that the manager of a business firm, the manager of a nonprofit social-service agency, the manager of a religious organization, or the manager of a political party would have something useful to contribute to the political process but a public manager would not?" He replies that "Public managers have expertise, and we should not ask them to wait quietly and politely until they are formally asked for their judgments." "The challenge," he asserts, "is not to prevent public managers from exercising leadership. The challenge is to accept that they will—and should—exercise leadership and, then, to ensure that the other institutions of society—from legislatures, to the press, to citizen organizations—carefully channel this leadership in ways that promote the general welfare" (221).

## Ethics and Entrepreneurship

Implicit in leadership, public management—old and new—and governance are questions of value. In this section, we consider Linda deLeon's (1996) work on ethics and entrepreneurship in particular, while in the next section, we turn to H. George Frederickson's (1999) work on ethics and the new managerialism in general.

After briefly reviewing the origins, assumptions, and criticisms of reinventing government, total quality management, and public entrepreneurship, deLeon turns to a discussion of the virtues and vices of entrepreneurs, noting that "what distinguishes entrepreneurs—whether in the public sector or the private—is that innovation is much more central to their role, and they exhibit a greater-than-average willingness to take risks in pursuit of their project" (497). She cites Peter Drucker's (1985) definition of an entrepreneur as one who searches for change, responds to it, and exploits it as an opportunity, and she cites as well Eugene Lewis' (1980) definition of the public entrepreneur as one who alters existing resource allocations by expanding or creating new organizational entities.

At the same time, deLeon points out that "critics of public entrepreneurship look askance at the private-sector variety, concerned that if civil servants become entrepreneurial, then 'individualism, profit, selfishness and shrewd calculation become the norms for public agencies as well as private business.'" Yet, deLeon also observes that the aspects of the entrepreneurial character—egotism, selfishness, waywardness, domination, and opportunism—are, "in fact, *functional* for the entrepreneurial role" (497).

Pointing to such well-known public entrepreneurs as Hyman Rickover, J. Edgar Hoover, and Robert Moses, deLeon cites Eugene Lewis, who suggests that all of them "demonstrated single-mindedness in the pursuit of their own ends, rather than 'corporate' good behavior" (Lewis 1980, 235). DeLeon argues that "each was iconoclastic and egoistic, mavericks who strove for power, sometimes veiling the true nature of their goals in order to win approbation and rewards from others" (497).

With regard to selfishness, deLeon again cites Lewis (1980), who writes: "The public entrepreneur sees the organization as a tool for the achievement of *his* goals" (237), and then suggests that these goals are substantive and involve "more than merely a quest for status and power" (498). In this connection, deLeon distinguishes between selfishness and self-interest by referring to Robert Solomon's example of eating dinner. "One's self-interest dictates that one should do it, but to do so is not selfish. It *would* be selfish, however, to try to eat someone else's dinner, too" (498).

Thus, deLeon argues, since we all act in our self-interest, it is specious to charge that entrepreneurs may act in self-interest. "Most people," she asserts, "prefer to act when their behavior is determined *both* by self-interest and by higher ideals" (498).

With reference to waywardness, domination, and opportunism, deLeon contends that entrepreneurs are wayward "because they require some freedom to innovate or experiment, outside the boundaries of the usual rules and procedures" (499). Entrepreneurs also seek "to realize a personal vision in the business or governmental sphere," while "[c]ritics of public entrepreneurship fear that this tendency will lead to tyrannical domination within what should be democratically run agencies of government." DeLeon points out, however, that "the same is likely to be true of *any* CEO; witness the universal admonition of consultants and organization development specialists that change will not occur unless it has 'support from the top'" (499).

As to opportunism, deLeon suggests that "[T]here are two types of entrepreneurs, whose very different characteristics may help account for the different moral judgments of those who value and those who fear entrepreneurship. The two types might be called the 'opportunistic' and the 'tenacious' entrepreneur" (499–500). The opportunist seeks profit and tends to have little staying power, while the tenacious entrepreneur sticks to a vision, pursuing goals despite many obstacles. Finally, deLeon observes that "At root, the reason the entrepreneur is valued is that his/her activity creates value" (500).

DeLeon concludes by maintaining that public entrepreneurs are "necessary agents of innovation in a business or governmental arena that otherwise would remain static. They are catalysts who bring together problems and solutions that otherwise would bubble chaotically in the convection currents of modern policy streams. Many of the attributes that provoke criticism—their egoism, selfishness, waywardness, opportunism, and domineering style—are the extremes of qualities that are functional for their role as innovators" (508).

Although entrepreneurship, according to deLeon, is not appropriate for all problems, it may be the only way to bring about helpful change in particularly difficult situations. Therefore, in light of the hopes of reinventors and the fears of their critics, deLeon suggests that "the public sector should encourage entrepreneurship but focus it on those situations to which it is appropriate and necessary." It also "should ensure that it remains ethical—by setting limits, by nourishing professionalism in the public service, and by facilitating widespread public participation in all aspects of the policy process." In the end, "Ethical entrepreneurship remains a useful and important means of finding better ways to achieve public purposes" (508).

## Public Ethics and the New Managerialism

H. George Frederickson (1999) argues that "managerialism itself is inherently less ethical and has a greater propensity for corruption regardless of the adoption of 'safeguards.'" He takes this position in the belief that, although it may appear to be a defense of the status quo, "it is always possible, especially in the name of administrative reform, to make things worse" (266).

In other words, Frederickson resists the popular view that the new managerialism is here to stay, and that the job of ethicists is simply to determine how to make government as ethical as possible under the circumstances. He argues that "there are points at which it is the duty of the ethicist to spit into the wind," and that we are at one of those points (266).

In the context of public choice theory, with its assumptions about self-interest, the National Performance Review (now known as the National Partnership for Reinventing Government), with its emphasis on cutting red tape, and the popularity of privatization, contracting out, and downsizing, Frederickson asks, "How far is it possible to go in cutting red tape and streamlining government procedures without harming our cherished rights and forgoing fairness?" He suggests that there is a trade-off between "a sharp reduction in the regulations that guarantee procedural due process and the substance of individual rights and quality of governmental fairness," and that "[d]espite the political slogans of those who are reinventing government, they cannot have it both ways—they cannot reduce procedural due process regulations yet guarantee fairness for individuals and groups protected by regulations" (268).

Frederickson also maintains that much of the red tape can be easily defended in the context of compassion and protection. "Much red tape," he asserts, "can be traced to the wish to protect citizens against possible harm by, for example, assuring the purity of food, the safety of flight, or the safety of drugs" (268). In noting that a lot of red tape is designed to influence many forms of human association, including schools and students, labor and management, and parents and children, Frederickson suggests that "Red tape is part of government programs of compassion, such as food stamps, aid to dependent children, Medicare, Medicaid, and the like." He also points out that, although there is no doubt that corruption has been part of these programs, [i]t is illogical to assume . . . that there would be less corruption in the absence of regulations." He asks: "In the passion for deregulation, is it possible that government will be less fair, citizens will be less safe, and we will all be less compassionate?" (268).

One of the most significant issues that Frederickson addresses is the tough choices associated with downsizing and our desire to have smaller government while retaining all the programs that we cherish. But even more provocative is the notion that "the federal bureaucracy has not really been downsized but simply relocated and hidden." As Frederickson says, "the only way bureaucracy could be saved was to hide it." Therefore, the situation today is that "[F]or every federal civil servant there are almost five others in the shadow bureaucracy, working for government but not a part of government. These hidden bureaucrats are in the defense contract companies, space contract companies, the Beltway bandits, and the nonprofit and nongovernmental organizations with governmental contracts" (272).

Thus, despite the claim that "the era of big government is over" and that we have "a government that works better and costs less," Frederickson asserts that "there is little evidence that government is any less expensive," because "most of the labors of those who once worked directly for government are now being done by contract in the shadow bureaucracy" (273). Embedded in this environment are a number of ethical challenges concerning equity, accountability, and even efficiency.

Frederickson concludes with a prediction that, in 2010, the ancient saying, "Today's problems are yesterday's solutions," will have come to pass. Managerialism, with its mix of deregulation, privatizing, downsizing, and market competition, will no longer be attractive, and will have become the ethical problem. In this regard, he offers several instances of the ethical consequences of deregulation, including the bailout of the savings and loan industry, telephone deregulation, which has resulted in deteriorating service at greater cost, and *E. coli* outbreaks, which demonstrate the woeful inadequacy of food inspection. Frederickson contends that "Such ethical breaches will increase over the coming decade, leading to a step-by-step process of re-regulation," driven primarily by the issue of fairness. "People understand that government cannot always protect their food and their environment. But they have little tolerance for unfairness, and deregulation is resulting in widespread unfairness" (276).

Finally, Frederickson asks, "If these predictions are accurate, what should we do now?" His answer: Advise our leaders to stop following the recipe for the new managerialism—"at least to the extent we make it clear that the efficiencies it buys are coming at a dear price in ethics" (276).

Our review of reinventing government and the new public management has identified several important interrelated themes and issues, including democratic governance, entrepreneurial behavior, accountability, equity, effectiveness, and efficiency. Although everyone, presumably, prefers an honest, efficient, responsive government, the purposes, priorities, and form of such a government are open to debate.

Questions about the effects of rules, regulations, and other constraints persist, along with issues related to customers versus citizens, the shadow bureaucracy, public monopoly, and political-administrative relationships. Moral complexities and perplexities abound.

Embedded in the moral complexities and perplexities of public management are trust, assumptions about human nature, and citizens' perceptions and expectations of government. Larry Terry (1998) tells us, for example, that, given its narrow, deterministic assumptions about selfishness, opportunism, and guile, public choice theory sends a message that public managers are not to be trusted and require extensive policing. But we must ask what kind of policing, since a major goal of the new public management is to liberate managers from stifling and stultifying constraints. Presumably, it is the policing of putative market discipline, rather than the policing of regulations, laws, and the public interest. It is the policing of the private sector.

At the same time, however, it is difficult to fathom how any concept of the common good or the public interest can be sustained by the adoption of private sector values and practices—a question raised by deLeon and Denhardt (2000)—and the substitution of those values and practices for the values and practices of the public service. Indeed, if lack of trust in government is a problem at present and public managers are not perceived by citizens as trustworthy, it is not apparent that this problem will be resolved by transmogrifying public managers into private managers. To paraphrase Terry Hartle (1985), such a change will leave public managers like Sisyphus, eternally pushing the rock of reform up a hill only to have it roll down again as it nears the top.

This is not to suggest, however, that public managers ignore entrepreneurship as a subset of leadership. In fact, we suggest, in line with Linda deLeon (1996), that too often the debate over entrepreneurial behavior in the public sector is framed in simplistic, either-or terms: either a public manager is entrepreneurial and, therefore, a loose cannon, or a public manager is a slave to the priorities and preferences of his or her political masters. Clearly, neither of these alternatives is viable for constitutionally informed administrative activity.

In our view, Behn (1998) is correct when he asserts that public managers are obligated to exercise leadership, to take the initiative, and to seize opportunities. But in no way does this imply mere opportunism, deception, or rogue behavior. Again, to cite deLeon (1996), the goal should be ethical entrepreneurship animated by a powerful and enduring sense of the public interest.

Ultimately, the point of such entrepreneurship, in our judgment, is to create what Mark Moore (1995) calls "public value." As we have suggested throughout this book, to have a real and lasting impact, ethics in the public service must be embedded in organizational policies, processes, and practices. It must be understood as an integral part of an agency's life, not a mere addendum or afterthought, and it must be tied directly and explicitly to the contributions that an agency makes as a public expression of our collective life. In the next chapter, we explore the connections between ethics, quality, and performance in the context of public value and the pursuit of the public interest.

# CHAPTER 13

# Ethics, Quality, and Performance

Almost 30 years ago, *In Search of Excellence* (Peters and Waterman 1982) was a best seller. Part of the burgeoning literature of management improvement, it expressed several principles that characterize the best-run companies: a bias for action, innovation, and loose-tight properties, meaning loose controls over employees and tolerance for individuality, but insistence on tight adherence to the central values of the organization. Indeed, attention to the values of an organization seems to be the most important lesson from the excellence literature: Effective management means articulation of values and reliance on people to live those values in the workplace.

More recently, many organizations, both public and private, have been involved in one way or another in initiatives designed to improve the quality of their operations and relationships—total quality management, quality circles, and empowerment, among others. These organizations, to varying degrees, have been searching for excellence. Some may have taken the effort more or less seriously than others; some may have been more or less creative than others. But regardless of the possible public relations angle or lip service that might have been paid or actual attempts to change things for the better, these concepts still resonate with many managers and workers. Some of it may be faddish, poorly understood, or poorly implemented; some of it may produce cynicism or at least skepticism among the seasoned organizational veterans who have seen management miracles come and go. But underlying it all is our aspiration to be better and to find meaning and fulfillment in what we do for a living and how we live our lives.

The point is that, given our need for meaning and meaningful relationships, as well as the central importance of work in our lives, we are trying to connect or reconnect our work with the rest of who we are, even as we struggle to achieve the bottom line or to get the job done. Which brings us to the specific question of organizational integrity: How can we build high-performance, high-integrity organizations? How can we create and cultivate excellent organizations with clear, value-driven missions that are more than words on a page—that, instead, enable employees to use their energy, intelligence, and ingenuity while insisting that the organization's central values are honored and practiced every day? And, perhaps, the hardest question of all: How can we demonstrate that our ideas and initiatives have actually led to increases in productivity and performance?

In this chapter, we first touch on a few of the many proposals for improving organizations, such as empowerment, quality of work life, and reinventing government. We maintain that all of these initiatives are of a piece—organizational attempts, on some level, to achieve the same fundamental goal: to add value to what we do in service of citizens and of ourselves. We also suggest that, although measuring value and performance is difficult under any circumstances, public managers need not be discouraged, but need to approach this issue with some new questions and new strategies.

We offer a moral, political-administrative, and functional framework for public managers to consider in their efforts to build high-performance, high-integrity organizations. The first part is the unified ethic that you are now familiar with; the second part is the concept of public value; and the third part is a conjoined organizational development/quality of work life approach to change. Together they can provide you with a morally informed foundation for advancing the dialogue, your career, and the public service itself.

## PERFORMANCE AND PRODUCTIVITY

There is no lack of advice on how to improve public organizations. For example, we are often told that support of the organization's leadership is always a plus—that leaders need to walk the talk, model behavior, and trust employees if the organizational culture is to change. These concepts are thought to be important because members of an organization quickly learn to read its values and ethical standards, especially through its budget, which is the public expression of how it allocates its resources. When the boss sponsors an ethics audit (a diagnosis of the organization's ethical climate), sets aside time for ethics training, participates directly in ethics training, and requires follow-up, ethics is perceived as important, something the organization takes seriously and values.

We are also told that organizational leaders must make it safe for employees to act ethically, not only in times of crisis or scandal, but on an everyday basis as well. The point has already been made in this book, however, that we are not off the hook if our leaders are not high-integrity performers. We all must ask ourselves whether we are meeting our own ethical, as well as performance, responsibilities, regardless of where we are in the organization. We must ask, too, about whether we tend to get caught up in groupthink and the team-player ethic, which may make it hard for an employee to exercise ethical responsibility without being ridiculed or ostracized.

We are also told that consideration should be given to including ethics in hiring, performance evaluation, and promotion decisions, and that, if the organization's mission includes ethical behavior, then it should be evaluated along with other competencies. We must note, finally, that most advice about performance and productivity does not address ethical concerns explicitly, even though such concerns are implicit in performance and productivity issues.

Consider, for example, Sandra J. Hale's (1996) essay, "Achieving High Performance in Public Organizations." Hale's position on high-performance organizations is similar to the U. S. Supreme Court's position on obscenity: "It's hard to define, but I know it when I see it." Hale argues that "We usually recognize a high-performance organization when we see one, but it is harder to define the attributes that contribute to the high performance [because] the attributes of high performance form a whole that is greater than the sum of its parts—they mesh into a vital system and lose their individual characteristics" (136). Nevertheless, Hale offers the following indicators of high performance:

- Anyone in the place can tell you the organization's mission and values.

- It is always looking into something new.

- Its customers' satisfaction level is high.

- A "failure" is considered a learning experience.

- Its employees frequently work in teams.

- The leader is a partner to the staff members.

- Others study and write about it, and everyone wants to take credit for its accomplishments.

- It can give relevant information on program results.

- It is a laboratory and its own best model. (136-137)

These characteristics, she notes, are similar to those offered by many others, but as she suggests, whichever list you consult, you are likely to find "two fundamental approaches to high performance in the public sector: orientation toward a mission and the customer and empowerment of employees" (138). We might add that these two approaches are clearly consistent with the reinventing government movement.

The key values of a high-performance organization, according to Hale, include learning, a focused mission, and a nurturing-community culture. A learning organization "places a premium on innovation, risk taking, training, the right tools, communication, and work measurement" (140). The second value—a focused mission—"guides both staff and the stakeholders" and "should be accompanied by an overall vision and values." "The key element of a focused mission is a customer-based orientation [since] a close correlation exists between a high-performance organization and satisfied customers" (142). Finally, a nurturing-community culture is characterized by teamwork, employee participation, flexible management, and reward and recognition.

Yet, attaining these key values in the public sector is difficult. Hale describes "six public management barriers to sustaining high performance: 1. Continuous improvement is difficult with constant change of leadership; 2. Essential recognition and reinforcement of employee innovations are blocked by the adversarial nature of politics; 3. The media are not interested in government's good news, so it's hard to develop a reservoir of respect; 4. Innovation is further blocked by controls piled on controls; 5. The standard government funding processes are major disincentives to saving; and 6. Elected officials disagree on executive branch missions and goals" (146–147).

This is probably familiar territory to you if you have spent much time in public management, and Hale's suggestions for achieving high performance are familiar as well to even casual readers of the management reform literature. The challenge, however, is to suggest strategies to overcome the kinds of barriers that Hale describes and to show that implementation of these suggestions has, in fact, led to performance increases. Thus far, the evidence appears to be rather thin.

This is not to say that the management improvement advice cannot or will not lead to performance increases. It is simply to acknowledge that "proving" the productivity improvements associated with any initiatives is terribly difficult, notwithstanding Hale's claim that "the existence of high-performance management formulas in the public sector is convincing evidence that high-performance does indeed exist there, despite the public sector's unique barriers" (149). Indeed, it seems to fair to say that even a beginning law student would not infer that formulas for improvement equal evidence of improvement.

Hale's essay is valuable, nonetheless, for its description of the real barriers to performance improvement in the public sector and the characteristics imputed to a high-performance and, by implication, high-integrity organization. It provides a benchmark for reflection and understanding. Ironically, it is also useful because its lack of substantive examples of productivity or performance increases raises the question of what qualifies as a reinvention or a performance achievement.

The danger here is that virtually any change, no matter how minor, can be classified as progress. As Peter Drucker (1995) observes, some initiatives such as "one-stop service" in welfare offices, supplying accurate information to clients, and essentially doing one's job are hardly innovative and deserving of special recognition or reward. On the other hand, given the barriers to innovation noted by Hale, they may be the necessary early steps toward more comprehensive and significant change.

Robert B. Denhardt's (1999) comments on human resources and productivity improvement further illustrate the need to go beyond standard prescriptions for public sector performance growth and to develop fresh approaches toward more convincing evidence of such growth. For example, in sketching the evolution of management by objectives (MBO), quality of work-life programs, quality circles, and incentive programs, he notes that one common assumption has been that improving the quality of work life would lead to a rise in productivity.

According to Denhardt, "studies seemed to show that improving the quality of work-life led to decreased absenteeism and turnover, greater job satisfaction, and greater commitment to the organization and its goals—all features that should improve an organization's productivity as a whole" (333). Unfortunately, although Denhardt may be correct, no documentation of these studies is provided.

But most telling for our purposes is Denhardt's discussion of experiences in productivity improvement (337-341). At the federal level, success stories include the claim that in 1997, the National Performance Review (NPR), by its own estimate, had "saved more than $137 billion, established approximately 4,000 customer service standards, cut more than 16,000 pages of bureaucratic red tape and regulations, and reduced the federal workforce by 309,000 positions." More specifically, the Social Security Administration conducted telephone and in-person interviews with more than 10,000 clients to help develop a more customer-friendly operation. As a result, it upgraded payment delivery, increased the number of bilingual support staff, and streamlined claim systems. According to Denhardt, "the im-proved toll-free service was recently ranked higher than even those provided by L. L. Bean and Disney." The Department of Energy reorganized its contract management process and reen-gineered its internal management systems, creating the Strategic Alignment Initiative. Denhardt claims that "the result was a more effective, responsive system of administration for stakeholders both within and outside of the organization" (339). We should note, however, that the source of this claim is the NPR itself.

At the state and local levels, Denhardt offers similar examples. In Iowa, for instance, state officials felt that citizens did not see the value of public service and did not know what they were getting for their tax dollars. "This failure to connect had contrib-uted to a sense of disengagement between the public and their government institutions. Citizen cynicism had degenerated into a lack of public participation." State administrators responded by creating results-oriented assessment systems, including com-piling information from stakeholders, formulating measurable performance goals and benchmarks, connecting this information to the state's budget, and integrating the performance indicators, benchmarks, and budget data into decision-making processes.

On the local level, "in Louisville, Kentucky, city workers rewrote the area's telephone directory as a means of facilitating more effective connections with citizens." Thus, the heading "Garbage Collection" is no longer hidden behind the heading "Department of Solid Waste Management," and "citizens can now contact agency personnel more effectively" (340).

These examples of productivity improvement are laudable in one sense, but almost laughable in another. Certainly, no one can dispute the benefits of a more responsive organization that is clear about its mission, principles, and priorities. But do these examples constitute a reinvented government? Should or could these changes have been made without the fanfare of the NPR? Aren't these changes things that one would normally expect in a reasonably functional organization? And why did it take the NPR to stimulate these changes?

Furthermore, it is worth noting that Denhardt's position on the NPR is in striking contrast to his position in his essay with Linda deLeon, "The Political Theory of Reinvention" (2000), discussed in the previous chapter. In that essay, he and deLeon were quite critical of reinvention, while here he cites the NPR claims as true and positive, and does not even question, for example, the veracity or disposition of the alleged $137 billion in savings. Nor does he go beyond general claims and specify the outcomes of the state or local initiatives.

One piece of advice that does link ethics with productivity and performance, although not in a direct causal sense, is offered by Gary Zajac (1997). Zajac argues that "ethics failure (corruption and other forms of wrongdoing) is equally powerful as shortcomings of efficiency and effectiveness in explaining popular desires for reinventing or even eliminating government." "The development of professional and organizational excellence," Zajac suggests, "is at least as important for the practice and image of the public service as the pursuit of excellence at the technical functions of government" (385).

In Zajac's view, despite strong anti-government sentiment found in American culture, reflected in the reinventing government movement as well as other reform initiatives, there are equally strong ethical claims on the public service that must be honored. Indeed, "public service ethics failure" itself is one factor that contributes to anti-government sentiment in this country. If true, it seems fair to say that the apparently oxymoronic phrase, "ethics in government," may mirror disappointment and disenchantment more than mindless anti-government ideology.

By ethical claims, Zajac is referring to "standards of right conduct which the public has legitimate warrant to demand of public servants and organizations. Right conduct refers not only to the honest management of public resources but also to respect for the rights and dignity of persons within and outside of public organizations." Zajac believes that "right conduct in government translates into a well-founded respect for, and trust of government on the part of the citizenry" (392).

Whether this assertion can be proved—whether respect and trust can be measured and demonstrated—ample survey data indicate that trust in government has plummeted since the 1960s; this drop in turn has important implications for public sector legitimacy and effectiveness. This decline has occurred despite the many accomplishments in government related, for example, to health care, food safety, law enforcement, technology, and national security. In any event, quantifiable or not, respect, trust, and legitimacy appear to be at least as important to the American public, if not more so, as visible technical achievements such as DNA testing, the Hubble telescope, and the Internet.

Our small, but illustrative, sample of the advice available to public managers for increasing productivity and performance captures the key themes and concerns in contemporary reform initiatives. Both advocates and adversaries of reinvention and new public management focus on quality, responsiveness, and efficiency in the delivery of public goods and services. The chief differences between them seem to lie in their respective concepts of the purposes and processes of governance.

As Nicholas Henry (2001) says, the reinventors are rebelling against both the traditional reformist public administration of the nineteenth century and the more recent administrative restrictions "that have resulted from a revisionist definition of corruption as waste and abuse as well as fraud." According to the reinventors, we must "unchain the bureaucrats from these outdated and crushing constraints, so that they may more effectively serve the public." On the other hand, Henry argues, "there is . . . much merit to the motivations of both the reformers of yore and corruption controllers of today." Their motivations, which encompass "cleaning up corrupt governments and protecting honest ones from corruption" (177), continue to be relevant to contemporary circumstances.

"The essence of the resistance to reinventing government," according to Henry, "is the fear that its loosening of traditional administrative controls will lead to more corruption in government" (178). But he concludes that "introducing the values of reinvention to governing will not inevitably result in less honest or less lawful government, as the critics of reinvention insist, and may induce more efficient, effective, and responsive government as the reinventers (perhaps rashly) promise" (180).

Thus, as Donald Kettl (1994) suggests, contemporary reform is mixed. Although the reinventors have made a valuable contribution in their recognition that top-down bureaucratic authority "no longer effectively steers public management" (180), the traditional approach remains valuable and can never be obsolete "so long as the United States is a government of laws" (54).

But governance in the United States is about more than laws. It is about principles and values, and it is about the public interest. It is about administering in a political environment, which means sustaining dialogue among competing interpretations of those principles and values and balancing the tensions in diverse policy arenas. It is about stewardship or trusteeship, which means public servants acting in behalf of citizens and sometimes presenting citizens with choices that only they can make. It is about responsibilities, obligations, and competencies (Green and Hubbell 1996).

The new managerialism drives many public agencies today. Managers are encouraged to emulate the private sector, which can be very confusing. For example, what may be considered to be appropriate behavior in a private organization may be considered to be misconduct in a public one. So when someone tells us that government should be run like a business, we might ask if that includes everything about a business, such as gifts and hospitality, as well as innovation and efficiency. The question, therefore, is whether effectiveness in government is to be defined according to business norms and standards, whether public managers must adopt business methods and measures as surrogates of market discipline, and, conversely, whether business is obligated to apply constitutional and ethical values to itself.

On the other hand, as Charles Garofalo (2000) points out, "Perhaps, our difficulty is in describing the establishment of goals, targets, priorities, and deadlines as 'business' methods, rather than as general management methods, which are applicable to all organizations. Perhaps, we also err in believing that there is an inevitable conflict between public service values and managerial excellence" (105).

## ETHICS AND PERFORMANCE

Let's now shift from performance advice to the relationship between performance and ethics, in the context of three caveats. First, we must be modest or tentative in our advocacy of devoting organizational resources to integrity, given the current paucity of concrete evidence of its efficacy or clear value-added benefits. Second, we must recognize that increasing performance or productivity is tricky under any circumstances, given the differing definitions, approaches, and applications associated with these terms. At this juncture, we are far from consensus. Third, we must acknowledge that it is not reasonable to expect ethics initiatives, including codes or training, to effect significant changes by themselves. Clearly, they must be part of a comprehensive strategy to address the major issues of contemporary governance.

At the same time, however, we must offer three qualifications of these caveats as well. First, scanty evidence of efficacy is not restricted to ethics initiatives. Proof of productivity or performance increases associated with any initiatives is difficult to accumulate as a rule. Today's reforms related to reinvention and new public management, for example, have been widely embraced without solid evidence to support their immediate or long-term potential. Second, despite the inevitable challenges in efforts to increase performance and productivity, we can draw on a wealth of available knowledge and experience to help us find our way. Third, this wealth of knowledge and experience includes the concepts, language, and strategies needed to identify the value-added benefits of ethics initiatives and to develop approaches to achieve them. We are not adrift in completely uncharted waters.

Let us begin by briefly considering productivity, particularly strategic measurement and total quality management. According to Henry (2001), many measures of governmental performance have been produced—on the local level, in fact, as many as 1,500 indicators—so the value of these measures is debatable. Therefore, what is being recognized is the need for a greater understanding of the process of public management, in order to help determine how performance measures are used and to what purpose.

As a result, "the use of performance measurement is now being conceived in terms of systems theory." We now think of performance measurement *systems* and the presence of six characteristics that are essential in the development of any performance measure: "its relevance, understandability, comparability, timeliness, consistency, and reliability." Henry argues that the "value of these measures is maximized when they are used to help link the functions of planning, budgeting, and managing into a coherent framework" (196).

Henry also tells us that "governments are experimenting with *Total Organizational Performance Systems* that are using performance measures to improve overall organizational performance by focusing on group, as opposed to individual, performance; organizational processes and flexibility; diagnosing performance for purposes of continuous improvement; and constantly measuring and recognizing cost improvements by individual departments." This approach, he says, "is predicated on many of the precepts of Total Quality Management" (196). Finally, Henry suggests that "The point of strategic measurement is to make the plethora of performance measures . . . both useful to, and useable by, top public managers" (197).

With regard to total quality management (TQM), Henry maintains that it is "designed to continuously improve, and, if necessary, transform the processes of the organization from top to bottom so that customers are fully satisfied with the organization's products, performance, procedures, and people." It also was the impetus for the introduction in 1987 of the Malcolm Baldrige National Quality Award, which was followed by the creation a year later of the Federal Quality Institute, since renamed the Federal Quality Consulting Group. "Federal agencies now compete for a Federal Quality Improvement Prototype Award and the President's Award for Quality and Productivity Improvement. State and local governments have developed similar awards" (198).

Yet, in spite of the impact of TQM on the public sector, Henry argues that it "is no panacea for the productivity problems of organizations, whether public or private." Even corporations, he suggests, have had mixed experiences with it, "including one hapless company that filed for bankruptcy shortly after it received the Baldrige Award." So, in Henry's view, "TQM addresses only some of the problems faced by democracies in enhancing their governments' productivity, and some problems it addresses not at all." For example, TQM could be effective in refocusing governments' mission as servants of the citizenry, in encouraging decentralization, or in stressing prevention of problems rather than solving them later. "But TQM simply fails to address those problems of productivity that are unique to the public sector" (199).

Some problems are systemic (e.g., governments are monopolies); some result from the lack of internal organizational authority found in the private sector; some relate to the need for the public sector to develop substitutes for profit to measure its productivity; and some concern the very different legislatively mandated missions of public agencies. All of these, coupled with a host of technical problems (such as defining customers, acquiring citizen feedback, and, significantly, the high turnover of top public executives), present serious and enduring challenges to proponents of TQM in the public sector.

Nevertheless, Henry does note that despite its public sector problems, TQM has been found to be helpful at the state and local levels in such areas as group decision making, commitment to stakeholders, and customer satisfaction. Thus, he concludes that "TQM's strengths for the public sector may reside more in its philosophy and less in its commandments and techniques, since TQM pressures management to think in terms of defining quality in client-based terms; of seeing the larger picture; or improving processes . . .of empowering employees; of instituting long-term strategic planning; and of never being content with the status quo" (201).

Embedded in existing reform proposals—including TQM as well as others, such as quality of work life (QWL)—are the principles, purposes, and priorities that also attach to ethics initiatives and organizational integrity. TQM and QWL specialists are already conversant with concepts such as autonomy, responsibility, and authority. Empowerment, job enrichment, work design, and feedback are fixtures in our management lexicon and are tied directly to such goals as lower absenteeism, lower turnover, more job satisfaction, and greater commitment to the organization and its purposes. Thus, the familiar aims of these familiar reforms are inseparable from the value-added aspects of ethics and integrity: minimum self-deception, hypocrisy, and rationalization; trust; positive accountability; judgment and intelligent use of discretion; and willingness to take responsibility.

We have not proved, however, that ethics initiatives increase performance—at least not with what you might accept as hard evidence—because the question "What difference do organizational ethics make?" has seldom been asked and has certainly not been answered. But the normative and logical case can be made that well-conceived, well-organized ethics initiatives, with follow-through, can make a real difference in organizational, professional, and personal performance.

More specifically, we believe that our triad consisting of the unified ethic, public value, and organizational development/quality of work life can provide a framework for moving toward the generation of more conclusive evidence of the nexus between public sector performance and integrity. We believe, as well, that resources directed toward integrity should be seen as investments, rather than expenses.

Before turning to our triad, however, let's review Menzel and Carson's (1999) summary of the available evidence on ethics and performance. Menzel and Carson claim, first, that both private- and public-sector managers recognize that "productive, high-performing units are value-driven units that place ethics high on their list of values" (252). Although we agree, we also maintain, as Menzel and Carson imply, that the link between ethics and organizational performance has not been definitively demonstrated. Concrete measures of the value-added aspects of ethics training, for example, have not been developed, nor do we have consensus on what would constitute evidence that ethics training leads to more effective performance. We also might add that ethics training, as currently conceived and executed, cannot reasonably be expected to add much value to organizational performance.

On the other hand, one might argue that this "cost-benefit" approach to ethics training is fallacious, since things such as trust, accountability, and responsiveness do not lend themselves to measurement or statistical analysis. We all share an intuitive sense that ethics is fundamental, and many believe that public organizations are obligated to pay substantive attention to it, in order to fulfill their constitutional responsibilities in as effective a manner as possible. But just as reforms, in general, including reinvention, new public management, and TQM, require evidence of efficacy and justification, so does ethics—at least in the cost-conscious, utilitarian environment of public management.

According to Menzel and Carson, one of the first attempts to investigate the ethics-performance connection was the work of Frances Burke and Amy Black (1990), who "conducted an exploratory study of organizational ethics and productivity by surveying sixty-nine executives and managers, approximately one-third of whom were from the public and nonprofit sectors." Although their findings "did not demonstrate a firm empirical link between ethics and performance," they did "recommend that agencies should create 'a leadership group focused on identifying ethical concerns and productivity measures'" (252).

A second attempt cited by Menzel and Carson in this regard was the work of Willa Bruce (1994), who surveyed municipal clerks about ethics in the workplace. Bruce concluded that managers and supervisors have a "substantial influence on employee ethics and, by extension, on organizational performance" (251).

Menzel himself also has explored the ethics-performance link. For example, in several surveys of city and county managers in Florida and Texas as well as of employees in two Florida counties, he asked whether "ethical climates of public organizations reinforce or detract from organizational values such as efficiency, effectiveness, excellence, quality, and teamwork" (Menzel 1993, 193). Hypothesizing that "as the ethical climate of an organization becomes stronger, organizational performance values will be strongly supported," Menzel concluded that "ethical climate has an important positive influence on an organization's performance.

Menzel (1996) also has investigated the "organizational consequences of ethics-induced stress in the public workplace." He defines ethics-induced stress "as a form of cognitive dissonance between an employee's sense of ethics and the ethical or not so ethical values found in the employee's workplace." The question was "whether ethics-induced stress resulted in decreased employee productivity, lower levels of job satisfaction, higher levels of conflict, and higher levels of employee turnover" (253).

Based on surveys of several hundred city and county managers in Florida and Texas, he found "strong statistical associations between managers' high levels of ethics-induced stress and impaired organizational performance. Specifically, as the level of ethics-induced stress increases, job satisfaction decreases, organizational conflict increases, and employee turnover is likely to be greater" (253). Menzel concludes his discussion by observing that, although no research has been reported on "how much ethics is needed in an organization in order to yield a certain dollar value in efficiency or effectiveness . . . .the literature . . . points to a single conclusion: High-performing organizations embrace, indeed prosper, as a result of strong ethical work environments" (254).

## THE TRIAD

We now turn to the triad—our framework for generating the value-added aspects of ethics initiatives, for going beyond conventional advice and exhortations, for beginning to reconfigure our understanding and definition of performance, and for designing, implementing, and evaluating organizational endeavors to create and sustain high-performance, high-integrity workplaces. As you recall, the triad consists of the unified ethic, the concept of public value, and an organizational development/quality of work life perspective. Since you are already familiar with the unified ethic, we touch on it here only briefly before moving to the other components.

### The Unified Ethic

The unified ethic, which combines principle, purpose, and character, provides the public manager with a practical moral basis for thinking, deciding, and doing. But the unified ethic also needs to be enhanced by an understanding of behavioral and organizational dynamics. The public manager can then incorporate the enhanced unified ethic into daily decisions, judgments, and interpretations. We suggested six advantages of the unified ethic, including reduction of moral stress, clarification of value conflicts and justification of our choices, and transformation of ethics into a routine, high-performance activity—providing a balanced approach to decisions that is consistent with the public management environment.

## The Concept of Public Value

The second component of the triad—the concept of public value—is drawn from Mark H. Moore (1995), *Creating Public Value: Strategic Management in Government*. Here, we will simply summarize Moore's main points and also touch briefly on his analysis of the ethical challenges of public leadership.

Moore argues that "the aim of managerial work in the public sector is to create *public* value just as the aim of managerial work in the private sector is to create *private* value" (28), and in this context, he offers six key points, as follows:

- First, "value is rooted in the desires and perceptions of individuals, [so] public sector managers must satisfy some kinds of desires and operate in accord with some kinds of perceptions" (52).

- Second, "there are different kinds of desires to be satisfied." Private management focuses on goods and services that can be produced and distributed through markets, while "others are for things produced by public organizations and are (more or less imperfect) reflections of the desires that citizens express through the institutions of representative government" (52). The central concerns of public managers are citizens' aspirations, expressed through representative government.

- Third, public managers "can create value (in the sense of satisfying the desires of citizens and clients) through two different activities directed at two different markets." One market, so to speak, involves the use of money and authority entrusted to public managers to produce things of value to clients and beneficiaries. Examples include the provision of parks, treatment for heroin addicts, and deployment of military forces. This is creating value through public sector production. The second market involves the creation of value by "establishing and operating an institution that meets citizens' (and their representatives') desires for properly ordered and productive public institutions." This entails oversight and scrutiny and the assurance of fair, efficient, and accountable public enterprises. Here, "[t]he demands of citizens, rather than of clients or beneficiaries, are being met" (53).

- Fourth, public managers must reassure the "owners" that their resources are being used well. This is distinguishable from satisfying clients or beneficiaries of a program. "The production and distribution of the organization's products must be fair as well as efficient" (54).

- Fifth, "what citizens and their representatives (as opposed to clients and beneficiaries of programs) 'buy' from public managers is an account of the public enterprise—a story contained in a policy" (54). In this connection, Moore likens a policy in the public sector to a prospectus in the private sector.

- Sixth and last, the public manager's world will change as citizens' aspirations change, along with methods for accomplishing old tasks. New problems emerge, so "[I]t is not enough . . . that managers simply maintain the continuity of their organizations, or even that the organizations become efficient in current tasks. It is also important that the enterprise be adaptable to new purposes and that it be innovative and experimental" (55).

This, in general, is the aim of public management. Public managers "must work hard at the task of defining publicly valuable enterprises as well as producing that value," and "they must be prepared to adapt and reposition their organizations in their political and task environments in addition to simply ensuring their continuity" (55). The remainder of Moore's book provides public managers particular advice for developing a concrete definition of public value to guide them in their political and organizational arenas, as well as strategies for producing public value as consistently as possible.

With respect to the ethical challenges of public leadership, Moore notes that we have two images of public managers. One is the public servant who is the faithful agent of political masters and whose only moral duty is to provide expertise to the achievement of policies sanctioned by legislatures, elections, or courts. The other image is the public executive as an independent moral actor who is required not only to express personal views of what is right and good, but also to resist and protest in the face of injustice or venality. Thus, we are ambivalent. We fear public officials who have their own views of public value and who may pursue them at society's expense, but we also fear public officials who blindly follow orders, who assume no responsibility, and who are not accountable.

Moore, however, proposes a third alternative, which he believes is closer to the reality of modern governance. "In this image, public executives are neither clerks nor martyrs. Instead, they are *explorers* commissioned by society to search for public value." They are expected to take the initiative and to be imaginative in their search, but they are also expected to be responsive to political authority. But "[t]heir most important ethical responsibility is to undertake the search for public value conscientiously" (299), by which Moore means that they are open about what they believe is valuable, and they subject their views to both political and administrative tests of effectiveness.

In the end, public managers striving to create and deliver public value are guided by both commitment to a cause and a capacity for diagnosis, reflection, and objectivity. They embody what Moore calls the managerial temperament "that is appropriate for those who would lead organizations that work for a divided and uncertain society" (308).

## Organizational Development and the Quality of Work Life

The third component of our triad is intended to furnish a practical and well-established method for operationalizing the unified ethic and the creation of public value, namely, organizational development, or OD, in conjunction with a quality of work life (QWL) approach. You will recall that in Chapter 5, we touched on Gerald Gabris' argument that OD may provide the basis for reconfiguring organizational culture and for building meaningful administrative ethics. Now we turn to Robert T. Golembiewski (1996), whose work on OD and QWL completes the triad.

Golembiewski first provides a few definitional features of OD that, in general, are germane to our concerns in the triad. For example, he suggests that OD "is explicitly value-loaded;" it "encompasses patterns of interaction for individuals and groups, structures for organizing work . . . and strategic purposes and policies;" it "makes much use of organization members" in organizational processes; it "empowers employees to take advantage of opportunities through . . . skill and capacity building;" and it "encourages appropriate changes in members' attitudes, interaction, and norms" (512).

Next, Golembiewski compares OD and QWL, observing that, although they tend to have different starting points, they are based on similar behavior science theories and share similar values. For example, the concept of self-actualization is applicable to both OD and QWL, and each shares with the other the values of security, equity, individualism, and democracy. Workers should be secure in their jobs, "free from anxiety concerning health, safety, income, and future employment." "Workers should receive fair compensation" (518). Work should be stimulating and provide opportunities for continued learning, and organizations should seek to create democratic workplaces.

Of special interest here, however, are the OD and QWL techniques that can be applied to ethics training and the creation of public value. Golembiewski touches on three sets of activities that appear particularly pertinent to our triad. First, there is survey-feedback, a classic design in OD and a popular approach today. The aim is to collect, through interviews or surveys, information on organizational processes and then furnish feedback to all organizational members at all levels. "Executives may be interested in the overall level of satisfaction with management in the organization, while each supervisory cluster also gets the results for its own unit." According to Golembiewski, "[s]uch data can be used for scorekeeping, with each unit comparing itself to departmental or institutional averages," and "the data can also inspire action plans designed to improve conditions in specific units, as appropriate" (520–521).

Second, there are technostructural activities, which include micro and macro levels of application. "At the micro level, the focus is typically on building needs-satisfying roles or jobs." Specific changes can be identified from "efforts to unfreeze communication and increase trust" (521). At the macro level, the focus is on system building or renewal, including attention to structure, culture, climate, and values.

The third category of activities in both OD and QWL programs concerns policies and procedures. Golembiewski provides three examples that illustrate the broad range of issues that these activities address and the types of solutions they produce. First is flexible work hours, with management flexibility concerning such issues increasing employee choice. Second is quality circles, which consist of small groups of employees, who meet periodically and who are often trained in group processes and diagnostic techniques. The goal is to induce continuous improvement; according to Golembiewski, they have substantial success rates. Third is total quality management which, as we have discovered, does not have convincing success rates, but has enjoyed some success, especially at the local level.

Golembiewski concludes his essay with a discussion of the success rates of OD and QWL. He suggests that "OD activities tend to have the intended effects most of the time" (522). Citing various surveys, he asserts that "OD success rates are high, in general, with the basic range being 60 to 80 percent. Public sector applications have somewhat lower success rates, but not by much. Different OD activities vary in their success rates, but even the lowest rates are attractive" (523). Furthermore, he states that much the same may be said about QWL, with success rates for various QWL activities clustered in the 75 to 85 percent range.

Finally, after noting the possibility or probability of fade-out of OD or QWL effects and, thus, the need for periodic "booster shots," Golembiewski closes by contending that the values in OD and QWL are especially appealing in representative political systems, that success rates in the public sector are attractive, though somewhat lower than in business, and that there is a foundation for OD and QWL applications in both theory and experience. We maintain that an OD–QWL approach, reconfigured around the ethical principles, issues, and concerns in the unified ethic and the creation of public value, can serve as the linchpin in effectuating the triad.

In this chapter, we tried to make several key points. For example, we tried to show that attention to values is an established part of public management. It is not some strange or radical idea. Whether it is TQM, empowerment, OD, QWL, or ethics, we are talking about adding value to our work and to our lives. We are talking about enabling public employees to build their skills and to use their talents in service of the common good. We are talking about designing and redesigning work, creating pride and purpose, and producing and delivering public value.

We also showed that, in spite of the volumes of advice on improving public management in the academic, practitioner, and self-help literature, we still know relatively little about the ethics–performance link. Prescriptions pertaining to building trust, providing feedback, and developing leadership are easy to find. What is hard to find is concrete evidence that following these prescriptions will lead to increases in integrity or performance. What is also hard to find are answers to questions concerning the real purposes behind the attempt to link ethics and performance. For example, we might ask about why and how a public manager would try to correlate ethics training and productivity increases, and whether, absent conclusive evidence of such a correlation, that public manager should cancel ethics training or not consider it in the first place.

We showed, too, that several factors intervene in the attainment of high performance in the public sector. Frequent reference is made, for example, to such variables as turnover of top officials, lack of respect for government, and the bureaucratic budget culture that penalizes managerial economy, effectiveness, and efficiency. Public managers operate in the midst of competing or conflicting missions, values, and priorities that often obstruct innovation and imagination.

Finally, given these and other constraints on public management, we, too, ended with a piece of advice: our triad, a model for clarifying and connecting ethical principles, for joining those principles to the fundamental purpose of public management—the creation of public value—and for drawing on well-established, reasonably successful methods to make that union real. In our judgment, in light of the diversity of organizational missions and circumstances under the public management umbrella, the specific value of our triad will have to be developed by particular public managers in particular agencies. We would not nor could not presume to prescribe organization-specific strategies. Each of us must strive, in our own way, to find and create public value in order to serve both the public and our own interest.

# CHAPTER 14

# Ethical Dilemmas in Hybridization and Outsourcing

Special ethical issues arise when public organizations combine with private ones. Public and private organizations operate in different environments and different ethical contexts. Public organizations have an inherently moral status, or moral agency, that is not normally associated with private organizations. Administrators in structures that combine public and private organizations are particularly vulnerable to moral dilemmas in that their responsibilities to their private organizations may conflict with their public moral charge.

A similar conflict may arise in purely public organizations in which the interests of the organization are inconsistent with those of the people it is charged to serve. However, in such cases the public organization experiences a moral temptation rather than a moral dilemma: The organization is obligated to serve the public and it would simply be unethical to sacrifice that obligation for the self-interest of the organization. In contrast, the private-public hybrid organization may have legitimate moral obligations to its stockholders and to its other clientele. When those moral obligations conflict with moral duties to the public, a moral dilemma, rather than merely a moral temptation, results.

In this chapter, we first describe "hybridization," the combining of public and private organizations. We then discuss some of the ethical dilemmas that arise in hybrid organizations. Next we focus on the type of hybridization that results from public outsourcing to private organizations, with emphasis on the outsourcing of prisons and military functions. We conclude with suggestions for minimizing the moral dilemmas that arise from the conflicting ethical environments of public and private organizations.

## HYBRIDIZATION

The term "hybrid," whose origin is in biology, has come to mean any mixture of distinct elements, such as hybrid automobiles. We therefore initially define public-private hybrids as "organizational forms that operate in the border area between state and market and which have to combine conflicting cultural orientations" (Karre 2010).

One form of hybrid is the public-private partnership, or PPP, which may be defined as a contractual agreement between a public agency (federal, state, or local) and a private sector entity. Through this agreement, the skills and assets of both sectors are shared in delivering a service or facility for the use of the general public. In addition to sharing resources, each party shares in the risks and potential rewards involved in delivery of the service or facility (National Council 2010). Common PPPs include government outsourcing of construction, defense, and transportation projects to private contractors.

Hybrids that are not the result of contractual agreements are not considered PPPs. For example, a company that is in court-appointed receivership is, in effect, a hybrid. In other cases, government agencies may have assumed control of an organization because of its importance to the social structure, as in, for example, the cases of automobile manufacturers and banks that were deemed "too big to fail" in early 2009.

Another form of hybrid emerges in the case of businesses that are heavily regulated, such as private airlines. In some sense, these may be considered PPPs because there is a contractual aspect to the relationship; however, the contracts are not between equals.

Yet another form of hybrid is the government-sponsored enterprise (GSE), which is an organization created by government to promote social goals. More specifically, GSEs are "privately held corporations with public purposes created by the U.S. Congress to reduce the cost of capital for certain borrowing sectors of the economy. Members of this sector include students, farmers and homeowners" (Walstreet 2010). Among the best known GSEs are the Federal National Mortgage Association (Fannie Mae) and the Federal Home Loan Mortgage Corporation (Freddie Mac).

The definition of "hybrid" can be extended to include organizations that combine state and privately funded nonprofit agencies. Private hospitals and universities fall into this category.

However one classifies hybrids, they share one common feature: They "combine conflicting cultural orientations" (Karre 2010). That feature is significant because it renders hybrid organizations vulnerable to moral dilemmas. They are under obligations to meet the private goals of the organization yet at the same time they are obligated to serve the broader interests of society. Such dilemmas would be minimized in a libertarian anarchy, such as that proposed by Robert Nozick (1980) or in a totalitarian socialist society, but they are inevitable in a mixed economy; the hybrid is a microcosm of the mixture.

Given the various ways in which government and private concerns can be combined, the question of who is a public administrator is murkier than one might initially suppose (Lan 1992). Some people, such as the head of a publicly funded welfare agency, are unquestionably public administrators, while others, such as private, independent grocers, are not. But there is a great deal of ambiguity in other areas. For example, the CEO of an automobile company whose majority stockholder is the federal government may not nominally be considered a public administrator, but he may be *de facto*. His employment is under the control of the government and his actions are likely heavily influenced by it. Furthermore, the public investment in the company gives the CEO a responsibility over public funds. If he misuses those funds, he betrays the stockholders.

However, in this case, the stockholders are not private individuals who voluntarily bought stock in the company; in essence, the entire society is the stockholder. Society's stake in the company includes, like that of any stockholder, the profit the company makes. In addition, the public may have other interests that differ from those of private stockholders. Those interests may include making more fuel-efficient or environmentally friendly automobiles, even if they result in less profit. As a steward of public funds and of the public interest, the CEO functions, at least in part, as a public administrator. One could argue that he is entirely a public administrator because the public financial interest in the company cannot neatly be separated from the private interest.

The administrator of a public grant at a private university also might be considered a public administrator, even if she is a full-time employee of the school. If she oversees public funds, she has the responsibilities of a public servant.

In 1988, the United States Congress required any educational institution that accepted federal funds to comply with Title IX regulations (National Organization for Women 2010). The law suggested that if an institution accepted any federal funding, it was potentially subject to federal oversight. Is any organization that accepts governmental assistance in effect a public entity? If so, its decision makers share at least some of the public stewardship responsibilities of public administrators.

Administrators of GSEs such as Fannie Mae and Freddie Mac have such responsibilities. Those organizations were created to perform a public service and their funding is significantly influenced by public policy.

The phrase "public administrator" appears to assume different meanings in different contexts. If the phrase applies only to people directly on a public payroll, then the automobile CEO, the grant administrator, and the GSE heads are not public administrators. But since our concern is with ethics, the question becomes whether such people assume the ethical responsibilities that are characteristic of public administrators—over and above the ethical responsibilities they would bear if they were fully private employees. The answer is clearly that they do.

But it may be best to avoid a semantic discussion concerning the meaning of the phrase "public administrator." More important are the potentially conflicting obligations of an administrator of an organization that has both public and private aspects. Those conflicting obligations pose moral dilemmas and raise the question of how to reconcile the public interest with the rights of private corporations and companies.

## ETHICAL DILEMMAS IN HYBRID ORGANIZATIONS

As we have argued elsewhere (Garofalo and Geuras 2006), the public administrator is a moral agent. An ethical agent, as we have defined it, performs his or her assigned duties in an ethical manner even if the goal that he or she is pursuing has no moral significance. For example, an executive in a candy factory may be motivated only by the prospect of improving the company's financial status, but he would be an ethical agent if he did so in an ethically flawless manner. A moral agent, however, is motivated by and pursues a moral value. For example, a social worker who is motivated solely by justice and benevolence is a moral agent.

Public service is, by its nature, a moral enterprise. Public service is dedicated to the social good, as the people discern it. In fulfilling their charge to promote the good of society, public agencies are collective moral agents; therefore, public administrators, individually, are moral agents. Unless one supposes that the public administrator is to make no moral decisions that promote the social good but only follow the dictates of the majority, no matter how flawed, the public administrator must be a moral agent. The contrary opinion is especially unrealistic when one considers that, on many important matters, the majority opinion is not readily available.

Moreover, the public administrator is an expert in his or her professional field. As we will argue in Chapter 15, The Competent Moral Agent, ethical decisions in a professional context require experience and expertise that the general public does not possess. The public administrator is charged with those professional ethical decisions just as he or she is charged with making other professional judgments.

Any mixture of private businesses and public organizations, therefore, presents the possibility of moral conflict. The public administrator is a moral agent, but the private employee is not, at least *prima facie*. If the decision maker in an outsourced organization is not a moral agent, he lacks the responsibility inherent in public service. If we consider him to be a moral agent by virtue of his function in the public interest, his duty to the business that employs him is compromised.

The modern public administrator is sometimes torn between loyalties and responsibilities. As we have seen, she may be caught between the interests of the public and those of her organization. Such a conflict is more a temptation to favor organizational loyalties over the public interest than a moral dilemma. But in the case of an administrator in a hybrid organization, the conflict can become a moral dilemma. The administrator of a private corporation that has contracted to perform a public service has dual loyalties: to the stakeholders of the corporation and to the public. So also do administrators of PPPs, GSEs, and other hybrids.

Let us suppose, for example, that Eleazar is a government-appointed CEO of an automobile manufacturing corporation over which the government has effective control. His charge is to improve the firm's financial condition so that it will no longer need government assistance. If he succeeds, the government will remove itself from the auto industry, which is not considered "inherently governmental." Both the government and the corporation have agreed to the overall plan, which also has the support of the public. The plan will work most efficiently if the corporation can sell a large volume of cars at a reasonable profit margin.

But the government also has another interest that reflects its moral commitment to the best interests of society: an environmental interest in reducing greenhouse gases. Such a reduction is considered beneficial to the health not only of the nation but of the entire world. However, to meet the goal of significant carbon reduction, the corporation will have to produce automobiles that are neither as profitable nor as popular as larger, less fuel-efficient vehicles.

Eleazar is given considerable discretion regarding how to run the corporation. The nongovernment stockholders strongly favor policies that would separate the government from the corporation, but the government strongly favors the health of the environment.

The case of Eleazar may not be especially challenging from a moral perspective. One might argue that Eleazar should do that which, in the long run, would promote the best interests of society as a whole. He might choose the environmental option for its evident benefits to humanity. Alternatively, he might think that society's interests will be best served if it unburdens itself financially from the automobile business. The differences in the choices, in this case, reflect different means to the same ultimate value, i.e., the best interests of society. In addition to his duties as a CEO and as a government employee, Eleazar is also a citizen and therefore he has a strong responsibility to his country.

Another case demonstrates a deeper moral conflict, between the interests of society and the rights of an individual. Siobhan is an administrator in a financial institution that has been taken over by the government because it was about to collapse and cause turmoil in the financial markets. She is on a board that decides whether to extend loans to applicants with uncertain financial status. She is under a governmental mandate to promote affordable housing for low-income people and the government is willing to underwrite some losses for her institution to meet that mandate. However, the public cannot be expected to accept too heavy a financial burden.

Siobhan has to set a criterion, at least for her personal voting practices as a member of the board, to determine whether or not to support an application. Without a criterion, she would not feel that she is carrying out her duties in a responsible manner. The criterion is not legally binding on anyone and is not morally binding on anyone but her. Yet she feels she must devise a criterion as a moral duty. Siobhan is only one member of the board, so her vote does not determine the final outcome. But her vote, even if it is overruled by others, is final for her. It is her moral choice.

Siobhan determines that a positive vote on a certain class of cases would inflict a potential financial burden that the public would choose not to accept. However, she considers people in that class to have a moral right to the benefit of the doubt, so she considers extending that benefit to be consistent with her charge to promote affordable housing. She sees her case as a conflict between the interests of society and the interests of the individual loan applicants.

If Siobhan were an administrator in a purely private corporation, she could in good conscience vote against risking financial loss by helping the applicants. She sees no reason why a private company would be obligated to risk its profits and the investments of its stockholders for the interests of private loan applicants. But she believes that her responsibility as a member of a public organization endows her with special moral obligations, one of which is to the people her financial institution is intended to serve.

Siobhan's situation is in no way unique. Social workers often must choose between the interests of their clients and the financial cost to society of giving those clients the best care. Decision makers in public health systems face the same issue of the rights of the individual versus the benefits to society. The increasing prevalence of hybridization will make such decisions more widespread. Moreover, the members of an organization that has functioned privately for many years may think that its ethical behavior will be unaffected when it becomes a hybrid. But such is not the case.

To fully understand the ethical significance of Siobhan's dilemma, we must recognize that she has a fourth responsibility in addition to her obligations to the organization, society, and the individuals she serves. She must balance all those interests on the basis of something distinct from any one interest, something that would dictate her moral decision at the expense of all the other considerations: ethics.

The significance of ethics as an ultimate determining factor that outweighs other considerations can also be seen in another case involving Eleazar, the automobile executive in the hybrid organization. In this case, he is considering a slight compromise in the safety of the automobiles his company produces to make them more fuel-efficient, more affordable, and more profitable. The compromise, which remains within legal requirements, is favored by the corporation, its stockholders, and the government. Let us further assume that the general population and the potential clientele are willing to accept the risk, knowing that, while some people are likely to die, the likelihood for any individual is small. In summary, all the stakeholders favor the compromise. But the issue is not thereby settled. Eleazar must make the decision, and he cannot ignore his own moral values. He may reject the compromise on purely ethical grounds.

One might object that to impose his own morality on the public is to reject his charge, as a *de facto* public administrator, to act in accordance with the will of the people. But the charge and the will of the people are not clear, even though they both clearly support the compromise. Is his charge to obey the public's opinions on all policy matters or to make his own judgments as a professional on the public's behalf? This question goes to the heart of the nature of the public servant. Is she a mere instrument of the specific desires of the public in each instance or does she have the more general charge to act as a professional with her own moral competence?

For example, some provisions of the Patriot Act may violate human rights yet remain perfectly acceptable to the public at large. Nevertheless, a morally committed legislator may not only be permitted but may be morally obligated to vote against the act because of its moral defects. Similarly, those charged with executing the act may use discretion in imposing it, even if they are certain that the public prefers more vigorous enforcement than is morally acceptable.

While all public administrators must make moral decisions, hybrids change the moral equation in two ways. First, hybridization increases the number of public administrators, at least in the *de facto* sense. The administrators of a hybrid organization make decisions on behalf of the public and are therefore agents of the public. Administrators of Fannie Mae and Freddie Mac who decided to give risky loans at the public expense—and with potential consequences for the national economy—were acting as public agents. So were the administrators of AIG who allowed large bonuses to employees while the company was being supported by public funds.

Before entering into an agreement with government to form a hybrid, executives of corporations must be aware that their moral status will change. If they are unwilling to commit themselves—and all their decision makers—to the ethical demands placed on public administrators, the corporation should not agree to hybridization. Likewise, unless absolutely unavoidable, government should accept no hybridization agreement with an entity that is neither willing nor competent to act as a moral agent of the public.

Second, hybridization introduces a new source of at least *prima facie* moral dilemmas. The executive in a hybrid organization has initial obligations both to the organization and to the public. Conflicts between those dual obligations require that decision makers exercise moral judgment different from that of an executive in a private organization with no public affiliation.

## OUTSOURCING

The ethical problems of hybridization are evident in contracting out, often known as outsourcing, which is one of the principal instruments of government. Outsourcing entails many of the problems associated with hybrids, including the issue of conflict between different ethical environments. The public administrator is a moral agent with ethical expectations different from those of the private contractor.

The issue is rendered more complex when one considers the reasons that are generally used to support outsourcing. Presumably, private organizations are more efficient in providing their services. That presumption is highly questionable, but even if it is true, the problems of conflicting environments remain.

The issues of public value and sovereignty are major sources of conflict. Barry Bozeman (2007) defines public values as "those providing normative consensus about (a) the rights, benefits, and prerogatives to which citizens should (and should not) be entitled; (b) the obligations of citizens to society, the state, and one another; and (c) the principles on which governments and policies should be based" (13). More specifically, public values comprise due process, accountability, responsiveness, sustainability, citizen participation, and integrity.

According to Bozeman (2007), public values are found everywhere in civil societies, and those values can fail when they are not reflected in the market or in public policy as a result of factors such as ineffective communication of values, benefit hoarding or capture of public goods and services by individuals or groups, and violations of subsistence and human dignity. Although public values do not necessarily require public provision of goods and services in all cases, their ultimate protection resides in the state.

Public values and sovereignty are therefore linked. Despite the shifting currents in our conceptions of public and private (whether in law, contract, or regulation), government is still officially the chief umpire and fiduciary. We also must acknowledge, however, that "delegations of government authority to private hands are not simple transfer decisions. They are decisions that potentially transfer sovereignty" (Verkuil 2007, 81). Thus, in the interests of democratic deliberation and decision making, it is important to examine the implications of outsourcing for public values in general and governmental capacity in particular.

Ronald Moe (1987) argues that sovereignty is "the single most important characteristic that separates the public and private sectors" (456). In light of the contemporary privatization movement, with its blurring of public and private responsibilities and functions, Moe's statement might strike us as quaint. Yet, one particular quality of the sovereign Moe offers seems to be especially relevant: "A sovereign is indivisible," meaning that "a sovereign cannot assign its attributes to a private party and remain a sovereign" nor can a sovereign "share its powers with another body claiming sovereignty" (456).

In Moe's view, the assignment of functions to the public or private sector necessarily includes the question of whether the performance of the function involves powers properly reserved for the sovereign. Clearly, however, despite Moe's contention (as well as many other scholarly struggles to define the nature and significance of sovereignty), contracting out of governmental functions proceeds apace, with little or no regard for either the theoretical or practical issues involved.

A critical problem in assessing the impact of outsourcing on public values and governance is the confusion that surrounds the meaning of "inherently governmental functions." Despite periodic attempts by legislators, executives, and judges to clarify and codify the activities that require performance by government employees, consensus on the nature of inherently governmental functions continues to elude us. Combined with the ideologically driven effort to shrink government, this uncertainty leaves state agents embroiled in the daily struggle to do more with less; putative cost savings are often the primary justification for outsourcing many traditional governmental responsibilities (Guttman 2004).

Underlying the effort to distinguish between public and private responsibilities via a definition of inherently governmental functions is the obligation to protect and promote public values

(Dudley 1996). Public organizations are charged with protecting and advancing those values through both moral and ethical agency. If governance is to serve that charge properly, organizations that act under it must adhere to its values and restrictions.

Contracting out is regarded as beneficial if the adherence to those values and restrictions (be they constitutional or administrative) is not onerous, argue David Rosenbloom and Suzanne Piotrowski (2005). Does this position implicitly assume that these norms do not interfere with private sector efficiency and profit but do interfere with public sector efficiency and effectiveness? Or, we might ask how contracting out can be beneficial if applying constitutional and administrative law norms is onerous. Thus, we are left to wonder by what alchemy contractors can adhere to public values, be efficient, and make a profit.

The specific issue is whether reliance on third parties "runs the risk of governmentalizing them, and thereby negating the initial logic behind their deployment" (Rosenbloom and Piotrowski 2005, 13). If third parties are qualitatively different from civil servants—more entrepreneurial, for example—then making them "accountable to public purposes may alter the qualities that made them desirable" and "by the same token, the desire to make the civil service more 'entrepreneurial,' 'customer-responsive,' and 'businesslike' may dilute or negate the qualities valued in the civil service at the start" (13). According to Guttman (2004), the preferred option to the present muddling through is that the executive branch and Congress view the federal workforce as a whole—with periodic reviews of personnel and procurement policy, increased transparency of the third-party workforce, and public comparison of the differing rules that apply to federal employees and nongovernmental actors in the performance of the government's work.

Guttman's prescription may not go far enough as a response to his diagnosis of the problem. In the context of public values and outsourcing, the presumed differences between the public and private sectors present a conundrum that may require more than reviews, transparency, and comparisons of state and nonstate actors. Indeed, it may require reconsideration of the basic assumptions underlying the outsourcing process, including what Charles Goodsell (2007) calls the conceptual bias in favor of outsourcing and against direct administration by government.

Consider the assertion that private sector advantages are lost with the imposition of public values on contractors. This implies that public values stand in the way of governmental efficiency and that efficiency is the prime value to be sought. Hence, the question: Do we want government to be as efficient as the private sector is purported to be if that means neglecting public values?

From the ethical standpoint, one must ask whether the public organization and the private outsourced organization address ethical issues in a compatible manner. More specifically, from the standpoint of the unified ethic, do both organizations ask the same ethical questions and do they answer them in the same way? The public organization must affirmatively answer the questions that capture the teleology, deontology, virtue theory, and intuitionism of the unified ethic: "Do our policies and procedures promote the interests of society as a whole?" "Do our policies and procedures adhere to rational ethical principles?" "Do our organizational culture and behavior strengthen the moral character of the organization as a whole and of its individual members? "Do our actions conform to our moral intuitions?" If the private organization responds affirmatively to all these questions and thus maintains a commitment to public values, then no ethical conflict will arise. However, considerations of profit and private interest may preclude such uniformly positive answers.

The fundamental issues that arise in the specific areas of prisons and the military have broad implications for outsourcing and for hybridization in general.

## Outsourcing Prisons

Prison privatization, like that of other public programs and services, has been explained or justified essentially on the basis of potential cost savings imputed to private sector efficiency, innovation, and competition (Lukemeyer and McCorkle 2006). Byron Price and Norma Riccucci (2005), however, suggest that cost savings is not the primary reason for prison privatization. Their research shows that "more plausible explanations for the decision to privatize revolve around political and ideological factors such as the overall political and ideological culture of the state," even states with Democrat-controlled legislatures (232).

Whether cost savings or underlying political and ideological factors are the actual driving force, questions concerning inherently governmental functions, sovereignty, and state action typically are excluded from deliberations and decisions to privatize prisons as public officials cope with stringent sentencing requirements, rising inmate populations, and mounting fiscal pressures. Therefore, we can easily stipulate that corrections policy and management, as both an inherent political responsibility with ambiguous and conflicting goals and an inherent governmental responsibility with authority over life and liberty, present difficult dilemmas to elected officials, public administrators, and private contractors alike (Morris 2007). Here, however, consistent with John J. DiIulio, Jr.'s (1990) and Sharon Dolovich's (2009) analyses, we focus not on the question of whether contractors can provide economical, efficient, or effective prison management but on whether they *should*, given the constitutional, philosophical, and moral issues involved.

On the constitutional level, both advocates and adversaries of privatization agree that the delegation or subdelegation of sovereignty to private contractors is permissible, at least in principle, if the people concur and the agents follow the people's instructions or act under the color of the state (Schichor 1998; Verkuil 2007). As a practical matter, however, the people clearly do not directly concur in privatization and, furthermore, cannot rely on their representatives for oversight of contractors or for determining which functions are inherently governmental and therefore are not to be privatized.

As Guttman (2004) argues, "the codification of the principle of inherently governmental functions into 'public law' is coincident with its negation in practice" (41). As a result of limits on federal personnel designed to control the growth of so-called "big government" via the private sector, we have had a "bipartisan belief that the polity would indulge in the fiction that Big Government does not grow if the civil service does not" (41), despite the fact that the shadow bureaucracy far outnumbers the size of the federal workforce. Thus, once again, we see privatization-as-ideology at work.

At the same time, however, we must acknowledge that delegation in general, and in the criminal justice system in particular, is well established in the United States and other western democracies. Professional associations license attorneys and physicians, for example, and many criminal justice functions, including community corrections, diversion programs, and bail bonding as well as prisons, are administered by the private sector through government contracts.

According to David Schichor (1995), the key question is how much legitimate use of coercive power the state can cede to the private sector. Schichor suggests, largely consistent with Moe (1987), that if the state gives up all or a large portion of its coercive power, it ceases to be a state because it loses its sovereignty, which is final and absolute authority and is at the heart of private-public concerns. Similarly, Michael Reisig and Travis Pratt (2000) contend that "coercive authority is integral to the state and cannot be delegated to the private sector" (215).

The chief philosophical and moral issues embedded in prison privatization relate to our notions of the size and scope of the state, our public values, and the implementation of punishment. Privatization is generally identified with the minimal state, an artificial construct that citizens endow with certain rights and responsibilities. Thus, the delegation or subdelegation doctrine justifies the transfer of authority to private contractors. In the case of prison privatization, the concept of the minimal state underlies the libertarian claim that since the individual citizen is the source of legitimate power, punishment is the exclusive right of the victim; the victim can in turn transfer this right to others, including private prison corporations (Schichor 1998).

It is difficult either to ignore or to minimize the ideological energy behind this claim and its disregard for intellectual and practical complexity. For example, alternatives to the libertarian minimalist state are by no means limited to a maximalist state eager to subjugate its citizens through oppressive bureaucracies. The social contract is just that—a social contract, not an individual contract, and individual rights are necessarily mediated and managed alongside societal rights. Thus, the transfer of prison management to for-profit corporations is not equivalent to turning prison management over to individuals or institutions prepared to reify the individualistic concept of punishment.

On the contrary, this claim overlooks the concrete concerns involved in prison management, such as discipline, parole decisions, and good-time computation, that are encapsulated by the exercise of discretion. These concerns must be managed regardless of the perspectives and proposals of libertarians or other privatization ideologues.

Punishment is a moral issue centered on the deprivation of freedom. It is administered by the state without the consent of the punished and may include pain, loss, or even death. Punishment symbolizes society's core values; it expresses moral judgments and reaffirms the moral order. The symbolism is significant, then, when a correctional officer's badge displays the name of a private corporation instead of the state. This reinforces the claim of private sector superiority over government: that private enterprise is able to provide public services as easily and efficiently as commodities and that profit-making from punishment is legitimate. But these observations do not imply that government prisons are necessarily effective. In fact, they are often overcrowded, violent, and ineffective (Schichor 1998).

One important question is whether privatization is the solution, particularly given the inherently governmental nature of incarceration as well as the ambiguous and competing goals associated with corrections. Another is whether the focus on prison privatization provides a real opportunity to reframe the debate and enables us to identify broader approaches and perhaps even solutions (Dolovich 2009).

Despite the clear moral implications of prison management, including the exercise of discretion in critical decisions affecting inmates' lives, advocates of prison privatization have attempted to revive a version of the politics/administration dichotomy by separating arrest and adjudication from detention. From this perspective, detention entails no exercise of discretion; it is merely implementation of the sentence handed down by the court. But as Anne Larason Schneider (1999) maintains, "because prisons deliver punishment ... there is no way to turn this into a technical administrative exercise devoid of discretion" (205).

Moreover, the attempt to resurrect the politics/administration dichotomy raises a larger issue, namely, a concerted effort to drain the moral content from prison management and to transform privatization from a free-market ideology intent on commodifying the public interest, perhaps even calling convicts customers, into a value-neutral process propelled only by the public will. As DiIulio (1990) argues, however, "to continue to be legitimate and morally significant, the authority to govern those behind bars, to deprive citizens of their liberty, to coerce (and even kill) them must remain in the hands of government authorities" (173).

## Outsourcing National Security

The rise of private military firms has been explained as essentially a response to global threats, instability, and conflicts following the end of the Cold War (Avant 2005; Feeney 2008; Mandel 2002; Markusen 2003; Minow 2009; Singer 2003). While the United States and the Soviet Union maintained a bipolar peace for four decades, the period since has seen an exponential increase in the number of corrupt, fragile, and even failing states in the developing world, an absence of effective state apparatuses in many nations, and important growth in the presence of nonstate actors, including terrorist organizations, multinational corporations, and drug cartels.

Combined with military demobilizations, this situation has provided a ready market for the large numbers of unemployed members of the armed forces of the former Soviet Union and its satellites, the United Kingdom, the United States, and other countries. Already trained and experienced, these demobilized soldiers have joined private security firms to provide advice, training, logistical support, and intelligence to a wide range of state and nonstate clients.

The rise of private security firms has also led to a number of recent efforts to understand their significance on the national and international levels, their implications for sovereignty and governance, and their relationship to a decreasing supply of military members, especially in countries that rely on all-volunteer forces. Thus, before turning to the specific normative issues implicated in privatized security, we consider three symposia sponsored, respectively, by the Princeton Project on National Security (2004), the McCormick Tribune Foundation (2006), and the New America Foundation (2008), in order to distill the themes and issues central to the outsourcing debate. Participants in the three symposia included academics, active-duty and retired military, attorneys, think tank representatives, and members of private security firms.

The general approach to outsourcing security can be framed as principle following practice, as an ideologically generated strategy driving practice, or both. Despite the two decades of experience with this issue, the symposia reflect the many remaining ambiguities, uncertainties, and unanswered questions. One assumption made by the symposia participants, however, was very clear: Regardless of the multiple challenges related to outsourcing, it is unlikely to disappear in the foreseeable future. Both the Department of Defense and the Department of State will continue to contract with private military companies despite an absence of credible data to support supposed private sector superiority over government, resource constraints in the face of

American global commitments, and post-conflict reconstruction requirements.

Nevertheless, a number of key concerns emerged from the symposia, including the numerous tradeoffs and dilemmas found in any policy realm. For example, regardless of the lack of convincing evidence to support the cost-savings claim, the political or ideological nature of outsourcing virtually precludes a serious challenge to this deeply held belief. The oligopolistic environment in which outsourcing occurs, the lobbying and campaign contributions by private military firms, and the political advantage of excluding contractor injuries and fatalities from official statistics combine to strengthen the status quo and simultaneously to undermine accountability and perhaps even adherence to the rule of law. Yet, no participant in any of the three symposia questioned the legitimacy of the conventional and invidious characterizations of the public service as inefficient, excessively bureaucratic, and inflexible.

In the symposium sponsored by the McCormick Tribune Foundation (2006), for instance, the claim was made that government bureaucracy is often the root cause of outsourcing decisions. In particular, it is difficult and time-consuming to get approvals through both military bureaucracies and civilian government agencies. Still, no one asked why these approvals are required in the first place, whether they should be rescinded, and what might be sacrificed by rescission or simply circumvention. If, as one participant argued, the civil service system is dead on arrival and it is too hard to hire and fire, are there practical alternatives that might obviate the multiple public-value problems associated with outsourcing?

A number of participants in all three symposia offered their opinions regarding the enduring enigma of what functions, if any, are inherently governmental. For example, the question of whether there should be a bright line on the use of contractors generated much discussion, with one participant suggesting that no function that would destabilize public trust or jeopardize the public's links to government should be contracted out. Although the complexities underlying this suggestion were not explored, there was general agreement that logistics, medical support, and foreign troop or security officer training are suitable for outsourcing.

When it came to prisons, detention centers, and interrogation, however, the bright line shifted toward opposing outsourcing, while acknowledging that contractors are already playing a large role in these areas. It was generally agreed that prisons, detention centers, and interrogation should not be outsourced because of the high propensity for abuse. Participants also agreed that governance should not be outsourced, nor should intellectual capital such as doctrine writing and military education (including ROTC, which was outsourced more than a decade ago). There was recognition as well that a significant consequence of outsourcing intellectual capital is the loss of the military's capacity to understand its own profession. Finally, there was broad agreement that the long-term implications of outsourcing decisions are typically overlooked in favor of short-term expediency.

Symposia participants offered several suggestions. First, outsourcing decisions should be driven by mission goals, not simply costs. There is need for less *ad hoc* decision making and more focus on meeting national security objectives. One particularly provocative proposal in this connection was that the decision on what we should and should not outsource comes down to two questions: What will the American people pay for? What will the American people stand for? Regrettably, there was no discussion of how these two questions might be answered, nor was there consideration of transparency in informing the American people of the purpose, scope, and implications of outsourcing.

Second, government should prohibit the use of private security contractors in active battle spaces and build up the capabilities of the State Department's Bureau of Diplomatic Security and the military police to assume security responsibilities. Third, the Military Extraterritorial Jurisdiction Act (MEJA) should be expanded to govern the actions of contractors in Iraq and Afghanistan not currently covered by the Uniform Code of Military Justice.

Fourth and finally, we should move away from reliance on the "flawed and widely misunderstood" term "inherently governmental" in deciding how and when to use contractors and focus instead on core competencies and mission success. Congress should identify redlined activities that must not be outsourced and require the military to maintain a resident capacity for any function that it does outsource. We might question whether these two suggestions are inconsistent and how, given the resource constraints as well as embedded cultural perspectives and practices, the military might maintain its own capacity for outsourced functions.

## Public Values and Outsourcing National Security

The Preamble to the United States Constitution includes provision for the common defense. Although defense has been described as the quintessential public good, its definition and delivery raise complex questions. In this section, we focus on two major areas: (1) public values and contracting out security; and (2) the moral standing of government and private contractors, including the significance of national security outsourcing for civil-military relations. Implicit in these considerations is the concern that conventional claims about private sector efficiency, public sector inefficiency, and cost savings for taxpayers are insufficient if our public values are to be honored more in the observance than in the breach and are to be integrated into our decisions and actions as members of the polity.

A quarter century ago, Dennis Thompson (1985) explored the ethic of structure and the ethic of neutrality in American public service to determine whether administrative ethics is possible. Not surprisingly, considering the strength and durability of these two phenomena, a significant omission in governmental outsourcing today is the absence of substantive attention to public values.

Given the press of the immediate, the conventional, and the expedient, elected and appointed officials rarely pay more than lip service to the moral implications and impacts of transferring public responsibilities and resources to private entities. Public administrators involved in outsourcing civilian or military functions do not have the time, the skill, or the inclination even to raise questions that might be perceived by their superiors and colleagues as unsettling or threatening to the outsourcing orthodoxy. Thus, the ethic of structure and the ethic of neutrality remain intact.

Private sector superiority is an article of faith among many policymakers, and public administrators as well as taxpayers are expected to suspend disbelief in the push to outsource public functions, including security. "Commercial concerns and lobbying rather than real gains to the nation and citizens" are the drivers of this process (Markusen 2003, 471). Yet, even cursory consideration of the logic underlying outsourcing reveals its fundamental flaws. For example, how can we expect a reputedly inefficient and ineffective bureaucracy, staffed by risk-averse, rule-bound bureaucrats, either to protect the public interest in contract negotiations or to serve as competent overseers of efficient, effective, and politically influential private military entrepreneurs?

With regard to the moral standing of government and private contractors, in the context of civil-military relations, one of the principal concerns is the relationship between the military and the community. If there is an active connection between the military and the community, then government must justify its use of military force to the public—and government does not have complete control over public perceptions and assessments of a war. On the other hand, as Jessica Wolfendale (2008) argues, "If a government uses a private military company, there will be little reason for the government to justify how and when force is used and the public will have little direct access to the experience of war. Private military companies are not representative of the community they serve, and this is a morally significant difference between these companies and national military forces and provides the strongest moral reason for preferring national military forces" (218). While Wolfendale may be somewhat overreaching in her depiction of the use of private military companies and the public's experience of war, her general point is well taken.

According to Wolfendale (2008), the moral standing of the military is conditional on the legitimacy of the state and how the state uses military force. In her view, military force is not morally valuable in itself because the end it serves is not intrinsically morally valuable. Similarly, private military companies are not morally independent from their employers and how they are used. If no intrinsic moral difference exists between national military forces and private military companies, is there a moral difference between them? Wolfendale (2008) answers that the chief reason why national military forces are morally valuable is that their personnel are members of the community. In countries with all-volunteer forces, the national military manifests its citizens' willingness to defend their common life and the life they share with their allies.

A government will try to justify its defense policies to the public because it is the community that will bear the costs of military action; once these justifications are in the public domain, criticism and debate become possible. Wolfendale (2008) concludes: "If we treat private military companies as morally equivalent to national military forces, we fail to recognize the emotional, political, and symbolic importance of the literal and symbolic relationship between national military forces and the community"(231).

In a similar vein, Elle Krahmann (2008) draws two important distinctions between the military contractor and the professional soldier. She believes that the primary feature of the military profession is ultimate liability or the willingness to give one's life as part of a professional ethos. The private contractor recognizes no such liability and swears no allegiance to the state or the constitution. "The military entrepreneur is not bound to anybody but him or herself" (255).

The second distinction is the profit motive. While the military professional ranks patriotism higher than financial rewards as motivation to join the armed forces, the contractor prizes monetary gain. Patriotism as a motivation is also undermined by the fact that most contractors are neither working for nor in their home countries. In Iraq, for example, military firms employ citizens from a wide variety of countries, including Colombia, Croatia, and Ukraine. Nationality and citizenship are irrelevant for contractors and their employees. "The military function of the military contractor is commodified and completely separated from his or her political person" (256).

Finally, Krahmann maintains that the net effect of the use of private military contractors is to introduce a new model of soldier, which poses fundamental political challenges for democratic control over the legitimate use of violence by undermining established civil-military structures of accountability. Private contractors may have no moral commitment to defending democracy or the state that hires them; patriotism is replaced by profit. Thus, "ensuring political control and accountability over the publicly sanctioned use of armed force is a fundamental aspect of civil-military relations within the democratic state" (261).

Colonel Matthew Moten (2010) notes the conflicts that arise when the military outsources its functions to private industry:

> Properly overseen, this military-industrial partnership can be a boon to national security. In many other cases, however-er, contractors have assumed responsibilities that heretofore were considered inherently military, such as logistical support, protecting installations and high-ranking officials, and developing professional doctrine. An army that depends on commercial enterprise to deliver its food and fuel is subcontracting its sustenance—an army travels on its stomach. An army that relies on contractors for its doctrine is farming out its thinking—an army fights with its brain as much as its arms. And an army that permits civilians to employ armed force on the battlefield tolerates mercenaries, the antithesis of professionals. (16)

A hypothetical example illustrates the potential moral conflicts that arise when the military function is outsourced. Kimon is an executive in a munitions corporation that has a contract with the government to produce weapons. His corporation is in the process of developing a new, high-powered weapon. The engineers determine that two options are feasible: The weapon can be made more accurate and damaging to its targets, or it can be made safer for the user. The more accurate model is less expensive and allows more weapons to be produced within a given period of time than the safer model.

The problem with the accurate weapon is that it has a greater chance of exploding and killing the person who fires it. However, this chance is only one percent greater than with the more accurate model. Given the number of firings, Kimon calculates that 20–30 users will lose their lives. Kimon must recommend which option should be chosen. Let us assume, for the sake of the example, that the corporation has no legal obligation to inform the government of the nature of the decision. Rightly or wrongly, the decision is under a broad category of technical professional matters that are left to the expertise of the corporation.

Kimon's choice would be difficult if it were only a military decision. However, he is the employee of a corporation with a responsibility to investors to turn a profit. Company profits will be maximized if the more accurate model, which it is cheaper and easier to produce in large quantities, is developed.

It may seem that the moral choice is obvious: Ignore profits and choose what is best for the country. However, some, such as followers of Milton Friedman (Friedman 1970), might argue that the corporation's overriding ethical responsibility is to its stockholders, who seek the highest possible profit. Notably, the conflict between profit and national interest would not arise if the weapon manufacture were not outsourced in the first place.

## A CAUTIOUS APPROACH TO OUTSOURCING

The contemporary blurring of public-private distinctions, the diffusion of sovereignty, and the ambiguities associated with the state-action doctrine present profound ethical problems for both public and private parties in polities pursuing privatization. The goal, however, is not to draw an irrefrangible bright line between the two sectors under all circumstances, but rather to encourage clarification and comprehension of each sector's inherent functions as well as its legitimate roles and responsibilities.

Democratic public service is by definition a moral enterprise that reflects the values that citizens support with their tax dollars and policy preferences. Public servants are by definition moral agents, experts, and stewards (Garofalo and Geuras 2006). Ideally equipped with moral competence (including fidelity to the public good, respect for citizen sovereignty, and prudence), public servants protect and promote public values such as citizens' exercise of self-rule, civility, and sustainability (Winston 2003; Bozeman 2007). The public servant/moral agent functions with a unified moral perspective, not drawing arbitrary distinctions among principles, character, and consequences. Ultimately, the public servant is an exemplar of citizenship and an agent of the common good.

At the same time, the public servant/moral agent is mindful of the morally tortuous environment endemic to public service and the potential conflicts between explicit moral questions and conventional political wisdom. Expressing moral skepticism about outsourcing prisons or national security, for example, may not be an expedient career move. Yet, if the public administrator is a moral agent, then she is obligated to raise moral questions rather than focus only on alleged economic benefits. The public servant/moral agent, more specifically, would not ask where to draw the line between the public and private sectors but rather where to draw the lines—the tactical line mirrored in the managerial approach to outsourcing versus the strategic line reflected in the default assumption of government as a junior partner of private enterprise. The public servant/moral agent would then reject both as distractions from the central issue: the advancement of moral and public values in the design and delivery of justified public services.

The public servant/moral agent, then, resists technocratic approaches to essentially democratic and moral concerns. As Mary Feeney (2008) notes, for example, many academic critiques of outsourcing national security call for better contract management and government oversight, which "would be a laudable position if the core problem in military outsourcing were a problem of contract violation." The "primary problem," however, "is of public values failure" (34). Therefore, the public servant/moral agent would commend Cohen and Eimicke (2008) for their analysis of the public ethics of contracting, including issues of campaign finance, conflict of interest, and corruption, and Phillip Cooper (2003) for his analysis of contract negotiation. The public servant/moral agent would, however, reject their managerial responses, namely, improved contract negotiation and management, to these normative challenges.

Finally, whether the issue is outsourcing prisons, national security, or other programs or services, we confront profound and perplexing questions concerning the melding of two distinct and, in many respects, incompatible organizational cultures. One set of questions that reflects the complexity of such a melding can be found in the case law on state-action doctrine, in which federal judges have attempted to distinguish between public and private actors in the context of protecting the autonomy of the private sphere, protecting individual rights from abuse by government surrogates, and preventing government from evading its constitutional obligations. Regrettably, judicial decisions in this realm have hardly been a model of clarity or consistency (Rosenbloom and Piotrowski 2005).

A more nuanced analysis of the nature of the private and public sectors might be helpful. Mark Moore (2002), for example, considers three key notions at the heart of the outsourcing model: customer service, the bottom line, and contracting out. Distinguishing among the purposes, practices, and obligations of each sector, Moore provides a valuable point of departure for developing a more accurate and textured view of outsourcing than is usually proffered.

Although analysis may tend to be outmatched by advocacy or ideology, and supporters and skeptics may define good governance differently, systematic approaches to outsourcing should help enhance our understanding and judgment as we navigate between mindless adulation and mindless condemnation of either the private or the public sector. Ultimately, then, we need to revisit common assumptions and assertions underlying the outsourcing of public services, both to assess the claims and evidence related to outsourcing's outcomes to date and to explore possible, probable, and preferable futures in the context of emerging forms of governance, globalization, and most important, public values and citizenship (Treverton 2005; Verkuil 2007).

Decision makers in hybrid or outsourced organizations must possess the moral competence that is characteristic of the ideal public administrator. Such decision makers must recognize that they are moral agents and they must demonstrate insight and sophistication in recognizing and confronting moral issues.

This conclusion has implications for the process by which governmental functions are outsourced or private organizations are allowed to partner with public organizations. If the charge of the public administrator to function as a moral agent applies to the private organization working in the public service, regulations must be imposed to ensure that the private organization functions in accordance with that charge. The charge of moral agency must be made clear and the responsibilities of the public agency must be specified. While such specifications will differ depending on the function performed, they will serve to codify the requirement that the organization advance public value.

Private organizations may find such agreements onerous and be reluctant to enter into them. Theoretically, the imposition of such burdens could virtually preclude private organizations from entering into government partnerships or at least put corporations in a commanding bargaining position. However, there is empirical evidence to the contrary.

In the case of *West v. Atkins* [487 U.S. 42(1988)], the United State Supreme Court concluded that the contracted physician working for a state prison operates "under the color of law" and is therefore subject to many or the same legal obligations of a government employee. Moreover, in the case of *Richardson v. McKnight* [521 U.S. 399 (1997)], the Supreme Court held that some of the immunities from lawsuit that are enjoyed by public employees do not apply to private contractors working in state prisons. In effect, this case established that the private contractor is in some respects more vulnerable than a purely public agency would be. Despite both rulings, private corporations continue to compete for prison contracts.

In some cases, extra incentives may be required to persuade private corporations to accept outsourcing contracts heavily laden with the requirements of moral and ethical agency that apply to public service. Although such incentives may be costly, advancement of public value is an appropriate public expense. If all reasonable incentives fail, insourcing may remain an option.

Unfortunately, there may be cases in which none of these options are possible and the public organization must do its best to ensure a successful partnership. Even in such cases, though, the public has strategies at its disposal. The ethical history of the organizations under consideration must be a factor that can outweigh the advantage of a low bidder.

The city of San Marcos, Texas, for example, entered into a contractual agreement with Kellogg, Brown and Root, a company that had engaged in questionable ethical practices (Batura 2010). In response to public outrage, the city reversed its decision. The problem could have been avoided if the city had taken the company's ethical history into consideration in the first place.

It is possible that the component of Kellogg, Brown and Root that was responsible for the work was blameless, and it may well have carried out its responsibilities under the highest ethical standards. But if all other incentives for the use of private organizations in the public service fail, ethical history surely should be a factor. Consideration of ethical history in the awarding of contracts also provides incentive to private organizations with any expectation of possible contracts with governmental agencies to develop more ethical organizational cultures.

Good intentions are not enough, however. Public organizations and private organizations with ties to public service must have ethical expertise in addition to ethical motivations. Intending to be ethical and having an ethical character are necessary conditions of ethical decision making, yet ethical decisions can be intellectually challenging. In the next chapter, we examine the development of the expertise needed to meet such challenges.

# CHAPTER 15

# The Competent Moral Agent

If you agree that the public administrator is a moral agent in principle, then the question becomes whether the public administrator can also be a moral agent in practice. To begin to answer this question, recall our summary in Chapter 11 of Kenneth Winston's (2003) discussion of moral competence as part of the practitioner's toolkit. For Winston, moral competence, which encompasses such attributes as fidelity to the public good, duty to civility, and prudence, is key for a practitioner of democratic governance.

As we observed, Winston's perspective on moral competence in governance complements our model of moral agency and moral action. But we also suggested that his analysis lacks an explicit moral basis for the democratic practice of governance while our model of moral agency, including the unified ethic, provides such a basis. We concluded that, although the unified ethic alone is not enough to resolve the enduring issues associated with administrative legitimacy, compliance, and integrity, without it the probability of developing and sustaining moral competence in public administration is highly doubtful.

In this chapter, we shift our focus to the practice of moral agency, specifically its application in the context of good governance and professionalism. In our view, moral agency, good governance, and professionalism constitute a triad analogous to the unified ethic, with each element inseparable from the others; in combination the three elements represent the practical expression of the unified ethic. First, we consider the link between public service motivation and moral competence. We then turn to an examination of the unified ethic and moral competence, followed by a discussion of the relatively scant literature on moral competence in public administration. We then attempt to situate moral agency and moral competence in a grounded framework. Within this framework we consider whether Kohlberg's post-conventional reasoning is consistent with moral competence in public administration or whether it is trumped by Kohlberg's stage four conventional reasoning. Finally, we offer some reflections and recommendations for both practitioners and scholars regarding possible next steps in the development of moral competence in administrative thought and action.

## PUBLIC SERVICE MOTIVATION AND MORAL COMPETENCE

As we have argued in this book and elsewhere (Garofalo and Geuras 2006), the public administrator is by definition a moral agent. Regardless of social- or self-identification, the public administrator ideally embodies and enacts the values embedded in the constitution, law, and policy. Moral agency is intrinsic and endemic in public service, and it is aimed at promoting morality.

The practice of moral agency first requires consensus on the nature and purpose of ethical governance as well as an understanding of the unified ethic, including its utility as a decision-making framework and its application as an integrative device for sustaining the moral point of view. Second, moral agency requires a consistent level of public service motivation, even in the face of market-oriented reforms. Third, moral agency requires internal and external support of its legitimacy in the administrative and policy process.

Moral agency, however, must be distinguished from ethical agency, which is morally neutral. For example, as we have noted, the morally observant pipefitter is an ethical agent while the civil rights worker is a moral agent. Yet, for reasons familiar to seasoned practitioners and scholars, the majority of public administrators function, at best, as ethical agents and, at worst, as instruments of convention or expediency. Therefore, once again, the salient question is how moral agency can be ensured and expanded within public service in general to foster genuine efforts to implement the litany of values commonly enunciated in official declarations and policies.

One of the most important but neglected aspects of the moral dimensions of public administration is public service motivation. Both public service motivation and ethics comprise many of the same elements, such as changing expectations of public servants, responses to reform initiatives such as new public management, and fluctuating levels of citizen trust. Both research traditions also encompass the motivation of individuals to choose public service careers and to adhere to values, norms, and rules that accompany the fiduciary responsibilities of moral agents (Maesschalck, Van der Wal, Huberts 2008). Therefore, as Gene Brewer (2009) suggests, public employees are more inclined than private sector employees to engage in work that is valuable to society, although some individuals who are motivated by service do not work in public organizations. "People in all walks of life can perform meaningful public, community, and social service, and these activities are vitally important to society at large" (3).

Public service motivation, which James Perry and Lois Wise (1990) define as "an individual's predisposition to respond to motives grounded primarily or uniquely in public institutions and organizations," is linked to public service ethics in regard to leadership, interpersonal relationships, and efforts to influence organizational culture and behavior (Moynihan 2008). Both are concerned with the promotion of pro-social behavior, the encouragement of voluntary rule-following even when it may be at odds with self-interest, the building of trust in government, accountability, and productivity.

According to Donald Moynihan and Sanjay Pandey (2008), the bulk of empirical evidence supports the existence of a public service ethic among public employees. On the other hand, Laurie Paarlberg, James Perry, and Annie Hondeghem (2008) suggest that applied-values management is significantly underdeveloped; they therefore propose a constellation of tactics to improve performance through management of the values that motivate public employees. It is in the context of this need to connect public service ethics and behaviors that we delineate the relevance of the unified ethic to the development of moral competence in the public service.

## THE UNIFIED ETHIC AND MORAL COMPETENCE

The unified ethic is, by nature, practical. If ethics does not affect the way we behave in everyday life, then there is no serious reason for studying the subject. Ethics can be described as a skill that people apply in virtually all their activities.

Kant (1949) notes that, while people can be ethical generally even without theory, theory is helpful in understanding the foundations of ethics; moreover, theory can inform us of the more subtle aspects of good behavior (22–23). Despite the differences among the four theories in our unified ethic, all agree in one important respect: Experience and practice, rather than theory alone, are necessary to the development of ethical competence.

Aristotle (1881), in setting forth the foundation of virtue theory, makes the case for experience and practice explicitly. He argues that habit is the means by which ethical virtue is acquired (31). To be an ethical person, one cannot merely read a theoretical treatise or think deep ethical thoughts; one must behave in an ethical manner. For Aristotle, being ethical requires not only the occasional ethical action but a pattern of ethical behavior over time. The propensity to act in a consistently ethical manner can be the result only of habituation, which comes through repeated ethical action in appropriate circumstances. For Aristotle, virtue is the habit of acting according to the mean between the extremes of excess and defect (43), but habits take time to be both acquired and manifested.

Aristotle also argues that experience is necessary for the proper application of ethical virtues. The disposition to choose the mean is not a set formula that tells us what to do in specific situations. Instead, the disposition to choose the mean is a propensity to act in a virtuous manner. He argues that there is no method for calculating the mean; instead, someone must recognize what constitutes the mean by an act of judgment. While acknowledging that there are universals in ethics, Aristotle recognizes that those universals are applied differently in different societies; one must therefore have experience with a society and the practices of individual communities within that society to understand how to behave in an ethical manner.

Alasdair MacIntyre (1984), the foremost contemporary advocate of virtue theory, makes practice not only a valuable source of expertise but also an essential element of ethics generally. He argues that ethical behavior must take place within the context of a practice, which he defines as follows:

> By a practice I am going to mean any coherent and complex form of socially established co-operative human activity through which goods internal to that form of activity are realised in the course of trying to achieve those standards of excellence which are appropriate to, and partially definitive of, that form of activity, with the result that human powers to achieve excellence, and human conceptions of the ends and goods involved, are systematically extended (187).

MacIntyre argues that ethics, like playing chess, playing music, or practicing law, has long-held socially accepted standards that form the means of judging activities within the norms of the accepted practice. All such activities require experience with the standard and its application in order to acquire expertise. Master chess players, musicians, and lawyers do not acquire their skills merely by understanding theory but by engaging in the activity and judging themselves against the standard.

All three of these activities require not only the personal experience of the individual but also the historical experience of others who have engaged in the practice over the years. The example of the attorney may illustrate this point best. While courtroom experience is essential to legal expertise, much of the experience with which the new lawyer is equipped is not his or her own. Instead, it is recorded in legal text, written decisions, and scholarly essays. In addition, the experience of colleagues in a law firm, while not the personal experience of the individual, is valuable experience nonetheless.

Martha Nussbaum (2007), another virtue theorist, argues that the virtues Aristotle finds praiseworthy are general characteristics that can often be exercised effectively only with proper attention to circumstances:

> The Aristotelian virtues involve a delicate balancing between general rules and the keen awareness of particulars, in which process, as Aristotle stresses, the perception of the particular takes priority. . . . Like rules in medicine and navigation, ethical rules should be help open to modification in the light of new circumstances; and the good agent must therefore cultivate the ability to perceive and correctly describe his or her situation finely and truly, including in this perceptual grasp even those features of the situation that are not covered under the existing rule (694).

Experience and practice are evidently important factors in developing the "keen awareness of particulars" and the "perceptual grasp" to which Nussbaum refers.

Deontology is another of the theory categories that form the unified ethic. In *Foundations of the Metaphysics of Morals* (1959), Kant acknowledges that his analysis is *a priori* and theoretical, but he also recognizes that application of his theory to real, practical cases requires relating his theory, specifically his formulations of the categorical imperative, to empirical circumstances. In other works, including his *Lectures on Ethics* (2001), he attempts to make such applications. As we have noted, the third formulation, rendered by Kant (1949) as ". . . all maxims ought, by their own legislation, to harmonize with a possible kingdom of ends, as with a kingdom of nature" (53), is the most ambiguous when applied to actual circumstances yet is especially useful in resolving moral dilemmas.

Indeed, contemporary philosophical ethical literature is replete with theories that attempt to apply Kant to empirical cases. Such philosophical analyses include those of John Rawls (2005), Onora O'Neill (2007), and Warren Quinn (2002). The variety and diversity of their analyses demonstrate the flexibility of Kant's theory when applied to the empirical world. To act in a Kantian manner, it is not enough to master Kantian theory. One must be equipped with experience in the real world to determine how one's own interpretations of empirical fact fit with Kantian theory. No formula can substitute for such experience, even within the Kantian theoretical framework.

The teleological tradition, with utilitarianism as its predominant form, makes experience and practice key features in ethical action. For the utilitarian, happiness is the desirable end of all moral action; the means of attaining happiness are determined by the practical considerations dictated by circumstance. While the traditionally accepted rules of morality, such as "Do not steal" and "Do not lie," are reliable guides, experience is needed to discern how to apply them, when to apply them, and when to make exception to them.

Mill (1979) argues that experience is essential in distinguishing between different qualities of happiness. He argues that to determine which of two sources of happiness is of a higher quality, one must ask the connoisseur who is fully experienced in both pleasures. From this authority, Mill argues, there can be no appeal.

For the intuitionist, experience is also an important aspect of developing ethical expertise. But one must be careful in using the word "experience" within the context of intuitionism.

The intuitionist G. E. Moore (1976) distinguishes his moral sense or intuition from any empirical sense, such as sight, hearing, or taste. Nevertheless, he argues that intuition is analogous to an empirical sense, such as yellow, in that both directly detect their respective properties and, in both cases, the properties are simple and are not subject to analysis into component parts. Furthermore, moral intuition would have no subject matter to which to apply itself without an empirically observed event that possesses the intuitive property. For example, while the goodness in giving money to the poor may not in itself be an empirical property, one would have to either observe or imagine such acts of charity in order to notice the intuited property of goodness within them.

It is reasonable to infer that experience and practice play important roles in the development of ethical expertise for the intuitionist. If moral intuition acts at all as empirical senses, it can be sharpened and enhanced by experience. For example, an accomplished artist can discern nuances of color that less experienced observers do not notice. A wine connoisseur can taste differences that most people do not notice. In neither case would the expert necessarily possess native abilities that the average person lacks. More likely, the experienced expert becomes more attuned to perceptual differences that others could recognize if they were more practiced in the exercise of their perceptual sensitivities. If there is a moral sense, and if it behaves at all in the manner of perception, one could reasonably conclude that the moral sense can also be more finely developed through experience.

In all four of the ethical theories that constitute our unified ethic, experience is essential to ethical competence and ethical expertise. It should come as no surprise that practitioners in specific areas are better equipped to make ethical decisions within those fields than are amateurs. Doctors, nurses, attorneys, and baseball umpires are simply more knowledgeable in their fields than are the untrained. This is not to say that theory can be dispensed with. Kant (1949), while affirming the general reliability of moral judgments of "ordinary people" without a theoretical background, nevertheless regards theory as necessary for highly developed ethical behavior (7). Even well-intended people often are confronted with difficult ethical issues and moral dilemmas. In such cases, both experience and theory are essential to reaching the best possible resolution.

Robert Audi (1998) adds another significant aspect of experience in the development of moral expertise. When one performs morally good actions, one experiences a satisfaction that is in itself intrinsically good:

> Far from being just a cognitive awareness of moral properties or the bare thought of moral propositions, many of these experiences have positive value in themselves, hence are the kinds of things worth realizing for their own sake. Our dignity consists partly in our capacity for such experiences. Morality is not just a means of promoting non-moral value or a conventional structure that enables us to survive. Its experiential manifestations are among the things that make human life worthwhile. (375)

This is not to say that theory is an irrelevant or minor factor in ethical decision making. Rather than excluding theory from the process, we argue that practice and experience should be included, together with theory, in a complete ethical decision process. Neither pure theory nor uninformed practice constitutes a comprehensive ethic.

We have argued that experience and practice are essential to sound ethical decision making. However, people do not enter a profession with extensive experience, so how can we reasonably expect sophisticated ethical decisions from people new to an organization? Moreover, the problem of experience is not unique to the neophyte. All people, no matter how long they have been in a profession or organization, are limited by their own personal histories. The problem is therefore that of sharing ethical experience.

## MORAL COMPETENCE IN PUBLIC ADMINISTRATION

In papers prepared for the 2009 annual conference of the National Association of Schools of Public Affairs and Administration, a number of administrative ethicists provided their perspectives on the nature and aim of moral competence in public administration. For example, James Bowman (2009) maintains that because public administration is justified by a moral purpose, ethics in policy is essential in laying the foundation for excellence in public affairs. According to Bowman, in a sense all competencies are ethical, so "a technically incompetent manager is just as unethical as an ethically deficient manager" (1).

Robert Roberts (2009a) suggests five ethics competencies: corruption detection, prevention of conflict of interest, constitutional competence, understanding the moral implications of public servants' actions, and providing tools for public administrators to engage in ethically driven organizational dissent. Jeremy Plant (2009) contends that "ethical competence is the ability to analyze situations and decisions using the three most commonly employed theoretical frameworks: outcome-based, rule-based, and character-based approaches" (1). Plant believes that ethical competence includes ethical awareness, motivation to serve the community and individuals, respect for law and regulations, personal integrity, democratic and constitutional values, decisiveness, and the courage to take needed action.

Similarly to Plant, James Svara (2009) argues that competence covers only part of what is required to be ethical. Besides knowledge of law, ethical models, the nature of governance, and skills in ethical reasoning, for example, public administrators need awareness, commitment, autonomy, courage, and understanding of their distinctive ethical context. To Svara, quality of mind and perception, commitment to norms that transcend knowledge or skill, and motivation to choose the ethical course are key to moral competence. Finally, Terry Cooper (2009) argues for a design approach to organizational ethics in which ethical problems and their causes are contextualized, with an eye toward designing new structures and norms or redesigning old ones.

This collection of papers is a welcome addition to the emerging focus on the context of ethics in public administration. It is a critical step in the effort to penetrate abstract or hortatory pronouncements on the importance of ethics in public service and to develop strategies for the activation of moral agency. If we are to transcend moral passivity and moral complacency in public service, the integrated and design approaches promoted by these and other scholars are vital to the evolution of moral maturation in governance. But much more needs to be done.

Public administrators, entrenched in compliance models, do not see themselves as moral agents responsible for governance rather than rule-following. They do not recognize the need to reify moral agency via appropriate commitments, skills, and expertise. They do not believe that post-conventional thinking is critical to the effectuation of moral agency. On some level, they may feel that such thinking is an improper assumption of authority, not only beyond the law but above it as well.

With regard to practical ethics in public administration, we are interested in contextualizing moral agency and moral competence. Standard scholarly approaches tend to identify the characteristics of morally competent practitioners but fail to explain how such practitioners are to be developed and nurtured—or the likelihood of that actually happening. Implicit in these approaches are assumptions, for example, that failures of moral competence result merely from an information or awareness deficit; these failures then lead to exhortations and prescriptions pertaining to analytical and decision-making skill, motivation, and integrity.

Although an information or awareness deficit may well figure into failures of moral competence, it is clearly not the only or even the most important factor in the neglect of moral agency. Organizational disincentives to adopt integrity-based, instead of or in addition to compliance-based, programs; disparate perspectives on ethics; and an anemic grasp of the fiduciary responsibilities of public servants combine to present formidable obstacles to substantive and systemic change.

To help elucidate the issue, recall the distinction between an ethical agent and a moral agent. The ethical agent performs admirably, breaks no laws or rules, violates no principles, and upholds established values. In Kohlberg's terms, the ethical agent functions at level four—law and duty—where most adults, including public administrators, function. The moral agent, on the other hand, is in service to morality itself and tilts toward Kohlberg's post-conventional reasoning, which entails an effort to discern the values underlying laws and rules and to act on those values whenever possible.

The qualification "whenever possible" is especially significant in enacting moral agency in public administration, given the multiple perspectives on the proper role of administrators in both management and policy. Mediating between conventional and post-conventional reasoning can present perplexing, even profound, dilemmas.

For example, in *The Ethics of Dissent: Managing Guerrilla Government*, Rosemary O'Leary (2006) discusses the case of Claude Ferguson, a career employee of the United States Forest Service who became a government guerrilla in response to the agency's decision to allow off-road vehicles, namely motorcycles, in the Hoosier National Forest. What is particularly relevant in our consideration of the challenges associated with realizing moral agency in a generally inhospitable organizational culture are Ferguson's clashing obligations as cited by O'Leary. Specifically, according to Forest Service Regulation 6173.53h (1974): "Involvement in Public Controversies. Employees are expected to avoid becoming involved in public controversies on matters of public policy. Disagreements as to either fact or policy should not, under any circumstances, be publicly aired through statements to the press or any other medium. . . ." This is followed by a declaration from the Code of Ethics for Government Service (1974) stating that "Any person in Government service should: Put loyalty to the highest moral principles and to country above loyalty to persons, party or Government department" (76). O'Leary poses the issue central to our analysis of moral agency and moral competence: how a public servant might make sense of the paradox these obligations raise (123).

How can or should a moral agent in public service make sense of the kind of paradox presented by the Ferguson case? Is the Ferguson case a prototype of the moral dilemmas faced by public administrators daily? For example, despite the general scholarly tendency to encourage Kohlberg's post-conventional reasoning among public administrators confronting moral dilemmas, making sense of the type of paradox in the Ferguson case depends on the administrator's personal and professional circumstances, skill in moral reasoning, and level of intensity regarding the issue. A veteran employee of the Forest Service, Ferguson felt passionately about environmental protection and public safety in the Hoosier National Forest, while his superiors, exercising their managerial prerogatives, dismissed these concerns to accommodate motorcyclists represented by the American Motorcycle Association.

On one level, the Ferguson case can be seen as a genuine dilemma, a conflict between two sets of right values, both perplexing and pervasive in public service, that originated in the organization's own policies and code of ethics. But at a deeper level, the dilemma is more complex than a clear conflict between a moral David and an immoral Goliath. In fact, the dilemma may be genuine but framed in different terms. For example, it is right to meet one's family and financial responsibilities, to pursue one's career or profession, and to contribute to one's agency and to citizens, all of which may be seen as placing one's loyalty to the highest moral principles. Neither sacrificing one's personal or professional interests and obligations nor sacrificing one's highest loyalty constitutes a solution independent of the other. Thus arises the need to put the paradox into a moral framework—the unified ethic—and to contemplate the questions associated with each of its elements.

At the same time, the paradox must be considered from an organizational perspective. Organizational structure and culture are well-known as either enablers or inhibitors of particular behaviors, and the individual moral agent is unlikely to be successful unless the organization's leadership is receptive to proposals or at least questions concerning policy change. Therefore, if the leadership is uniformly intransigent or retaliatory regarding policy dialogue, let alone dissent, then other options may need to be explored, depending on the specific conditions in a specific organization.

If, however, managers are open to diversity of opinion, the potential guerrilla may choose to propose that the agency adopt an approach, perhaps similar to Carol Lewis' (1991) ethics impact statement, that requires explanation and justification in advance of any major policy initiative, such as the decision in the Ferguson case to allow motorcycles in the Hoosier National Forest. Such a proposal may be based on the prospects for increased trustworthiness and credibility that the agency could incur as well as on its intrinsic democratic and ethical nature. Thus, depending on circumstances, this paradox might be resolved without engaging in guerrilla actions.

## THE FRAMEWORK OF MORAL COMPETENCE

Making sense of the ethical and professional conflicts embedded in an organization's policies and code of ethics requires much more focus and detail than is contained either in exhortations to public servants promoting post-conventional reasoning or policies and regulations that ignore the competing values inherent in ethical dilemmas and the motivation, skills, and resources required to resolve them. In this section, we probe these concerns in the context of moral competence. We consider this competence in terms of moral development, the ethic of structure and the ethic of neutrality, and the ethics-administration dichotomy.

Much of the research on moral development in public administration has centered on the Kohlberg model, discussed in Chapter 9. The work of Debra Stewart and Norman Sprinthall (1991, 1993, 1994), for instance, led to the creation of the Stewart-Sprinthall Management Survey (SSMS), which is designed to measure the moral development of public administrators through the use of moral dilemmas. Other scholars, including Laura Lee Swisher, Ann-Marie Rizzo, and Marsha A. Marley (2005), have explored both the Kohlberg perspective and the neo-Kohlberg perspective formulated by James Rest in his Defining Issues Test (DIT). While the two perspectives differ in their conceptualizations of the developmental process, stages of cognitive development, and methods of evaluation, both models share a concern for post-conventional reasoning in the general population. This concern is shared by administrative ethicists, particularly with respect to the moral reasoning and judgment of public servants.

As noted, administrative ethicists often promote post-conventional reasoning by public administrators. Yet, given the predominant finding by administrative ethicists of the prevalence of level four (law and duty) reasoning among public administrators, the motivations and mechanisms behind the shift to post-conventional perspectives on natural rights, the social contract, and universal moral principles are not self-evident.

There is another potential flaw in Kohlberg's post-conventional reasoning. The flaw may be not in Kohlberg's theory itself but in common interpretations of it. In emphasizing the importance of abstract principle at the highest level of ethical thinking, Kohlberg appears, at least to some scholars, to slight the importance of experience and of the particularity of circumstances to which the principles apply. Carol Gilligan (1982), for example, argues that Kohlberg's analysis suffers because it is derived essentially from the experiences of men rather than women. At a more general level, Gilligan's criticism may be understood as demonstrating the overemphasis of principle and theory at Kohlberg's highest levels, to the near exclusion of experience.

This also appears to be the understanding of Hubert L. Dreyfus and Stuart E. Dreyfus (1991):

> The same polarity appears in feminism where the Kohlberg scale, which defines the highest stage of moral maturity as the ability to stand outside the situation and justify one's actions in terms of universal moral principles, is attacked by Carol Gilligan in the name of an intuitive response to the concrete situation. (230)

The phenomenon of cognitive disequilibrium can help explain a possible shift from conventional to post-conventional reasoning. In the context of the Kohlberg model, cognitive disequilibrium means that the public administrator's experience, rather than academic analysis and encouragement, might serve as the trigger of change in her level of moral reasoning. She gradually recognizes that her professional skills, defined and delimited by the organization, are inadequate to mediate effectively the moral dilemmas she faces virtually every day. Like the administrators in Morgan and Kass' (1993) treatment of the American odyssey and ethical crisis of career public servants, she confronts a constellation of values, including accountability, efficiency, and legitimacy, that produces profound stress in moral reasoning and moral decision making. But her experience triggers only the possibility, not necessarily the probability, of moving to a higher level of moral reasoning, given the general stance of most public organizations.

If Morgan and Kass (1993) are correct, we can easily conclude that the individual, even the collective, moral stress experienced by many public administrators is no match for the loss of conscience, judgment, and heart induced by the bureaucracy (Hummel 1994), the power of the ethic of structure and the ethic of neutrality promoted by the bureaucracy (Thompson 1985), or the ethics-administration dichotomy embedded in the bureaucracy (Garofalo 2008).

Our second key concern in the context of moral competence is the now-familiar question of whether post-conventional reasoning is appropriate for public administrators. On the one hand, post-conventional reasoning is consistent with moral agency in public service, with its implied accountability, autonomy, and responsibility. On the other hand, post-conventional reasoning is clearly inappropriate for public administrators functioning at Kohlberg's law-and-duty level, with its implied respect for proper authority, rules, and compliance. Therefore, urging public administrators to adopt post-conventional reasoning without specifying the risks, strategies, and tradeoffs is incomplete at best.

Moral development, motivation, levels of moral reasoning and judgment, cognitive disequilibrium, and professional as well as personal conflicts constitute a daunting array of complex and perplexing concerns. Whether it is observing obvious ethical infractions, struggling with subtle, hard-to-prove violations of ethical principles and standards, or analyzing and managing competing values and priorities, motivated practitioners require intellectual, administrative, and ethical tools to cope and perhaps even succeed. Yet the academic literature often fails to consider context—the actual circumstances surrounding administrative ethics—including the prevailing incentives, constraints, and sanctions in public organizations.

Key to contextualizing moral competence is recognition of behavioral variations associated with position, experience, and level of moral development. For example, some practitioners may function as ethical agents, meeting their responsibilities in a compliant, morally neutral manner, while others may function at relatively low levels on the Kohlberg scale, focusing on reciprocity and survival. Clearly, if the organization aids and abets such behaviors, the likelihood of substantive ethical growth, including acknowledgment of moral agency, is slim to none.

An important perspective on these and related issues is Howard Whitton's (2009) capacity-building approach to ethical competence. Whitton argues that core values require competent interpretation in context; that is, ethical problems must be identified before officials can reason about them and apply particular values in a given situation.

For Whitton, a focus on the values-laden political and administrative arena in which the public official is a moral agent is critical to contextualizing James Rest's four components of moral behavior: sensitivity, judgment, motivation, and character. But prior to interpretation, reasoning, and application of core values is competence itself—what the practitioner should be able to do based on knowledge and skills as well as appropriate attitudes and values. Therefore, the principal objective of competency-based ethics training for public administrators is to develop skill in identifying ethical issues and in making defensible decisions. Ultimately, according to Whitton, ethical competence comprises six components: problem identification; problem solving; advocacy, self-awareness, and consensus building; subject-matter knowledge or grounding in ethics standards; law and policy; and attitude and commitment.

Whitton's model for developing moral competence deserves serious consideration by practitioners and scholars. Yet, consistent with his depiction of public administration as an "inchoate normative environment" (238), there is reason to question the viability of his proposal, at least in the near term. Although he has gone further than many others in contextualizing administrative ethics and has tested his model via video case scenarios in Australia, Bulgaria, Estonia, Latvia, Lithuania, New Zealand, and Nigeria with some promising results, he appears to have made two dubious assumptions: (1) Leadership is motivated to accept his contention that its "primary task is to develop a coherent ethical institutional culture, and to ensure it is sustained to enable individuals to do their ethical duty unthreatened" (254); and (2) Leadership possesses the requisite commitment and skill to accomplish this task. While we applaud Whitton's imagination and energy, we believe that before his model is endorsed, let alone adopted, more evidence is needed regarding the role of leadership and the extent to which the outcomes of his project have been absorbed by the participating agencies.

Our position is generally consistent with the perspectives of James Bowman and Russell Williams (1997), James Bowman and Claire Connolly Knox (2008), and Gerald Gabris (1991). Bowman and Williams and Bowman and Knox find that public organizations tend to have no coherent ethics strategy, and Gabris "questions whether conventional management practices found in most public organizations make the possibility of a higher administrative ethics . . . rather meaningless and hypocritical" (205). He argues that "mere advocacy of ethical principles is not enough," especially "because real-world constraints make the practice of substantive ethics an elusive, complicated, and in some instances dangerous activity" (206).

According to Gabris, the disconnect in public administration between espoused and actual ethics is induced by several familiar bureaupathologies, such as hierarchy and organizational socialization, tolerance of suboptimal conditions, and defensive routines. These bureaupathologies in turn contribute to what he claims is a Machiavellian environment characterized by deceit, manipulation, and other dysfunctional and unethical behaviors. Yet, despite this portrayal of administrative ethics, Gabris believes that public organizations can become less Machiavellian via the implementation of organizational development, which promotes such values as trust, dignity, and excellence and provides a foundation on which to build ethical principles. While Gabris may be correct in his support of organizational development interventions and ethical growth, he appears to have made the same dubious assumptions offered by Howard Whitton, namely, that leadership is currently prepared to initiate such change and has the skill and commitment to see it through.

Finally, we all need to be reminded that during the past half century public organizations in the United States have enthusiastically adopted compliance-based ethics programs (Roberts 2009 b). Pressure to regulate financial conflicts of interest involving public employees; attacks on government for the traditional triad of fraud, waste, and abuse; the impact of the Watergate scandal on perceptions of public service ethics; the reinventing-government movement and the expansion of outsourcing; and the U.S. Sentencing Commission guidelines have led to the adoption of compliance-based ethics programs based on "the gradual realization that they offered many more advantages than integrity-based programs do. Specifically, they could provide a certain level of immunity from illegal actions undertaken by organizational employees. Equally important, they lowered the expectations for organizations and reduced the pressure to implement integrity-based programs" (262). This, despite the recognition by many critics of the deficiencies of compliance-based programs, such as their neglect of individual conscience, independent thought and judgment, and the range of ethical dilemmas confronted by employees every day.

Roberts concludes that organizations have no incentive to consider the possible integration of compliance-based and integrity-based ethics programs, largely because compliance-based programs "reduce potential organizational penalties for illegal actions by their employees . . . and "integrity-based plans make it much more difficult for organizations to respond to criticism of their policies and actions because it is more difficult to distinguish between permissible and impermissible actions by employees" (273). Moreover, compliance-based approaches "reinforce the ethic of neutrality, whereas integrity initiatives empower employees to challenges organizational policies and actions" (273). Nonetheless, Roberts argues that, despite the disincentives for the adoption of a fusion model, organizations "have an obligation to place equal emphasis on compliance- and integrity-based approaches policy" (273). Roberts seems to be suggesting that organizations are obligated to recognize and reward moral agency and moral competence.

## RECOMMENDATIONS FOR ORGANIZATIONAL CHANGE

We have argued that experience and practice are essential to sound ethical decision making and action. Yet, people do not enter a profession with extensive experience, so how can we expect sophisticated ethical decisions and actions from those new to an organization? Moreover, the problem of experience is not unique to the neophyte. All of us, no matter how long we have been in a profession or organization, are limited by our personal histories. The challenge, then, lies in sharing ethical experience.

In this context, we offer three recommendations intended to ensure that the experience of an organization is retained and thus becomes collective organizational experience. Our recommendations are not easy to implement, largely because they may threaten self-protective organizational cultures. Nevertheless, under the assumption that public administrators are moral agents intent on serving the public, they may be willing to commit to such change to better fulfill their charge.

First, organizations must be amenable to their decision makers discussing moral issues. Professionals show no reluctance to discuss nonethical problems, recognizing that such discussions are natural aspects of professional behavior. Ethics is often set aside as a distinct matter, something over and above professional competence. However, for a public administrator who by definition is a moral agent, ethics is not an adjunct to professional competence but central to it. Thus, public administrators must be able and willing to address the ethical aspects of their professional obligations and performance.

Such communication, furthermore, must be open to all decision makers. Opinions must be shared and discussed to arrive at the best collective decisions. Organizations are hierarchical, so decisions are unlikely to be entirely democratic. Those at the highest levels will undoubtedly make final ethical decisions and, presumably, take responsibility for them. But involving all decision makers benefits the organization in three ways. First, the public nature of the conversation ensures transparency. Second, the diversity of opinions expressed almost certainly strengthens the decision-making process. Third and perhaps most important, all decision makers benefit by contemplating and reaching conclusions on ethical issues of professional concern. Even if only one person ultimately makes the final decision, that decision becomes part of the ethical experience of all involved.

A second form of open ethical discussion occurs in the context of the entire profession rather than solely in the organization. The common ethical experience of public administration professionals should be included in scholarship and research, and it should be extended to the practitioner in clear and comprehensible formats. The daily experiences of practitioners should inform theoretical analyses and recommendations.

Conferences, papers, and journal articles are usually considered primarily academic exercises. Public service professionals, however, have every reason to engage in those activities if they help improve performance. As moral as well as ethical agents, public administrators must recognize ethical development as part of professional competence. Such activities need not be limited to practitioners. Terry Cooper (2009) recommends discussions of fundamental ethical issues at professional meetings such as the conferences of the American Society for Public Administration and the National Association of Schools of Public Affairs and Administration.

We suggest that such conferences include both administrators and academics in discussions of specific ethical issues that arise in administrative practice. Such discussions would help blur the line between the professional public administrator and the scholar. Eventually, the dichotomous relationship between them might become a continuum along which both are engaged in the same enterprise: serving the public interest.

Our second recommendation is more significant in terms of current organizational practice. We recommend that organizations preserve their ethical history in written form. It is commonplace for organizations to keep written records of budgetary and personnel decisions, but there is no similar expectation that organizations retain written records of ethical discussions, ethical decisions, and the reasoning behind them. Such records would be invaluable in filling the gap between the limited experiences of individuals and the collective experiences of the organization.

Akin to John Rohr's (1989) recommendation related to the use of Supreme Court decisions as guides for policymaking, we believe that the preservation of an organization's ethical history provides an opportunity for all members to contribute to the organization's collective experience (whether or not they agree with the final decisions). We recognize that keeping such ethical records will require significant changes in the culture of many public organizations, despite the increased emphasis on transparency and tolerance.

Our third recommendation is an adaptation of Carol Lewis' ethics impact statement, discussed in Chapter 5. Every policy or procedure, from its initial draft to its final implementation, should be accompanied by an analysis of all relevant ethical aspects. As Lewis notes, managers must develop the skills necessary to do their work properly, and ethical analysis is among those skills (Lewis and Gilman 2005, 257.) No proposal is considered without an analysis of budgetary implications; we recommend a similar treatment of ethical considerations. Indeed, the only reason to exclude an ethical impact statement is to maintain the fiction that ethics is a peripheral issue, not the essential business of the public organization.

Once an ethics impact statement is written, it becomes part of the organization's ethical history. The statement incorporates the experiences of the organization and the profession and then applies them to the specific issues addressed by the policy. The ethics impact statement incorporates past experiences as its foundation and becomes part of the organization's present and future experience.

We recognize that the disincentives associated with ethical development are pervasive and powerful in the public sector. Like other substantive reforms, ethical change is perceived as disruptive, offering only speculative long-term benefits and high immediate costs. Compliance, on the other hand, is comforting and comfortable. If differing understandings of the nature of public service (for example, the public servant as a competent moral agent versus an obedient bureaucrat) and differing interpretations of the public servant's responsibilities are not acknowledged, the practical advantages of compliance and moral neutrality can continue to be enjoyed.

We also acknowledge that our recommendations are predicated on a level of moral competence and commitment that is unlikely without reframing public service ethics, including "a reinvigorated conception of ethical public administrators, their obligation to resolve ethical dilemmas, and their covenant with the public, not as experts but as citizens in league with their fellow citizens" (Garofalo 2008, 351). Despite the pervasive and powerful disincentives that discourage ethical growth, however, reform in public administration has not been driven only by economic or rational forces. The competing drivers of reform have included demands for greater social equity, democratization, and empowerment as well as the humanization of the public service (Wise 2002). Therefore, we conclude that the central challenge in administrative ethics centers on the legitimacy of public servants as moral agents who are competent in the discernment, interpretation, and management of the values at stake in service to the public interest.

# CHAPTER 16

# Wrap-Up and Key Points

In this book, we have traveled down many paths to reach the same goal: a fresh perspective on the role, responsibility, and rewards of American public administration. This perspective consists of several things, including the unified ethic; the need for both compliance and judgment in decision-making; the influence of organizational structure, culture, and moral stress; and the importance of prudence, personal identity, and an ethical style. Each of these elements interacts with the others to weave a web of challenges, obligations, and opportunities, and each, in itself, constitutes an essential piece of the bureaucratic puzzle. Our aim has been to provide a map of this administrative terrain that will help to guide us toward our ultimate destination: fulfilling careers in high-performance, high-integrity organizations.

## COMMON ATTITUDES TOWARD ETHICS IN PUBLIC ADMINISTRATION

The following list, while not exhaustive, describes most of the different attitudes that people have toward ethics in their professions. When you examine the list, try to determine which entry, combination of them, variation on their themes, or other description best applies to the general attitude in your organization. You might also ask how yours might best be described, using the list as a basis. In addition, you might consider whether your attitude concerning ethics has changed since you began reading this book.

## Ethics As a Threat

Some people fear any mention of ethics in their professions. Not all people who take this attitude are unethical. Some may be very ethical in their personal lives but exempt their professional conduct from the same ethical standard that they apply at home. Others yet may be admirably ethical both at home and in their professions but fear ethics as something negative, accusatory, and judgmental.

This reaction to ethics is essentially emotional. Since it has no common source—people fear ethics for a variety of different reasons—there is no single antidote to it. However, much anxiety concerning ethics may be borne of unfamiliarity with the subject and a lack of confidence in one's ability to address ethical issues. We hope that this book helps to alleviate those sources of fear, or "ethics aversion syndrome," as we named it in Chapter 3.

## Ethics As an Externally Imposed Impediment

People who adopt this attitude do not fear ethics but consider it an annoyance. They believe that ethics is a barrier to attainment of professional goals, imposed by some source outside of the profession, such as a religion or a group of annoying moralists. Public administrators who share this view believe that ethics is not naturally part of their responsibilities and that, therefore, a public agent would, in the ideal professional situation, have no need whatsoever for ethics. To such people, ethics merely makes public administration more difficult and less productive than it ought to be.

This attitude reflects the failure to realize that ethics is part of one's professional life rather than a foreign intrusion. This attitude is especially to be avoided in the public service where, as we showed in Chapter 3, ethics is a fundamental aspect of the profession.

## Ethics As an Internally Imposed Hurdle

Some people think of ethics as something intrinsic to the profession, but, like the hurdle in a hurdle race, an obstacle in the way of attaining one's goals. Unlike the people who see ethics as an externally imposed impediment, people who take this attitude recognize that ethics is part of the job. Nevertheless, they still regard ethics negatively as a part that causes difficulty in reaching a desired end. Such people may think of ethics as constituting an aspect of the test of the true professional, who is able to overcome difficulties to attain the ultimate prize. They would not, however, regard ethics as an inherent part of the goal of their activities.

This attitude entails a more positive view of ethics than do the previous two. However, even this attitude is not optimal in public administration, where ethics is not an obstacle to success, but an essential element in successful public service.

## Ethics As a Component of the Job

This attitude is still not ideal as a public administrator's attitude, although it is better than any of the previous three entries on our list. Such an attitude suggests that the public administrator's profession has numerous separate parts, of which ethics is one. But as we have noted, the charge of the public administrator and the mission of his or her agency is essentially ethical. The public agency expresses the values of the society at large and is given the responsibility of fulfilling those values in an ethical manner. Ethics is not just a part of the job; ethics is the job.

## Ethics As a Defining Feature of the Profession

We have attempted to show that this is the most appropriate attitude for the public administrator. The goals that the society assigns to the public agent are ethical in that they express values that the society considers significant. The responsibility that the public agent has to attain those goals is also ethical in that it is based upon a public trust rather than a quest for profit. Furthermore, the manner in which the public agent pursues those goals must also conform to the standards of ethical behavior that the society expects from its stewards.

In public administration, the good professional is, by definition, the ethical professional. He or she does not distinguish the ethical component from other aspects of public service but regards them all, including the ethical, as one interwoven whole.

## Ethics As a Unifier

The signature quality of the ethical public administrator is integrity, the moral wholeness that belies moral fragmentation as natural and productive. Ethical public administration calls into question the assumptions and conduct of conventional management and what passes for political realism, which is often nothing more than the status quo of power, expediency, and hypocrisy, none of which can be justified, but only rationalized. Therefore, in promoting the unified ethic as the fundamental moral and functional framework for public service ethics, our central message is that the unified ethic reflects our nature as human beings and the inseparability of principles, consequences, and character in everything we do, personal and professional.

The real world of public administration is already familiar with ethics in some form, even though it may tend to be superficial and legalistic. We are trying to broaden and deepen that understanding in order to promote moral maturity, integrity, prudence, and democratic values. The possible benefits from such a broader and deeper understanding include greater institutional legitimacy and public trust as well as personal and professional growth and pride.

Ethics is often believed to be a great divider. It is said to divide judgmental people from people who want merely to live their lives without interference from others. Ethics is also often thought to divide those who make judgments against each other.

People with different ethical beliefs on matters such as abortion and capital punishment seem in diametric opposition. In ethical theory, the situation is the same: ethical theorists disagree with one another. In the workplace, ethics often seems opposed to productivity.

In this book, we have seen that ethics, when fully understood, unifies rather than separates. Although people with strongly held ethical views often oppose each other, any such opposition is trivial compared to the conflict in a world in which ethics does not exist. Self-interest divides people far more than do ethical considerations, which introduce concern for others and for society as a whole. Despite disagreements among ethical people concerning what constitutes the public good, they are unified in their dedication to the public good.

The workplace reflects the unifying power of ethics. Although ethical restriction may appear often to inhibit practical concern for the bottom line, the contrary is the case at a deeper level. Especially in public administration, which exists to serve the public rather than turn a profit, ethics ensures that the social good is always paramount over any private interest. Ethics is the font of responsibility, without which an agency cannot function. Rather than interfere with productivity, ethics inspires an agency to meet its mandate most effectively, efficiently, and cooperatively. The ethical foundations of the organization unify its purpose and its process.

Ethics also unifies the functioning of the individual with the public organization. The ethics of the individual and the ethical responsibility of the organization to promote the public good form an integrated whole. Without that integrity, neither the individual nor the organization performs its proper function. The unity of the ethical individual and the ethical organization forms a consummating unity in the society to which the public administrator and the public agency are committed.

In Chapter 3, we discovered that there is also unity in the apparent diversity among ethical theories. Our unified ethic demonstrated that the divisions among teleology, deontology, virtue theory, and intuitionism are ultimately illusory. The teleologist's ultimate concern for happiness is not, as it might appear, opposed to principle but actually depends on it. Happiness will never be attained without principle as a guide. Moreover, the teleologist's ultimate admonition, "Promote happiness," is itself a principle. On the other hand, the deontologist's principles would mean nothing without teleological considerations. Principles such as "Do not steal" and "Do not lie" are considered important because they have an impact on the social interest.

Nor can virtues be separated from either the public interest or principle. A characteristic such as honesty or benevolence is a virtue because of its relation to the social order and the rules of morality. As independent as our intuitions may seem from the considerations of the teleologist, deontologist, or virtue theorist, those considerations are undeniably factors that influence our moral feelings.

The theme of unity is expressed in the succession of the decision-making exercises that appeared in the book. In Chapter 4, the exercises were explicitly tied to the unified ethic. After each ethically problematic case, a list of questions, derived from the four main ethical theories, was presented. The aim of the exercise was to discover a resolution that responded to the question in a coherent manner reflecting the unified ethic. In Chapter 8, the list of questions was not made explicit, but the decision maker was to address the examples armed with the fundamental concepts implicit in the questions. In Chapter 9, those fundamental concepts were shown, through consideration of additional examples, to form part of a unified ethical style. The notion of an ethical style, when fully understood, extended the theme of unity to the individual within himself or herself because an ethical style, when fully understood, is the essence of a person's individuality.

Chapter 14 discusses the unity of public and private organizations in the form of hybridization and outsourcing. Here again, the basis of the unity is ethical. Hybrid organizations, we argue, must display moral agency because they are under a public charge. The moral agency required—the commitment to the public good—is the unifying factor in hybrid or outsourced organizations as well as in purely public organizations.

Ethics is the core of all the unities that we have discussed. The common core of values integrates the individual, the organiza-tion, and the society into a common community. Ethical unity within a community constitutes its integrity, but ethical discord entails disintegration. The public administrator should encounter not a choice between ethics and public service or even a mere compatibility between them, but ethics in public service.

Our moral lives are lived in community. We are all moral col-laborators who retain our moral identity regardless of pressures to the contrary, and acknowledgment of our ineradicable moral identity is the first step in reducing moral stress and renewing ourselves as moral agents. We found that the typical Type A and Type B personality categories might be conflated into the Type E personality, which combines the best of both. The Type E personality is spiritually healthy, centered, and self-aware; disciplined, restrained, and moderate; and, above all, morally mature. Developing a Type E personality is the second step in reducing moral stress and restoring our moral strength.

We recommended, too, that organizations would be well ad-vised to acknowledge moral stress and its costs, as reflected in such maladies as absenteeism, turnover, and burnout. Failure to recognize moral stress and its consequences is part of the failure to recognize the true ethical dimensions of the workplace, includ-ing the widespread mismatch between tasks and tools.

If you, as a public manager, wish to increase productivity, qual-ity, and performance in your area of responsibility, you might consider the possibility that the daily pathologies that you have come to take for granted may well be related to unacknowledged, and therefore untreated, moral stress. You might also consider the possibility that these daily pathologies result from the fact that when your employees are confronted with a real ethical dilemma—with competing claims, interests, and values—they have no place to go for real help.

In this regard, then, as we draw to a close, we ask you to ensure that the undeniable ethical content of all you do as a public administrator is considered in the daily routines of your workplace. We ask you to stretch your moral imagination, recognizing that, as Lewis (1991) observes, government is ethics institutionalized for pursuing the public good. We challenge you to apply your skill, experience, and discretion to the task of incorporating the moral point of view into the decisions you make, the rewards you provide, the sanctions you impose, and the culture you help to create. Reconfiguring the public service must begin with the ethically enlivened and committed individual willing to exercise leadership as a responsible risk-taker.

## FURTHER RESEARCH AND REFLECTION

The work of this book is not finished and never will be; the pursuit of ethics is an endless task. We attempt here to provide some aspects of the subject for further consideration. We expect to examine them in further research, and we hope that you will analyze them to enhance your understanding of ethics in your profession.

### Performance Linked to Ethics

As we noted earlier in this conclusion, there is a sense in which, for the fully professional public administrator, there is no need to "discover" a link between ethics and his or her profession. Public administration is by its very nature ethical. Fully professional public administrators recognize that they are ethically bound to promote, in an ethically proper manner, the values with which the society entrusts them. Ethics is so essential to the profession that to look for a link between the two would seem to misconceive both.

Nevertheless, it would be helpful to produce convincing empirical evidence that ethical organizations maximize the bottom line better than organizations that pay less attention to ethics. Common sense suggests that the ethical organization satisfies its public charge better, but solid evidence would make the case stronger. In Chapter 11, we noted that research has provided some evidence to support the practical efficacy of ethics in public organizations, but the research is incomplete—perhaps inevitably so.

Perhaps the best that the individual public agent can do to confirm that efficacy is to look at his or her own immediate environment and ask some central questions: Does ethics make a difference in the organizations with which you are familiar? Were you ever in an organization that would have functioned better if it had been more ethical? Were you ever in an organization that would have functioned better if it had been less ethical? Would you rather work with ethical coworkers than unethical ones? The mere contemplation of those questions suggests that the answer is self-evident.

## Agency Adaptation

This book discusses ethics in public administration in general. If our message is to apply fully, it must be adapted to the specific natures of each organization. For some, such as health and legal agencies, ethics will naturally play a more evident role than in others, such as those concerned with public groundskeeping. Furthermore, different agencies, regardless of their charge, may have developed different organizational cultures in which ethics has played a stronger or weaker role.

Because of such differences, each public agency is at a different ethical level and has different ethical issues. In the course of applying the contents of this book to your agency, we invite you to perform an ethical assessment and overview by asking such questions as:

- What are the primary ethical commitments with which the society has charged my agency?

- How ethical is it in discharging its duties?

- What can be done to improve ethics in my agency?

Remember that to find areas of possible ethical improvement in an agency is not to condemn the agency. None is perfect, even as no individual is perfect. We all can and should seek to improve as much as possible.

## Healthy Skepticism Toward Reforms

While we should all seek ways to make our agencies more ethical, we must not seek the quick cure-all. Chapter 10 revealed that reforms such as reinvention of government, managerialism, "running public agencies like businesses," and others with equally creative names—some of which may have been applied to your agency—are seldom as successful as advertised.

There are several reasons for the mixed results of such sweeping projects. As we noted earlier, each agency is different, and consequently, no general solution is likely to apply universally. Secondly, public agencies are more complex and under more subtle influences than the supporters of such "magic bullets" often comprehend.

Rather than look for some sweeping cure-all, we perhaps would do better to recognize that ethical improvement comes gradually and develops from small, incremental changes rather than from sweeping reforms. The internal ethical cultures of organizations must improve. To impose ethics "from above" is to accede to the misconception, evident in some of our previously mentioned flawed attitudes toward ethics in public administration, that ethics is an externally imposed barrier rather than an inherent aspect of the work of the public administrator.

Such impositions suggest that the people imposing the reforms know more about the public administrator's job than the public administrator does.

The best defense against such external impositions is internal reform. It is the responsibility of every member of the organization to improve its ethical organizational culture on a day-by-day, decision-by-decision basis. But the greatest burden rests on the highest-ranking members of each organization. They set the tone for the entire agency, and they make it easier or harder for those at lower ranks to effect improvement.

## Creating Public Value

The phrase "creating public value," introduced by Mark H. Moore (1995), is not to be misunderstood. The public charges the agency with attaining values. Moore does not mean to suggest that public agencies should create new tasks for themselves to build larger empires. Instead, Moore recommends that public agencies focus on creating valuable goods and services that are in keeping with the values with which the public charges its stewards through the mechanism of government.

Those values, such as empowerment to the disadvantaged, protection of the aged, and education for the general populace, are often stated generally. The public agency must determine the more specific elements of those values and the means of attaining them. Such determinations are the responsibility of the professional. Moore mentions, as examples of those determinations, provisions of parks, treatment for heroin addicts, and deployment of military forces. Each agency must use its expertise to discover the innovative ways in which the needs and desires of the public can best be served.

Moore discusses another sense in which the public agency creates value. Value can be created in the ethics of the process by which the agency performs its duties. Agencies must devise reasonable means of oversight and scrutiny to assure the public that it is being properly served, and in an acceptable manner, for the best result.

In using the term "creating public value," Moore emphasizes the creative aspects of the public agent's work. The fully ethical public agent must not be a mere follower of orders, but must also provide creative answers to the question, "What should be done in the public interest?" In answering that question, the public agent must display an understanding of value in general, knowledge of the specific values that the agency is best equipped to promote, and the innovative talent to discover new ways to serve them. The combination of abilities needed to answer that question may be called the "creative ethical consciousness" of the public agent.

That creative ethical consciousness is also evident in the unified ethic. In understanding and applying the unified ethic, one cannot merely follow rules in a formulaic manner, as some deontological thinkers would suggest. Nor can the follower of the unified ethic merely add up the most evident "happy" and "unhappy" results of alternative actions and produce a bottom line figure in order to calculate the correct moral choice.

The practitioner of the unified ethic applies rules and calculations with judgment and combines those more easily specified guidelines with a respect for the moral intuitions and with a concern for the aspects of human character that the moral act exemplifies. In applying the unified ethic, one uses the same talents that define the creative ethical consciousness. Under the unified ethic, one reaches ethical decisions as the result of a creative act based upon the understanding of values rather than on the basis of mere obedience to a formula.

The creative aspect of the unified ethic enables one to develop one's own ethical style. Like an ethical decision under the unified ethic, an ethical style is idiosyncratic, creative, and imaginative. While the ideal ethical thinker must possess some of the attributes of a research scholar, he or she must be, at least in part, an artist.

# Afterword

We are interested in your opinion and reaction to what we have offered here and will appreciate your taking the time to communicate with us. Please let us know if you found the book useful, in general, and what parts, if any, you found especially relevant to your particular concerns.

Were your expectations met? Did they change the more you read? Has your understanding of ethics, quality, and performance in your own work setting increased? We hope that your answers to these questions is yes. We hope that this book has met your expectations as they unfolded, that your expectations were enhanced and expanded by the ideas we presented, and that the connections we made among ethics, quality, and performance help to enrich your life in the public service.

Your feedback will probably be most helpful if you send it in stages. In other words, although we are interested in your immediate response after you complete the book, we are also interested in your response after you have had an opportunity to reflect on the book and apply it in whatever ways seem appropriate to you in your particular work setting. In any event, we appreciate the time you have spent with us, and look forward to hearing from you.

**Dr. Dean Geuras**
*Department of Philosophy*
*Texas State University*
*San Marcos, TX 78666*

**Dr. Charles Garofalo**
*Department of Political Science*
*Texas State University*
*San Marcos, TX 78666*

# References

Anas, B. December 27, 2009. *http://www.dailycamera.com/news/ci_14077758* (accessed May 25, 2010).

Apple, R. W. June 23, 1996. *http://topics.nytimes.com/topics/reference/timestopics/subjects/p/pentagon_papers/index.html* (accessed May 5, 2010).

Aristotle. 1881. *The Nicomachean ethics of Aristotle*, trans. F. H. Peters. London: C. Kegan Paul & Co.

Aristotle. 1980. *The Nicomachean ethics*, trans. D. Ross. Oxford, UK: Oxford University Press.

Associated Press. September 27, 2006. *http://www.msnbc.msn.com/id/15024576* (accessed May 11, 2010).

Audi, R. 1998. An axiology of moral experience. *The Journal of Ethics* 2:355–375.

Austin, J. L. 1975. *How to do things with words*. Cambridge, MA: Harvard University Press.

Avant, D. 2005. *The market for force: The consequences of privatizing security*. New York: Cambridge University Press.

Batura, S. April 10, 2010. *San Marcos Local News. http://www.newstreamz.com/2009/04/08/county-cuts-out-of-kbr-deal* (accessed April 10, 2010).

Behn, R. 1998. What right do public managers have to lead? *Public Administration Review* 58:209–224.

Behn, R. D. 2003. Creating leadership capacity for the twenty-first century: Not another technical fix. In *For the people: Can we fix public service?* eds. J. D. Donahue and J. S. Nye, Jr., 191–224. Washington, D.C.: Brookings Institution Press.

Bentham, J. 1970. *An introduction to the principles of morals and legislation*, eds. J. H. Burns and H. L. A. Hart. London: Athlone.

Blunt, R. 2001. *Organizations growing leaders: Best practices and principles in the public service*. Washington, D. C.: The PricewaterhouseCoopers Endowment for the Business of Government.

Bok, D. 2003. *Universities in the marketplace: The commercialization of higher education*. Princeton, NJ: Princeton University Press.

Bowman, J. S. 2009. Ethical competency in public service: A roundtable discussion paper. Conference of the National Association of Schools of Public Affairs and Administration, Crystal City, Virginia.

Bowman, J. S., and C. C. Knox. 2008. Ethics in government: No matter how long and dark the night. *Public Administration Review* 68:627–639.

Bowman, J. S., and R. Williams. 1997. Ethics in government: From a winter of despair to a spring of hope. *Public Administration Review* 57:517–526.

Bozeman, B. 1987. *All organizations are public*. San Francisco: Jossey-Bass.

Bozeman, B. 2007. *Public values and public interest: Counterbalancing economic individualism*. Washington, D.C.: Georgetown University Press.

Brewer, G. A. 2009. The possibility of an ethical dimension of public service motivation. Paper prepared for the International Public Service Motivation Research Conference, Indiana University – Bloomington, June 7–9.

Bruce, W. 1994. Ethical people are productive people. *Public Productivity and Management Review* 17:241–252.

Brumback, G. 1991. Institutionalizing ethics in government. *Public Personnel Management* 20:353–364.

Burke, F., and A. Black. 1990. Improving organizational productivity: Add ethics. *Public Productivity and Management Review* 14:121–133.

Burns, J. M. 1978. *Leadership*. New York: Harper & Row.

Chase, G. 1984. Bromides for public managers. Case N16-84-586, Kennedy School of Government. In *Managing in the public sector, 5th ed.*, ed. G. Starling. 1998. Fort Worth, TX: Harcourt Brace College Publishers.

Chase, G., and E. Reveal. 1983. *How to manage in the public sector*. Reading, MA: Addison-Wesley.

Code of Ethics. 1994. American Society for Public Administration. Washington, D. C.

Cohen, S., and W. Eimicke. 2008. *The responsible contract manager: Protecting the public interest in an outsourced world*. Washington, D.C.: Georgetown University Press.

Conger, J. A. 1992. *Learning to lead: The art of transforming managers into leaders*. San Francisco: Jossey-Bass.

Cooper, P. J. 2003. *Governing by contract: Challenges and opportunities for public managers*. Washington, D.C.: CQ Press.

Cooper, T. L. 1998. *The responsible administrator, 4th ed*. San Francisco: Jossey-Bass.

Cooper, T. L. 2009. Ethical competence and organizational design: A NASPAA roundtable paper. Conference of the National Association of Schools of Public Affairs and Administration. Crystal City, Virginia.

deLeon, L. 1996. Ethics and entrepreneurship. *Policy Studies Journal* 24:495–510.

deLeon, L., and R. B. Denhardt. 2000. The political theory of reinvention. *Public Administration Review* 60:89–97.

Denhardt, R. B. 1993. *The pursuit of significance: Strategies for managerial success in public organizations*. Belmont, CA: Wadsworth Publishing Company.

Denhardt, R. B. 1999. *Public administration: An action orientation, 3rd ed*. Orlando, FL: Harcourt Brace College Publishers.

DiIulio, J., G. Garvey, and D. F. Kettl. 1993. *Improving government performance: An owner's manual*. Washington, D.C.: The Brookings Institution.

DiIulio, J. J., Jr. 1990. The duty to govern: A critical perspective on the private management of prisons and jails. In *Private prisons and the public interest*, ed. D. C. McDonald, 155–178. New Brunswick, NJ: Rutgers University Press.

Dolovich, S. 2009. How privatization thinks: The case of prisons. In *Government by contract: Outsourcing and American democracy*, eds. J. Freeman and M. Minow, 128–147. Cambridge, MA, and London, England: Harvard University Press.

Dreyfus, H. L., and Dreyfus, S.E. 1991. Towards a phenomenology of ethical expertise. *Human Studies* 14:229–250.

Drucker, P. F. 1985. *Innovation and entrepreneurship*. New York: Harper & Row.

Drucker, P. F. 1995. *Really* reinventing government. *The Atlantic Monthly*. February 1995:1–8.

Dudley, L. 1996. Fencing in the inherently governmental debate. In *Refounding democratic public administration: Modern paradoxes, postmodern challenges*, eds. G. L. Wamsley and J. F. Wolf, 68–91. Thousand Oaks, CA: Sage Publications.

Feeney, M K. 2008. Public values and private armies: Militaries, mercenaries, and public values. Unpublished paper presented at Research Workshop on Public Values and Public Interest. University of Copenhagen, Denmark.

Fox, C. J. 1989. Free to choose, free to win, free to lose: The phenomenology of ethical space. *International Journal of Public Administration* 12, 6:913-930.

Frederickson, H. G. 1997. *The spirit of public administration*. San Francisco: Jossey-Bass.

Frederickson, H. G. 1999. Public ethics and the new managerialism. *Public Integrity* 1: 265–278.

Friedman, M. 1970. The social responsibility of business is to increase its profits. *New York Times Magazine*, Spetember 13, 1970.

Fund, J. August 20, 2009. *http://online.wsj.com/article/SB10001424052970 2035506045743610719684584300.html* (accessed May 11, 2010).

Gabris, G. T. 1991. Beyond conventional management practices: Shifting organizational values. In *Ethical frontiers in public management*, ed. J. S. Bowman, 205–224. San Francisco: Jossey-Bass.

Garofalo, C. 2000. Can elephants fly? Peter Drucker and governmental reform. *Journal of Management History* 6:94–110.

Garofalo, C. 2003. Toward a global ethic: Perspectives on values, training, and moral agency. *The International Journal of Public Sector Management* 16, 7:490–501.

Garofalo, C. 2008. With deference to Woodrow Wilson: The ethics-administration dichotomy in American public service. *Public Integrity* 10, 4:345–354.

Garofalo, C., and D. Geuras. 1999. *Ethics in the public service: The moral mind at work*. Washington D.C.: Georgetown University Press.

Garofalo, C., and D. Geuras. 2006. *Common ground, common future: Moral agency in public administration, professions, and citizenship.* Boca Raton, FL: Taylor & Francis.

Girdano, D. A., and G. S. Everly, Jr. 1979. *Controlling stress and tension: A holistic approach.* Englewood Cliffs, NJ: Prentice-Hall.

Gilligan, C. 1982. *In a different voice: Psychological theory and women's development.* Cambridge, MA: Harvard University Press.

Golembiewski, R. T. 1996. Facilitating organizational development and change. *Handbook of public administration, 2nd ed.,* ed. J. L. Perry, 511–526. San Francisco: Jossey-Bass.

Goodsell, C. T. 2007. Six normative principles for the contracting-out debate. *Administration & Society* 38, 6:669–688.

Green, R. T., and L. Hubbell. 1996. On governance and reinventing government. In *Refounding democratic public administration,* eds. G. L. Wamsley and J. F. Wolf, 38–67. Thousand Oaks, CA: Sage Publications.

Guttman, D. 2004. Inherently governmental functions and the new millennium: The legacy of twentieth-century reform. In *Making government manageable: Executive organization and management in the twenty-first century,* eds. T. H. Stanton and B. Ginsberg, 40–65. Baltimore, MD: The Johns Hopkins University Press.

Guy, M. E. 1991. Using high reliability management to promote ethical decision making. In *Ethical frontiers in public management,* ed. J. S. Bowman, 185–204. San Francisco: Jossey-Bass.

Hale, S. J. 1996. Achieving high performance in public organizations. *Handbook of public administration, 2nd ed.,* ed. J. L. Perry, 136–150. San Francisco: Jossey-Bass.

Hartle, T. W. 1985. Sisyphus revisited: Running the government like a business. *Public Administration Review* 45:341–351.

Heifetz, R. A. 1994. *Leadership without easy answers.* Cambridge, MA: The Belknap Press of Harvard University Press.

Heifetz, R. A., and M. Linsky. 2002. *Leadership on the line: Staying alive through the dangers of leading.* Boston: Harvard Business School Press.

Henry, N. 2001. *Public administration and public affairs, 8th ed.* Upper Saddle River, NJ: Prentice Hall.

Hitt, W. D. 1990. *Ethics and leadership: Putting theory into practice.* Columbus, OH: Battelle Press.

Hummel, R. P. 1994. *The bureaucratic experience, 4th ed.* New York: St. Martin's Press.

Jones, J. H. 1981. *Bad blood: The Tuskegee syphilis experiment.* New York: The Free Press.

Kaboolian, L. 1998. The new public management: Challenging the boundaries of the management vs. administration debate. *Public Administration Review* 58:189–193.

Kant, I. 1949. *Fundamental principles of the metaphysics of morals,* trans. T. K. Abbott. Upper Saddle River, NJ: Prentice Hall.

Kant, I. 1959. *Foundations of the metaphysics of morals,* trans. L. W. Beck. New York: Bobbs-Merrill.

Kant, I. 1989. *Fundamental principles of the metaphysics of morals,* trans. Thomas K. Abbott. New York: Collier MacMillan Publishers.

Kant, I. 2001. *Lectures on ethics,* ed. J. B. Schneewind, trans. P. Heath. Cambridge, UK: Cambridge University Press.

Karre, P. M. April 10, 2010. *http://www.hybridorganisations.com* (accessed April 10, 2010).

Kettl, D. F. 1994. *Reinventing government: Appraising the national review.* Washington, D.C.: Brookings Institution.

Kidder, R. M. 1995. *How good people make tough choices.* New York: Fireside.

Kohlberg, L. 1981. *The philosophy of moral development.* San Francisco: Harper and Row.

Krahmann, E. 2008. The new model soldier and civil-military relations. In *Private military and security companies: Ethics, policies and civil-military relations,* eds. A. Alexandra, D. P. Baker, and M. Caparini, 247–265. London and New York: Routledge.

Kravitz, D. September 9, 2008. *http://voices.washingtonpost.com/washingtonpostinvestigations/2008/09/report_finds_partisan_meddling.html* (accessed May 11, 2010).

Lan, Z. January 1992. Goals, rules, and effectiveness in public, private, and hybrid organizations: More evidence on frequent assertions about differences. *Journal of Public Administration Research and Theory,* 2:5–28.

Laurent, A. 1999. Stacking up. *Government executive magazine*, February 1, 1999, 1–6. *http://govexec.com/gpp/0299over.htm* (accessed May 24, 2010).

Leazes, F., and S. Campanelli. 1996. My sister's keeper. In *Ethical dilemmas in public administration*, eds. L. Pasquerella, A. G. Killilea, and M. Vocino, 39–48. Westport, CT: Praeger.

Lerner, A. W., and J. Wanat. 1993. *Public administration: Scenarios in public management*. Englewood Cliffs, NJ: Prentice Hall.

Lewis, C. W. 1991. *The ethics challenge in public service*. San Francisco: Jossey-Bass.

Lewis, C. W., and S. C. Gilman. 2005. *The ethics challenge in public service*, 2*nd* ed. San Francisco, CA: Jossey-Bass.

Lewis, E. 1980. *Public entrepreneurship*. Bloomington, IN: Indiana University Press.

*Los Angeles Times*, April 23, 2010. *latimesblogs.latimes.com/comments_blog/2010/.../sec-staffers-download-porn-while-wall-street-crumbled.html* (accessed April 23, 2010).

Lukemeyer, A., and R. C. McCorkle. 2006. Privatization of prisons: Impact on prison conditions. *American Review of Public Administration* 36, 2:189–206.

MacIntyre, A. 1981. *After virtue*. Notre Dame, IN: Notre Dame University Press.

MacIntyre, A. 1984. *After virtue: A study in moral theory*. Notre Dame, IN: Notre Dame University Press.

Madison, James. 1787–1788. Federalist no. 51. *The federalist papers*.

Maesschalck, J., Z. Van der Wal, and L. Huberts. 2008. Public service motivation and ethical conduct. In *Motivation in public management: The call of public service*, eds. J. L Perry and A. Hondeghem, 156–175. Oxford, UK: Oxford University Press.

Mandel, R. 2002. *Armies without states: The privatization of security*. Boulder, CO: Lynne Rienner Publishers.

Markusen, A. R. 2003. The case against privatizing national security. *Governance: An International Journal of Policy, Administration, and Institutions* 16, 4:471–501.

Mazzatti, M. September 24, 2006. *http://www.nytimes.com/2006/09/24/world/middleeast/24terror.html* (accessed May 11, 2010).

McCormick Tribune Foundation. 2006. *Understanding the privitaza-tion of national security*. *www.mccormicktribune.org/publications/privatization2006.pdf* (accessed March 23, 2009).

Menzel, D. C. 1993. The ethics factor in local government: An empirical analysis. In *Ethics and public administration*, ed. H.G. Frederickson. Armonk, NY: M.E. Sharpe.

Menzel, D. C. 1996. Ethics stress in public organizations. *Public Productivity and Management Review* 20:70–83.

Menzel, D. C., and K. J. Carson. 1999. A review and assessment of empirical research on public administration ethics. *Public Integrity* 1:239–264.

Mill, J. S. 1979. *Utilitarianism*, ed. G. Sher. Indianapolis, IN: Hackett Publishing.

Minow, M. 2009. Outsourcing power: Privatizing military efforts and the risks to accountability, professionalism, and democracy. In *Government by contract: Outsourcing and American democracy*, eds. J. Freeman and M. Minow, 110–127. Cambridge, MA, and London, England: Harvard University Press.

Moakley, M., and K. Power. 1996. Changing standards and hard choices: A problem in personnel administration. In *Ethical dilemmas in public administration*, eds. L. Pasquerella, A. G. Killilea, and M. Vocino, 75–83. Westport, CT: Praeger.

Moe, R. C. 1987. Exploring the limits of privatization. *Public Administration Review* 47, 6:453–460.

Moore, G. E. 1976. *Principia ethica*. Cambridge, UK: Cambridge University Press.

Moore, M. 1995. *Creating public value: Strategic management in government*. Cambridge, MA: Harvard University Press.

Moore, M. H. 1903. The subject matter of ethics. In *Twentieth century philosophy: The analytic tradition*, ed. M. Weitz. Toronto: Collier McMillan.

Moore, M. H. 2002. Privatizing public management. In *Market-based governance: Supply side, demand side, upside, and downside*, eds. J. D. Donahue and J. S. Nye, Jr., 296–322. Washington, D.C.: Brookings Institution Press.

Moore, M. H., and G. Sparrow. 1990. *Ethics in government: The moral challenge of public leadership*. Englewood Cliffs, NJ: Prentice Hall.

Morgan, D. F., and H. D. Kass. 1993. The American odyssey of the career public service: The ethical crisis of role reversal. In *Ethics and public administration*, ed. H. G. Frederickson, 177–190. Armonk, NY: M.E. Sharpe.

Morgan, P.W., and G.H. Reynolds. 1997. *The appearance of impropriety.* New York: The Free Press.

Morris, J. C. 2007. Government and market pathologies of privatization: The case of prison privatization. *Politics & Policy* 35, 2:318–341.

Morris, T. 1997. *If Aristotle ran General Motors.* New York: Henry Holt and Company.

Moten, M. 2010. *The Army officers' professional ethic: Past, present, and future.* Carlisle, PA: U.S. Army War College.

Moulton, J. 1924. Law and manners. *The Atlantic Monthly* 134:1–5.

Moynihan, D. P. 2008. The normative model in decline? Public service motivation in the age of governance. In *Motivation in public management: The call of public service*, eds. J. L. Perry and A. Hondeghem, 247–267. Oxford, UK: Oxford University Press.

Moynihan, D. P., and S. K. Pandey. 2008. The role of organizations in fostering public service motivation. *Public Administration Review* 67:40–53.

Nagel, T. 1978. Ruthlessness in public life. In *Public and private morality*, ed. Stuart Hampshire, 75–91. Cambridge, UK: Cambridge University Press.

National Academy of Public Administration. 1997. *Managing succession and developing leadership: Growing the next generation of public service leaders.* Washington, D.C.: NAPA.

National Academy of Public Administration. 2002. *Strengthening senior leadership in the U.S. government.* Washington, D.C.: NAPA.

National Council for Public-Private Partnerships. April 10, 2010. *http://www.ncppp.org/howpart/index.shtml#define* (accessed April 10, 2010).

National Organization for Women. April 10, 2010. *www.now.org/issues/title_ix/history.html* (accessed April 10, 2010).

New America Foundation. 2008. *Changing the culture of Pentagon contracting. www.newamerica.net/publications/policy/changing* (accessed March 23, 2009).

*New York Times.* July 1, 1971. *http://www.nytimes.com/books/97/04/13/ reviews/papers-final.html* (accessed May 5, 2010).

Northouse, P. 2001. *Leadership: Theory and practice, 2ⁿᵈ ed.* Thousand Oaks, London, and New Delhi: Sage Publications.

Nozick, R. 1980. *Anarchy, state, and utopia.* Oxford, UK: Blackwell.

Nussbaum, M. 2007. Non-relative virtues: An Aristotelian approach. In *Ethical theory: An anthology,* ed. R. Shafer Landau, 684–700. Malden, MA: Blackwell.

Office of Public Service Values and Ethics. 2002. *The ethics infrastructure in the public administration.* Treasury Board of Canada Secretariat. *www.tbs-sct.gc.ca* (accessed May 24, 2010).

O'Leary, R. 2006. *The ethics of dissent: Managing guerrilla government.* Washington, D.C.: CQ Press.

O'Neill, O. 2007. Kantian approaches to some famine problems. In *Ethical theory: An anthology,* ed. R. Shafer Landau, 553–564. Malden, MA: Blackwell.

Organization for Economic Cooperation and Development (OECD). 2001. *Public sector leadership for the 21ˢᵗ century.* Paris: OECD.

Osborne. D., and T. Gaebler. 1992. *Reinventing government: How the entrepreneurial spirit is transforming the public sector, from schoolhouse to statehouse, city hall to the Pentagon.* New York: Addison-Wesley.

Osborne, D., and P. Plastrik. 1997. *Banishing bureaucracy: The five strategies for reinventing government.* New York: Addison-Wesley.

Paarlberg, L., J. L. Perry, and A.Hondeghem. 2008. From theory to practice: Strategies for applying public service motivation. In *Motivation in public management: The call of public service,* eds. J. L. Perry and A. Hondeghem, 268–293. Oxford, UK: Oxford University Press.

Perry, J. L., and L. R. Wise. 1990. The motivational bases of public service. *Public Administration Review* 50:367–373.

Peters, T. J., and R. H. Waterman. 1982. *In search of excellence.* New York: HarperCollins.

Plant, J. F. 2009. Ethical competence and the 2009 NASPAA standards: Three challenges. Conference of the National Association of Schools of Public Affairs and Administration, Crystal City, Virginia.

Pops, G. M. 1994. A teleological approach to administrative ethics. In *Handbook of administrative ethics*, ed. T. L. Cooper, 157–166. New York: Marcel Dekker.

Price, B. E., and N. M. Riccucci. 2005. Exploring the determinants of decisions to privatize state prisons. *American Review of Public Administration* 35, 3:223–235.

Princeton Project on National Security. 2004. *The privatization of national security. www.middlebury.edu/administration/refia/conferences/princeton .htm* (accessed March 23, 2009).

Quinn, W. 2002. Actions, intentions, and consequences: The doctrine of double effect. In *Ethical theory: Classical and contemporary readings*, ed. L. P. Pojman. Belmont, CA: Wadsworth.

Rainey, H. G. 1983. Public agencies and private firms: Incentives, goals, and individual roles. *Administration & Society* 15, 2:207–242.

Rawls, J. 2005. *A theory of justice*. Cambridge: Belknap Press.

Rawls, J. R., R. A. Ullrich, and O. T. Nelson. 1975. A comparison of managers entering or re-entering the profit and nonprofit sectors. *Academic Management Journal* 18, 4:616–622.

Reisig, M. D., and T. C. Pratt. 2000. The ethics of correctional privatization: A critical examination of the delegation of coercive authority. *The Prison Journal* 80, 2:210–222.

Roberts R. 2009a. A competency approach to public service education. Conference of the National Association of Schools of Public Affairs and Administration, Crystal City, Virginia.

_____. 2009b. The rise of compliance-based ethics management: Implications for organizational ethics. *Public Integrity* 11, 3:261–277.

Rohr, J.A. 1989. *Ethics for bureaucrats, 2nd ed.* New York: Marcel Dekker.

Rosenbloom, D. H. and S. J. Piotrowski. 2005. Outsourcing the constitution and administrative law norms. *American Review of Public Administration* 35, 2103–121.

Rost, J. C. 1991. *Leadership for the twenty-first century*. New York: Praeger.

Sanger, D. E., and T. Shanker. April 17, 2010. *http://www.nytimes. com/2010/04/18/world/middleeast/18iran.html* (accessed May 11, 2010).

Sartre, J. P. 1948. Dirty hands. In *Three plays*, 1–52. New York: Alfred A. Knopf.

Schall, E. 1997. Public sector succession: A strategic approach to sustaining innovation. *Public Administration Review* 57, 1:4–10.

Schein, E. H. 1992. *Organizational culture and leadership, 2ⁿᵈ ed*. San Francisco: Jossey-Bass.

Schichor, D. 1995. *Punishment for profit: Private prisons/public concerns*. Thousand Oaks, CA: Sage Publications.

_____. 1998. Private prisons in perspective: Some conceptual issues. *The Howard Journal* 37, 1:82–100.

Schneider, A. L. 1999. Public-private partnerships in the U.S. prison system. *American Behavioral Scientist* 43, 1:192–208.

Selye, H. 1974. *Stress without distress*. Philadelphia: Lippincott.

Simon, H. A. 1957. *Models of man*. New York: Wiley.

Singer, P. W. 2003. *Corporate warriors: The rise of the privatized military*. Ithaca, NY: Cornell University Press.

Solomon, R. C. 1999. *A better way to think about business*. New York: Oxford University Press.

Starling, G. 1998. *Managing in the public sector, 5th ed*. Fort Worth, TX: Harcourt Brace College Publishers.

Stever, J.A. 1988. *The end of public administration*. Dobbs Ferry, NY: Transactional Publishers.

Stewart, D. W. 1993. The impact of demographic, professional, and organizational variables and domain on the moral reasoning of public administrators. In *Ethics and public administration*, ed. H. G. Frederickson, 205–219. Armonk, NY: M.E. Sharpe.

_____ 1994. Moral development in public administration. In *Handbook of administrative ethics*, ed. T. L. Cooper, 325–348. New York: Marcel Dekker.

Stewart, D. W., and N. A. Sprinthall. 1991. Strengthening ethical judgment in public administration. In *Ethical frontiers in public management*, ed. J. S. Bowman, 243–260. San Francisco: Jossey-Bass.

Stossel, J. 2004. *Give me a break*. New York: HarperCollins.

Svara, J. H. 2009. The elements of administrative ethics. Conference of the National Association of Schools of Public Affairs and Administration, Crystal City, VA.

Swisher, L. L., A. M. Rizzo, and M. A. Marley. 2005. Update on moral reasoning and theory in public administration: A neo-Kohlbergian perspective. In *Ethics in public management*, eds. H. G. Frederickson and R. K. Ghere, 70–94. Armonk, NY: M.E. Sharpe.

Terry, L. D. 1995. *Leadership of public bureaucracies: The administrator as conservator*. Thousand Oaks, CA: Sage Publications.

Terry, L. D. 1998. Administrative leadership, neo-managerialism, and the public management movement. *Public Administration Review* 58:194–200.

Thompson, D. F. 1985. The possibility of administrative ethics. *Public Administration Review* 45:555–561.

Timmins, W. M. 1990. *A casebook of public ethics and issues*. Pacific Grove, CA: Brooks/Cole.

Treverton, G. F. 2005. Governing the market state. In *High-performance government: Structures, leadership, incentives*, eds. R. E. Klitgaard and P. C. Light, 89–111. Santa Monica, CA: Rand.

United States Congress, Senate Record Vote Analysis, 103rd Congress, 1st session, September 7, 1993, Page S-11031, Vote No. 248.

United States General Accounting Office. 2003. *Human capital: Succession planning and management is critical driver of organizational transformation*, GAO-04-127T. Washington, D.C.: GAO.

Verkuil, P. R. 2007. *Outsourcing sovereignty: Why privatization of government functions threatens democracy and what we can do about it*. Cambridge, UK, and New York: Cambridge University Press.

Vocino, M., and G. Tyler, 1996. The library and the FBI: Ethical decision making under pressure. In *Ethical dilemmas in public administration*, eds. L. Pasquerella, A. G. Killilea, and M. Vocino, 49–57. Westport, CT: Praeger.

Walstreet, U. April 10, 2010. *http://www.unlockwallstreet.com/news-tools/ financial-Glossary/term/government-sponsored-enterprise-gse* (accessed April 10, 2010).

Whitton, H. 2009. Developing the "ethical competence" of public officials: A capacity-building approach. In *Ethics and integrity in public administration*, ed. R. W. Cox, iii, 236–255. Armonk, NY: M.E. Sharpe.

Williams, B. 1978. Politics and moral character. In *Public and private morality*, ed. Stuart Hampshire, 55–73. Cambridge UK: Cambridge University Press.

Williams, D. 2000. Reinventing the proverbs of government. *Public Administration Review* 60:522–534.

Winston, K. 2003. Moral competence in the practice of democratic governance. In *For the people: Can we fix public service?* eds. J. D. Donahue and J. S. Nye, Jr., 169–187. Washington, D.C.: Brookings Institution Press.

Wise, L. R. 2002. Public management reform: Competing drivers of change. *Public Administration Review* 62:556–557.

Wittmer, D. P. 1994. Ethical decision making. In *Handbook of administrative ethics*, ed. T. L. Cooper, 349–372. New York: Marcel Dekker.

Wolfendale, J. 2008. The military and the community: Comparing national military forces and private military companies. In *Private military and security companies: Ethics, policies and civil-military relations*, eds. A. Alexandra, D. P. Baker, and M. Caparini, 217–234. London and New York: Routledge.

Wuthnow, R. 1996. *Poor Richard's principle*. Princeton, NJ: Princeton University Press.

Zajac, G. 1997. Reinventing government and reaffirming ethics: Implications for organizational development in the public service. *Public Administration Quarterly* 20:385–404.

# Index

### Strategic Public Management: Best Practices from Government and Nonprofit Organizations

*Edited by Howard Balanoff and Warren Master*

Complex management issues in the public sector can't be addressed with limited, short-term fixes. Strategic, well-conceived approaches are critical to meet your organization's long-term needs. Through expert advice and real-world examples, this book presents the solutions that today's public administrators are putting into practice to address a variety of challenges, including planning and managing core mission functions, integrating new technology, and pursuing measurable results. Nineteen contributors representing local and federal government, nonprofit organizations, and the academic world offer guidance, direction, and examples that focus on the many areas of concern to public sector professionals.     ISBN 978-1-56726-276-6 ■ Product Code B766 ■ 192 pages

### Human Resources Framework for the Public Sector

*Dixon Southworth*

This book offers a fresh, new perspective on human resource (HR) management with the first comprehensive theoretical framework for work performance, tying HR theories, concepts, and concerns to public administration. With the introduction of the Work Performance Framework, Southworth offers a roadmap for work performance in the nonprofit and public sectors that focuses on three fundamental objectives of HR programs and services: build human resource capacity, build performance, and build community.     ISBN 978-1-56726-238-4 ■ Product Code B384 ■ 282 pages

### Transforming Public and Nonprofit Organizations: Stewardship for Leading Change

*James Edwin Kee, MPA and Kathryn E. Newcomer, PhD*

In the public and nonprofit arenas, leaders face the unique challenge of protecting the public interest while implementing organizational change initiatives. To succeed, these leaders must build organizations that are "change-centric," carefully weigh and prepare for the risks of change, and develop a change-oriented leadership style that authors call transformational stewardship. This book provides public and nonprofit leaders and students of leadership, management, and organizational change with theoretical knowledge and practical tools for accomplishing change goals while protecting the broader public interest.

ISBN 978-1-56726-227-8 ■ Product Code B278 ■ 301 pages

### Achieving Project Management Success in the Federal Government

*Jonathan Weinstein and Timothy Jaques*

The authors offer a realistic cross-section of the project management discipline in the largest single enterprise in the world–the U.S. federal government. Based on research and interviews with a wide variety of project managers who shared their lessons learned and advice, this book offers practical guidance and insights to federal leaders, project team members, and others involved with project management in the government.

ISBN 978-1-56726-275-9 ■ Product Code B759 ■ 300 pages